Captives

Captives

*How Rikers Island Took
New York City Hostage*

Jarrod Shanahan

VERSO
London • New York

First published by Verso 2022
© Jarrod Shanahan 2022

1 3 5 7 9 10 8 6 4 2

Verso
UK: 6 Meard Street, London W1F 0EG
US: 388 Atlantic Avenue, Brooklyn, NY 11217
versobooks.com

Verso is the imprint of New Left Books

ISBN-13: 978-1-78873-995-5
ISBN-13: 978-1-80429-055-2 (EXPORT)
ISBN-13: 978-1-78873-998-6 (US EBK)
ISBN-13: 978-1-78873-997-9 (UK EBK)

British Library Cataloguing in Publication Data
A catalogue record for this book is available from the British Library

Library of Congress Cataloging-in-Publication Data
A catalog record for this book is available from the Library of Congress

Typeset in Sabon by MJ & N Gavan, Truro, Cornwall
Printed and bound by CPI Group (UK) Ltd, Croydon, CRO 4YY

Dedicated to Kalief Browder, New York's boldest.

Contents

Introduction:
If You Build It,
They Will Fill It

Obscenity

On the evening of September 24, 1954, a woman locked on the fourth floor of New York's House of Detention for Women (HDW) was accused of making an obscene comment toward a guard. Escorted to her cell as punishment, the woman—identified by officials only as a "narcotic addict"—loudly denied the charges, protesting the injustice of her treatment. Her defiant clamor fell on sympathetic ears: other women inside rose to her defense, shouting protestations of their own. In response, the guards shut off the lights for the entire floor, much as one might send a recalcitrant child to bed early. Nevertheless, consigned to the dark, the women took to their cell windows, broadcasting rebellion to other floors of HDW. At least one of those floors joined in, while their message reverberated among people in the bustling streets of Greenwich Village below.[1]

For two hours the women set small fires, clanged their metal cups against the bars, and shouted protests to the unruly crowd that gathered on the sidewalk, until the onlookers were forcibly dispersed by a detachment of fifteen cops. The spirited demonstration inside ended only with the arrival of acting jail superintendent Loretta Moran, roused from the comfort of her home by their direct action, who restored the lights. Flanked by guards who just hours earlier had shut the women up in the dark, the official toured the jail to speak face to face with HDW's captive population, who shared their grievances.[2]

As social anthropologist Orisanmi Burton observes, "Jails and prisons seek legitimacy through their alleged ability to impose order on captive populations, thereby defending the order of society at large." Incidents like the rebellion at HDW challenge this legitimacy. By shattering the "surface order" these institutions must display to the broader society, such "production of disorder" is therefore "a powerful weapon for captive populations."[3] In the aftermath of this well-publicized incident, the local press held the New York City Department of Correction (DOC) to account, prompting it to respond directly to the women's charges of poor conditions in the facility with promises of reform.

For its part, DOC blamed the disorder on persistent overcrowding; a lack of medical, psychological, and psychiatric treatment services; untrained staff; and pervasive idleness in the facility—a familiar refrain from jail administrators, leaning heavily on factors that can only be remedied by increases in their own budgets. A subsequent internal investigation reiterated these findings, to which it added two telling details. First, it was commonplace at HDW for women to be denied basic rights, such as visitation, as they suffered the facility's abysmal conditions. Second, women classified as "narcotic addicts" suffered the additional indignity of being forced to wear blue chambray dresses that marked them as a particular class of prisoner. Filling out this picture, the *New York Herald Tribune* reported that, contrary to DOC's claims that the conflict began in a common area, the unrest had actually begun in a room called "the Tank," an added level of captivity—and indignity—for women deemed narcotic addicts. Responding to media scrutiny, city officials demanded DOC get the situation at HDW under control. The New York City Board of Estimate promptly pivoted, from pleading poverty with regard to the city jails, to discovering $108,794 in available funds, which was passed along to DOC in hopes it would help calm the facility.

Jail administrators have long cultivated the art of explaining prisoner unrest in terms flattering to polite society—and supportive of higher budgets and more power for corrections departments. The primary cause of this disturbance, however, was more than a mere amalgamation of poor conditions, and surely not a deficit of institutional capacity; it was instead fundamentally tied to the broader historical moment that produced it.[4]

As the Great Migration from the Jim Crow South redoubled following World War II, New York City saw a sizeable influx of African American residents, ultimately numbering in the millions. In New York they faced a Northern variety of segregation: marginalization from employment and housing, and criminalization by police, courts, and jails. The typical prisoner at HDW at this time was black, between twenty-five and thirty years of age, hailed from outside of New York State, possessed an elementary school education, and was locked away on charges of "disorderly conduct," drug possession, or sex work for an average of five months. These women were designated second-class citizens from birth and denied adequate housing, employment, and treatment before the law; in turn, they were deprived of their freedom for "crimes" attendant to daily survival. Perhaps they had believed a better life was in store for them in New York City, but HDW made plain a truth that Malcolm X would argue a decade later: "If you black you were born in jail, in the North as well as the South ... As long as you south of the Canadian border, you South."[5]

The reality of life in New York for these women was consignment to the lowest tiers of the labor force, whether in precarious legal employment or the harsh world of informal economies. In either case, they were subjected to perennial harassment by the cops, who represented the social order that simultaneously exploited their labor and made their daily lives as difficult as possible. Once imprisoned, these women struggled to eke out a dignified existence, packed for upward of three years into a cramped and squalid facility never intended for more than temporary detention.

Surely the conditions inside jails constitute social ills sufficient to justify rebellion, but they are only part of the story. The
deeper context in which such uprisings unfold is a broader and
more complex social terrain: a racialized social order defined
by human disposability and held together by violence. When
carceral facilities are thus situated, the question begging explanation is not "Why do people sometimes rebel?" but "Why,
most of the time, don't they?"

A Monument to Those Who Conceived It

The setting of these dramatic events was a twelve-story facility overlooking Sixth Avenue, resembling an art deco high-rise
and marked simply "Number Ten Greenwich Avenue." Though
nondescript by design, the facility nonetheless stood out. "The
idea was to make it look not like a jail at all but like a new
apartment building," writes essayist Tom Wolfe. "In the place of
bars there are windows with a heavy grillwork holding minute
square panes. The panes are clouded, like cataracts. Actually,
the effect is more like that of the power plant at Yale University,
which was designed to resemble a Gothic cathedral, but, in any
case, it does not look like a jail."[6] HDW was adjacent to the
Jefferson Market Court in Greenwich Village, known for lively
night sessions revolving around illicit street life, especially sex
work. While the jail had become notorious in New York City
long before the events of 1954, like many jails and prisons, its
life began as product of a hard-fought campaign by Progressive
Era reformers, including the local temperance movement and
the Women's Prison Association.

Prior to the opening of HDW in 1932, women detained
awaiting trial simply lived in police station cells pending the
outcome of their cases. Legal scholar Clarice Feinman describes
a status quo in which detained women, mostly "mendicants,
prostitutes, vagrants, or elderly" were, regardless of age, offense,
or health, "housed together, often in a common cell, and it was
not unusual to have mothers with babes-in-arms among the

women. They slept on wooden benches in unsanitary, vermin-infested surroundings." Sentenced women were confined on Welfare Island (previously Blackwell's Island, and known today as Roosevelt Island) in a dangerous and squalid facility notorious for over a half century before HDW took its place. The opening of HDW was thus a victory for jail reformers, who pinned their hopes of fixing conditions in the city system on the erection of new jail facilities. The *New York Times*, which has rarely met a new city jail it did not celebrate in the rosiest of terms, praised the ample sunlight, air, and "boarding house" feel of this new facility, where cells were "called rooms, and rightly so." When HDW opened, one reformer called it "a monument to those who conceived it." In short order, this remark would prove accurate—albeit far from the compliment intended.[7]

Reflecting on the infamous jail, the revolutionary scholar Angela Davis recalls, "I used to look up at this building almost every day, trying not to listen to the terrible noises spilling from the windows." In 1959, Davis was a new arrival to the city, thanks to a Quaker-run exchange program that placed Southern black students in integrated schools in the North. This had brought the teenager from Birmingham, Alabama, to Manhattan, where she attended Elizabeth Irwin High School in Greenwich Village, just down the street from HDW. The distressing sounds she heard "were coming from the women locked behind bars, looking down on the people passing in the streets, and screaming incomprehensible words."[8]

Davis was not alone in taking note of the suffering on display in Greenwich Village; given the jail's central position in this bustling area, it was hard to ignore. Just a year after its opening, overcrowding at the facility was already earning criticism from the reformers who had fought for it to open. HDW had been designated for a small population of pretrial detainees, but almost immediately upon its opening, DOC had begun using HDW for its *entire* female population, packing in detainees and prisoners serving sentences upward of three years. Often, space was so limited in the facility that women were doubled up in the small, dark cells. A contemporary photograph shows how many women bided their "recreation" time: sitting in the dingy hallway just outside these cells. The reformers who had campaigned for the opening of this jail, it turned out, had no control over how it was used.

By the mid '50s, this unfavorable view of the jail had taken hold in DOC itself. In the wake of the September 1954 disturbance, DOC's new commissioner, Anna M. Kross—a pioneering suffragist, court reformer, and herself an advocate for the construction of HDW—made no excuses for the facility. She called it "a shocking penal anachronism." As for the women who rebelled there, Kross was even more direct: "I don't blame them one bit."[9]

Shocking Penal Anachronisms

By Kross's own account, the DOC she inherited in 1954 was still in the era of "horse and buggy." Then as now, DOC oversaw what was effectively a massive and diffuse county jail, including "remand facilities" for detainees and "sentence institutions" for convicted prisoners who were serving short sentences. Manhattan, Brooklyn, Queens, and the Bronx hosted borough-based remand facilities called "city prisons"; these held accused men while they awaited trial and caged city and state parole violators, as well as sentenced prisoners who were serving ten days or less. The Manhattan facility remains colloquially known as "the Tombs." The Tombs, named after its Egyptian revival architecture, dated back to 1838, when it had been erected on a public execution site that was older still. This was the facility of which one prominent visitor—Charles Dickens—wrote, "Such indecent and disgusting dungeons as these cells would bring disgrace upon the most despotic empire in the world!" The Tombs was rebuilt twice following Dickens's visit, with the third incarnation opened in 1941, connected to the New York County Court at 100 Centre Street.

The Brooklyn facility, commonly known as the Raymond Street Jail, had been constructed over a century earlier, in 1836, and remodeled in 1909. Similarly, the Queens County Jail (now City Prison Queens) opened in 1875, while the Bronx City Prison was the newest jail, built in 1938. By and large these were crumbling facilities, designed for short-term incarceration numbering in the days, and inadequate to detaining the rapidly climbing jail population of the postwar years. Most notably, this network of pretrial detention jails had no presence on Rikers Island.[10]

Rikers Island is a patch of reeking landfill plopped into the East River between LaGuardia Airport in Queens and Hunts Point in the Bronx. In 1954, the island was accessible only by a ferry system, which limited the island's capacity for daily traffic. The contemporary cliché that many New Yorkers cannot find Rikers on a map was doubtless truer in 1954, as the largely undeveloped island cut a slender figure in the city's institutional landscape. Nonetheless, it was a looming presence for New York City's sentenced male prisoners. The city and state correctional systems divided custody such that the city was responsible for detaining people prior to their trials, and for incarcerating people serving clearly defined (or determinate) sentences of a year or less; it also held those serving indeterminate sentences stretching from six months to three years, the extent of which were at the discretion of the parole board. Rikers is sometimes referred to as a prison, but this is not technically correct. The facilities on Rikers are *jails*, a term that designates their use for pretrial or short-term incarceration conducted on the county, not state, level. Rikers was at this time still a facility for sentenced men; pretrial populations would come later.

In 1954, male prisoners serving sentences of less than six months wound up at the Rikers Island Workhouse, largely for offenses such as disorderly conduct and public intoxication. If they were aged sixteen to thirty, and serving time on their first misdemeanor, they may have been sent to the New Hampton Reformatory in Orange County, New York, to perform agricultural labor. Prisoners serving more than six months were locked up in the Rikers Island Penitentiary. In both cases, the petty crimes prisoners were accused of and the working-class composition of these facilities befitted the historical role of the workhouse and short-stay jail: they were repositories of proletarians who refused to observe the dictates of the wage relation and the discipline it entailed, or else were simply in the way of the surface order that the state strove to cultivate.[11]

Anna M. Kross was a reform commissioner, brought in by the incoming mayor, Robert Wagner Jr., to fix the embarrassing mess that the city jails had become as a postwar spike in incarceration played out against institutional inertia. Bearing the mantle of the New Deal, with which his father and namesake was associated in the minds of working-class New Yorkers, Wagner undertook a sweeping expansion of city employment and institutional capacity. The effort aimed to cohere a powerful working-class base among municipal workers and trade unionists, and to generate widespread consensus for a Keynesian social order. His so-called New Deal for New York would be managed by union leadership and Democratic politicians, who would serve to temper unrestrained market development, providing robust social services and public sector employment. As part of this vision in the city jails, Kross endeavored to replace the untrained and often brutish guards who oversaw the city's captives with experts steeped in the social sciences—jailers who would approach incarceration from a clinical perspective, and endeavor to solve the social ills that led to people being locked up in the first place.

In postwar New York, the only thing that seemed impossible was that the future would resemble the past. Kross's struggle to remake DOC was therefore not unique; in this period, the governance of New York City was defined by two increasingly polarized camps. On one side stood humanistic liberals like Wagner, who approached the administration of social order as a project of generating the consent of the governed and administering their lives through robust public spending, legalistic trade unions, and a small army of experts trained in the social sciences. On the other side stood forces of brute repression, who believed that administering a well-ordered society began with a policeman's club and ended with a jail cell. This latter pole would in short order adopt the banner "law and order."

Make no mistake: both camps swore allegiance to the capitalist order and believed in the ultimate legitimacy of whatever means were necessary to protect it—something that would become especially clear amid rebellion against capitalism and white supremacy in the ensuing decades. But they remained two distinct visions of the postwar order, and how it was to be achieved and maintained. And while the law-and-order camp was nascent in Kross's day, her twelve-year stewardship of DOC coincided with the emergence of a powerful political base for it.

When Kross condemned DOC as antiquated, she counterposed a medical model for understanding criminality that sought to undertake nothing short of "human engineering," in her words. Kross was very much an orthodox product of the Progressive Era. She followed the trail blazed by the likes of social work pioneers Josephine Shaw Lowell and Louisa Lee Schuyler, and Katharine Bement Davis, the first female commissioner of DOC (a distinction often wrongfully applied to Kross). These reformers pursued a distinct course of public administration by deploying courts and carceral facilities to function as agencies of social work—dramatically expanding, in the process, the role of police, courts, and jails in the lives of working-class people.

By the late nineteenth century, the emergent problems of urban administration—including the prevention of outright proletarian insurrection, but also more fundamental questions of sanitation, public assistance, and care for the needy and delinquent young—proved too daunting for localist machine politics. As cities expanded, governance was seized by experts representing the specializations of medicine, law, and public administration. As historian David Rothman demonstrates, this was an era in which probation, juvenile courts, and all manner of progressive prison schemes were deployed by an ascendant class of university-trained social managers as a humanistic alternative to discredited institutions of punishment and social control.[12]

By mid century, when she took over DOC, Kross was part of an international movement of what criminologist David Garland calls "penal welfarism." This approach to public administration combines "the liberal legalism of due process and proportionate punishment with a correctionalist commitment to rehabilitation, welfare, and criminological expertise."[13] This was not mere benevolence; it was a distinct paradigm for how social order could be maintained in a capitalist society defined by the concentration of property and power in a small set of hands. To meet the problems of this society, Kross believed jails could be repurposed to produce well-adjusted workers, if only these jails could be built properly and run by the right people.

Accordingly, Kross's reform agenda rested on two vital elements. The first was to wrest control of the city jails from the paramilitary organization of uniformed staff, with its hierarchical culture of insularity and distrust of outsiders, and to establish the dominion of civilian experts over DOC. The second was to create the proper jail infrastructure to allow these experts to properly administer New York City's working class. This would require significant expansion of the city system: namely, the construction of new jails and other infrastructure designed to facilitate rehabilitation.

Social change, however, does not unfold as the coherent application of a single individual's clever plans. It is instead produced by the clash of antagonistic forces vying through contests large and small to impose their will on human events. Ultimately, Kross was able to get much of the infrastructure she wanted—most notably, a bridge connecting Rikers Island to the mainland, which greatly improved vehicular access and opened the land to significant carceral development. But Kross had little control over how these facilities would actually be run, who would administer them, and, ultimately, who would govern the city in which jails play such an important role. "We plan," runs an old Yiddish proverb, "God laughs."

Captives

This book tells the story of the postwar struggle for who would run New York City, beginning with Wagner's New Deal for New York and Kross's penal welfarism, and culminating in the triumph of the twin figures we today call neoliberalism and mass incarceration. Following legal scholar James Forman Jr., *Captives* endeavors to treat these immense social processes "as the result of a series of small decisions, made over time, by a disparate group of actors."[14] What follows is, then, not an exhaustive history of these scourges. It is instead a view of this epoch through the figure of the city jail, with an emphasis on the small decisions and daily struggles of disparate actors who crisscross its institutional world. "The relationship between structure and agency is dialectical," writes postwar historian Thomas Sugrue, "and history is the synthesis."[15] Ultimately, in charting the unfolding of this dialectic, *Captives* tells the story of how the Rikers Island of today—and the social order it represents—came to be.

Despite its central role in reproducing social life in New York City, the existing literature on this pivotal historical period makes scant reference to the city jail system. Most prominently, the system is absent from Joshua Freeman's canonical study of this period, *Working-Class New York*.[16] This is unfortunate given the millions of working-class New Yorkers—disproportionately black and brown—who cycled through it during the period Freeman lionizes as the apex of US social democracy; meanwhile, he celebrates the emergence of city unions, one of the most powerful of which was that representing jail guards. "I am invisible, understand," recounts the narrator of Ralph Ellison's 1952 novel *Invisible Man*, "simply because people refuse to see me … When they approach me they see only my surroundings, themselves, or figments of their imagination—indeed, everything and anything except me."[17] Freeman and others who omit the jail and its denizens from the history of postwar New York not only erase the people whose lives played out in the city's jails system, on one side of the bars or the other, but also play directly into the city's strategy to conceal the most dramatic expressions of social problems by quarantining them behind high walls.

As the 1954 rebellion at the House of Detention for Women demonstrates in a radical sense, the boundaries between the jails and the rest of the society are in fact quite porous. Jails are blunt yet essential tools by which capitalist order is maintained and negotiated. Therefore, they are just as vital, if not more so, to their given societies than other institutions—factories, schools, political parties, and unions—that might be easier to plumb for progressive politics or more pleasing to look at. Yet the political deployment of the jail represents, in a most extreme form, the conflicts and contradictions that define a given social order: it is at once a key terrain on which that order is inscribed and the grounds where it is contested. When struggles and scandals break out of jails and into the wider public discourse, they tend to threaten the legitimacy not just of the jail as an institution, but of the broader society it serves to prop up.[18]

As the reader is surely aware, the unfolding conflict in postwar New York was characterized by persistent violence—at times routine to the point of banality, at times spectacular. Any effort to depict the violence of structural racism, and incarceration in particular, is a fraught undertaking. To present violence in graphic detail risks turning human misery into an entertaining commodity, all in the name of proving things that most readers already know: the United States is an incredibly violent society, especially for working-class black people, and US prisons are places where sadism and brutality thrive. With this in mind, I strive to present violence judiciously, in the service of what the reader likely doesn't already know. The book's most violent episodes constitute a series of events central to the unfolding of New York City carceral history, and the history of the city itself, that have been scarcely documented, will be completely unknown to the vast majority of readers, and that polite society would happily forget. Their recounting therefore attempts to balance a respectful explication of violence undergone by real people in the recent past with the historian's responsibilities to record events as they transpired, and to foster greater understanding of the world we inhabit today.

The reader might be surprised to discover that Rikers Island cuts a modest shadow in the book's early chapters. The explanation for this is simple: in the immediate postwar period, Rikers Island was not the central node of working-class life that it would later become. Further, while the central concerns of this book limit much of its discussion to New York City by necessity, many of the trends explored herein can serve as case studies of national phenomena, including postwar dislocation, deindustrialization, Black and Brown Power, the law-and-order movement, the so-called punitive turn in governance, and the creation of the largest captive population on earth. In the case of the New York City fiscal crisis, the attendant onset of neoliberalism as the city's governing paradigm and the massive prison boom that came in its wake, New York was not simply emblematic of national changes, but a testing ground for a ruling-class offensive that was subsequently carried out on a national scale.

To make sense of the rise of Rikers Island as a central figure in New York City and the country at large, *Captives* looks beneath the surface order of not just the jail, but New York City as a whole. It finds there a crowded field of contending powers whose struggles shape the unfolding of long-term historical events. This entails spending considerable time dealing with mayors, DOC commissioners, and other custodians of social order whose employment hinges on the biennial ritual of voting. The definitive actions of its story are, however, extraparliamentary conflicts between captors and the jailed, cops and the policed, rank and filers and union brass, civil servants and their bosses, black militants and the old guard of white power, small groups of committed radicals on both sides, and, ultimately, the forces of law and order against the world. Sometimes this constant push and pull breaks the facade of surface order in spectacular scenes suitable for the silver screen. But most of the time, it plays out in minutiae, across vast expanses of unremarkable days in the lives of its contestants. This antagonism, fueled by the violent contradictions at the heart of capitalist social relations, drove the unfolding of postwar history, culminating in the Rikers Island of today. Given the central focus on the Rikers Island penal colony, a word is in order about its unique origins.

To Build a Bigger Jail

The Rikers Island jail complex, long an accepted fact of daily life in New York City, has not always existed. Located on the tribal lands of Wappinger, Matinecock, and Lenape, the low-lying ninety-acre island was expropriated by the Dutch and became the legal property of one Abraham Rycken in 1664. The most famous of the Riker clan, as the family's name came to be spelled, is Richard Riker. Historian Eric Foner describes how Riker "played a pivotal role in what abolitionists called the Kidnapping Club. In accordance with the Fugitive Slave Act, members of the club would bring a black person before Riker, who would quickly issue a certificate of removal before the accused had a chance to bring witnesses to testify that he was actually free." Though the island is not named after Richard Riker, and he was not the family's "patriarch," as is often claimed, this historical coincidence has nonetheless captured the imagination of contemporary activists who compare the Kidnapping Club to police and court practices that disproportionately impact black New Yorkers.

Between 1851 and 1855, the Riker family sold the island to the Totten family in two pieces. It subsequently served as a training camp for Northern regiments in the Civil War and was used as a haven for black New Yorkers fleeing the racist mob violence of the 1863 draft riot. By 1884, when the city purchased the land, the island had been most recently used as a fertilizer plant.[19]

In 1884, one massive agency department, the Department of Public Charities and Correction, oversaw a teeming network of asylums and jails clustering the city's poorest and most abject people—including a large population of recent immigrants—into miserable quarters just down the river on Blackwell's Island. The island's various institutions—almshouse, workhouse, lunatic asylum, penitentiary, hospital—had porous boundaries that blurred their various intended functions. They comprised a general repository of working-class New Yorkers either unable to work for a wage (and thus requiring city aid), unwilling to work for a wage (and thus requiring discipline), or simply redundant to the city's workforce (and thus requiring warehousing). Escapes were common at Blackwell's, as were fatalities from diseases like smallpox that spread rampantly. The infamy of Blackwell's in New York City in the late nineteenth and early twentieth century was much akin to that of Rikers today.

By the late nineteenth century, reformers were pushing to modernize Blackwell's. They sought to differentiate its mass of surplus workers into more easily administered populations beholden to their own specific set of experts and bodies of social science. The purchase of Rikers "to build a bigger jail" was celebrated by the *New York Times* as an occasion that would "draw a very distinct line of demarcation by territorial restriction between institutions for the relief of the distressed, and those for punishment of the guilty." This demarcation was anticipated by the 1896 bifurcation of Public Charities and Correction, which created the New York City Department of Correction as a distinct institution free from the burden of "public charity." This was in keeping with the movement in private philanthropy to divide the guilty from the unfortunate, who were funneled into increasingly ornate administrative agencies, such as social work, that could oversee and engineer working-class life. The construction of a bigger jail on Rikers, however, would prove more difficult to achieve; the Rikers Island of 1884 was hardly the ideal site for a jail. Its low-lying shore and unstable soil required considerable development before any large-scale construction could be undertaken.[20]

In the 1880s and '90s, Blackwell's generated a steady stream of scandal, most famously through journalist Nellie Bly's 1887 undercover exposé of the Women's Lunatic Asylum, which was ultimately published as *Ten Days in a Mad-House*. In 1883 a grand jury found conditions at Blackwell's overcrowded, with two prisoners often placed in cells made for one, and recommended that it be expanded—findings reiterated by another grand jury in 1886, a year when 700 cells in the penitentiary held 1,100 prisoners. While Rikers had been purchased to replace the jails on Blackwell's, the city government consistently balked at the expense of leveling the island and building a modern jail there. The sentiment of the time was captured by New York Board of Aldermen president Patrick McGowan: "Palaces for prisoners, I won't vote for it." But there was a way to mitigate the costs, which the city had eyed from the very beginning: prisoner labor. Through forced labor, the New York Times raved in 1900, "Riker's Island, bought by this city in 1884 for $180,000, can be turned into a property worth several million without the expenditure of a cent."[21]

In an early experiment in incarceration on Rikers Island, the island was used in 1893 to contain four Chinese Americans who had contracted leprosy—and who quickly escaped across the East River, inaugurating a long history of daring escapes. In the mid 1890s, Rikers became a daytime worksite for Blackwell's prisoners, transported by ferry each day to fill in the island's shallow coastline with the city's trash, including rubble from the excavation of the subway system. The first permanent carceral structure on the island, the Branch Workhouse, was constructed in 1897 but could not hold prisoners overnight until a freshwater pipe was built in 1903. This piece of infrastructure enabled the continuous habitation of Rikers Island, which has continued to the present day.

Working on Rikers was the worst job in the city jail system, and the prisoners were disproportionately black, compared not just to the city but to the jail system itself. Many toiled on the island's farm, growing produce for use by city agencies. The majority, however, worked at the backbreaking process of filling out the island's shoreline, expanding it from ninety acres to the 440 that stand today. The labor these prisoners performed was dangerous and disgusting, as the combustible landfill was prone to ignition, swarmed with rats, and emitted odors that raised complaints miles away in multiple boroughs. Their living quarters were mostly dangerous wooden-frame structures, which proved easy to escape for anyone who dared to hazard the swim across the East River, which ran more swiftly than it does today due to less infrastructure impeding the current.

DOC also experimented with cement barracks, including the 1914 construction of a soundproof structure with solitary confinement cells. These were meant to house anarchist political prisoners like Frank Tannenbaum, who were agitating prisoners on Blackwell's Island as part of the revolutionary fervor of the time. For a short time, the island was repurposed as a rehabilitative site for accused narcotic addicts. But this population could not, or would not, keep up with the harsh work required of them, which bore no resemblance to the ideology of "rehabilitation" in which it was couched; this was simply hard labor. The almost four decades that preceded the opening of the penitentiary, largely erased in contemporary accounts of the island, were defined by punishing forced labor that literally laid the groundwork of the Rikers Island penal colony, from its expanding shoreline to the very foundation of the penitentiary.[22]

As plans for a "model penitentiary" dating back to the 1880s languished on drawing boards, the crisis of Blackwell's Island—rechristened Welfare Island in 1921—became too much for the city to countenance. This was especially so as the corruption of Tammany Hall, a Democratic Party patronage machine, was assailed by Progressive Era reformers who fought to redesign jails so that they might mold prisoners into good proletarians. Further, the 1895 bifurcation of Public Charities and Correction had stipulated no new construction on Blackwell's Island. When the teeming facilities there were condemned as dangerous firetraps, the city was at last spurred to act. Progress on Rikers was stilted due to recurring fiscal crisis and the onset of the Great Depression. Nevertheless, as DOC consistently reminded City Hall throughout this period, the use of forced prisoner labor helped keep the costs down.[23]

The new jail on Rikers opened in mid 1935—also the year of its first escape. Draped in the noble vestments of the Progressive Era, the Rikers Penitentiary was celebrated as a model jail. It was overseen by renowned progressive penologists Austin MacCormick, who was tapped as DOC commissioner by the progressive Republican mayor Fiorello La Guardia, and Richard McGee, the new penitentiary's warden. The penitentiary on Rikers featured an array of rehabilitative programming, an impressive library, and, most strikingly, a state-of-the-art seven-story hospital meant to provide the entire DOC with facilities for everything from minor medical care to serious surgery. Despite its auspicious beginning, however, the plans of the reformers soon came to naught. Budgets fell short of MacCormick and McGee's vision, and World War II drained New York City of the working-class men who would ordinarily languish behind bars. When the city's jail population began its postwar climb, the intent behind the penitentiary was all by forgotten. Taking office in 1954, ensconced in the highest ideals of penal welfarism, Anna M. Kross endeavored to bring it back. That is where *Captives* begins.[24]

Sites of Civic Unity?

C.L.R. James remarks somewhere that historical controversies are always about the present. This book is no exception: it is saturated with the historical moment that produced it and the personal circumstances of its author. Like millions of New Yorkers before me, I became intimately acquainted with Rikers Island by virtue of being locked up there. Unlike those who languish on the island for years on end awaiting trial, I was fortunate enough to be serving a sentence of forty-five days, roughly the average stay, in the Eric M. Taylor Center (EMTC), the island's facility for sentenced men and contemporary heir of the penitentiary and workhouse. To make the best of a bad situation, I endeavored to learn as much about the institution as I could. As I became ever more enmeshed in the Kafkaesque reality of New York City's punishment system, I could always hear the sage words of my attorney, a squat, mustachioed, septuagenarian movement lawyer named Jesse Berman. Midway through deciphering for me the ridiculous theatrics and tragic absurdity of criminal court proceedings, Jesse would stop himself and clarify, lest it had not occurred to me: "It's all shlock."

At Rikers I beheld and experienced the degrading treatment to which tens of thousands of New Yorkers are subjected each year by guards who answer to nobody. Their behavior toward us prisoners under their watch ranged from callous indifference to aggressive hostility. It was not uncommon for a guard to shout threats and obscenities into a crowded room of prisoners for no particular reason, aimed at nobody in particular. Rules were enforced arbitrarily, and the prisoner handbook enumerating our rights was confiscated as contraband. My visitors were berated and intimidated. They were subjected to invasive strip searches, as was I on a routine basis. My mail—a vital lifeline to the outside world—came in episodic spurts, with no explanation. I also experienced the violence and humiliation of aggressive shakedowns by the island's Emergency Services Unit, an elite band of warrior guards clad in ornate riot gear who tore through EMTC's dormitories with no explanation, dumping everyone's meager possessions on the floor, shouting abuse and threats. All the while, they sought to bait prisoners into a fight the prisoners would surely lose. On more typical days, discipline was maintained by verbal abuse and threats of time in "the box"— the island's expansive system of punitive solitary confinement —while the threat of violence remained just beneath the surface. Nevertheless, I was consistently reassured by just about everyone I spoke with that this was the calmest male facility on the entire island—by a mile.

This was a place for discarded people, where nobody cared if you lived or died. There was nothing to do but look at the calendar. Days were characterized by expansive idleness, waste, and enforced stupidity. The rapper Lil Wayne, who spent eight months at EMTC in 2010, describes life there as "days spent doing too much of fucking nothing."[25] I felt myself becoming meaner, jealously guarding my pitiful property and increasingly courting conflict that I knew could end in disaster. One night a prisoner experienced violent seizures, and a rookie guard sent out an emergency call. When his commander arrived, he ignored the prisoner and scolded the rookie for calling something as trifling as a prisoner's health crisis an emergency. My friend in the next bed over, who knew I was a writer, remarked: "Put that in your book—that man could have died. If he hadn't pulled the pin, they would have taken twenty minutes to come."

On the outside, my fellow prisoners had largely spent their lives cycling in and out of shelter systems, working precariously or informally as petty drug dealers or shoplifters, following the dictates of substance dependence, and being perennially swept off the streets and into the city's jails. Many of them had experience in facilities across the island; for some, Rikers was almost like a second home, and for some of those who dealt in informal economies, occasional captivity was simply the cost of doing business. Sitting in EMTC, I was keenly aware of the dualism the place embodies: at the same time that Rikers is removed from the city, a space of enforced isolation surrounded by the East River, it is also thoroughly constituted by New York City, and, in turn, constitutes it.

In the exercise yard, I would do as many consecutive dips as possible, staring directly at the Empire State Building through four layers of razor wire fence and across the glimmer of the East River. All day, flights coming in and out of LaGuardia Airport buzzed overhead. From my dormitory window I could see planes taking off and landing, and the steady stream of traffic across the mile-long bridge connecting the island to Queens. Conversations buzzed about the New York streets, to which all of us would soon return, and new arrivals streamed in on a nearly daily basis, bringing with them their own unique stories of misadventure in the city's behemoth punishment system.

One day, I was staring longingly at the skyscrapers of Midtown Manhattan, doing my best to recount what life looked like outside their ground floors (mind you, the last place on earth I'd want to be if I were free). Then it struck me: where I was standing was not only just as central to New York City as Times Square; it was, in fact, Times Square's necessary opposite. Rikers absorbs the symptoms of social problems the city is unwilling to address at their root, among the populations who resist the imperative to work for a wage, offend public order, or else simply refuse to leave when the ruling class wants its neighborhood back. Just as one overturns a log and observes the bugs that enrich the soil, if you turn over the sanitized spectacle of contemporary Times Square—or Williamsburg, the Lower East Side, Long Island City, and all the rest—you see Rikers.

I landed on Rikers as part of a crackdown on anti-police street rebellion in New York City in the wake of the August 2014 uprising in Ferguson, Missouri—protests that would come to define the Black Lives Matter movement. This was an exhilarating time in which the courage and determination of masses of anonymous people transformed the political terrain of the United States, sowing the seeds of a struggle that still rages on in the wake of the 2020 George Floyd Rebellion. This movement also occasioned the rise of the Blue Lives Matter movement, organized through New York City's powerful Patrolmen's Benevolent Association, and the rise of a resurgent right across the United States, which would culminate in the election of Donald Trump on a platform of "law and order." Meanwhile, City Hall was pushed and pulled into impossible contortions, satisfying nobody, as the philanthropic juggernaut Ford Foundation plied the Black Lives Matter movement, to the tune of tens of millions of dollars, to keep its horizon business-friendly. These distinct poles, occasionally fighting it out in the streets and always jockeying for position behind the scenes, would help define the city's political terrain for years to come. Watching these antagonistic forces clash on the battlefield of New York City politics has informed the present study immensely.[26]

While at Rikers I began hearing talk about a campaign to close down the penal colony. This organizing work began with the Campaign to Shut Down Rikers, a group of prison abolitionists responding to the death of Kalief Browder. Browder, an African American teenager, spent three torturous years at Rikers while refusing to plead out on specious charges, only to take his own life after he was finally exonerated. At Rikers, Browder stood up to victimization at the hands of guards and his fellow prisoners, and upon his release he spoke out against the ordeal the city's punishment apparatus had put him through. Honoring Browder's profound acts of refusal, Shut Down Rikers demanded the jail be closed, with no replacement, thus forcing the city to begin solving its problems without resort to the police baton and the jail cell. Seizing the momentum that Shut Down Rikers had built, however, the Ford Foundation–funded #CLOSERikers campaign began to campaign for the creation of a network of skyscraper jails to replace Rikers. It was a plan that would not end the island's legacy of violence and debasement, but, as abolitionist organizer Bryan Welton remarked to me at the time, spread Rikers across the city.[27]

The cornerstone of this jail-expansion plot was the Independent Commission on New York City Criminal Justice and Incarceration Reform—often called the Lippman Commission, after its chair, former judge and longtime court reformer Jonathan Lippman. Composed of criminal justice reformers, veterans of the punishment system, and, of course, emissaries of New York City real estate, the Lippman Commission generated several important studies supporting the closure of Rikers Island and its replacement with new jails.

The problem with Rikers, Lippman and his cohort argued, was that it was not living up to the social potential of a jail. According to Lippman's plan, police, courts, jails, and ancillary nonprofits should be some of the strongest threads cohering the city's social fabric. And so, yet again, jail reformers pedigreed in the social sciences sought to repurpose jails toward the purported public good. "The new jails should be integrated into their surrounding neighborhoods," the report argues, "both in terms of design and uses," including retail space on the ground floor and spaces for community meetings. The local jail, argues Lippman, can and should be a "site of civic unity," tying communities together at their heart, both geographically and socially. As prison scholar Judah Schept described a similar jail-expansion plot, this plan "both framed and limited local responses to social issues, so that incarceration was simultaneously the problem and the solution."[28]

Shortly after being released from Rikers—at four o'clock in the morning in desolate Downtown Brooklyn, after being kept up all night—I met with the geographer Jack Norton, an expert on incarceration in New York State, to discuss what I had experienced and how to make sense of it. "The first thing you need to know about Rikers," Jack told me, "is that it began as a reform." This began my study of the historical role that reformers like Lippman had played in the formation of the Rikers Island of today, and why their plans had gone so horribly wrong. Jack shared with me his notes on the early infrastructure of Rikers, and we subsequently collaborated on an article titled "A Jail to End All Jails," based largely on this research, which was an important influence on the present study.[29]

I subsequently studied and wrote about Rikers and its related history with Zhandarka Kurti, Jayne Mooney, Tyler Wall, Nadja Eisenberg-Guyot, Abby Cunniff, David Campbell, Nate McDonough, Maud Pryor, CUNY Struggle, and the research committee of No New Jails NYC. This last organization opposed the construction of Lippman's new jails, guided by a mantra that has tremendously informed the present study: "If you build it, they will fill it." An earlier draft of *Captives* was submitted as my doctoral dissertation in environmental psychology at the CUNY Graduate Center, chaired by my advisor Susan Saegert, alongside committee members Cindi Katz and Jayne Mooney. I also had the honor of two outside readers: Rebecca Hill, whose work on the history of police and corrections unions influenced the present study tremendously; and John Garvey, who shared his considerable wisdom on the period, including an unpublished manuscript on the significance of the Civilian Complaint Review Board fight of the mid 1960s (in which he was a teenage participant). Ben Mabie at Verso provided outstanding support in carrying the project to completion. I am also greatly indebted to Bennett Stein of the New York City Board of Correction (BOC), who went above and beyond in providing me with archival documents, providing valuable feedback on draft material, and even inviting me to a lunchtime talk with BOC staff, where I presented segments from *Captives* chronicling the history of that agency and engaged in a lively discussion.

The work of an archival researcher is titillating yet fraught. Much of the history I have unearthed relies on either capitalist journalism or an outright DOC perspective—even material from the prisoner-run *Rikers Review*, which, though putatively written by prisoners, bears the imprint of DOC administrators throughout. Wherever possible I have foregrounded the voices of people who have been locked in the city's cages. In the case of prisoner memoir (of which a few excellent examples can be found from this period) and prisoner testimony, I have largely taken them at their word. This is so, in no small part, because prisoners' accounts of certain key events in the story that follows are demonstrably more reliable than accounts of guards and their sympathetic scribes—especially in the case of the large staff riots that form the narrative's bloody culmination. Even where ambiguity persists regarding who to believe, I do not fret bending the stick too far in favor of the prisoners' perspective; to do so would be impossible. Due to limitations inherent in the archival research of carceral institutions, the following account remains unavoidably skewed toward the view from the desk of DOC administration. I am consoled only by the fact that even from this vantage—which, we can surmise, is purged of count-less acts of violence, deprivation, and everyday indignity—the picture that emerges remains quite damning.

1

The Era of Horse and Buggy

A New Deal for New York

Human caging at Rikers Island began as a reform.[1] By the early 1950s, however, the progressive spirit of its founding commissioner, Austin MacCormick, and warden, Richard McGee, was largely forgotten at the Department of Correction. The shift was part of the zeitgeist in a city that seemed rudderless in the aftermath of World War II. When Anna Kross, a Russian-born lawyer and judge, took over DOC in 1954, she inherited facilities taxed to the absolute breaking point by the bottom tiers of the New York City working class.

Since the end of the war, the yearly DOC census showed that the total number of prisoners cycling through the system had more than doubled, from 49,330 to 110,048. In September of 1954, DOC reached what was then an all-time high of 7,921 prisoners in captivity—for whom there were only 4,276 cells. The Manhattan House of Detention, or "the Tombs," was rated for a capacity of 824, and in 1954 its population peaked at 1,660. In Brooklyn, the Raymond Street Jail, rated for 465, peaked at 848. City Prison Queens, rated for 199, peaked at 316. City Prison Bronx, rated for 239, peaked at 423. In Greenwich Village, the House of Detention for Women (HDW), rated for 401, peaked at 452. And the Rikers Penitentiary and Workhouse, rated for 1,887 and 1,000 respectively, were thronged with 3,759 total prisoners—roughly 2,200 at the former and 1,548 at the latter.[2]

An internal City Hall memo illustrates how overcrowding was justified in this period. "The so-called stated capacity of an institution," it reads, "does not necessarily indicate the number of inmates that can be housed there. The normal capacity can be temporarily increased during *peak load periods* by the use of double decked bunks, the placing of cots in corridors and the use of quarters normally used for other purposes." By this reasoning, short-term immiseration during "peak load periods" was excusable if it did not affect, in the long run, the functioning of the institution. This kind of grim calculus would define DOC management for decades to come.[3]

Upon taking office, Kross's administration anticipated a further population climb of 17 to 22 percent in the coming five years, due to "municipal population growth, an increase in adolescent crime, and increased police activity." This estimate would prove conservative. Meanwhile, DOC's response had been stopgap measures like packing multiple people into single cells and the conversion of nonresidential facilities to makeshift dormitories. "Recently many agencies of the City of New York started a drive in which summonses by the thousands were issued to landlords for failure to maintain living conditions as required by the laws of this City," wrote Kross's chief architect in a 1954 internal memorandum. "About all that can be said is that we are very fortunate that prisons were not included in these inspection trips. Very obviously we cannot operate within the laws regulating housing standards, means of egress, ventilation, sanitary facilities, and likely many more."[4]

The Rikers Island Workhouse provides a concrete illustration. The facility was fashioned in 1950 out of disused penitentiary workshop and warehouse space. In converting it to a Workhouse, DOC meant for 900 prisoners to share forty-three toilets, twenty-three urinals, and seventy-five water faucets— thoroughly unpleasant ratios in themselves. By 1954, however, the census had reached its peak of 1,548. Under these conditions, beds discarded as inadequate by other city agencies—including hospitals, police stations, and homeless shelters—were packed into every conceivable space, including the auditorium, recreation rooms, and even the chapel, "not more than one foot apart." Clothing and bedding were in chronic short supply. Individual guards were responsible for the custody of upward of 200 prisoners at a given time. Workhouse warden Edward Dros conceded: "We can no longer say that there is any program of rehabilitation, recreation, or therapy existent at this institution and it remains no more than a mere over-crowded hostelry, unworthy of the name of a correctional institution." This, for a population experiencing the myriad health effects of hard living on the outside, including withdrawal from alcohol and drugs.[5]

The disorder at DOC was emblematic of a city government that, just a decade after beloved New Deal progressive Fiorello La Guardia had left office, had become awash in the kind of graft and corruption that the likes of La Guardia had fought for decades. The two mayors who followed La Guardia, William O'Dwyer and Vincent Impellitteri, both left office amid charges of widespread corruption. By 1953, as political scientist Richard Flanagan puts it, "New York did not feel governable without La Guardia." DOC itself had been implicated in several scandals, including the granting of special privileges to an imprisoned gangster connected to the Democratic Party clubhouse Tammany Hall. Neglect at the institutional level was not just abetted by a disorganized city government, but actively supported. Mayor Impellitteri even refused to release the findings of a city investigation into DOC commissioner Albert Williams for multiple charges, including corruption and anti-Semitism in staffing. The city jail system, Impellitteri believed, was best left alone.

This crisis of leadership proved an opportunity for the younger Manhattan borough president, Robert Wagner Jr. Perhaps his biggest asset was his name; his father, Robert Wagner Sr., was a former New York senator associated with New Deal programs like social security, public housing, and the National Labor Relations Act. The latter, which granted legal recognition to private labor unions while enshrining bargaining rights within a regimented labor bureaucracy, is commonly called the Wagner Act. Drawing on nostalgia for the salad days of the Democratic Party, Robert Wagner Jr. challenged Impellitteri on the platform of "a New Deal for New York." He commanded a broad appeal in a time of disarray among Democrats, including the ambiguity of a name that allowed both Irish and German voters to imagine him as a fellow countryman—some of whom may have believed they were voting for his father, who passed away several months before the election. When Wagner was elected mayor in 1953, he sought a new commissioner to reform the scandal-plagued DOC. He turned to Anna Kross. In addition to being a stalwart progressive and loyal Democrat, Kross was also a friend of his father. [6]

It is impossible to situate Kross's tenure as DOC commissioner without understanding Wagner's concurrent mayoralty, and vice versa. Before Wagner's 1953 campaign, New York's unionists were likely to vote with either the American Labor Party (an offshoot of the Socialist Labor Party), or still another offshoot, the Liberal Party. Unlike today, general election results could split three or four ways among serious contenders. In order to unseat the fellow Democrat, Mayor Impellitteri, Wagner drew on his New Deal pedigree to court a labor base. He promised to formally recognize city unions, which had hitherto operated on the fringes of legality and lacked the powers of formal representation and collective bargaining. He also promised to expand the city infrastructure: hospitals, schools, housing, and other bread-and-butter public goods. This strategy paid off: Wagner won, with significant support from city unions. However, much was expected in return. At DOC, the unique tensions produced by this new era of New York City politics would converge in an increasingly crisis-driven mode of daily operation. In the tumult of postwar New York, Kross attempted an ambitious restructuring of the agency in the spirt of penal welfarism, the belief that carceral facilities could serve a positive social function akin to welfare services, if administered by experts in the social sciences. And as the control of city workers grew, Kross's efforts to place DOC under the dominion of civilian experts would meet with resistance from the ascendant force of New York City's jail guards.[7]

Enter Anna Kross

Anna M. Kross was sworn in as commissioner of New York City's Department of Correction on New Year's Day 1954. The *New York Times* lauded her as "a unique and woman jurist whose ability, example, and integrity have made her a civic symbol." The *Rikers Review*, a prisoner magazine produced at the adult school of the Rikers Island Penitentiary by a carefully vetted group of male prisoners, wasted no time beginning its twelve years of uncritical acclaim for Kross. "We can expect changes and improvements very shortly," the editors wrote, "for Commissioner Kross brings to the job the type of mind which inquires and then acts." Born Anna Moscowitz in 1891, Kross's working-class Jewish family emigrated from Russia in a ship's cargo hold when she was two years old, with Kross the only child of three to survive the passage. Kross came of age in a Chrystie Street tenement on Manhattan's Lower East Side, adjacent to the Allen Street brothel district, where she observed police harassing and arresting female sex workers while largely accommodating the male clients soliciting them. As an adolescent, Kross attended public school, worked in an apparel factory, and tutored fellow immigrants in English before attending Columbia University's Teachers College and completing a law degree at New York University at age nineteen.[8]

As a teenage law student, Kross began monitoring women's night court and advocating for the provision of clothing to the poor women tried there, many of whom were sex workers who reported victimization by the New York Police Department's Vice Squad. Through these efforts, Kross became involved in the provision of legal and material assistance to imprisoned women, to help them become law-abiding wage laborers. Kross was given a small office, courtesy of DOC, where she and a growing network of progressive reformers effectively functioned, under the aegis of the department, as social workers. As a private law practitioner from 1923 to 1934, Kross primarily represented labor unions, while campaigning for civil rights, women's suffrage, Irish Home Rule, and the establishment of a Jewish state in Palestine. "I love to match my wits against men," a young Anna Moscowitz told a reporter. "It is great fun, and I just love to beat them. You ought to see how foolish men feel when I win a case."[9]

Kross caught the eye of Judge Warren Foster, a Tammany Hall appointee, and was invited to speak on his behalf in his 1916 electoral campaign for a seat on the county-level Court of General Sessions. Kross delivered forty-four addresses on behalf of Foster. Though he lost the election, the campaign initiated Kross into Tammany Hall's insular inner circle. Growing up Jewish on the Lower East Side, Kross had viewed the Tammany as most non-Irish outsiders did: a nexus of electoral graft. But through her dealings first with Foster and later Tammany giants Charles Murphy and Al Smith, who also came of age in immigrant families in Lower Manhattan slums, Kross came to appreciate the organization. It was, in her eyes, a kind of unconventional social service provider that used the apparatus of the state to help recent immigrants establish themselves and become acculturated into the dictates of wage labor in the New World. More importantly, it was to be a potential vehicle for her own program of progressive court reform, which would require considerable political backing.

Kross's support for a progressive approach to managing working-class life led her to join the clique behind Al Smith's 1918 successful gubernatorial campaign. In Smith's entourage, Kross mixed with powerful political figures like Belle Moskowitz and Robert Moses, who similarly viewed the Tammany machine as vehicle for a reform agenda. Kross served under Moses on the Reconstruction Commission, which was responsible for the professionalization of the New York State government under the Progressive Era principles of modernization, centralization, and the elimination of redundancy. Like Moses, Kross played politics not for personal enrichment or fame, but to advance her own vision for transforming the city's terrain. The legacy of Robert Moses would be the dramatic alteration of public space in New York City and State. Kross, by contrast, had an eye on the city courts. Kross was granted a position on the city's magistrate court in 1933, and was robed by Smith himself. The ceremony was indicative of Kross's ascent in city politics, which she had played for almost two decades, sometimes winning, sometimes losing. "But in this game," she later remarked, "you can't cry when you lose. It's part of the gamble."[10]

In her efforts to remake the city courts, Kross also enjoyed the continual support of at least one Republican, her former New York University classmate Fiorello La Guardia. During his tenure as mayor, from 1934 to 1945, Kross had a friend in City Hall despite their nominal party difference. Long before the 1954 HDW rebellion discussed above, Kross toured the facility with La Guardia, hoping that seeing the conditions would help spur him to undertake reforms to women's incarceration. La Guardia told her he could put a stop to the women's criminal careers if he could simply find them all husbands. Unamused, Kross pressed the mayor for actual reforms. La Guardia suggested installing a curtain in front of the bathroom area to abet modesty—a solution Kross dubbed "the La Guardia curtain." This patronizing proposal is emblematic of the obstacles Kross faced in applying even the most basic principles of penal welfarism to the city's punishment system.

As a judge, Kross distinguished herself as a reformer in Family Court, Domestic Relations Court, and Women's Court. This was in addition to Adolescent Court, Wayward Minors Court, and Home Term Court—three "social courts" Kross helped establish that synthesized the court system with the emergent practices of social work. This new approach to punishment significantly expanded the role of the courts in the lives of working people, under the principle of making the system more humane. These courts introduced new authorities into the lives of working people—the judge, the prosecutor, the social worker—with considerable power over matters unrelated to the law: where they worked, how they kept their homes and got along with their families, how often they or their children attended school, and so forth.

Kross believed that the field of corrections should be professionalized and placed under the firm control of social scientists. In so doing, her hope was that the jail would not merely respond to criminal acts, but consider the prisoner as raw material to be reshaped by incarceration. Such reforms, Kross wagered, could only be won through playing the game of city politics. "There isn't a judge on any one of our benches from the highest to the lowest," she later declared, "who is there by virtue of what he knew, but rather by whom he knew, including myself." Accordingly, Kross's tenure as DOC commissioner occurred no more in a political vacuum than had her rise in the courts.[11]

Hysteria in the Community

The 1954 rebellion at HDW discussed in the introduction did not arise from circumstances peculiar to the city jail system. Rather, it was deeply imbricated in a wider political and historical context, including the massive demographic shifts underway in North America. The mass migration of this period from the US Black Belt and Puerto Rico can be traced to mechanization of agriculture that disrupted local economies. Suddenly, large numbers of landless, unskilled, and historically oppressed laborers and their families had to seek out more stable livings in larger cities, where they could find employment opportunities. New York City was a top destination. Once in New York, young people in particular were disproportionately unemployed, due to a combination of overt discrimination and structural disadvantage resulting from differential access to education and employment experience.

Now outside of the Jim Crow regime that played a large part in many black families' decisions to move north, black workers found in New York a colder and more impersonal form of structural racism that was nonetheless omnipresent in their lives. This included, as historian Eric Schneider observes, a "declining job base; the influx of African-American and Puerto Rican youths into a hostile environment; public policies that wiped out neighborhoods, ignored the displaced, and reinforced segregation; and the gradual abandonment of the city by better-off whites." It would be a mistake to reduce this to simply the effect of ideological racism. "Racism," write Stuart Hall et al., "is not simply the discriminatory attitudes of the personnel with whom blacks come into contact. It is the specific mechanism which 'reproduces' the black labor force, from one generation to another, in places and positions which are race specific." In 1950s New York, the mechanisms of this reproduction consigned black workers to bottom tiers of a labor market that was in profound transformation.[12]

So-called urban renewal was immensely disruptive to the racialized lower strata of the city's working class, and a dire shortage of legally mandated replacement housing resulted in a housing shortage alongside elimination of entry-level manufacturing work. Despite its rapid expansion during this period, public housing could not accommodate the staggering numbers of dislocated people, as a growing class fraction of transient residents floated between inadequate living quarters on the margins of the city's poorest areas. Moreover, the war had dislocated traditional forms of authority, empowering adolescents and women to leave school and domestic work in favor of blue-collar jobs that endowed them with considerable freedom in their interpersonal lives. High school enrollment plummeted. A lucrative trade in nightlife, including sex work, beckoned to New York City's youth. This was the situation faced by black servicemen returning home from a war waged in the name of anti-fascism and equality.

In the mainstream press, if not the popular imagination, a potent metonym for this postwar dislocation became the youth gang. Gangs provided structure and direction for young people navigating this moment of dizzying social upheaval, amid their widespread exclusion from formal employment. In his textured study of the youth gang phenomenon of 1950s New York, Schneider argues gangs were "rooted in a working-class world turned upside down." The distinctly outlaw culture of the gangs provided a path for young people excluded from long-term lawful employment to find their place in the world. However, the police perceived it as a direct challenge to traditional forms of authority. This was especially so when youth revolt involved black and brown men's efforts to build complex associations, which were sometimes unruly and otherwise placed a bold and organized claim on the use of public space.[13]

"I've never seen a situation so dismal," Irish writer Brendan Behan once remarked, "that a policeman couldn't make it worse." True to form, the New York Police Department (NYPD) responded to this chaos of life in working-class black and brown communities by adding more violence. Deploying the time-honored tactic of unbridled brutality—"muss 'em up," as they called it—police endeavored to control these youth with violence and arrests that flooded jails and created crippling disorder in the lives of people swept off the streets and kept away from their families, jobs, and daily lives for indeterminate amounts of time. These tactics also fed perceptions of a growing youth crime problem while exacerbating the tension and disorder in the streets that had catalyzed the creation of gangs in the first place. In 1954, NYPD launched "Operation All-Out," an aggressive street-level, arrest-intensive strategy responding to the perceived spike in quantifiable street crime. The initiative contributed to a rising arrest rate, and with it the rising population of city jails. Just a month after Kross took office, DOC's census reached a fifteen-year high. In Kross's words, an "unprecedented increase in violent crime particularly as it involved our youth has created almost hysteria in the community."[14]

NYPD's crackdown on the supposed crime wave of the postwar years was stridently opposed by a long-standing coalition of black leaders, including Adam Clayton Powell Jr., and organizations including the National Association for the Advancement of Colored People, the Civil Rights Congress, the Communist Party, local churches, and unions affiliated with the Congress of Industrial Organizations. The tradition of black resistance to NYPD extended back decades, to the beginning of the Great Migration from the rural South. These groups organized against police killings, for which the cops were never indicted, as well as the everyday indignities black—and increasingly, Puerto Rican—New Yorkers suffered at the hands of the cops. However, this uneasy coalition came apart in the 1950s, as the Cold War set in and the Communist Party's fidelity to the Soviet Union became increasingly alienating. Nonetheless, it represented a tradition of responding to crime wave sensationalism by pointing to the structural racism at the core of black and brown life in New York City, including the brutal violence and daily indignities with which NYPD upheld the color line.[15]

Then as now, explanations in official society typically emphasized the aberrant or dysfunctional culture, especially in family life, of the people committing crimes. A sophisticated 1952 study by the *New York Times*, for instance, pointed to the war mobilization, under which "families are once again on the move, women are entering the labor market, and the number of 'latchkey kids' is growing." The white establishment's perception of this crime epidemic, which began during the war, was from the start explicitly racialized. Tabloids wrote of the "Harlem crime wave," as if its conditions were not general across the city's working class. Politicians' emphasis on specifically juvenile crime would also come to define the federal government's earliest efforts to manage the urban disorder, undertaken by the Kennedy administration beginning in 1961. Such policy, argues historian Elizabeth Hinton, "aimed to change the psychological impact of racism within individuals rather than the impact of the long history of racism within American institutions."[16]

A 1962 study commissioned by Mayor Wagner, the first of its kind to deal with the problem of youth unemployment in New York City, sheds considerable light on the material roots of the crisis that DOC confronted in the city's jails. The study found that from 1950 to 1960, wages increased 57 percent on the national level, 60 percent in the nation's cities, and only 44 percent in New York City. While New York boasted the nation's largest manufacturing sector, with upward of 950,000 workers, these jobs typically fell on the low-waged end of manufacture—

such as textile, apparel, and leather—which were overrepresented in New York. The finance, insurance, and real estate sector, along with ancillary white-collar industries, experienced the highest rate of growth. Meanwhile, manufacturing, and especially apparel, was declining, sowing in its wake high unemployment in the lowest tiers of the city's workforce. These trends portended still more dramatic changes ahead.

The result of this transformation was an astounding number of young people "drifting in a tide of discouragement and frustration": some 76,800 youths from fourteen to twenty-four were out of school and either unemployed or relegated to part-time work. Additionally, youths from ages fourteen to nineteen, and those without high school diplomas, were likeliest to be unemployed. The report warned of a deepening crisis to come, due to an increase in youth seeking work, a decrease in high school completion, a shift in New York City demographics toward non-white populations with generally less educational and work experience than their white counterparts, and an "accelerated trend ... to increased demand for skilled and educated workers and a decrease in opportunities for the unskilled and undereducated."[17]

The correlation between this racialized unemployment epidemic and the rising rate of incarceration is striking. In 1958 DOC conducted a study of 3,296 adolescent and adult male inmates sentenced to terms on Rikers Island. Of this sample, a startling 1 percent could claim "a history of being fully employed," or of having "remained at a job steadily [with] regular attendance."[18]

The political and economic changes undergirding the much-vaunted youth crime waves were not limited to the youth of New York City, nor were they unique to the 1950s. "Massive suburban migrations and the 'deindustrialization' of the cities" in the postwar period," writes historian Raymond A. Mohl, "had devastating consequences, including job losses, deteriorating neighborhoods, concentrated poverty, and more intense patterns of racial segregation." While New York City remained a manufacturing hub well into the 1970s, the percentage of the city's workforce laboring in manufacture had been on the decline since 1910. The average manufactory was small-scale, clustered around ancillary businesses and services in "external economies" producing limited runs of commodities on a "flexible" model. This model represented a lucrative source of employment for many working-class New Yorkers, though long-standing ethnic and racial protectionism and male chauvinism combined to restrict most desirable jobs to white men. And even these jobs were not to last.

As historian Joshua Freeman notes, "As soon as a product became standardized and began to be sold in large quantities, its production was moved out of the city, and often out of the region entirely." As the ranks of the poor and unemployed swelled, so too did the populations of the city's jails, thanks to a response to social crisis that leaned heavily on those institutions to manage growing unemployment and the attendant disorder it sowed throughout working-class life. In turn, this move only exacerbated that crisis by further disrupting the social life of some of the city's poorest people.[19]

Flotsam and Jetsam

Kross once referred to the city jail population as "people of all social and economic stations of life and from the far-flung corners of the earth ... first offenders as well as the recidivists, the 'flotsam and jetsam' of our urban culture, the alcoholics, the drug addicts, the prostitutes, the homosexuals and other social misfits." But their common ground was more homogenous than such language lets on. A majority of detainees were simply unable to afford bail—a fact Kross acknowledged. "About one fourth of our detained prisoners have bail set at less than $250," she remarked. "It is self-evident that the individuals who are held in detention in default of bail are not usually our dangerous criminals nor our high-powered racketeers. They are the small-fry who do not have the means to put up bail." Kross later put this more bluntly: "The real crooks are out! Whether it's $25,000, $50,000, or $100,000 bail, you notice they get it somehow. But the poor devil with $500 bail that's the equivalent to $100,000, they're [in jail]!"[20]

Then as now, addiction and incarceration went hand in hand. Kross was known for her long-standing position that the "socially sick," as the *New York Post* phrased it, did not belong behind bars. "Year by year," reflected Kross's medical director, Rose C. Boyer, in 1961, "there is no lessening of the number of sentenced to the Department because of various manifestations of 'disorderly conduct' or other euphemisms for deviate behavior stemming from acute or chronic alcoholism." These prisoners most often committed no offense more serious than creating an annoyance in public, and their incarceration was simply a means by which cops kept surface order on the streets. "Their incarceration on what has been aptly called 'the revolving door' basis," Boyer complained, "represents the neglect of government and society in not providing proper facilities for their rehabilitation … *Sweeping them under the rug of Correction is the easiest way out for the busy law enforcement agency.*"[21]

Kross's DOC avoided explicitly addressing the racial composition of its prisoner population, befitting a general outlook that could be called race blind. In fact, it is easier to find data on the racial composition of DOC prisoners for the early 1910s than for the 1950s. Thankfully, a study on bail for adolescent detainees conducted by DOC and New York University in 1956 sheds some light on the racial composition of jail populations during this period, and the structural inequality underlying it. The study looks at a large sample representing the 10,924 adolescent detainees who cycled through the system in 1956, in detention ranging from short-term imprisonment in City Prison pens, to incarceration at the Rikers Penitentiary.

In a marked departure from the turn of the century, when European immigrants were heavily represented in the city system, by 1956 99.3 percent of the prisoners surveyed were US citizens (16.9 percent of whom born in Puerto Rico). The disproportion of the black population is striking: 37.1 percent of the total jail population was listed as black, despite black people only registering at just under 14 percent on the 1960 New York City census. The survey found that black people and those with Puerto Rican heritage were likelier to stay longer in jail, receive harsher penalties for the same crimes, and, above all, have greater difficulty making bail. Concretely: 44 percent of white detainees, 37 percent of Puerto Ricans, and 27 percent of black detainees were released on bail.[22]

Black revolutionary Sundiata Acoli, first incarcerated in New York City in the late 1950s, witnessed firsthand this marked racial disparity in tandem with deplorable conditions. "I came face to face with the stark reality of the American system of 'justice,'" Acoli recalls. "I saw with my own eyes that over-crowded, inhuman, sadistic environment ... I saw depraved, sadistic guards club brothers into unconsciousness. I saw sick addicts or just plain mentally disturbed prisoners slash their wrists, hang themselves with sheets, or burn themselves in a pile of blankets and newspapers." Roy Caldwood, a black Harlemite who took up work as a DOC guard in 1955, found the jails' racial division of labor reflected that on the outside. At Hart Island, Caldwood observed, "black inmates were always assigned the hardest, dirtiest work: shoveling coal for the island's power house or digging graves at Potters Field, a section of Hart Island where the city buried indigents when no family member claimed them ... Black prisoners dug and shoveled, white inmates worked as clerks." Even at the height of New York City's putative social democratic polity, the city's jails served as repositories for the racialized strata of the working class for whom the city's official society had no good use. In 1954, their ranks were only growing, inside and outside of jail walls.[23]

2

The Chasm

Professional People

By 1954, the city's half-hearted attempt to match the influx of "flotsam and jetsam" with increased carceral capacity had consistently fallen short for over a decade. "Custodial staff"—as Department of Correction commissioner Anna M. Kross called uniformed guards—had grown by 40 percent, from 882 to 1,237. Civilian staff, however—including medical staff, psychologists, psychiatrists, educators, and social workers—had scarcely increased (from 424 civilians in 1945 to 443 by 1954). Moreover, practically all of the new positions were manual labor, unrelated to prisoner programming or so-called rehabilitation. One psychologist and one psychiatrist were stretched across the entire DOC system, including Rikers Island, at a time when it was only accessible by a time-consuming ferry ride.

The ratio of civilian experts to custodial guards, Kross declared immediately upon assuming office, "must be increased several-fold so that not only a more adequate amount of treatment service may be rendered directly to inmates but in order that the professional personnel may be adequate in numbers to guide and direct the uniformed personnel in its program activities with inmates." This authority structure would represent an inversion of the traditional power dynamics of a jail system ruled by the uniformed guards; Kross wanted the civilians to dictate to the guards how the facility should be run. However, as Mayor Wagner strove to empower municipal workers' unions through his New Deal for New York, Kross would face opposition from an increasingly organized and independent body of jail guards with little interest in the garrulous theories of criminology or the latest insights of the social sciences.[1]

When Wagner tapped Kross for the commissioner position, she replied: "Just give me the trained professionals," meaning college-educated civilian experts. By 1953, only $50,000 of DOC's $8.7 million budget was allocated to "rehabilitation." By Kross's math, DOC was spending only two cents a day per prisoner toward programming that was even nominally rehabilitative. Kross also found the department lacking "minimal standards of medical care," treatment for drug addiction, alcoholism, or age-related afflictions. Sentence institutions needed a treatment program "to include reception, diagnostic, classification, medical and social treatment services, vocational guidance and counselling, education, vocational training, recreation, and separation services." Kross's program aimed to bolster not only clinical care but also education. "Investigation of the educational backgrounds of our prisoners in 1954," the administration later reflected, "disclose that there was a great necessity to raise the level of the 3 Rs ('Reading, Writing, and Arithmetic') of many of our prisoners before they could be taught vocational skills that might open up the world of social acceptability and offer economically rewarding employment to them."[2]

In a 1954 address to the American Prison Association, Kross invoked the spirit of professionalism that had animated DOC under Austin MacCormick and Richard McGee two decades prior. "Formerly," she reflected, "we had a sizeable social service department, a modern medical service, classification, a staff of psychiatric and psychological personnel—in brief, a roster of professional people." Wagner's New Deal for New York, Kross wagered, was the setting in which the spirit of this period could be recaptured. Rehabilitation would become the watchword of Kross's administration, driven by two progressive mantras: "We must abandon the notion that we are merely jailers or keepers"; and "We must do a job of human engineering." The first represented a fundamental shift in the power relations inside DOC from the custodial to the civilian—or, at least, the conversion of the former to the latter. The second defined the task of expert rule in the tradition of penal welfarism.[3]

The Rikers Island Hospital provides a concrete illustration of the downward trend in civilian staffing and medical facilities in the decade and a half preceding Kross's administration. Opened in 1935 as an ambitious seven-story monument to progressive penology, the hospital had succumbed to neglect during the war years. It never recovered. A DOC medical report later summarized its descent:

> In the 1940's the hospital [had] begun to deteriorate. The zest of the initial interest exhibited by the visiting staff had been tempered by the time-consuming problem of transportation. Visits to the hospital took too much time out of a busy day. The service needs of the Second World War made heavy inroads on the staff of visiting and consultant physicians. Those who left did not return at the close of the war nor were they replaced. By 1954, when the current administration took office, there was no visiting staff to speak of. The operating rooms were literally in wraps, no surgery having been performed in more than ten years. Essential equipment, viz., sterilizers, autoclaves, x-ray apparatus, developing tanks, electrocardiograph, etc., etc., were either in need of repair or replacement. Essential supplies were inadequate or missing.

As an avatar of this degeneration, when Kross inherited the hospital, the entire surgical floor was used exclusively for storage.[4]

In terms of staffing, the hospital had just six positions for resident physicians, of which only three were filled; only one of them was licensed. These overworked physicians were assisted by six part-timers, working shifts totaling a few hours each day, despite a daily census in excess of two hundred prisoners, who suffered from the myriad health impacts of hard living prior to their incarceration. DOC could only manage fifteen dental sessions per week, and the dentist simply pulled out the problem teeth, regardless of whether they were salvageable. The barrier to hiring presented by the arduous daily trip to Rikers was likely secondary to that posed by the low wages medical professionals earned at DOC compared to employment elsewhere. Nonetheless, it was a strong disincentive, and the residents DOC could entice to the job were most often "foreign physicians who stay only until they can get State licenses."[5]

The emphasis on civilian professionals was especially apparent in Kross's administrative restructuring of DOC, as seen in her hires for the department's newly defined central positions. Kross appointed as first deputy commissioner Harry Manuel Shulman, a sociology professor at City College, with extensive consultancy experience in policing and incarceration. Kross selected as second deputy commissioner Frederick C. Rieber, a lawyer with experience in Army intelligence and eight years at the New York City Department of Investigation (DOI), a dogged anti-corruption watchdog within city government. Rieber would lead DOC's legal division. For the position of DOC secretary, Kross tapped Arnold H. Wallack, a Harvard-trained sociologist and political scientist working in the public relations industry. Wallack would provide public relations for DOC, in addition to overseeing inmate social services. It's difficult to imagine which of these three men—the sociology professor, the DOI rat fink, or the Ivy League PR maven—would have been most objectionable to the average rank-and-file jail guard.[6]

Kross immediately ran into insubordination and attempts among rank-and-file guards to subvert her plans. A surprisingly candid 1958 interview with Kross on the CBS radio program *This Is New York* demonstrates the resistance Kross encountered, and the belligerence with which she met it. Kross begins the interview complaining about the spate of damaging leaks emanating from DOC that cast the guards as demoralized and questioned her leadership. She complains that in a "reprehensible and contemptible procedure," employees had taken their grievances to the press instead of to her and, in doing so, had distorted reality "in a fashion that made it look as if things were completely out of control—which they never were since I've been commissioner!" This she attributes to retribution for her anti-corruption reforms.

"I found that it was due to the fact that in my cleanup, I had been stepping on toes," Kross remarks. "When I'd inquire, 'Now why do we do things in this fashion?' I was told, 'That's the way we always do it.' I was also told I should not be surprised that correction officers or police—those were the words used to me, I quote the actual words—are entitled, they think they're entitled, to a gratuity!" Pressed by the interviewer, Kross clarifies that she is referring to bribery, from prisoners and their families: "selling favors, having to pay for that which a prisoner was entitled to." She continues: "Someone said I stopped the gravy boat. I said there'd be no gravy boat in the Department of Correction at my time, and I'm proud to say we reduced it to an irreducible minimum." Kross is talking here about corruption. But corruption is only as interesting as far as it reveals power dynamics that unfold in the ordinary, lawful functioning of an institution. In this case, the struggle over "gratuities" and the cutthroat posturing on both sides evince the most fundamental cause preventing Kross's application of penal welfarism in DOC: control over the daily operation of the city jails was firmly in the grip of the guards themselves. "That's the way we always do it," they told her. And they were not ready to surrender this domain without a fight.[7]

Custodians

In a 1961 overview of the Department of Correction's capacities, Kross's medical director, Rose C. Boyer, calls particular attention to

> the difficulties stemming from the differing values of the two disciplines—the custodial, on the one hand, and the medical on the other. To the custodial officer, understandably, an inmate's need for medical services is an inconvenient incident interfering with the routine of his functions and responsibilities. To the physician, the fact that the sick man is being held in security custody and the service he can render is thereby limited, is the

44

inconvenient interference. Each is thwarted in his relation to his basic function and responsibility. The chasm of [this] dichotomy is difficult to bridge.[8]

Boyer downplays considerably what was in fact the fundamental dividing line stratifying DOC: the chasm between the civilian experts and the uniformed staff.

On one level, this was an *inconvenient* overlap of different functions operating within the same cramped and stressful workspace. Boyer seems content to leave the matter there, perhaps for the sake of diplomacy. The chasm ran far deeper, however; it was, and remains, fundamental not just to the daily business of the city jails and its jailers, but the broader question of how society itself should function. In this pithy observation, Boyer had distilled the question that would define postwar New York: Who will run the city? Would it be the humanistic technocrats, steeped in the science of public administration, and other professional fields replete with specialized bodies of knowledge about proletarian dysfunction? Would order derive from the enlightened consent of the governed—and administered— masses, through the careful architectonics of social managers? Or would order emanate from a cruder and more direct source: the clubs of the city's cops and guards? This chasm was not simply a matter of ideas, but dissonant power blocs fighting for control. Their conflict would not be settled with appeals to morality or justice, but by incessant struggle for dominion over city institutions.

While the state of this uniformed staff in 1954, though significantly larger than the force of civilian experts, was scarcely better, the guards had one valuable asset that would appreciate in utility as time went on: the power of collective action. City unions would not be legally recognized as bargaining agents until later in the Wagner administration. But DOC's rank-and-file guards had, by this point, long been organized in the Correction Officers' Benevolent Association (COBA). COBA was formed in 1901 as a kind of benefit pool, namely to socialize expenses stemming from sickness and death among guards. In the subsequent decades, COBA and similar groups—especially the more powerful Patrolmen's Benevolent Association (PBA) of the New York Police Department (NYPD)—expanded beyond the narrow function of their origins to become lobbying organizations that partnered with city politicians to pass legislation that improved benefits and working conditions for their members. In the 1930s and '40s, COBA pushed legislation earning DOC guards an eight-hour day, the elimination of permanent night work, and the enactment of a formal command structure within DOC that standardized promotions and created the bedrock for career work in DOC. Still, COBA largely remained adjunct to the politicians it would enlist to push such legislation.[9]

A dramatic departure from this cloakroom politics came in summer and fall of 1953, when COBA and DOC Commissioner Albert Williams, Kross's predecessor, burst onto the city stage. The primary issue seems to have been the COBA demand for sick leave on par with police, fire, and sanitation. Williams argued this was a matter of law, not DOC policy. More fundamental, however, was the question of how much respect Williams owed COBA. The union was testing its power.

Accordingly, COBA and Williams vied for Mayor Impellitteri's support, amid claims of bad faith and retaliation. Their feud escalated to the point at which Williams stripped all DOC uniformed staff, from rookie guards all the way to wardens, of their metallic badges. Some even lost their right to carry a gun outside the jail—a cherished perk of uniformed DOC employment. A subsequent meeting of roughly 400 COBA members voted unanimously to demand Impellitteri terminate Williams, appending to their resolution a letter accusing the commissioner of "acting like a little boy who, having been spanked cries, 'I'll get even with you' and then proceeds to pull out his mother's flower bed." The municipal labor publication *The Chief* sided with COBA, depicting Williams, in the spirit of the season, as a Thanksgiving turkey awaiting the axe of "DISMISSAL." The mayor stuck with Williams, but Impellitteri's 1953 loss to Wagner gave them what they wanted. However, there were upsides to the Williams administration that many of the guards would miss when he was gone—most notably, his absence from their day-to-day affairs.[10]

Taking office with the cloud of this conflict still hanging low, Kross noted "a backlog of building operations, pending and delayed for a variety of reasons, a commissioner for several years under attack, a city naturally Democratic suffering because of party disunity, and inadequate budgetary provisions; all of which added up to the low and discouraging morale of staff." This was, however, not a problem merely reducible to wages, benefits, political legitimacy, or departmental efficiency. Nor was it limited to New York City's jails.[11]

Writing in 1950, Trinidadian Marxist intellectual C.L.R. James reflected on the lessons of his twelve years of residence in the United States and his extensive study of its society. "What is it the people want?" James asked. "That 'full employment,' 'better working conditions,' 'more leisure,' 'security' is what people want—this is a doctrine which reduces mankind to the level of horses and cows with an instinct for exercise." Surely James, who closely followed the US labor movement, was aware of struggles nominally waged toward these ends. But there was something deeper, he argued, toward which US workers strove. "The industrial workers, automobile workers, miners, railwaymen, marine-workers, rubber-workers, and in addition the millions who are not organized," James concluded, "want to manage and arrange the work they are doing without any interference or supervision by anybody."[12]

James, and virtually all Marxist observers of US society in this period, looked with great optimism to the nation's manufacturing, extraction, and transportation workers as constituting important bases from which American workers could assert their collective power. These were not, however, the only jobs in which Americans from working-class backgrounds strove to realize the yearning for freedom and self-determination that was so endemic to the age. Nor was it the only place they were finding social power. The cops and jail guards of the postwar period were steered by the same desire for autonomy over their work conditions as were industrial workers. Of course, New York's streets and jails were not factories or docks, and the human beings administered were not inanimate objects—though they were often treated that way, or worse. When cops and guards demand control over the conditions of their work, respect for the most basic human dignity of the people they oversee becomes just another obstacle to be overcome by collective action. Thus, the growing quest for autonomy and social power among cops and guards put them at fundamental odds with the human lives that constituted the raw material of their labor. Instead of promoting the interests of the class from which they sprang, however, this growing power bloc set out to serve itself.

Progress through Crisis

"The institution is crowded," opined the editors of the *Rikers Review* shortly after Kross took office. "No successful rehabilitation program can be instituted within an overcrowded prison, because vital segregation of inmate's 'personalities' or 'types' cannot be fully practiced … While this concept is not new by any means," they concluded, "progress toward this goal has been agonizingly slow." Though by all appearances run by prisoners, the *Review* was in fact administered by civilians in the adult education program and almost never criticized Department of Correction or jail conditions directly. In this rare instance of open grievance against DOC, the editors did not pose a challenge to Kross, but merely reiterated her consistent talking points from this period. To meet the threat that overcrowding posed to her agenda, Kross demanded from the onset the hasty construction of additional jail facilities, including a remand facility for adolescent detainees (who were hitherto mixed with adults), and a facility for sentenced female prisoners (who were grouped with detainees in the Manhattan House of Detention for Women).

Additionally, the Kross administration sought an expanded design for projects already underway: the Brooklyn City Prison (to become the Brooklyn House of Detention for Men), a City

Prison in Queens, and extensive improvements to the penitentiary on Rikers Island. City politics had taught Kross, as it had
taught her contemporary, the megalomaniacal builder Robert
Moses, that executive power may not be infinite, but it could
almost always be expanded.

In addition to deploring the "horse and buggy" conditions she
inherited, Kross also found the executive office of DOC to be
insufficiently sophisticated and poorly centralized. Kross complained of "an administration characterized by divided authority
and extreme decentralization of responsibility, with consequent
lack of control by the Central Office over institutional policy."
This meant that each facility was in effect run independent of
any central coordinating body, creating a powerful de facto rule
of order that largely trumped written departmental policies. To
a penal welfarist like Kross this was an obstacle to be overcome,
while to guards it afforded considerable leverage and autonomy
in their daily work. Kross also found DOC lacked strong executive positions "for such essential services as medical care, social
work, education, industries and personnel." The solution would
be the insertion of still more civilian authorities into the daily
work of DOC's guards.[13]

Despite the turn to experts at the top—or perhaps because
of it—the Kross administration worked assiduously to keep the
uniforms on its side. Its first major action was the restoration
to DOC's 1,100 guards of their badges, which had been taken
away by Williams during his feud with COBA. These badges
were not a necessary component of the guards' job but instead
represented the hard-won efforts of COBA to place them on
equal footing with NYPD. The badges were a symbol, in other
words, of the guards' ability to command respect from the city's
civilian leadership, while marking them with the same kind of
special social status enjoyed by the cops.

Though this gesture was in part symbolic, it was nonetheless an important token of Kross's intention to cooperate with
guards amid a program of restructuring they were sure to find
profoundly unsettling. Kross's first major change to the jail
system also came in response to the wishes of the guards: the

1954 closure of the Rikers Island Workhouse and its relocation to nearby Hart Island—a move demanded by COBA. Despite Kross's promises for redoubled civilian hires, of the 135 new positions created in 1954, ninety-eight were guards. Contrary to her wishes, this hiring pattern did not modify the ratio of custodial to civilian staff. But the opening of the new workhouse at Hart Island, along with the recent rebellion at HDW, in which women caused a raucous hours-long public disturbance, Kross's DOC reasoned, necessitated the addition of more guards.[14]

More, More, More

It was no mystery why DOC was scrambling to find adequate jail beds. As DOC administrators never tire of pointing out, the city jail system has no control over the volume of prisoners it receives; that is the domain of the police, who make arrests, and the courts, which determine bail and sentencing. At the exact moment Kross was attempting to move the jails away from warehouses for the city's unwanted, NYPD was doing its best to keep them packed to capacity. Kross's fellow Wagner appointee Francis Adams assumed leadership of a scandal-plagued NYPD in 1954, announcing plans to root out corruption and demanding a larger staff—in Adams's case, to the tune of 5,000 new cops. That very month, citing ascendant crime statistics in a dramatic televised address, Adams pushed a tough-on-crime posture, deploying dragnet-style "drives" against street-level illegality, which targeted "undesirables" for offenses like loitering. Kross made no secret of her disagreement with these tactics. Writing in 1954, her office argued: "We know the resultant products of [Adams's] intensive police drives. Our overcrowded detention and sentence institutions can already attest to that fact."

The cops were only concerned with clearing the streets in the short term; meanwhile they were thronging jails with people whose lives would be even more disordered when they got out. "The end result" of this approach, Kross argued, would "be that we will need MORE police, MORE prosecutors, MORE courts,

MORE judges, and bigger and stronger bastilles to hold our prisoners." Here a contradiction emerges—which would define Kross's commissionership and set the stage for the unfolding of events beyond it—between a pursuit of progressive reform on a societal level, and the adequate administration of jails within the existing state of affairs. Kross attempted to square this circle by adopting the jail as a site of potential social good. She committed to this strategy even as the city's increasing reliance on police and courts to solve social problems necessitated *bigger and stronger bastilles.*[15]

Looking back on its tenure in 1965, the Kross administration conceded, "We are all too conscious of the limitations of ... attempting to relieve the problems of overcrowding through the expedient of spending more and more money to build more and more jails designed to hold more and more people who should never have been sent to jail in the first place." Ultimately, while DOC could not divert prisoners from its custody, they argued: "We have at least done the next best thing. We have initiated a far reaching and comprehensive building program, carrying its various phases to completion as quickly as funds have been made available." By accepting the strictures of a municipal commissionership, Kross agreed to work within parameters limited to the provision of optimal conditions for those placed in DOC custody. The pursuit of penal welfarism, therefore, led Kross to the creation of more and more new jails. "If we had more policemen we'd need more jails," Kross remarked in 1958, "but that wouldn't solve the problem." Within the narrow parameters of humanely administering DOC, however, overcrowding wrought by the police solution to social disorder was itself the problem— to which new jails were the solution. And Kross would build them, seeking "progress through crisis in a constantly volcanic situation." Such was the struggle to shift the balance of power from the uniformed staff to civilian experts.[16]

3

War of Position

Revolt of the Guards

In December 1955, New York County district attorney Frank S. Hogan announced charges against eight guards at the Tombs, who were accused of selling a variety of perquisites to prisoners. For fifty cents, the complaint charged, prisoners could leave their cells and take a stroll down the cellblock's bridge. For one dollar, they could visit another cell, or enjoy a steak sandwich in their own. Cash could be smuggled from the outside but would always arrive fifteen dollars shy of the original amount. A quart of Scotch, worth roughly seven dollars on the outside, netted thirty-five dollars, while "economy sized package deals" priced at just twenty-five dollars paired outside food with whiskey. An arrangement with the jail's underground gambling circuit netted guards an unspecified cut in exchange for smuggling in cards and dice, and, more alarmingly, razor blades. But it was the smuggling ring's VIP package—a party for six in a linen room, catered with cold cuts and whiskey, for a total of eighty-five dollars—that ultimately resulted in the racket's downfall, after one of the attendees informed to the district attorney in exchange for a plea deal.

Eight guards in total were arrested, and in a turn of events constituting red meat for the press, it was revealed that one of the guards had numerous prior convictions for petty crimes, including theft, and two others had been arrested for murder and rape, respectively, though had not been convicted. Commissioner Anna M. Kross expressed anger that the district attorney had not coordinated the investigation with her office, claiming: "If I had been taken into their confidence, we could have gone much further in the matter. I still don't think the problem is resolved." But even Kross was not above suspicion. Soon there were three parallel investigations of the city's jails, by the New York County Grand Jury, Department of Correction (DOC), and the Department of Investigation (DOI). Kross's foes attempted to hang the scandal around her neck. However, she was not cowed, even after suffering a minor personal scandal of her own: Kross had hired relatives for DOC positions, including her husband, Dr. Isidor Kross. Unsubstantiated claims of misappropriated commissary funds added to a growing cloud of suspicion. "I'd never resign under fire," Kross defiantly avowed. She meant it.[1]

Though it was a public relations disaster in the short term, the scandal was not necessarily a bad thing for Kross, who by her own estimation continued to enjoy Mayor Robert Wagner Jr.'s "100 percent" support. Leaning into the scandal, Kross called within days for a "complete reorganization" of the uniformed staff, constituting what she claimed to be the largest personnel shift in DOC history, including wardens, deputy wardens, and captains. The plan also unfurled a new organizational table for these positions, introduced the additional position of assistant deputy warden, and reinstituted warden positions at three institutions where they had fallen into disuse. Kross was embracing the crisis, in a calculated attempt to shift the balance of power in her favor.[2]

Kross did all this in accordance with Wagner's Career and Salary Plan, a key aspect of his so-called New Deal for New York that rationalized the employment hierarchies of municipal organizations, mitigating individual and structural corruption—along with the comparative worker autonomy that comes from decentralization—with the trade-off of higher wages. However materially beneficial for workers such an action might have been in the long term, it is worth emphasizing how disruptive it would be for guards up and down the chain of command, many of whom were not breaking any rules. The resistance Kross met attests to this. In March of 1956, in a move almost certainly unprecedented in DOC history, representatives from all three uniformed staff unions—the Correction Officers' Benevolent Association (COBA), the Correction Captains Association, and the Association of Wardens and Deputy Wardens—along with other powerful uniformed officials, including Warden Thomas McDonnell of the Rikers Island Penitentiary, bypassed Kross and grieved the restructuring directly to Wagner. Threats hung in the air of a 1,400-guard march on City Hall. Wagner had been caught unawares by the bold maneuver and was forced to dispel swirling rumors of Kross's impending termination.[3]

During this time, Wagner had become less vocal in his defenses of Kross but nonetheless remained loyal. In response to the mounting pressure from the unions and the grand jury, he convened a special committee to evaluate the recommendations of the latter and use them to improve DOC. Kross, always one to steer into crisis rather than away from it, said of the grand jury's findings: "I might have written that report myself." In short, she declared victory and kept moving. It worked. The guard unions were just as correct about the opportunity of the moment as they were mistaken in their estimation of their opponent.[4]

Kross's victory relied on more than just outmaneuvering the heavy-handed union brass. Just weeks after the grand jury's initial report, Kross received a show of support from an association of jail wardens who assembled at Manhattan's House of Detention for Women (HDW). These high-ranking DOC officials expressed confidence in Kross's restructuring on the grounds that it replaced "acting" titles (which did not come with a boost in salary) with full positions; converted warden positions whose perks had included free food and lodging at the institution to ordinary salaried positions (with an attendant doubling in salary to reflect the loss of provisions); and refrained from bringing outside administrators into the new institutional structure developed under the Career and Salary Plan. The following week, Kross undertook another shake-up, including reassigning twelve wardens and deputy wardens—a move that elicited little resistance. This dance established a pattern that would define the remainder of the Kross administration. In August of 1956, Wagner established a forty-hour work week for cops, firefighters, and jail guards, which further sweetened the pot. The unions were playing ball with Wagner, and with Kross.[5]

The Situation

Ultimately, COBA and the other unions were far less interested in fighting Kross than they were in fighting for three key demands Kross could, for now, continue to deliver: better wages and benefits for guards, more guards, and, above all, more DOC facilities. In 1958 COBA had passed a resolution "Urging Creation of Additional Facilities for Inmates and Appointment of 150 More Correction Officers." Far from opposing it, Kross reprinted this resolution on the front page of *Correction Sidelights*, the official staff newsletter. Indeed, Kross had argued from the beginning, "While there is a great rank and file pressure for improved working conditions and salary schedules, these improvements will be obtained only with the transformation of correctional personnel from a purely custodial to a treatment force." Kross understood these maneuvers, however politically expedient, as supporting the implementation of a penal welfarist agenda.

DOC subsequently changed the time for guards to reach the maximum salary of $4,850 from five to three years. Kross had placated union leadership. But this did not necessarily mean the sentiment would be shared by rank-and-file guards, who do the actual work and often have political interests that stand in direct antagonism to union leaders. These guards, Kross wagered, could be won over to a more studied approach to custody—if the price was right. When first confronted with Wagner's New Deal for New York, DOC's unions had bristled against change. But now, they were clearly coming to understand its benefits. In exchange for their cooperation, Kross was willing to expand DOC's uniformed workforce and its collective power, as well as grow the capacity of the New York City jail system to hold

New Yorkers captive. If it occurred to her that the guards had a remarkably different vision for how the jails should function, this did not sway her course.[6]

On April 26, 1958, the women of HDW, packed well over capacity with a census of 513, once again staged a spectacular rebellion. After being locked in their cells for the evening, women took to their windows as they had in 1954, shouting, setting their sheets on fire, and raining crockery and flaming linen down on the street below. In the process, they attracted a crowd of onlookers estimated at 1,000. If the motivations of the 1954 rebellion had to be deciphered by investigators, this time the message was clear: "They were not being given enough to eat," explained the *New York Times*, and "a girl who had protested this had been beaten." The paper's source was the women themselves. Nevertheless, in the following days anonymous sources inside DOC alleged that Kross had covered up three assaults against guards and had told police who arrived to investigate: "Don't make an arrest. I'll take care of the situation. This is my problem." Subsequently, Kross had done nothing to discipline any of the forty women who had taken part. This bolstered the charge, allegedly widespread among guards, that Kross was "more sympathetic to inmates than she was to her officers."[7]

Subsequent events, however, followed a familiar pattern for Kross. The media rediscovered city jail conditions all over again; the jails, it was revealed, were at an all-time-high capacity of 8,032. COBA issued apocalyptic condemnations of the conditions, urging additional hiring. Wagner demanded an investigation, and Kross took some heat. But the scandal did not stick. Kross followed the events with her largest staff shake-up in four years, but there was not to be another revolt of guards. The three unions representing uniformed DOC workers met once again at City Hall—but this time they met not with Wagner but with a representative, and when they spoke of Kross, they lavished praise on her reform administration. Meanwhile, Kross was hard at work successfully striking down an austerity measure that would trim fifty-six guards from DOC's ranks—and from the dues base of COBA.[8]

This did not mean Kross gained unquestioned control of the system. The guards' struggle took the form of daily resistance to civilian power, management from above, and any impediments to their capacity to do the job with arrogant autonomy. "Generations to come will trace the fundamental history of the modern United States in the contrast between workers and employers," wrote C.L.R. James in 1950. "It is in these, what the workers demand, what they get, the millions of conflicts over grievances large and small, the interminable friction and jockeying for position, it is here that in the eight hours where the workers expends his life, his blood, his energy, it is here that the basic forces of modern life are in action."[9] Though it is highly unlikely James had them in mind, the work of jail guards in this period was no exception.

As they soon realized, however, the most effective way for rank-and-file guards to resist Kross's policies was not by creating a spectacle on the city stage. Indeed, such a move would only call more attention to them. Instead, they opted simply to ignore civilian leadership and continue to run the facilities as if Kross did not exist. "When rehabilitation was first introduced to this island" in the early Kross years, Rikers prisoner J. Rogers recalls, the guards

> tried to fight it either by ignoring it or giving those whose jobs were connected with it a hard time. In their resentment, or maybe one should say—their insecurity, they laughed at the "bug" doctors and derided the school program. The guards that were placed in those quarters for security measures made it so miserable for the participating inmates that most of them, out of fear of such constant prejudicial treatment, just quit, with others not wanting to take their places for fear of the same treatment.

Such was the day-to-day resistance playing out against her vision for the City jails, beneath the fragile peace Kross was able to broker at the top.[10]

The Board of Correction

The conflict between Kross and the guards produced a result likely unanticipated by either side. While Kross brokered peace with the unions, the mayor's promised investigation into DOC remained to be conducted. In a move reminiscent of her contemporary Robert Moses, Kross was originally announced as the chair of the mayor's committee to investigate DOC. By the time the commission met, however, and the story had garnered negative press, this had been chalked up to a "misunderstanding"; the chair, they announced, would instead be city administrator Charles Preusse. His findings did not mark a banner moment for Kross. Preusse sided with COBA, taking Kross to task for extreme micromanagement verging on autocracy. As the *Times* put it, "It can be assumed she did not welcome all the language or the recommendations in the report."[11]

The report was, however, heavy on rhetoric and short on concrete consequences. In this sense, Preusse's report was surely recognizable to the Tammany Hall veteran as a political victory, especially as it expanded the department's staffing to the tune of $500,000, spread over ninety-six positions, some of them administrators overseeing rehabilitation and other civilian branches of DOC. Like the grand jury and DOI reports, which it largely accepts as given, the majority of the Preusse report is nothing Kross had not already said about the backward facilities and administration of DOC. Indeed, it corroborates that the whole department was in need of modernization, which translates to an increase in funding and capacity. Kross had mastered the jail administrators' hallowed pastime of turning practically any criticism of carceral institutions into an occasion for expanding their resources and capacity.[12]

Even Preusse's attempt to check Kross's power strengthened it. Instead of returning to de facto decentralized authority held by local uniformed administrators, Preusse called for the establishment of a civilian oversight and planning body, the Board of Correction. Preusse proposed the BOC be modeled on similar lay boards in other states, like those in California and

Massachusetts. The purpose of such boards was not simply to check the power of the executive, but to provide long-term continuity amid the disruptive and often unpredictable turnover of correction commissioners—itself a victory for the civilian side of jail administration. Additionally, Preusse cited BOC as providing "a voice for the imprisoned segment of the population," which it found lacking in present carceral administration. BOC was tasked with long-term planning, conducting oversight over the city jail system, developing construction plans for new infrastructure, evaluating department plans through a penal welfarist lens, and regularly reporting on their activities and findings. For her part, Kross could not resist pointing out that she had in fact called for a civilian oversight board upon taking office.

With the issuance of Preusse's report, and Kross's swift acceptance of its findings, the *Times* effectively declared it the denouement of the crisis begun with the Tombs scandal and kindled by the revolt of the guards. The influential newspaper expressed full confidence in Kross.[13]

4

The Lesser of Two Evils

A Pastel Dungeon

The day after his committee's report on DOC was issued, Mayor Robert Wagner Jr. oversaw another milestone for the administration of Anna M. Kross: the opening of the Brooklyn House of Detention for Men (BHD) on Atlantic Avenue in Downtown Brooklyn. "We can never be happy about prisons," Wagner declared. "But looking at this modern new facility I have a sense of pride in that it is intended to help make better citizens of those who have lost [their] way."[1] The Department of Correction celebrated BHD as heralding a new era in its carceral facilities, writing: "The modern Brooklyn House of Detention for Men now replaces the antiquated, century-old *Bastille* dungeon known as *Raymond Street Jail*. We trust that the pioneering programs in rehabilitation and counselling, to be started here will be as far removed from the old custody concepts as the new architecture is from the old penal dungeon it replaces." Standing eleven stories tall with an 817-cell capacity, the $10.6 million maximum security facility had even been compared, DOC claimed, to the United Nations building in Midtown Manhattan—on the outside, of course.[2]

The facility represented a modified version of the plans Kross had inherited for a detention facility in Brooklyn, which by January of 1954 was already under construction. In DOC's telling, BHD's provisions included twenty-eight "spacious, light and airy dayrooms," along with "spacious, light and airy" cell blocks, "facilities for extensive segregation; modern medical treatment; provisions for recreation and religious needs; a library; closed circuit TV; a physical interior as light, airy and clean as modern design will permit," organized "to conform with modern prison management methods." Additionally, the facility was adjacent to a borough court, connected via an underground tunnel. Kross had modified a key aspect of the original plan, replacing space intended for a warden's quarters—obviated by the abandonment of the maintenance pay structure—with office space for so-called community-based service providers. Pointing to its airy, bright, "colorful and modern" facilities replete with "cell walls in pastel colors," the *New York Times* celebrated "a thoroughly modern jail" combining "the utmost in modern jail facilities."[3]

Beneath all the airy, bright, and colorful rhetoric, however, BHD was very much an ordinary jail. In fact, it was a particularly nasty one, complete with steel bars, scarce sunlight, and minimal facilities for programming or recreation. In this respect it was very similar to Manhattan's House of Detention for Women (HDW). Further complicating the Kross administration's gloss on BHD, the facility was almost immediately converted into a remand center for adolescent detainees, as part of an effort to centralize adolescent detention and segregate adolescents from adults. Retreating from the florid language of DOC's published materials, Kross admitted the inadequacy of BHD for this task in February 1957, when adolescents were moved into its barred, maximum-security cellblocks—of which DOC itself could not muster a single photograph for its *1956 Annual Report* that did not appear dark, bleak, and almost medieval in its design. Kross tried to spin the situation as best she could. Despite all these shortcomings, and the unplanned presence of adolescents, she tersely declared that "this new building is far better than any other available now."[4]

Most inauspiciously of all, the detested Raymond Street Jail, which BHD was constructed to replace, was not shuttered upon the opening of the new facility, but remained in use until 1963. The facility had been on the chopping block since at least 1930, when it was bitterly denounced by DOC commissioner Richard

C. Patterson Jr., who said it had "every vicious feature which has been condemned by modern penologists, sociologists and social workers in the last thirty or forty years." Despite Patterson's indignation, it would be another thirty or forty years before anything was done about it.

In 1957, City Parks commissioner Robert Moses, eager to convert the site to a playground as part of a development plan for Brooklyn's Fort Greene neighborhood, wrote to Kross: "I would appreciate it if you'd let me know whether or not there is substance to the ridiculous rumor which is going around to the effect that you want to continue the old Raymond Street Jail in use indefinitely." For her part, Kross insisted DOC's hands were tied until the city freed up funds for its proposed adolescent remand facility. The urgent task of a new adolescent facility, which Kross had declared upon assuming office, was tied up on the planner's board, slated during this period for construction on the Hunt's Point peninsula in the Bronx. "Commissioner Moses is extremely anxious to vacate 'Raymond Street Jail,'" Kross wrote later that year, "and we are even more anxious to comply with this request. Unfortunately, we have 648 prisoners in this ancient prison who cannot be relocated until this project is completed." In short, the opening of BHD, which was meant to conclusively close the notorious Raymond Street Jail, effected no such thing.[5]

Acute Problems

Upon taking office, Kross singled out two populations whose institutions required particular attention, and more generally, whose welfare had concerned her since her early days in the courts: women and adolescents. To address conditions at HDW, Kross campaigned for a sentence facility, so that the original intent of HDW for pretrial detention could be realized. Additionally, in keeping with the national zeitgeist, Kross had singled out adolescent criminality as both a challenge facing society and a particular issue facing DOC. "Adolescents in our prisons," wrote Kross's administration in 1956, "represent one of the most acute problems facing our city. The publicity which our local newspapers give to juvenile delinquency, school adolescent problems, gang wars, and adolescent narcotics can be taken as a barometer for the adolescent problem in our prisons." This sense of crisis had not been conjured out of thin air; the average number of detained adolescents had doubled in the previous three years alone from 400 to 800. Moreover, DOC was doing very little with this population. Kross identified the admixture of adolescents and adults in remand facilities, and the lack of substantive education and programming, as two primary challenges facing her administration.[6]

Prior to 1954, sentenced adolescents had been locked in their cells from 3:30 p.m. until 7:00 a.m. With the addition of more staff, time allowed outside cells was extended to 9 p.m., and a number of penal welfarist pilot programs introduced. Chief among them was a new school. In 1959, Kross used prisoner labor and salvaged materials to convert a Rikers Island warehouse into Public School 616, an accredited public high school for prisoners. A firsthand account by a student named M. Jones describes an intake process where, upon admission, the student was given a tour of the facility and given a choice between academic or vocational training (the former contingent on an aptitude test). If PS 616 improved the immediate situation of a select group of adolescents locked up at Rikers—even after expansion, its capacity was 350, less than half DOC's adolescent population—the school also normalized the presence of young people on the island, paving the way for the future expansion of adolescent facilities on the growing penal colony.[7]

Infrastructure expansion progressed elsewhere in the system. In 1959, the Rikers Island Penitentiary was renamed the Correctional Institution for Men (CIFM), comprising an adolescent division in dormitories fashioned from warehouse space adjacent to the main penitentiary building, and an adult division, composed of the original jail. In 1962, Kross opened the C-71 facility for sentenced adolescents, named the Adolescent Reformatory. Though it would be expanded significantly in the coming decades, comprising the lion's share of the massive facility known today as the Anna M. Kross Center, C-71 was originally two X-shaped buildings connected to CIFM, containing single cells, with a rated capacity of 496. In 1961 DOC opened the Queens House of Detention for Men, next to Queens Borough Hall in Kew Gardens. With sufficient DOC capacity achieved at last, the Raymond Street Jail was closed in June of 1963.[8]

Interested Citizens and Volunteers

Kross had long complained that the Department of Correction was "a stepchild of the city," in reference to the latter's apathy and unwillingness to provide proper resources. Absent substantive funds for prisoner programming, Kross invited volunteers and, increasingly, nonprofit organizations to fill the gap between what the prisoners required and what the city was willing to spend on them. These included clergy, philanthropists, and the twelve-step programs Alcoholics Anonymous and Narcotics Anonymous. As prison scholar Clarice Feinman argues, it was among the great progressive novelties of her administration that Kross fulsomely deployed these groups to provide a variety of services for prisoners. Beyond vocational training and the so-called three Rs—reading, writing, and arithmetic—"P.S. 616 also set out to open and extend cultural and creative horizons" through collaboration with groups like the American Association of Variety Artists and the Joseph Papp Shakespeare group, in addition to two nonprofit organizations, the Heckscher Foundation for Children and Young Audiences, Inc. The school also had its own student paper, *The Open Mind*.[9]

At HDW, partnerships included the Quakers, Salvation Army, National Council of Jewish Women, and the Friendly Visitors, Inc. These organizations provided material support and volunteer hours in rehabilitative programs. The Friendly Visitors, a group pioneered by Kross, acted as an adjunct to the HDW staff and assisted in implementing rehabilitative services to the prisoners. Their organizational goals were: "1. to make the institution more habitable; 2. to organize vocational training courses; 3. to better the recreational facilities; 4. to aid released women; 5. to acquaint other public-spirited women with the need, and to ask them to join in the work."

The Friendly Visitors served to bring a number of charitable and nonprofit organizations into the jail to provide services neglected by the state, such as the Manhattan United Church Women, the Key Women, the Pilot Club of New York, the Ladies of Charity, Jewish Family Services, the Woman Federal Jurors, and the Women's Conference of the Society for Ethical Culture. The ranks of the Friendly Visitors included the writer Max Wylie, providing him with much of the access he drew on in his highly laudatory portrait of Kross in the book *400 Miles from Harlem*. Additionally, DOC's staff publication, *Correction Sidelights*, appeared thanks to an anonymous "group of executives 'with a heart,' of a well-known printing firm in this City, who have been generously donating paper 'off-cuts' for use in our adult and adolescent training program."[10]

On the citywide level, the Kross administration would later reflect, "Volunteers have contributed yeoman service [in] social service work, psychological testing and classification, education, library service, recreation, counseling, occupational therapy, aftercare planning, and … aftercare services." Advertising the success of this programming, DOC touted the story of "Mary H." as a flagship study in the benefits of such programming to forging a docile workforce out of the city's jail population. "Overweight and untidy in appearance, Mary H. had not completed her High School education and was being hindered thereby psychologically and materially." As a prisoner at HDW, however, Mary was discovered to possess above-average skills in language and typing and received her GED, while also qualifying for the English Regent School, which could lead her to a degree at the City University of New York. Upon release, "after several abortive attempts which she was psychologically prepared for," Mary landed a job as a private secretary. "Naturally enough her problems were not all resolved immediately, but her self-confidence and self-esteem were sufficiently strengthened to allow her to accept her situation and patiently work toward the desired end."[11]

There was, however, a problematic side effect to this close partnership between charity workers and DOC. In 1965, decades of simmering scandal at HDW reached a boil thanks in large part to a young Bennington College student named Andrea Dworkin, who would later become a world-renowned feminist theorist. As a teenager, Dworkin was briefly jailed at HDW after protesting against the escalating war in Vietnam and subsequently spoke out against the deprivation, depravity, and abuse at the Greenwich Village facility, including sexual abuse by intake staff. Though accounts of its indignities and abuses had long emanated from the jail—literally streaming from the windows down to the Greenwich Village sidewalk—as a white college student, Dworkin was more appealing to the press than the working-class black women who were the facility's more typical victims. Her testimony against HDW garnered national press and put DOC on the defensive.[12]

In response, the nonprofit and religious organizations who worked at HDW defended the facility and denounced Dworkin. The ecclesiastical staff of HDW distinguished itself by ecumenically rushing to defend the facility. HDW's rabbi even claimed anyone "who hadn't been in a prison before would be shocked in any prison." Joining the chaplains, representatives from the Salvation Army; the Women's Prison Association, the City Episcopal Mission Society, and the Society for Ethical Culture joined forces to pen a letter to every city newspaper. It read:

> The people of New York who pay the taxes for the upkeep of the House of Detention for Women deserve an honest and accurate picture of conditions there. We have been appalled by the exaggerated and distorted descriptions given by news media. It is hardly recognizable as the institution we know. As interested citizens and volunteers, we have worked thousands of hours yearly in every corner of this institution; we meet inmates face to face in visits and conversations daily. We are qualified to set the record straight!

What followed was a categorical denial of the experiences of Dworkin and other survivors of the horrors of HDW. In six bullet points, the authors defended the institution, rebutting charges of staff brutality. On the contrary, "the attitude toward these economically, culturally and emotionally starved women is one of understanding and sympathy." Kross reprinted the letter on the cover of *Correction Sidelights*.[13]

Why would so many people ostensibly dedicated to making life better for HDW's prisoners line up to deny the abysmal conditions they suffered? The answer helps situate the social position of these organizations, which exist in expanded form in the present day. The nonprofit organizations that provide services in carceral facility or court system likely seek in earnest to improve conditions for incarcerated people, usually as part of a penal welfarist approach to public administration. These organizations tend to be staffed by compassionate people who wish to do good in the world and are willing to work thankless jobs under dangerous conditions. From their position within the institution, nonprofits can make small but important contributions to the quality of life and dignity of powerless people trapped in vulnerable and miserable positions.

In their day-to-day work, however, nonprofits operating behind bars must accept a partnership with the facility's administration, effectively becoming part of the punishment apparatus. Threats to the legitimacy of punishment become threats to the legitimacy of their own charitable work, and to the access that made their work—and funding, and often their very jobs—possible. Ultimately, these nonprofits have no choice but to facilitate the perpetuation and expansion of carceral institutions, lending them ideological cover and practical support under the auspices of doing good deeds.[14]

Roaches and Mice

Andrea Dworkin was only the most famous of the former prisoners of the House of Detention for Women who emerged telling horror stories. Those who found the most sympathetic ears were, like Dworkin, sentenced on protest-related charges. These included Benita Cannon, Barbara Pliskow, and Helena Lewis, participants in the campaign by the Congress of Racial Equality (CORE) against white supremacist hiring practices in the Building Trades Union. In 1963, they spent five days in HDW on charges of disorderly conduct. The trio emerged describing hellish neglect amid squalor and casual brutality: women screamed in agony for medical treatment, to the indifference of guards; clothing and blankets arrived filthy and stained; grimy mattresses emitted dust when touched; rats roamed the halls unafraid of humans; basic amenities like toothpaste and soap had to be begged, or else purchased with sexual favors or simply done without; a rudimentary cocktail of pills for withdrawal was indiscriminately administered for all maladies; and double-celling in already-tiny cells resulted in an arrangement by which, in Lewis's words, "either my roommate or I had to stand on a cot when the other one had to pass. We took turns getting in or out of the cell. Also, one of us had to stand on our cot when the other wanted to get to the toilet or the washbin in the cell."[15]

These conditions were also regularly described, though to less fanfare, by the facility's more typical prisoners. "Oh God, roaches and mice," an anonymous HDW prisoner recalls. "The place was corroded with them. The back of my neck was all broken out with some kind of bites while I was there. And this rat, I saw it right in my cell." Another young prisoner describes erecting clotheslines at night in order to pin up candy bars and other food that would otherwise be eaten by mice. She recalls:

There was two in a cell at the old House of D., and you had to sleep in these bunk beds. But the problem was, if you slept on the top bunk you got all the roaches falling on you from the ceiling and the walls. If you slept on the bottom bunk, you had to deal with the mice. So it was like a choice of the lesser of the two evils.

HDW warden Mary Lindsay denied the accounts coming out of the jail, going so far as to claim there was no pest problem. Lindsay even feuded with Dworkin in the pages of the *Village Voice*. She also joined with Kross to declare the only serious problem facing HDW was overcrowding—incidentally, not DOC's responsibility.[16]

Amid heightening scandal surrounding HDW in the 1960s, journalist Sara Harris conducted an investigation of the facility and the women who called it home. She found all the media accounts of the facility—tales of squalor, neglect, and casual brutality—substantiated by numerous women she interviewed. In the process, Harris developed a composite of the jail's majority demographic. Black women, who represented by Harris's estimation 60 percent of the population, were by and large

daughters and granddaughters of former sharecroppers, the poorest people in the South, who poured into New York during the Great Depression and the decade immediately following. They were told that marvelous opportunities for advancement existed in New York and that there was no "color problem" there. They were told that Negroes lived in houses with electricity, running water, and indoor toilets. They were told that the living would be easy in New York and that their children would go to the same schools and have the same possibilities of making decent lives for themselves as white children did. To them, New York was the "promised land" where they and their children could, at long last, lay their burdens down.

And what they found were the dirty, uncared-for slum ghettoes of Harlem and Brooklyn's Bedford-Stuyvesant and East New York, and basically the same sunup to sundown working hours they'd known down South. They found that they were no better off in New York than they'd been in the South. And they found that in one important way they were worse off than they'd been, because, now that they were already in what should have been the "promised land," they had no hopes of deliverance anymore.

These women had watched their families fall apart amid alcoholism, drug addiction, an extreme employment precarity; their options were often limited to sex work and day labor pickup areas like the one Civil Rights activists Ella Baker and Marvel Cooke dubbed "the Bronx slave market," where women stood by, forcing smiles as their muscles were literally squeezed by prospective employers to evaluate their strength for domestic work. When finally swept off the streets for "crimes" related to survival or despair, often in street-level arrests by slum-trawling beat cops called "ragpickers," these women were not particularly shocked by the indignities to which they were subjected. Some came to consider the facility home.[17]

Resignation among some prisoners did not, however, dull the low-intensity struggle constantly waged in the facility between prisoners and their jailers. In 1965 alone, prisoners set at least thirty-five "malicious fires" to protest conditions and to demand access to sedatives that would make their time in jail more bearable. "We did some funny things there," recalls an anonymous HDW prisoner.

> At night, before we were locked in, some of the inmates would sprinkle Rice Krispies along the corridor. Then when the night officer tried sneaking up on us to see if we were doing anything that wasn't allowed, the crunch of the Rice Krispies under her shoes would warn us that she was coming. She would get so mad 'cause she couldn't catch us.

Widespread lesbian practices, ranging from romantic love to violent coercion, thrived at HDW, with the guards either apathetic, or, in some cases, active participants themselves. The institution took token measures to demonstrate its opposition to romantic relationships, such as offering only "femme" haircuts in its beauty parlor. In response, "butch" women and transmen would simply steal razors or break light bulbs and use the shards to cut their hair. The masculine-presenting "stud broads" had a single garment available—the men's undershirt—but nonetheless incorporated it into a sophisticated system of coding that built forbidden relationships into the institution's daily life. Women also used sex to gain access to contraband by seducing prisoners and guards alike, thus cultivating supply chains that circulated food, cigarettes, and narcotics throughout the facility.[18]

HDW remained a great shame of the city, not least because it was out in the open, with its prisoners within shouting distance of the street below; hence it could not be buried from the public mind for long. In 1960, the city freed up $50 million for DOC's "long neglected" Capital Building Program, which included the construction of an entirely new women's facility on North Brother Island, in the East River near Rikers. The Dworkin scandal added expediency to this plan, as it spawned a number of city and state investigations into the facility. In response, DOC made a loud public showing of removing almost 150 women to a special section of the Brooklyn House of Detention—only to quietly move them back to HDW before the year was out. In a bizarre historical irony, for a short time DOC even plotted an atavistic return of its women prisoners to Welfare Island (previously known as Blackwell's, today known as Roosevelt Island), from which the women's facility was evacuated in ignominy a quarter century earlier. Building on a city island, DOC argued, was not simply cost effective, but allowed for a "horizontal design," to replace the vertical design largely discredited by the scandals of HDW. "Replace this vertical monstrosity," Kross had said of HDW, "with a horizontal layout that has a full rehabilitation program." It would be over a decade before the facility opened, and it would be located not on North Brother Island or Welfare Island, but on Rikers.[19]

A similar fate befell the adolescent remand facility. DOC originally planned for two facilities, one of which was to be located on a city-owned plot of land in the South Bronx. The area had long been a garbage dump and contained a network of scrapyards and an asphalt production facility. Kross hoped that development of this "eyesore" would not conjure the common response to jail construction, when "community organizations arise like mushrooms, vociferously clamoring that the prison be located elsewhere ... anywhere ... but not in their neighborhood." However, Kross was not the only one with eyes on this property, and DOC was ultimately outmaneuvered by local developers. Adolescents were moved to the Brooklyn House of Detention as a stopgap measure while Kross effected a construction plan for a permanent adolescent facility. When finally completed, the adolescent jail would be one facility, not two, and it too would be located on Rikers Island.[20]

5

An Island Metropolis

Manpower Development

Since its establishment as penal colony in 1903, Rikers Island had been home to sentenced male prisoners, and accessible only by ferry. At the end of 1959, when the entire population held captive by Department of Correction was 7,391, the population at Rikers was 2,596. These prisoners were mostly concentrated in the penitentiary, but small populations lived in the workhouse and adolescent reformatory. Writing in 1961, an anonymous prisoner at Rikers Penitentiary reflected on the island's division of labor and leisure, conceiving of it as an "Island Metropolis":

> Every facet of life that is incorporated in a small town has its reasonable facsimile on our island. We have our movie, hospital, dentist, library, band, fire dept., ballteam, employment agency (Vocational Service), Chapels, clinic, tailor, grocery store, butcher, school, welfare agency (Social Service), psychologist, restaurant (Mess-Hall), shoe repairer, laundry, printer, plumber, furniture store (Bed Shop), courthouse (Disciplinary Board) and even a jail (Isolation).[1]

A humorous advertisement run in the *Rikers Review* in the summer of 1962 announced positions for dishwashers, porters, housemen, maintenance men, short-order cooks, kitchen help, busboys, and waitstaff. Open to prisoners with definite sentences, the imaginary positions offered $140 to $220 monthly, in addition to free room and board, year-round employment, and transportation to work provided.

In all seriousness, work programs for adult males were available to far more prisoners than were the adult education classes. Commissioner Kross developed and modified the workshop capacity of the penitentiary, adding to the traditional industries of industrial machine repair, printing, and bed manufacturing the fields of auto maintenance, barbering, baking, and garment machine operation. Kross also introduced the Inmate Wage Incentive Plan, offering wages in the city jail system, paid directly to prisoners for the first time ever. The Incentive Plan was augmented by the introduction of a further retraining initiative funded by the Manpower Development and Training Act of 1962. MDTA was a federal program designed to combat nascent deindustrialization by retraining workers whose jobs were being automated out of existence. The US Department of Labor argued that MDTA was "the major vehicle for providing unemployed and underemployed disadvantaged groups with those skills necessary for entry into the competitive labor market." It was part of a "quiet revolution" in labor policy, DOL claimed, as it "considered the criminal offender as a manpower resource." The occupations it was geared toward at Rikers included machine operation and metal fabrication, as well as maintenance, gas-appliance repair, and shipping.[2]

Another program developed locally in DOC, called Restoration of Youth Through Training, focused on adolescent prisoners. RYT preselected adolescent prisoners based on a remarkable criteria: their perceived aptitude at operating IBM punch card data-processing machines. The city subsequently provided qualified candidates with job placement and post-release services. According to one RYT report, the prisoners encountered in DOC custody were

likely to live in marginal, impoverished, culturally deprived sections of the community. Their previous employment record is sporadic, a sequence of short-term jobs interspersed with frequent periods of unemployment. When they have worked, the jobs are likely to be low-skilled and low-pay. The jobs for which they qualify are decreasing in numbers because of technological advance and changes in the occupational structure. Not only is the number of jobs decreasing, but because more young workers are entering the market, the competition for entry-level jobs is tougher.

This was the reality that programs like RYT endeavored to remedy by working with incarcerated people. In 1963, the emphasis of job training at Rikers was shifting to "fields in which the demand for trained workers exceeds the supply": "typewriter repair, food service and preparation, graphic arts, plastic fabrications." Additionally, training at HDW was introduced for garment workers—a more stubborn, though lower-waged, New York City industry—through the Amalgamated Clothing Workers Union.

These programs constituted a recognition of profound shifts in blue-collar occupations in New York City away from manufacturing-based employment toward a service-based economy. But however noble their intentions, equipping urban prisoners with these new skills was largely shoveling against the tide. As historian Thomas Sugrue argues, so-called manpower theory underlying MDTA and RYT "explained unemployment as the result of individual educational or behavioral deficiencies, and deemphasized the structural causes of joblessness." Even the training meant to acclimate workers to new occupations outside traditional manufacture, like RYT, was premised on the idea that widespread unemployment was due to workers' lack of skill. The sad fact was there simply were not enough good jobs to go around. Most cruelly, prisoners regularly emerged from the city's jails only to find employers—and unions—averse to hiring them for jobs for which they had been trained while locked up.[3]

This is not to say that most—or even a majority—of prisoners at the Rikers Penitentiary were employed in sustained activity throughout their days. Indeed, these programs represented a select minority of prisoners and, like PS 616, were woefully inadequate to the growing population of boys and men held captive on Rikers. The account of one anonymous prisoner, incarcerated in the penitentiary in 1962, provides an in-depth view of daily life in that facility that was likely far more common than all Kross's ambitious programs put together. He describes serving a six-month sentence while doubled up with another man in a maximum security cell:

> At first I was unassigned for approximately a month and a half, we just laid around and done nothing. We stayed at the block all day and just played cards. We had designated days for going to the showers and the library, and so forth, but until you were assigned by the captain who was in charge of assigning inmates their respective jobs, you just laid around in either block 2 or block 3 and done nothing ... They have a television in the blocks, every block has a television, but it's pretty hard when you try and get 400 guys looking at one little television ... At night we lock in, doors would open at about 7:15, and you get your hot water to make coffee and so forth, and everyone's locked in at 7:30 ... lights are out at 9 o'clock.

The interviewer asks if he has a reading light and he responds that he does, but that it's useless on the bottom bunk. She asks if he ever saw a caseworker and he says no. Getting back on the institutional routine, he continues:

> As soon as you come back from chow you're locked in and you're generally not let out of your cell until 9 o'clock in the morning. You're in your cell until after the count, you have to have your bed and everything made up before the count, which is at 8 o'clock ... And after the count you still lay up because, they have what they call the house gang, they clean the block, until that's finished you have to stay in your cell, sometimes it's 9:30, then you come out and by the time you get out and settle down and sit down and play a game of bridge it's time to go to chow ... After you come back from chow, you lay around in the afternoon until about 3:30, just in the block. Sometimes they have "in or out," it depends on the officer that's on, if he wants to bother to open up the cells, you know for the guys who'd rather lock in and read in the afternoon, or if they wanna just stay out, it depends

on the officer who's on, but if you got an officer that doesn't want to open up the cells you gotta stay out until 3:30 in the afternoon, then everybody locks in for the count at 4 o'clock, you lock out at about 25 after 4, 4:30, and from then you just lay around for a little while and wait until you go to chow again. After you come back from chow, you stay around in the dormitory until 7:15 til the doors open up, you get your water. Then you just lock in your cell again for the rest of the night til they wake you up in the morning, 4:30, 4 o'clock it depends on what officer is on in the control room to put the radio on. You know, in the front of the block they have a radio. It's a very good radio they have too, if they put it to good use occasionally, but sometimes they like to put it on blasting, tear your eardrums out, just to get you up in the morning. It's pretty ridiculous at times.[4]

Here we see the prevalence of what Kross called "the 'lock-'em-up-forget-about-'em' policy," to which she declared an end in 1954. Its prevalence, eight years into her administration, does not indicate a lack of effort on Kross's part, but the intransigent resistance on the terrain of daily institutional life by the uniformed guards who oversaw these facilities. Kross and her loyal circle of subordinates could only be in so many places at once. Rather than fighting her on the main stage of city politics, they elected instead to simply ignore or outright subvert the civilian agenda for remaking the jails. Kross's agenda nonetheless continued, and would bring with it still more carceral infrastructure in which the struggle for power between civilians and guards would play out.[5]

Reception and Classification

During this same period, Kross used prisoner labor to repurpose an old wardens' quarters vacated by the elimination of maintenance positions into an on-site Correctional Academy for staff. Off-site, Kross partnered with City College and New York University to offer an associate's degree in administration of correctional institutions. At the former, this was open only to DOC employees, while at the latter, academic workshops were limited to wardens and deputy wardens. Additional university partnerships included a course on correctional administration at Long Island University, leadership training through Cornell University, and a partnership with Borough of Manhattan Community College establishing courses for guards on Rikers Island and enabling civilian staff to attend courses at BMCC's campus.[6]

Beginning in 1956, coordination with the New York City Community Mental Health Board brought mental health programming for select prisoners for the first time. The program fell far short of the pressing mental health needs of a jail system dealing with, as Kross's administration indelicately put it, "the social deviates, the homeless, various categories of alcoholic and narcotic addicts, prostitutes, the mentally retarded, the senile, and all the sorry motley crew who can't quite manage to steer clear of the law" and instead "fill our prisons to overflowing without any benefit either to themselves or to the community." An analogous psychotherapy program included the ecclesiastical authorities in a program of faith-based counseling. Yet another Kross novelty was the "Social Hygiene Project." Under this pilot program, aimed at preventing syphilis and other sexually transmitted infections, male prisoners were tested upon admission to sentence institutions, while all arrested women simply accused of being sex workers were forcibly tested and administered a penicillin shot.[7]

Hiring for clinicians during this time was eased by the incorporation of medical staff into the Career and Salary Plan, with attendant raises in pay, and the size of the medical workforce was increased by adding positions and filling vacancies. But the problem of long vacancies persisted. In 1962 Kross came under fire from medical staff for referring to DOC's doctors and dentists as "generally of low quality," claiming that in most cases "the only physicians that can be hired at present rates are those too old for active office practice, those with unfortunate personalities and those physically and mentally handicapped." The following year the New York City Department of Health took over the provision of medical services in DOC facilities, which the Kross administration welcomed as "a Department fully equipped for the two-pronged task of medical care for our inmates and the safeguarding of the community against the possible spread of infection." DOC would continue to be responsible for hiring nursing staff, administrative and clerical workers, and social service staff. The quality of health care, however, would not improve.[8]

In a somewhat ironic twist, now freed from primary responsibility for medical care, the Kross administration could pursue the pet project of its civilian care program, a complex institutional nexus of academic institutions, clinicians, and social workers. Upon taking office, Kross's administration observed how idleness and lack of proper classification had resulted in "conflicts among inmates and between inmates, smuggling and institutional traffic in contraband stolen within institutions or brought in from without, and homosexual practices." In response, Kross aimed to combat the "unsound" policy by which "cell blocks were permitted to be dominated by the prisoners, under an open-cell policy that exposed tractable and submissive inmates to the aggressions of assaultive, larcenous, and homosexual prisoners, owing to a lack of custody and program staff to develop normal community life and provide protection to the prisoners." Central to this undertaking was the practice of classification.[9]

The question of the proper classification of prisoners has posed a consistent problem since the earliest days of large-scale incarceration, which in New York City dates to the founding of Newgate Prison in 1797. Classification hinges on the peculiar ideological tryptic of incarceration, which combines the contradictory imperatives to protect society from a sentenced person, punish the person, and also rehabilitate them. It is ultimately an administrative problem: its proper exercise is meant to minimize violence, negative publicity, and behaviors deemed unacceptable from a management position, such as contraband smuggling and flagrant homosexual behavior. Above all, classification is meant to make carceral facilities more easily governable. Driven by the imperative to improve classification, Kross's penal welfarist program exercised considerable influence on a major capital construction project that would shape the future of Rikers Island, beginning with the facility that today bears the name Eric M. Taylor Center, originally known simply as C-76.[10]

A Penological Milestone

The C-76 facility (meaning simply "Capital Project 76") was originally conceived as a replacement for the Hart Island Workhouse, which was by all accounts decrepit, squalid, and in violation of city fire code. In 1957 DOC contracted plans for C-76 as an ordinary workhouse. Originally intended for Hart Island, DOC subsequently chose Rikers, "to take advantage of the savings that are possible by operating two institutions in the same general area, and to take advantage of the larger acreage available for a meaningful inmate work program." C-76 was meant to absorb and centralize sentenced male prisoners from the Hart Island facility in a more functional workhouse setting. Its prospective capacity was 1,200, with plans for a subsequent annex that would bring the maximum to 2,000. It would include special housing for alcoholics, narcotic addicts, traffic offenders, and non-supportive fathers, who were to be housed in dormitories emanating in a chevron pattern from either end of a long rectangular administrative building, traversed by a 396-foot corridor. "Observation should become a keyword in the development of the design," stated the architectural plans, a joint project of DOC, Department of Public Works, and the architectural firm Brown & Gunther. "All areas such as dormitories, rooms, cells, toilets, showers and dayrooms should be designed for ready observation."[11]

The most prominent feature of C-76—its overwhelming reliance on dormitories housing upward of eighty prisoners—came not from penal welfarism, but rather concerns over the facility's price tag. "Because of cost limitations," the designers remarked in the facility's plan, "it is necessary to house most of these inmates in dormitories rather than private rooms. It is recommended, however, that the dormitories be divided into separate areas by low partitions, giving some degree of privacy and at the same time permitting observation by the guard." Scarcity of funding delayed the project in its early phases. "Interestingly enough," DOC chided the city administrators, "the World's Fair for New York City is scheduled to be held in 1964 and, from experience gained in the 30's when the last World's Fair was held here, we can expect an unprecedented increase in our inmate population."[12]

By the time C-76 made it to the advanced planning stages, the facility had been rechristened the New York City Reception and Classification Center for Men. Upon the intervention of Kross, who insisted that "the physical environment of an institution bears directly on an inmates health, mental attitude, and response," the original plans had been modified, at least rhetorically, such that "a maximum of light and air is made possible through spaciousness and layout of building design." Familiar themes returned. "Walls are painted in harmonizing blends of pastel shades that lend a tone of pleasant brightness within the institution and seem to blend in with the spreading green lawns on the outside. It is all calculated to lift the spirits not only of the inmates but of the institutional staff as well."[13]

Despite sharing much of the pastel-shaded rhetoric that had accompanied the practically medieval Brooklyn House of Detention for Men, C-76 was clearly meant to be a different kind of facility. The new prisoner was intended to undergo a ten-day program, beginning with an orientation and followed by a number of psychological tests and interviews conducted by civilian staff. Prisoners would be screened based on their need for further psychological and psychiatric testing, and would be funneled accordingly into a track adequate to their mental state, overseen by a director of classification. Based on the ruling of the director, an institutional assignment officer would place prisoners in housing, including "special study project housing areas" for prisoners of particular clinical interest.

"Candidates" selected for these projects would be given additional psychological tests by rehabilitation counselors and meet with civilian experts over the following days. Casework on all prisoners continued until the tenth day, when they would be assigned housing and work by the Classification Board, and be sent from the intake wing of the facility to the housing area for settled prisoners, where they would serve their terms. The $10 million facility officially opened in January of 1965. However, later that same year, DOC complained of inadequate staffing to implement the processing program and persistent overcrowding. Until their abatement, the department reported, "the Reception & Classification Center facilities will be needed for housing purposes, and many of the scheduled activities must be held in abeyance." This abeyance would be permanent.[14]

This Will Be a Beautiful Institution

An undated recording from this period documents an anonymous prisoner's experience at the recently opened C-76. Asked, with Kross present, to evaluate the facility, the twenty-eight-year-old white prisoner replies: "If all the inmates were working in here, it would probably be a lot smoother running, you see. I have a lot of inmates that aren't working over here presently because they just don't have the jobs." He is quick to add: "There's no comparison like from here to the pen [penitentiary]. It's clean. It's very clean, and it's kept clean too ... I'm saying this from my heart. I'm not just saying it just because ... the commissioner is here. It's the cleanest institution I've ever been in in my life, and I've been in a few."

The prisoner continues to balance the positive assessment he clearly perceives to be expected of him with his actual assessment of the institution. "I like this institution," he hedges. "The dormitories are alright. They have a pretty nice setup too. But presently, they don't have a complete set of rules that are abided by all of the officers. Some officers will come in and turn the TV off at eight o'clock; some officers will have no this, and no that, no showers, showers at this time, no showers at this time; such and such, like there's no orders or nothing yet."

At this point the interviewer interrupts: "Well, because it's new." At which the prisoner quickly corrects himself: "Well, once it gets operational this will be a beautiful institution."

"Yes," the interviewer responds, "that's right."[15]

This attempt to force the party line indicates Kross and her subordinates were not naive about the grandiosity of DOC's penal welfarist program and the difficulties of its application. Nonetheless, they coveted the public perception that Kross was winning the struggle for the jails. In 1965 the administration remarked, with some bitterness, that it had taken eleven years to actualize a blueprint for "what must have seemed like a very simple measure"—bathing facilities and dayrooms in every cellblock at the Rikers Penitentiary.

A particularly embarrassing incident came in the fall of 1962, thanks to a two-part documentary for ABC television called "The Big Revolving Door: The Portrait of a Prisoner." The program followed prisoner John Rigby through his Rikers experience and back onto the streets. To the chagrin of administration, the filmmakers adopted the prisoner's perspective, even allowing Rigby to narrate. Rigby described two distinct realities: the flowery version of the city jails promoted by Kross, and the reality of daily life in institutions run by guards, where brutality reigned. He even claimed that the music piped into the dining hall, a vaunted environmental reform under Kross, was only played when Kross was present and was turned off as soon as she left. Kross, it seemed, was being placated by staff while her directives were constantly resisted by the custodial forces.[16]

Such was the bedrock reality for many prisoners beneath the facade of Kross's penal welfarism. But however far it may have remained from the lived experience of the average prisoner, this ideal served as the backbone of Kross's plans for DOC. All the major steps DOC took during this period were packaged as part of a much-larger strategy, which Kross understood as being fulfilled in small increments across time, toward a radically new approach to punishment in New York City. Less incremental, however, was the island's explosion of new infrastructure.

6

Build, Build, Build

Renovation for Rehabilitation

"Swing the crane," rhapsodized the *Rikers Review* in 1964. "Sink the girders. Sound the rivets. Almost before an inmate can leap or duck out of the way, a building is being born here. Since the beginning of the year, it's build, build, build. It's a lively little cadence, noisy but very constructive. It tolls of big things in the making here at Rikers."

An immense infrastructure program was underway. "It almost looks like an atom bomb hit a bull's eye right on the Island," wrote Warden Henry Noble in a 1960 message to prisoners. Though Kross had from the beginning expressed skepticism about building more jails to house prisoners who did not belong behind bars, the expansion of the island's carceral capacity during this period was justified by a philosophy of "renovation for rehabilitation." Writing in collaboration with Deputy Warden Emil Joehnk, the *Review* editors argued: "The present administration of the City's Correction Department has undertaken a vast program of rebuilding in order to foster a clime conducive to reform. Some of the building has to be done, some of it doesn't, but all of it is being done to help the inmates."

Under this philosophy, the *Review* explained, new buildings "will follow the prescribed pattern of being different from the accepted mode of a prison: "[Quadrants] are erected with louvered windows instead of bars; cafeteria styled eating areas, where inmates are seated at individual tables, are substituted for the cruder type tables." The facilities would be replete with "recreation day rooms with showers in every block; an enlarged library and commissary; corridors connecting cell blocks with all work industries; and corridors connecting clinic with hospital." These were the advantages of building horizontally that Kross had celebrated, capitalizing on the ample real estate of Rikers Island to move beyond the "vertical monstrosity" of facilities like the House of Detention for Women.[1]

"It is the opinion of the Correction Department," penitentiary prisoner David Ruskin wrote, "that there must be a constant exchange of discovery, improvements and experience. This great building program is to facilitate these ideas. It will play a great part in the rehabilitation programs set up in this Institution to help the inmate find his rightful place in life."[2]

Behavioral Sciences

Beginning in 1961, Rikers was used as a training ground for students at the New York University graduate school of social work as part of Kross's plan to bolster university partnership with the Department of Correction, strengthening in the process the grip of civilian experts on its institutions. When Borough of Manhattan Community College began offering a degree program at Rikers, the Kross administration called it "a giant step forward unparalleled in the annals of any municipal system anywhere else." Such casual grandiosity may seem laughable. But this claim referred not to the accomplishment of instituting an associate's degree in correctional studies, but what was meant to come next.[3]

In 1960, Kross unveiled an ambitious proposal for another new facility at Rikers, the Institute of Behavioral Sciences. This would not be a jail but a center of research and higher education. Planned to solidify and formalize the ties Kross had been assiduously building with New York City universities, in addition to philanthropic organizations, including the wide-ranging nonprofit partnerships Kross introduced in the previous six years, the institute was to be a center for undergraduate, graduate, and postgraduate study in a number of fields in the human sciences. The study was not to be done by the prisoners, but on them, with no discussion of compensation, privacy, or consent.

With the city's captives as test subjects, the institute would function "as social laboratory for advanced students in psychology, psychiatry, education, anthropology, sociology, public administration and law to test methods of the various disciplines as applied to the fields of crime, delinquency, and correction." Kross's proposal for the institute delineated the minutia of complex division of labor between civilian DOC staff, university staff, DOC guards, student interns, fellows, research assistants, and, of course, the commissioner. Prisoners, the raison d'être for this knowledge production facility, were naturally at the bottom of the pyramid.[4]

Upon taking office, the Kross administration asserted the prisoners "in our institutions provide an important 'natural' laboratory for research and study of important socio-medical problems of public health, viz: alcoholism, narcotic addiction, geriatrics, sex deviation, and mental illness." Kross envisioned turning Rikers Island into an archipelago of public institutions overseeing sundry dysfunctions of working-class New Yorkers, guided by an explicitly medical model, in collaboration with universities and nonprofit organizations holding aloft the banner of Progressivism.

Kross's plans for the institute also shed light on what she meant by the oft-repeated mantra that too many people were being locked in jail. "The Institute," her administration hoped, would "result in many more students entering careers in correction and allied areas than enter these fields at present." This would be a project to broaden "allied areas" administered by experts. Kross's position was therefore not to be confused with that of the decarceration movement that would arise a decade later. The problem, in her view, was not that too many people were policed or incarcerated. Rather, it was the specific figure of the non-rehabilitative, "worse-than-useless dumping ground" of the traditional custodial jail. To Kross, this meant it was a necessity to build new, better carceral facilities, with a broader field of social application. And building them on Rikers Island—where the growing daily traffic of prisoners, construction workers, and supplies was hindered by an antiquated ferry system—would require a bridge.[5]

The Final Piece of the Puzzle

By 1961, the dual forces driving the Kross administration— persistent overcrowding and the imperative to lay the foundation for a science of progressive penology—led Kross to devise an impressive program of expansion and centralization of DOC facilities. Construction on C-76 and improvements on the Correctional Institution for Men had overwhelmed the island's ferry system; clearly, logistical trouble was ahead. Additionally, a 1957 plane crash on Rikers Island, in which prisoners had played a vital role in pulling survivors from the East River, raised safety concerns surrounding the ability of emergency services to access the island in case of another crash or comparable exigency. And in the most banal sense, the ferry was simply a hassle.[6]

On the eve of unveiling a massive capital project for developing the island, DOC argued that the "expansion of the present New York City Correctional Institution for Men, Adult and Adolescent Divisions, and the building of two new sentence institutions at Rikers Island, makes it imperative economically and operationally that a bridge to Astoria, Long Island be constructed." The reasons were numerous: "In operating an island institution, serviced by ferry alone it must constantly suffer interruptions. Personnel recruitment is made difficult, work schedules cannot be maintained, deliveries are delayed, emergency service is halted, and visitors suffer long waiting periods. Ferries are halted due to fog, storm and mechanical breakdowns. This is a serious situation in an operation of this magnitude."

The following year, this list would include two more carceral facilities long in search of a home. "After repeated failures to secure adequate sites," wrote Kross's administration in 1962, "the City Planning Committee supported this Administration's plea for a bridge to Rikers Island. It is here that we plan to centralize our future sentence institutions (male and female), and to locate our long-sought-for, adequately designed Adolescent Remand Shelter." The bridge thus made Rikers Island DOC's obvious choice for both its adolescent and women's jail.[7]

In a 1961 letter to the State Commission of Correction, Commissioner Kross outlined sixteen reasons for them to support the bridge to Rikers Island. The bridge, she argued, would "directly connect 500 acres (largely unused because of its remoteness to the mainland of New York City.)" It would also eliminate DOC's $250,000 yearly ferry budget, and an estimated $200,000 in work hours lost due to ferry travel. Delivery fees and time lost to contractors for travel would be eliminated. Overall, Rikers Island's "practically unlimited land" could be home to new carceral institutions easily accessible from the mainland by emergency services, public transit, and employees. Parking on the island for the visiting public would "improve public and labor relations." The *Rikers Review* supported the bridge as doing away with "the long outmoded and sometimes tardy ferry that presently serves as mainland linkage," adding, "We all look forward to seeing such a bridge constructed, of course looking at it, someday, from the Queens side of the river." With the support of the State Commission of Correction, the bridge was adopted in the city's public works budget with the ambition of being completed by 1966.

The impact of the bridge was threefold. In the short term, it meant that a cluster of capital projects could proceed on Rikers Island, meeting long-standing needs and upgrading facilities that in many cases constituted a dereliction of the city's most basic legal responsibilities to its incarcerated people. In the longer term, this move allowed for the development of Rikers Island toward what Kross imagined would become a state-of-the-art center for progressive penology, soon to be renowned the world over. Most fundamentally, however, with the bridge in place, the largely barren or underused surface of DOC's sprawling New

York City property became the logical place for all future jail expansion in the city. The bridge became the centerpiece of an ambitious infrastructure expansion strategy, centered around Kross's penal welfarist vision, that opened the island's largely undeveloped surface to almost-unlimited carceral uses by a city increasingly leaning on police and jails to manage its social problems. With the best of intentions, Anna M. Kross had paved the road, quite literally, to the Rikers Island of today.[8]

Who's Going to Occupy Them All?

Addressing prisoners in 1961, Warden Henry Noble argued, "The Commissioner and all members of the Department of Correction do hope that the situation will be such that we never have to use these buildings or any other confinement facilities." Drunker still with penal welfarist zeal, the *Review* wondered: "Who's going to occupy them all, when we go home, and no new inmates arrive?" This was wishful thinking. The swelling ranks of the New York City jail population showed no signs of abating as the attitudes that undergirded this jail expansion began to harden. In 1965, after eleven years of what she called "progress through crisis in a constantly volcanic situation," a seemingly exasperated Kross administration declared: "Our major responsibility is to preserve law, order, and outward decency." Seldom if ever do the words "law" and "order" appear together in Kross's voluminous body of literature. Yet here she frankly admits not only that her administration serves law and order above all else, but that its experiments in rehabilitation had yet to come to fruition.[9]

When Kross took office in 1954, she argued that efforts to get the jail system in basic working order were a necessary step to realizing her vision. Twelve years later, she was singing roughly the same tune. Her administration argued: "When our correctional institutions have been rendered habitable, when space is available and staff is no longer overwhelmed by sheer numbers of prisoners, then re-evaluation and rehabilitation of those who are imprisoned may really have a chance to function properly." In 1955, Kross had declared: "The 'lock-'em-up-forget-about-'em' policy of the past is over." But by 1965, despite modest advances in programming and some basic improvements to infrastructure, DOC was still very much a custodial organization. What had changed was that now there was a larger, and ever-expanding, carceral network under DOC command.[10]

In 1964 the DOC census reached an all-time high of 12,288. The population had been steadily rising since the end of World War II, while the New York City population itself remained flat. Meanwhile, New York City itself was fast becoming a very different place. Mayor Wagner himself later recalled witnessing firsthand, roughly midway through his mayoralty, a change in the racial composition of the jails: "You could see the change taking place, where it was almost 70 percent or more blacks and Spanish people from Puerto Rico." During Wagner's mayoralty, the DOC population had shifted from majority white to majority black and brown. "In the old days," he observed, "it was mostly the whites, the poor." But by the end of his term, Wagner reasoned, most white New Yorkers had advanced beyond the economic strata that was regularly incarcerated.

This offhand remark acknowledged something Wagner would be hard pressed to admit during his mayoralty: the New Deal for New York, like the New Deal itself, had disproportionately assisted white workers. During Wagner's term, the earning gap between white and black workers widened as the shift of New York's economy away from manufacture subjected black workers to higher rates of unemployment, relegating them to the bottom tiers of the city's labor force. The growing population of black and brown prisoners in the city system thus attested to the other side of Wagner's social contract, which left a considerable portion of black and brown New Yorkers out of the spoils of postwar New York. There was growing consciousness among many in these communities that radical action had to be taken to remedy a situation that would otherwise not change. On one visit to Rikers at the end of his term, Wagner asked a warden why so many black prisoners suddenly sported beards. He was informed, "Black Muslims have begun to recruit here now, and they're recruiting in the prisons."[11]

In 1957 the *Review* dedicated three pages to a beginner's guide to Islam, by a prisoner named Muhammad Zahir, meant to facilitate understanding of Muslim prisoners. That same year, Rikers Island Penitentiary prisoner J. "Trip" Davis, sports editor for the *Rikers Review*, departed from the athletic events of the island's various prisoner sport leagues to comment on the proposed Civil Rights Act. Davis considered the act to have been "juggled, modified, and compromised to such an extent, that what started out as a giant step, has degenerated into an infinitesimal faux pas." Nonetheless, Davis argued: "A new school of thought is in existence... the church is playing the part it so courageously played in pre-Civil War days. Elijah Mohammed is slowly gaining power among the people. The South is fighting back. The NAACP is fighting for Civil Rights all over the United States." To this, Davis added the growing resistance to European imperialism in Africa and the Middle East: "The Mohammaden tribes of North Africa want their heads, as tokens of years of oppression; just as Henri Christophe, the King, and Jacques Daselines, 'The Tiger,' wanted their heads, during the turn of the eighteenth century, for the tricks played by that who-faced Napoleon Bonaparte on Toussaint L'Ouverture."[12]

This expression of black militancy in the pages of the *Review* was a novelty for the publication. It would become a thoroughly unremarkable sentiment among DOC prisoners in the coming decade. While it was fanciful to imagine Rikers as an island metropolis unto itself, it was undeniable that the place was part and parcel of New York City, a metropolis increasingly defined by social crisis.

7

The End of an Era

City in Crisis

"New York City is the greatest city in the world," opined the Republican *Herald Tribune*, "and everything is wrong with it." These words launched a broadside at the administration of Robert Wagner Jr. in advance of the 1965 mayoral election. Under the banner of "New York City in Crisis," the paper spent a month decrying soaring poverty and rising unemployment, spotlighting failing schools, and warning, in world-weary prose, about simmering racial tension, crumbling infrastructure, and the flight of middle-class whites from the city to the suburbs. The Wagner administration's record spending had not alleviated these problems, the fiscally conservative paper alleged, but had in fact exacerbated them, while feeding a bloated and ineffective city bureaucracy. Wagner, the paper argued, had set the city up for fiscal crisis. More broadly, the paper echoed much of what people at the bottom of the city's class hierarchy in particular had been saying for decades: beneath the facade of the postwar boom, New York City was coming apart at the seams.[1]

The series was, in part, a response to a cash-strapped Wagner's request to finance the city budget on borrowed money for the first time since the Great Depression. It was also part jeremiad against so-called big government. Ideology aside, however, the *Herald Tribune* stories publicized a growing web of cracks in the facade of Wagner's feel-good New York. While the series underscored the downward mobility of all blue-collar workers amid deindustrialization, it was especially unforgiving when it came to questions of structural racism, as recorded in disparities of income, housing, employment, education, and welfare statistics for black and Puerto Rican New Yorkers. Above all, the blitz served to foreground the inability of Wagner's administration to take seriously the cauldron of racial animosity these conditions engendered. "This is becoming a white collar city," a declassed dress manufacturer presciently complained, "with blue collar people." And the availability of positions to this dwindling blue-collar workforce was predetermined in large part by race.

In a 1961 article for the *Rikers Review*, penitentiary prisoner M. Grice reflected on these changes: "Machine age and industrial progress have made it compulsory to have some sort of technical knowledge and education. As production increases … the uneducated and unskilled are left hanging at the cliff's edge." Yet the author does not despair. "There are no patents on skill and knowledge … Each of us were endowed with these at birth, we need only to exercise them to succeed!" Similarly, in 1964 the *Review* ran, on its inside cover, an advertisement for the adult school, bearing the likeness of President Lyndon B. Johnson, overlaid with his words: "We have entered an age in which education is not just a luxury permitting some men an advantage over others. It has become a necessity without which a person is defenseless in this complex industrialized society."[2] But who had access to what kind of education and how it could be put to use were also questions thoroughly imbricated in the city's racialized class structure. These were not matters to be magicked away by appeals to universality.

Working-Class New York

The attacks waged against Wagner in the mid 1960s belied the successes of his tenure as mayor. Employment increased practically every year of Wagner's term, most prominently in the public sector, which grew from 347,400 in 1960 to 563,200 by 1970, when it boasted more "employees than the garment, banking, and longshore industries put together." Of this massive workforce, historian Joshua Freeman estimates roughly "half of it performed functions common to most municipalities: elementary and secondary education, police, fire, sanitation, highways, parks, and general administration. The other half were employed in New York's version of social democracy ... hospitals, public housing, higher education, and mass transit."[3]

Thanks to Wagner, this immense public sector was also prosperous and, increasingly, unionized. Wagner kept his campaign promises, though he did so with the calculating political savvy that had won him office. Mayor Wagner courted comparisons between his labor legislation and his senator father's 1935 National Labor Relations Act, known as the Wagner Act. However, unlike the latter, very little concrete change followed Mayor Wagner's declaration of recognition for municipal unions. In fact, what he called his "Little Wagner Act" was no act at all, but a series of executive orders. Wagner slowly and cautiously legitimized city unions as bargaining agents, establishing dues checkoff and selectively recognizing representatives. This enabled him to give strategic preference to his allies while disciplining his foes, and generally to keep a tight grip on the balance of power. Accordingly, the rank and file of unions were largely kept under control by labor leaders designated as partners to city management—the same arrangement that had animated the spirit of the original Wagner Act. Mayor Wagner's executive orders would not become codified into law until the 1967 Taylor Law, which built prohibitive penalties for strike action into a broader recognition of a bureaucratic management structures for the state's public sector unions. Therefore, the growth of New York City's municipal workforce under Wagner was contingent on its governability. Legal recognition severely limited unions' ability to exercise their most potent weapon, the strike. [4]

Under his Career and Salary Plan, Mayor Wagner rationalized and standardized salary scales and lines of promotion under an anti-corruption strategy that considered sunlight the best disinfectant, receiving widespread approbation. However, the program owed its popularity not only to its advancement of meritocratic values, but also to the increases it brought to salaries; in the first year alone, Wagner spent an additional $27 million on salaries over the previous budget. Thus, Department of Correction staff unions who had initially opposed Commissioner Anna M. Kross became ever more cooperative as the maximum guard salaries increased 94 percent during her tenure, and that of captains by 105 percent, attaining pay parity with New York Police Department, which had for decades been a central demand of the Correction Officers' Benevolent Association. In 1960 Wagner helped eliminate the Lyons Law, which mandated that city workers live within city limits, paving the way for a stark geographic divide between the increasingly well-off police and jail guards, and the working-class communities of black and brown New Yorkers they often interacted with most. The result was best dramatized by James Mangold's 1997 neo-noir film *Cop Land*, which depicts NYPD cops' lives in an insular white-flight enclave far removed from the city, which they consider nothing short of enemy territory.[5]

Simultaneously, the Wagner administration forged ahead of even Johnson's so-called War on Poverty, not just in public expenditure, but in the manner, almost inconceivable to the present imagination, by which it was financed—taxation. With little organized opposition to increased taxation among the city's political players, Wagner was able to consistently raise taxes on businesses as well as a variety of goods and services, including cigarettes, taxi rides, restaurant meals, and even tickets to entertainment events like baseball games and movies. While some of this was offset by the growth of wages during this period, Wagner's taxation per capita, which rose from $178 per fiscal year in 1954 to $467 per year in 1965, outpaced the rise of average wages. Wagner also increased the city's receipt of state aid by a staggering 187 percent during his tenure. This influx of funds into city agencies, coupled with the successful courtship of city unions, helped Wagner break from Tammany Hall and chart his own course. In the 1961 campaign, union members provided the shoe leather vacated by Tammany machine operatives with whom Wagner had broken, and Wagner was able to campaign openly against "bossism" and "the clubhouse" in the name of the highest ideals of liberalism. The result was a Wagner victory, a new charter giving the mayor extensive control over the city budget, and a new electoral base, rooted in the dramatic expansion of public services and public employment. But the economic basis of this expansion was not to last.[6]

Nothing at All

When Wagner and Kross came to power in the mid 1950s, the US labor force was enjoying the salad days that Freeman chronicles, replete with record rates of unionism, enabled by the senior Wagner National Labor Relations Act, and an average yearly increase of 3.6 percent in real wages throughout most of the decade. City unions saw a boom under Wagner, due both to the legal recognition he extended to them and to the growth of the public sector. These factors combined to make New York City's teachers, sanitation workers, and transit workers into powerful forces in city politics. It also created the same opening for the city's cops and jail guards. While Wagner claimed the mantle of the New Deal for New York, the large-scale public investment in these growing workforces was in fact part of a national trend buttressed by high industrial profits. Nonetheless, the postwar boom would soon run into several problems, beginning with what economist Robert Brenner calls "the weight of fixed capital."[7]

As the US rode high on the economic prosperity under which Wagner brought the New Deal to New York, the nation's fixed capital—machinery, physical plants, infrastructure—was becoming ever more outdated, and its profit rate diminishing. Meanwhile, unions struggled to stave off the impact of a slowed profit rate on wages. The largest US firms used their size and influence over the market to discourage competition from firms able to produce at lower costs. When lower-cost firms were able to penetrate commodity markets, the larger firms, tied to older fixed capital, were more inclined to meet the lowered prices than to completely overhaul production or exit an industry in which they were being outproduced.

This meant that large firms would increase production in order to enjoy larger yields of a diminished profit rate, in addition to living off their fat; they also increasingly opted to incur debt. On the most basic level, in response to an oversupply of commodities, all that competing firms could do was produce more commodities. Thus, a race to the bottom ensued, as firms eliminated as much labor as possible from their production processes, creating a paradoxical arrangement—unique to capitalism—in which there are commodities with no buyers, piled up alongside a surplus of unemployed workers. "This is the law governing capitalist production," writes Karl Marx, "arising from the constant revolutions in the methods of production themselves, from the devaluation of the existing capital which is always associated with this, and from the general competitive struggle and the need to improve production and its scale, merely as a means of self-preservation, and on pain of going under."

Simultaneously, decades of US labor militancy in manufacture, though ossified by this point into legalistic unions that largely acted as junior partners to management, had raised the cost of US workers considerably in manufacturing industries that had grown on the backs of workers paid low wages. For New York City, this meant the flight of manufacturing jobs from the city. By 1970, researchers found the unemployment rate for black youth in working-class neighborhoods approaching 35 percent, double what it had been in 1960.[8]

"Manufacturing jobs have been declining rapidly and steadily," the City Planning Commission's acting chairman wrote in a 1963 memo to Wagner. "Only in a limited sense can the current increase in white collar employment be considered a compensating gain, since a large proportion of New York City residents are dependent upon blue-collar jobs." Wages for black and Puerto Rican young people during this period were markedly lower, and unemployment significantly higher, than among their white peers, with significant barriers to entry and advancement in most desirable fields. This was also true of the workforce in general, where black people and Puerto Ricans who overcame structural barriers (such as differential access to education) and subjective barriers (like hiring discrimination) were nonetheless consigned largely to blue-collar manual labor—the area hit the hardest by the loss of manufacturing jobs. None of this occurred in a political vacuum. "At the very moment that civil rights struggles promised to reduce employment discrimination," writes Freeman, "the kinds of entry-level jobs that had provided a level of economic stability for earlier waves of newcomers diminished in number, creating overlapping racial and economic divides within the city and its working class."[9]

The mounting crisis of capitalism in the United States was, like every aspect of US society, inextricable from the color line. "As automation spreads," wrote black militant autoworker James Boggs in 1963, "it will intensify the crises of capitalism and sharpen the conflicts among the various sections of the population, particularly between those working and those not working, those paying taxes and those not paying taxes." New Deal programs like Social Security had been widely popular among white and black workers alike. But as Boggs predicted, the coming crisis would produce perennial "outsiders," expelled from the productive process altogether, and against whom reactionary politicians would attempt to play workers. "Out of this conflict will grow a counter-revolutionary movement made up of those from all social layers who resent the continued cost to them of maintaining these expendables," he wrote, "but who are determined to maintain the system that multiplies the number of expendables. This in turn will mobilize those who begin by recognizing the right of these displaced persons to live, and from there are forced to struggle for a society where there are no displaced persons."[10]

During Wagner's tenure, the nonwhite working class in New York City had grown dramatically. Between 1950 and 1970, the city's black population more than doubled, from 747,608 to 1,668,115, and its Puerto Rican population more than quadrupled, from 187,420 to 817,712. Meanwhile, the overall city population remained virtually flat. As comparatively affluent whites withdrew from the city, taking their taxes with them, racially stratified economic inequality persisted, exacerbated by the decline of manufacturing work. This dynamic was met head on by civil rights movement agitation, and soon, direct action on the part of the movement's more militant offshoots. While Wagner had black and Puerto Rican voters to thank for both of his reelections, he did not address race as an issue distinct from economic inequality. For this, he relied on tit-for-tat arrangements with appointees and allied politicians, such as Harlem's J. Raymond Jones, to manage working-class black New Yorkers, who were growing increasingly restive as the long civil rights movement picked up steam.

"You can spend two hours talking to him," an anonymous civil rights leader told the *Herald Tribune*, referring to the mayor, "and come away thinking what a nice man he is. Then, when you get around to figuring out exactly what you've gained, you suddenly realize that he's given you nothing at all."[11] This arrangement would not stand.

8

Battle Lines

Awakening from the American Dream

On July 16, 1964, a group of black teenagers walked through the white Yorkville section of Manhattan's Upper West Side, where they attended school. They were accosted by a white building superintendent named Patrick Lynch, who interrupted his work of watering flowers to turn the hose on them and shoo them away. He reportedly told them, in an Irish brogue, "I'm going to wash all the black off of you." In response, at least one of the boys, fifteen-year-old James Powell, chased Lynch into the building. Lynch escaped unharmed. As Powell emerged, however, he was approached by an off-duty NYPD lieutenant, Thomas Gilligan, who drew his weapon. Gilligan opened fire, pumping two bullets into Powell's body and ending his short life. Gilligan insisted he had been menaced with a knife, which many witnesses disputed. What is undisputed is the killing was the catalyst for a rebellion that would shake the city's white establishment, and serve as a vision of the future for dozens of major American cities.

Spontaneous demonstrations began immediately, met with a heavy police presence. Demonstrators on the scene confronted police, shouting, "This is worse than Mississippi!" The next night, the Congress of Racial Equality (CORE) and the National Association for the Advancement of Colored People (NAACP) organized a sanctioned Harlem protest nearly fifty blocks north. However, many in the crowd had no stomach for the nonviolence these groups advocated, and clashes erupted between Harlemites of all walks of life and NYPD. As historian Marilynn S. Johnson argues, "the first major ghetto uprising of the 1960s was underway."[1]

Nearly a week of looting, vandalism, and violent clashes with NYPD ensued in Harlem and the Brooklyn neighborhood of Bedford-Stuyvesant, with hundreds of arrests and injuries, one death, and upward of a million dollars in property damage. NYPD's response echoed the repression that had occasioned the rioting in the first place, including wanton beatings and "warning" shots fired at crowds of black New Yorkers. As Harlemite Abayama Katara later recalled:

> I saw people I had known all my life, the same people that broke up the fights around the block, that screamed and called the cops when rumbles started, these same people that had stopped us from killing ourselves in our futile attempts at gaining manhood by gang wars—they were out in the street with bricks and bottles in their hands.[2]

Herald Tribune journalist Barry Gottehrer, who would assume the role of mediator of race relations in Harlem under the next mayor, John Lindsay, understood the Harlem riots as the symptom of a failing black leadership class. "Between the absentee leaders, the rioters, the looters, the opportunists, and the respectable people," wrote the paper, under his direction, "there was little or no communication. The middle class, which might have bridged the gap, was sorely missed." Katara begged to differ: "Housewives, young bloods, pimps, pushers, whores, bloods with so-called 'good' jobs," he recalled, "were all in the streets telling the man in the only way they knew how that black people had started to awaken from the 'American dream.'"[3]

Langston Hughes similarly captured the zeitgeist in the poem "Death in Yorkville (James Powell, Summer, 1964)":

How many bullets does it take
To kill a fifteen-year-old kid?
How many bullets does it take
To kill me?

How many centuries does it take
To bind my mind—chain my feet—
Rope my neck—lynch me—
Unfree?

From the slave chain to the lynch rope
To the bullets of Yorkville,
Jamestown, 1619 to 1963:
Emancipation Centennial—
100 years NOT free.

Civil War Centenntial: 1965
How many Centennials does it take
To kill me,
Still alive?

When the long hot summers come
Death ain't
No jive.[4]

For his part, Wagner convinced Martin Luther King Jr. to take
to the streets in order to quell the rebellion. After he agreed,
King learned that Wagner intended to offer no concessions to
the enraged black New Yorkers. The New Deal scion simply
wanted King to use his charisma and political clout to stop the
rioting.

Wagner's efforts were futile. The riots signaled two important transformations in American political life. The first was a
growing bifurcation within the civil rights movement. Neither
Martin Luther King Jr., heeding Wagner's call, nor his fellow
civil rights leaders Bayard Rustin and James Farmer proved able
to restore order, as crowds called Rustin an Uncle Tom for urging

people to disperse and to otherwise resist in nonviolent ways. The second was the rise to prominence of an explicitly reactionary movement that would come to be called "law and order." Indeed, just hours after Powell's killing, presidential nominee Barry Goldwater took the podium at the Republican National Convention, where he denounced "violence in the streets" and called for a crackdown on the disorder in America's cities.[5]

Support Your Local Police

To NYPD rank and filers, the growing movement against police brutality and killings was an affront to police power, plain and simple. This was an important moment in NYPD history, when the low-ranking cops' union, the Patrolmen's Benevolent Association (PBA), was coming into its own as a political power in the city. Like the Correction Officers' Benevolent Association (COBA), PBA had originated as a pool to cover the risks of injury, disease, and death, and had morphed over time into a member-advocacy organization. Initially denied union recognition, police were included in a 1964 amendment to Mayor Wagner's executive orders, granting PBA the full powers of a city union. This was largely a formality, however, as under Wagner PBA already enjoyed the same recognition and esteem as other municipal unions, if informally. But legal recognition also cemented the power of PBA to act independently of City Hall, and solidified the legal standing and political clout of the union's activism to follow.

Wagner's recognition of municipal unions helped bolster the power of PBA to take independent action. Especially since the insurgent victory of patrolman John Cassese, elected president in 1958, PBA had become increasingly antagonistic toward City Hall and any perceived enemies of the cops' ability to do their job however they saw fit. Under Cassese, PBA took aim at Wagner-appointed NYPD commissioner Stephen Kennedy, who had refused to bargain with the union and had taken the provocative step of banning police from working part-time jobs in their time off. In response, PBA undertook direct action, conducting ticketing slowdowns that curtailed city revenue. Anti-Kennedy slogans sounded over the police radio, and the increasingly frustrated commissioner bugged squad cars in an effort to find the culprits. Where COBA's revolt of guards failed, PBA's initiative against Kennedy succeeded: Wagner, who needed the union's support to stay in power, pushed Kennedy to resign in 1961. A new power had flexed its muscle in City Hall. While PBA was the last to be formally recognized, this was not its endgame; indeed, it would never be enough for PBA to be just another city union.[6]

In 1965, the final year of Wagner's mayoralty, PBA tested its newfound power in a campaign against a relatively mild plan to restructure NYPD's Civilian Complaint Review Board. The CCRB had been established as a concessionary measure in 1953, amid scandal surrounding NYPD's internal review of brutality complaints. Its name, however, was deceptive. The original CCRB was in fact composed of three NYPD officials, accountable only to the commissioner, and in practice did not represent a departure from the status quo. By 1964, a panoply of community organizations representing black and Puerto Rican neighborhoods called for the establishment of a board composed of actual civilians. Support for this plan grew amid a rash of suspicious deaths in custody and murder confessions apparently elicited using "the third degree"—a euphemism for wanton brutality.

Support for a reformed CCRB extended even to the Guardian Association, an organization of black cops. However, this group was outmatched and outnumbered by a growing force of white cops mobilizing in response to the civil rights movement and the procedural revolution in the Supreme Court led by Chief Justice Earl Warren. This latter movement was not simply directed from above by PBA leadership but represented dynamism between the firebrand Cassese and a growing base of support for right-wing politics within NYPD.[7]

In May 1964, operating under the banner of the "Committee to Support Your Local Police," a front group for the ultra-right

John Birch Society (JBS), one hundred right-wing activists picketed NYPD headquarters, denouncing the plan to restructure the CCRB. They chanted "fight the reds, support the blue," waved American flags, and displayed signs whose messages included "Police Are Our Last Line of Defense against Communism." Founded in 1958, JBS was an offshoot of the National Association of Manufacturers, a far-right organization of petit bourgeois business nationalists anchored in corporations who had vehemently opposed the New Deal and the US presence in the United Nations. They particularly opposed the encroachment of the federal government on local power structures in both the Jim Crow South and the North, identifying the liberalism underlying the Warren Court and civil rights legislation as a symptom of communist infiltration of the US government.

Building on the long-term history of anti-communism among US police, the JBS fought to empower law enforcement against its malevolent enemies: an invasive federal government that sought to impose civil rights legislation on the states, and on the local level, civilian review boards. Conveniently, this served to buttress localized white power structures, suddenly vulnerable to federal enforcement of civil rights legislation, especially after the Civil Rights Act of 1964—JBS's most active year. Regardless of whether they believed the group's often-outlandish conspiracy theories about communist subversion, JBS was a natural ally to cops who opposed civilian oversight, whether from the civil rights movement, the federal government, local police review boards, or anyone else, including their city's mayor.[8]

The growth of this nascent law-and-order coalition coincided with *Brown v. Board of Education* and other victories for formal racial equality; in turn, these court decisions spurred the mobilization of both organized efforts like the JBS as well as informal backlash across the entire South. The Warren Court also delivered several rulings strengthening due process dubbed "the criminal law revolution," most famously Miranda rights and greater protections against unreasonable search and seizure. Police across the country perceived this as an affront to their control over working conditions, which it most certainly was—perhaps especially to their role as de facto enforcers of the white power structure, acting outside the law to discipline nonwhite people in Northern ghettos and the Jim Crow South alike. The growing backlash against civil rights and civil liberties reached a high-water mark in George Wallace's abortive primary campaign for the 1964 Democratic presidential nomination, which, along with the growing influence of the John Birch Society, captured the imagination of enough NYPD cops that Wallace bumper stickers had to be removed from their cruisers. The celebration of Wallace and opposition to civilian review of police were therefore part of one coherent movement, aimed at protecting what the celebrated essayist and novelist James Baldwin called their "arrogant autonomy"—the coveted ability of cops to do their jobs however they see fit, with no limits to the violence, degradation, rule breaking, or outright illegal acts this entails.[9]

The month after the 1964 Support Your Local Police rally, PBA sponsored a similar rally outside City Hall, where the new board was being debated by city council. This time, there were 1,200 in attendance. Speaking inside, PBA president Cassese called the restructured board "a deliberate and unwarranted affront to the police of New York City," while Kennedy's successor, Michael J. Murphy, decidedly friendlier to PBA, warned that if the measure passed, "police would be hesitant to act, fearful of the second-guessers and the Monday-morning quarterbacks." This mobilization was enough to get the plan scuttled for the time being, as the city council was justifiably shaken by the strident opposition it encountered. For his part, Mayor Wagner wanted nothing to do with the political minefield surrounding the CCRB. In fact, he decided not to run for office again. But the issue figured prominently in the 1965 election, when John Lindsay championed the issue, finding in the *Herald Tribune*'s "City in Crisis" series a readymade campaign, pinning the rapidly eroding social fabric of New York City on Wagner. Wagner responded to the series, which Lindsay later called his "raison d'être for running," by letting *New York Herald Tribune* editor Jock Whitney know he could "shove it up his ass."[10]

Falling in Love

Candidate Lindsay was particularly responsive to black and Puerto Rican concerns about structural racism and police brutality, which had come to a boil with the Harlem riots the previous summer. Lindsay's victory at the polls would test the power of City Hall to oversee the actions of its increasingly powerful police in the face of an organized pushback from the communities they had long terrorized with impunity. Backed by a PBA emboldened by Wagner's legitimation of municipal unions and the considerable expansion of its ranks, the cops were now poised to flex their muscle. The election provided an opportunity. The young, charismatic Lindsay was the clear favorite to win. However, he faced a surprising challenger, one who represented the growing white resentment against postwar liberalism: *National Review* editor William F. Buckley Jr.[11]

Shortly before announcing his candidacy, Buckley appeared before 5,600 members of NYPD's Holy Name Society and pledged full allegiance to the nascent political coalition of law and order. He opened the speech by declaring "a general atmosphere of hostility toward the police force" that made their supporters akin to an oppressed minority. Buckley proceeded to praise the "restraint" of the police in Selma, Alabama, who had violently repressed civil rights marchers led by Dr. Martin Luther King Jr. the previous month. "Nobody is more sacrosanct," he declared melodramatically, "than the man who strikes a policeman. No man more guilty than the policeman who strikes a defensive blow." Buckley went on to address the recent murder of civil rights activist Viola Liuzzo by the Ku Klux Klan in Alabama: "So the lady drove down a stretch of lonely road in the dead of night, sharing the front seat with a young Negro identified with the protest movement; and got killed." He hedged: "Why, one wonders, was this a story that occupied the front pages from one end to another, if newspapers are concerned with the unusual, the unexpected?" Ostensibly without a sense of irony, Buckley then likened his own support for NYPD, for which he felt publicly besieged, to that of a Franco supporter in Spain. The speech generated considerable controversy, not least because of the allegedly spirited response it received from the assembled cops.[12]

In his subsequent campaign announcement, Buckley doubled down on the themes of law and order, arguing that "until such a moment as the crime rate is reversed," New York needed "a much larger police force, enjoined to lust after the apprehension of criminals even as politicians lust after the acquisition of votes." Buckley naturally gravitated to the controversy surrounding the Civilian Complaint Review Board. "Under no circumstances," he droned ominously, "must the police be encumbered by such political irons as civilian-review boards—or by any other contraption whose presumptive concern is for advantageous political relationships, rather than for law and order in our streets." Moreover, Buckley's choice for city council president—Rosemary Gunning, from the anti–school integration Parents and Taxpayers (PAT), among the vanguard of the growing white reaction against housing desegregation—supported the mistaken idea that the forces of reaction among New York City's downwardly mobile ethnic whites had an unlikely friend in the aristocratic Yale wordsmith. In reality, of course, Buckley was an unrepentant patrician who must have struggled to mask his disgust for the plebes who now threw their support behind him.[13]

"In the summer of 1965," recalls Buckley campaign aide Neal B. Freeman, "the NYPD fell in love with Bill Buckley." Some police openly donned "Buckley for Mayor" buttons and even booed Lindsay, while in uniform, at campaign appearances. Yet Buckley was never a completely serious candidate. When asked what he would do if elected, Buckley memorably replied: "I'd demand a recount." The impact of his campaign was, as intended, not to place Buckley in Gracie Mansion, but to provide a vehicle for a right-wing political movement in New York City capable of pushing back against both the weakened foe of postwar liberalism and the ascendant power of rebellion from below. The campaign largely succeeded in uniting many downwardly mobile whites in the outer boroughs with so-called law-and-order organizations like PBA, a growing political force in whose footsteps the Correction Officers' Benevolent Association would soon follow.[14]

Successful political actors need a social base. The expansion of boroughs like Brooklyn and Queens earlier in the century had created a growing base of white homeowners, whose entire lives were sunk into a small piece of property in largely segregated neighborhoods. By the 1960s, the city had become markedly blacker and browner, and the once-firm borders isolating white neighborhoods began to dissolve—at the exact time the city was running aground financially, and increasingly unable to keep up basic services like garbage collection. Many affluent whites took advantage of the segregated suburbs the federal government was eagerly subsidizing through highway construction and home loans. Those who stayed behind faced urban decay, as in the case of neighborhoods like Brownsville, Brooklyn, where city disinvestment and an aging housing stock catalyzed a dramatic deterioration in a relatively short amount of time. Housing desegregation also coincided with aggressive campaigns by civil rights organizers to desegregate workplaces and schools, which were similarly suffering from deindustrialization and underfunding, respectively. This created the notion that the corresponding influx of nonwhite people was the cause of these changes. Whether or not white New Yorkers truly believed this, it was a palpable myth.[15]

As historian George Rawick put it in 1964, "Every white worker knows that either a victory for Negroes would mean that white workers would share more equitably the burden of unemployment, or something will have to be done to end unemployment." The absence of a collective, multiracial response to the growing crisis in New York City's housing stock and social institutions engendered a white reaction to desegregation in the form of anti-taxation groups, vigilante resistance to housing desegregation, and support for the arrogant autonomy of the police. This was surely not true of every white New Yorker—and, as political scientist Michael Javen Fortner points out, there were plenty of middle-class black New Yorkers supportive of law and order policies, albeit as a last resort amid systematic under-funding of their communities. But when local white business leaders and other elites like Buckley sensed their opportunity to capitalize on the crisis in the outer boroughs to advance their own class agenda, a decisive mass of the white working class chose to align with their white social betters—against working-class black and brown people. The CCRB controversy was an important milestone in the development of this alliance, the law-and-order coalition.[16]

"If New York City is ungovernable," candidate Lindsay had declared, "then we're all doomed." This hypothesis would soon be tested, as Lindsay inherited a whirlwind of racialized economic insecurity that made its presence felt on New York City's streets and inside its jails. By the end of John Lindsay's term as mayor, one particular piece of city property would be synonymous with urban disorder and the city's increasingly punitive response to it: Rikers Island.[17]

9

Crossing the Rubicon

A Bridge of Hope

On November 22, 1966, Mayor John Lindsay formally opened the bridge between Rikers Island and East Elmhurst, Queens. Though the island remained within the legal jurisdiction of the Bronx, Rikers thus joined Queens with this extension of Hazen Street across the East River. The forty-foot-wide bridge stretched just over a mile, and for the convenience of vessels belonging to the coast guard and LaGuardia Airport, its three traffic lanes and pedestrian walkway gradually inclined to an apex of fifty-two feet above water. The Republican Lindsay spoke off the cuff that day, riffing that the feats of famed planner Robert Moses had met their match in the mammoth bridge, and suggesting Queens Borough president Mario J. Cariello, a Democrat, ask President Johnson "to do something about these jet aircraft noises" from La Guardia. Still smarting from his crash course in city politics, the mayor lauded the Department of Correction band for not going on strike on the eve of their performance—as the transit workers had done on the first day of his mayoralty.

"Mention should be made," underscored Lindsay's preparatory notes, "that the bridge will pay for itself within ten [years]." In those same notes, the subject of the speech itself is listed as: "Emphasis on economies and money saving." The mayor was sure to cover this ground, having cast himself as the fiscally responsible foil to the supposedly extravagant public spending of his predecessor, Robert F. Wagner. The bridge was calculated to save $500,000 yearly on the elimination of the ferry service alone, in addition to twelve days of wages per DOC staffer previously compensated port to port for the ferry trip, the elimination of delivery fees, and a savings of 20 percent on the estimated $45 million of construction projects slated to reshape the island in the coming years. These included the Correctional Institution for Women, the Adolescent Remand Shelter, and a nearly $10 million expansion of the island's power plant. Lauding the bridge's role as the linchpin of progressive infrastructure projects present and future, Lindsay dubbed the structure the "bridge of hope."[1]

Flanking Lindsay at the foot of the bridge was new DOC commissioner George F. McGrath. Whereas Wagner had leapt at the appointment of Anna M. Kross, Lindsay had dragged his feet for months to appoint a new DOC commissioner, suggesting a marked decline of interest in the agency that would define his mayoralty. Lindsay waited until mid-March to offer the position to McGrath, former Massachusetts state commissioner of correction. The child of Irish immigrants, McGrath hailed from a large Catholic family in Boston, where his father worked as a bricklayer. McGrath began his jail career as a social worker at Charlestown State Prison, worked as a researcher at Harvard, and subsequently earned a law degree at Boston College, where he also taught criminal law.

Kross hailed McGrath as "rehabilitation minded; not just lock them up and throw the key away." Indeed, he seemed in Kross's mold. Yet, as commissioner in Massachusetts, McGrath had also distinguished himself by calling in the state police to violently repress a rebellion at Walpole State Prison, just days after taking office. "You don't give in to inmates under any circumstances," he had reflected, earning him plaudits from the *New York Times* as a "firm prison hand." McGrath's salary of $25,000 was 25 percent more than the city had paid Anna Kross.[2]

McGrath appeared to represent a continuation of Kross's program of rehabilitation. Echoing her belief in human engineering, DOC's 1966 *Annual Report* opens with the sage words of nineteenth-century statesman Daniel Webster: "If we work upon man's immortal minds, if we imbue them with high principles, with the just fear of God and love of their fellow men, we engrave on these tablets something which no time can efface, and which will brighten and brighten to all eternity." McGrath himself underscored this theme in an introductory essay to the report titled "Is Our Investment in Prison Justified?" McGrath argued that rehabilitation, achieved through programming aimed at assisting the lawbreaker in becoming a law-abiding citizen, was not only socially desirable and individually ethical, but also the legal obligation of DOC. Interestingly, the city charter had little to say on the matter, only calling for the "care and custody of felons, misdemeanants, and violators of local law" held in its facilities. McGrath's generous reading of this mandate seems to have derived from his conviction—in keeping with both the penal welfarist program of Kross and the political philosophy of the Lindsay administration—that "in most cases the crime the individual was convicted of is merely a symptom of more basic underlying problems which are not effected [*sic*] by mere custody or punishment."[3]

McGrath shared Kross's conviction that prisons are "in a very real sense, agencies of crime prevention." Hence, the expansion of DOC facilities and programming was the logical response to an increase in quantifiable crime. However, as under Kross, the time when these facilities could truly do the job for which they were designed always seemed to fall on the proverbial day after tomorrow. "Once the Department can house the inmate population, space-wise and with institutions designed and reconverted for rehabilitative purposes," claimed the 1966 report, echoing years of sentiments under Kross, "a great deal more can be done than is currently being accomplished." As ever, DOC singled out crowding as the primary obstacle. By 1966, the average daily population for the entire system was above 10,000, and all facilities were above rated capacity. Some situations were especially grave. Already in 1965, the House of Detention for Women had reached a peak of 760, 166 percent of its stated capacity. Despite Kross's best efforts to rationalize DOC's expansion and plan for the future, the situation remained dire.[4]

"The Department of Correction has not had a planned growth," wrote Mayor Lindsay's 1966 Task Force on Correction, part of an expansive study of the city government meant to maximize the "good government" campaign he had waged against Wagner. "Organizational changes have been made but they have not kept pace with the prodigious development of the agency," which included a budget approaching $30 million and a capital budget more than that figure for the coming five years alone. Chaired by progressive penologist James V. Bennett, and boasting none other than Austin MacCormick and Richard McGee, who had overseen the auspicious opening of the Rikers Island Penitentiary, the task force lauded Kross for having "transformed the agency from one whose chief emphasis was on custodial problems to one stressing rehabilitation as well as safekeeping." They attributed the shortcomings of her program to "budgetary and legal restrictions."[5]

The chief culprit the task force identified as hindering a robust penal welfarist program was not an external obstacle but the structure of DOC itself. Namely, they argued, the "semi-military" hierarchy of the agency, combined with the civil service requirement for vertical promotions, fostered an institution resistant to substantive change. "Consequently, a central organizational structure suited largely to conventional custodial needs, making only reluctant accommodations to the new correctional philosophy and program characterizes the Department." At root, they found "an *uneasy truce between the custodians and the rehabilitators*," which had characterized the Kross years, kept afloat by the significant material gains enjoyed by uniformed staff amid the city's postwar prosperity. It was a frank observation. In no uncertain terms, the task force named the subterranean conflict that had been playing out daily in DOC institutions since the revolt of guards and Kross's deft brokering of superficial peace. This constant push and pull played out not over wages and benefits, which Kross used to keep the guards satisfied, but over a much more coveted prize: control of the city jails. And this uneasy truce, always tenuous, would be supremely tested in the years to come.[6]

The task force also found the present level of cooperation between DOC and the courts, police, probation, public health, and mayoral officials to be "haphazard," "ad hoc," and largely in response to crisis. Accordingly, they proposed the formation of an interagency council to take the place of the Board of Correction. The latter, the task force argued, had insufficient resources, and its role was poorly defined. Therefore, it should be "reorganized, redefined, and more clearly delineated," or else eliminated. This was partly a reference to BOC, which never distinguished itself as independent from Anna M. Kross, having fallen into semi-dormancy. "The board had been virtually non-functioning for years," board member Barry Gottehrer recalled. Earlier that year, an announcement by BOC chair Ethel Wise that the board need not meet for the second consecutive month due to "no material for an agenda" earned a harsh rebuke by member David A. Schulte Jr., which found its way to the desks of Kross, then, in the final days of her term, Lindsay and the entire BOC. There was, Schulte argued, plenty to discuss. He was surely correct.[7]

In response to the task force, the Board of Correction wrote both the mayor and Commissioner McGrath, concurring with the recommendation for an interagency council but defending their own role as a watchdog group directly accountable to the mayor. After several vacillations—including the December issuance of letters to each BOC member announcing the dissolution of the board—Lindsay ultimately reversed course and allowed BOC to continue as a watchdog organization. While the interagency board envisioned by the task force would never take shape, BOC would, in fact, endure. As we will soon see, the agency was to assume something of an activist role in DOC in the coming decade, while overseeing an unprecedented expansion of the city's carceral capacity on Rikers Island, enabled in no small part by the bridge that Lindsay and McGrath had dedicated on that fateful November day.[8]

Traversing the Rikers Island Bridge for the first time, one feels in their stomach an uncanny pressure as the bus engine gears downward in approach of its apex. At midpoint, this hump is abruptly overcome, and for a split second one becomes airborne, suspended between the free world left behind and the prison world toward which one now surges. Gravity, that unseen force of nature, pulls inexorably toward Rikers Island. Long afterward, the passenger is left with the lingering memory of that fleeting moment when the upward climb has been overcome, but the inevitable descent has yet to begin. Mayor Lindsay's dedication of the bridge marked such a moment for the New York City Department of Correction, and for New York City itself, which would be henceforth drawn, irresistibly, toward Rikers Island.

A Fun City

In many ways the Rikers Island Bridge serves as an apt metaphor for Lindsay's mayoralty itself. It connected the city's period of postwar prosperity eulogized by so many liberal historians, and the images of disorder and racial strife with which New York remains associated in the public imagination to the present day. As New York spiraled out of control, the Kennedyesque Lindsay often seemed like a man from a different time. To a large extent, he was. The tall, handsome, clean-cut, and charming congressman from Manhattan's East Side "Silk Stocking" district was a species of Republican held over from the mid nineteenth century and soon to be extinct. Lindsay was a traditional progressive, part of a lineage stretching back through Thomas Dewey, Fiorello La Guardia, and Theodore Roosevelt, all the way back to the reformers who had grappled with Tammany Hall patronage in the late nineteenth century in the name of scientific principles of urban management.

Lindsay's campaign platform paired themes of fiscal austerity and distrust of bureaucratic machine politics with a steadfast belief in the formal equality of all people before the law, which Lindsay traced back to the Republican Party of Abraham Lincoln. As a member of Congress, Lindsay had been instrumental in passing the 1964 Civil Rights Act. Racial discrimination was anathema to his pro-business, individualistic vision of liberal harmony amid optimal free market completion —facilitated, if need, be by interventionist city and state governments. This position made Lindsay an ally of President Johnson, whose Great Society agenda fueled a strong welfare state aimed at redressing America's racial order with anti-poverty spending and civil rights legislation. Partisan rivalry prevented their closer collaboration.[9]

When Johnson assembled the National Advisory Commission on Civil Disorders in 1967 to study the torrent of racialized urban unrest in US cities, he tapped Lindsay as vice chairman. Lindsay and his staff, largely composed of youthful idealists, penned the striking introduction to the final report of what is commonly called the Kerner Commission, after its chair, Illinois governor Otto Kerner. With profound brevity, they summarized the new mayor's outlook in words that could almost have flown from the pen of James Baldwin: "What white Americans have never fully understood—but what the Negro can never forget—is that white society is deeply implicated in the ghetto. White institutions created it, white institutions maintain it, and white society condones it." Correcting the structural inequality inscribed in the very geography of the modern city was, in their estimation, the primary task of the moment, lest violence and "mob rule," the desperate response to unaddressed structural inequality in US society, consume America's cities. Their progressivism bridged a moral imperative to right the historical wrongs of structural racism with the practical necessity of uninterrupted development of the free market, unhindered by racial animosity and urban insurrection. "The alternative [to mob rule] is not blind repression or capitulation to lawlessness," the authors argued, but a reasoned reckoning with the country's past, and the legislative rectification of racial and economic inequality facing the nation's poorest people. "It is time now," they implored, "to turn with all the purpose at our command to the major unfinished business of our nation ... to adopt strategies for action that will produce quick and visible progress ... to make good the promises of American democracy to all citizens—urban and rural, white and black, Spanish-surname, American Indian, and every minority group."[10]

Quaint civic pieties aside, the near-apocalyptic vision the Kerner introduction invokes, of "the continuing polarization of the American community and … the destruction of basic democratic values," was not only justified on the basis of the immense crisis facing the present; it was also prescient. Lindsay, however, remained optimistic that the course could be reversed. When the Transit Workers Union had launched a strike on the first day of his term, crippling New York City for almost two weeks, the mayor notoriously strove to put a positive spin on the myriad symptoms of urban crisis amassing around him. "I still think it's a fun city," he remarked.[11]

Lindsay nonetheless recognized the explosive situation he had inherited. His "fun city" was ground zero of a maturing complex of postwar contradictions: deindustrialization, attempts at housing desegregation, and the rapid urbanization of a racialized underclass. Amid these crises, Lindsay would be directly challenged, in a way Wagner never was, by a rightward-shifting segment of New York whites. While this emergent bloc included elite figures like William F. Buckley, it also included a critical element of working-class people affected by deindustrialization and urban disinvestment—those either too poor to join the white flight or simply determined to stay behind. Historically sympathetic to the cops, who often hailed from the same ethnic white, outer-borough neighborhoods that served as Buckley's base, this class fragment became ever more dedicated to untrammeled police power as urban crisis heightened, elite politicians like Lindsay appeared oblivious to their concerns, and cops emerged as an organized political alternative to permissive liberalism.[12]

However, the law-and-order coalition was not the only game in town. The Patrolmen's Benevolent Association (PBA) may have been louder, but Civilian Complaint Review Board (CCRB) reform, civil rights, and the burgeoning movement for black and brown power in New York City enjoyed a long-standing reservoir of support, only broadened by the freedom movement agitation in the South. Malcolm X, in particular, helped over-come the morass of the 1950s and bridge the black nationalism of the early century—typified by the Pan-Africanism of Marcus Garvey—with a new generation emerging in tandem with the civil rights movement and the revolutions in Africa and across the so-called Third World.

By Lindsay's arrival, this underground current had been gaining momentum for some time. The original civilian review board from 1954 had been the product of demands, in response to widespread claims of racialized brutality gone unchecked, by a panoply of organizations including the Urban League, Ameri-can Federation of Labor, the American Civil Liberties Union, the American Jewish Congress, and National Association for the Advancement of Colored People (NAACP). In February of 1961, black nationalists—including radical poets LeRoi Jones (better known as Amiri Baraka) and Maya Angelou, and activ-ist Mae Mallory—staged a raucous demonstration inside the United Nations to protest the assassination of Congolese prime minister Patrice Lumumba, explicitly connecting local struggles against structural racism with an international black struggle. Even amid the so-called classical phase of the civil rights move-ment, which was said to be the apex of a focus on targeting de jure discrimination in the Jim Crow South, James Baldwin noted the political significance as inhering far beyond demands for mere desegregation. "The movement," he wrote, "does not have as its goal the consumption of overcooked hamburgers and tasteless coffee at sleazy lunch counters."

When James Powell was killed in Harlem in 1964, the Con-gress of Racial Equality (CORE) and NAACP were among the initial organizers of demonstrations against police brutality and murder; however, the crowd escaped their control, augur-ing militant offshoots from the civil rights movement to come. By the time PBA took to picketing its opponents, it had been watching CORE do so for several years, including at precincts where cases of brutality had been reported. This nexus of left organizations and campaigns, part of a long-standing New York activist milieu dating back to the heyday of the Communist

Party, represented a viable adversary for the ascendant forces of law and order. This was a powerful tradition of subversion from below, with a formidable social base among working-class black and brown New Yorkers. Throughout Lindsay's tenure, these blocs would continue to clash around the enduring question of civilian oversight of the police, as the sunny optimism of the postwar liberal tradition, which Lindsay represented par excellence, increasingly fell on deaf ears.[13]

Your Life May Depend on It

In May of 1966, flanked by NYPD commissioner Howard Leary, Lindsay announced the heralded restructuring of the Civilian Complaint Review Board. It would include seven members, four appointed by the mayor and three by the NYPD commissioner. Under the supervision of a high-ranking police official, the board would have no disciplinary authority, nor could it make specific disciplinary recommendations. Like most civilian review boards, the new CCRB was toothless: it was designed to perform opposition to NYPD while possessing no formal power. The CCRB was a measured compromise designed to appease activists without upsetting police power. But the Patrolmen's Benevolent Association, fresh off their ouster of a sitting NYPD commissioner and emboldened by the political movement of police across the country, was not in the mood for compromise. Instead, PBA was pushing hard, capitalizing on the law-and-order coalition to expand its role in city politics. But on a more basic level, as Barry Gottehrer recalls, rank-and-file cops "believed the rhetoric of the PBA's campaign against the civilian review board—the picture of the policeman with his hand tied behind his back—and, because they felt themselves the real victims, forced to answer for all of the city's failures, the man on the beat began to hate the mayor and his people and what they believed he stood for."[14]

PBA and the Conservative Party, on whose line Buckley had run, filed a ballot initiative to repeal the new CCRB so quickly their people produced two independent but nearly identical initiatives for the Board of Elections. The campaign drew on the nastiest elements of New York City politics, especially the city's growing racial panic, but also the anti-communist language of John Birch. "I'm sick and tired of giving in to minority groups," spat PBA president John Cassese in a press conference announcing the campaign, "with their whims and gripes and shouting." Cassese also claimed CCRB proponents were communists. Anti-CCRB advertisements, funded by PBA, pulled no punches. One depicted a vulnerable young woman exiting the subway at night and declared: "The Civilian Review Board Must Be Stopped. Her Life, Your Life May Depend on It." Another claimed, in language that can still be found today: "With a Review Board, It May Be the Police Officer Who Hesitates, Not the Criminal." In short, the PBA-led campaign argued that NYPD must be allowed to dispose of undesirables however they saw fit. Otherwise, the state of crisis—which many New Yorkers felt to be intensifying with the passage of time—would degenerate into utter chaos akin to that of a failed state.[15]

The pro-CCRB campaign, led by a Lindsay-sponsored umbrella group called Federated Associations for Impartial Review (FAIR), was largely incoherent and ineffectual, and failed to rally support. It evinced the weaknesses of an anti-police brutality movement that had been purged of communists. Rather than take on the reality of structurally racist police violence, FAIR believed it was adequate to point out the nefarious supporters of the anti-CCRB referendum, which included the John Birch Society and the American Nazi Party, and draw high-profile support from senators Robert F. Kennedy and Jacob Javitz. Vacuous slogans like "Join the Forces of Progress—Not Hate!" and "Don't Let the Bigots Ruin Our City!" sidestepped the lived experience of violent police in black and brown communities, appealing instead to the moral sensibilities of middle-class white liberals. The CCRB election, therefore, was hardly a referendum on the power of policing in New York City, though the police surely felt it as a challenge to their arrogant autonomy. The debate was instead framed in a way that pitted a small group of middle-class liberals against a much-larger array of conservative forces that had propelled Buckley into the spotlight. Meanwhile, the movements for liberation—the black and brown nationalists, the communists, the working-class activists, and other radicals who had long fought against police violence—were left out of the debate entirely.

Either disbelieving the prevalence of police brutality or unwilling to tackle it as a political issue, FAIR argued that police brutality was a rare phenomenon, and that the CCRB could prove it. "A Civilian Review Board," one flyer boasted, would "help, not only those who have complaints, but it would prove that police brutality is not as prevalent as has been alleged." The CCRB, it concluded, promised to "raise the morale of the slum dwellers and ... help reinstate a respect for law and order among the citizens of our city." Under the heading "Better Understanding," another flyer declared: "There is no longer any reason for anyone to take his grievances to the street, since the new Board guarantees a fair hearing to all."[16]

Unable to take the issue of police brutality seriously and thus build meaningful ties with the black and brown New Yorkers for whom it was a visceral reality, the liberals behind the CCRB campaign effectively conceded defeat in advance. In the process, they fed the perception among working-class whites, pushed by Buckley and others in the New Right, that left-leaning politics was inherently concerned with either the abject or the affluent, and had nothing to say to most working people. It was surely true that the groups involved in FAIR talked to one another instead of to the New Yorkers who would decide the fate of the CCRB. Relying on the star power of its endorsers and the supposed political extremism of its opponents to shock and scandalize the general public, FAIR was content to offer virtually nothing in the way of a positive politics, especially to the people most impacted by police violence. The campaign was a bust.

In a stinging blow to Lindsay and New York State's celebrity senators, the CCRB was defeated by ballot referendum. Their star power, it seemed, was no match for Cassese, a mere police patrolman bearing a message of militant white power whose time had come. PBA had blazed an independent path in city politics, one that the Correction Officers' Benevolent Association would follow soon enough. "They had won extraordinary rights to prevent investigations after incidents had occurred," reflects Gottehrer. "Now they were looking for the right to reject consultation before the fact as well." As PBA pushed for an expanded role in city politics, and rank-and-file cops demanded unrestricted power over their work, liberals offered no serious alternative to law and order.[17]

In marked contrast to the milquetoast sloganeering of the pro-CCRB campaign, a militant tradition confronting NYPD had been in formation for over a decade. In April of 1957, a young black Harlemite named Johnson Hinton observed cops clubbing a black man on the corner of 125th St and Seventh Avenue. Hinton commanded the police to stop, telling them, "You're not in Alabama—this is New York!" The cops responded by beating him severely, fracturing his skull, and arresting him for felonious assault. Hinton, it turned out, was a member of the Nation of Islam, and a congregant of Mosque Number Seven, under the leadership of Malcolm X. Within an hour and a half, fifty of the NOI's Fruit of Islam security force gathered under the command of Malcolm X outside the precinct where Hinton was held. "I told the lieutenant in charge," Malcolm later recalled, " 'That man belongs in the hospital.' They called an ambulance."

Under Malcolm X's leadership, the Fruit of Islam followed Hinton to Harlem Hospital. "Negroes who never had seen anything like this were coming out of stores and restaurants and bars and enlarging the crowd following us," he continued. "Harlem's black people were long since sick and tired of police brutality. And they never had seen any organization of black men take a firm stand as we were." Before Hinton was released, thousands of people had gathered outside the precinct. Under the leadership of Malcolm X, Harlem became an important base of operations for the Nation of Islam, and subsequently his Organization for Afro-American Unity, until his 1965 assassination. But the militant tradition Malcolm had established in Harlem did not die with him.[18]

White Tigers Eat Black Panthers[19]

In 1967, a new tendency in black militancy emerged. Founded in Oakland in 1966, the Black Panther Party was based on the Revolutionary Action Movement (RAM), a radical black nationalist organization founded in Philadelphia; the Lowndes County Freedom Organization, a project of the Student Non-violent Coordinating Committee (SNCC) in Alabama under the direction of Stokely Carmichael; and the teachings of Malcolm X. The group's platform drew heavily from the current of black nationalism responding to the failure of post-*Brown* integration and the proceduralism of the mainstream civil rights movement with demands for an independent black polity achieved *by any means necessary*. "We want freedom," began the Panthers' Ten-Point Program. "We want power to determine the destiny of our Black community." True to the spirit of the age, the New York City chapter of the Black Panther Party was founded in 1968, just weeks after Martin Luther King Jr.'s assassination. Two of its earliest members were Sekou Odinga and Lumumba Shakur, from Jamaica, Queens. The duo had become politicized while incarcerated at Great Meadow Prison, where they had organized a rebellion against discriminatory hiring and subsequently joined Malcolm X's Organization for Afro-American Unity.[20]

The New York Panthers drew members from different backgrounds. Many had roots in street gang culture. "All I am is an ex-Disciple," Panther Afeni Shakur later reflected, referring to the street gang of which she had been a member, emblematic of a violent subculture replete with drugs and brawls. "But I'm able now to use the things that I had when I was a Disciple, the desire to survive ... in a manner that has nothing to do with just having fun and cutting somebody. It has to do with something greater than that." Sympathetic to Malcolm X, though more immersed in the local bar scene than politics, Shakur happened across Bobby Seale speaking on the corner of 125th Street and Seventh Avenue. She joined the Party shortly thereafter.[21]

By contrast, Kuwasi Balagoon lived comfortably as a paid tenant organizer financed by Great Society anti-poverty initiatives, organizing rent strikes, pressing for building repairs, representing tenants in court, blocking illegal evictions, and using withheld rents to pay for repairs while agitating for collective ownership. But, over time, Balagoon was drawn toward a more militant approach to politics. When he traveled with other tenant organizers to Washington, DC, to release a rat in Congress in protest of slum conditions, his New York delegation ended up skirmishing with police under the rotunda. Balagoon went on to join the Central Harlem Committee for Self-Defense, organizing against the encroachment of Columbia University on black neighborhoods. During the 1968 occupation of the university, Balagoon and his comrades broke through the right-wing student blockade surrounding an occupied building in order to bring food and water to the rebels inside. Balagoon subsequently decided, "Working as I did as paid opposition was only a sham, making black people believe that things were getting better." He began following SNCC chairman H. Rap Brown, read Robert Williams's *Negroes with Guns* and *The Crusaders*, studied Mao Zedong's "Little Red Book," and joined the Black Panthers shortly after the Party came to New York. His story was representative of a militant turn among black radicals in this period. As Black Panther George Jackson wrote from a California prison in 1970: "Pure nonviolence as a political ideal … is absurd. It may serve our purpose to claim nonviolence, but we must never delude ourselves into thinking we can seize power from a position of weakness, with half measures, polite programs, righteous indignation, loud entreaties." He concluded: "Long live the guerrillas!"[22]

In keeping with their program and diversity of influences, the New York Panthers organized around tenant issues, against school segregation, and against police brutality. The group's influence extended far beyond their official membership, including inspiring the Young Lords, a group of militant Puerto Rican activists tracing their roots to a 1950s Chicago street gang. The NYPD took immediate notice. In August of 1968, two young Panthers were beaten and arrested for demonstrating outside the Party's Brooklyn office at 780 Nostrand Avenue, on the pretext that they did not have a sound permit. The pair wound up being charged with assaulting an officer and resisting arrest. When they appeared in court, their Panther comrades packed the gallery in solidarity. PBA president Cassese later claimed, quite improbably, that the group of Panthers "cursed at" and "spat upon" the arresting officer, while presiding judge John Furey and the court officers did nothing to intervene. To make matters worse, two days after the duo's arrest, two cops responding to a distress call near the Panthers' office had been wounded by an unknown shooter. Cassese claimed that "war has been declared against the Police department," promising to issue "get tough" directives from PBA, for cops "sick and tired of taking it on the chin."[23]

Despite his tough talk, however, Cassese was merely chasing after the militancy of his union's rank and file. Several days earlier, an independent organizing group within NYPD had broken ranks, declared itself an independent entity, and issued "get tough" directives of its own. Calling itself the Law Enforcement Group, the hard-right organization had emerged from a rank-and-file petition calling for Furey's removal, which had taken on a life of its own and soon escaped the control of PBA leadership. LEG released a seven-point program to rival the Ten-Point Program of the Panthers, calling for a grand jury to investigate the "coddling" of criminals, the abolition of even the police-led CCRB, the removal of civilians from police clerical duties, and, most tellingly, to "contact and wholeheartedly support the United States Senators who are trying to prevent another Warren Court." Ira Glasser of the New York Civil Liberties Union called the document an "undisguised declaration of war against the black militants." It was that, and more. LEG represented the most sophisticated expression of the law-and-order opposition movement that had been building within NYPD's ranks for years, goaded on in part by Cassese himself, but part of a broader national zeitgeist of reaction against postwar liberalism, the Warren Court, civil rights, and challenges to traditional structures of white power—chief among them the police.[24]

LEG's banner action came in early September, at the arraignment of three Panthers for another altercation with police. During the days leading up to the arraignment, a flyer had circulated in station houses urging cops to "support your fellow policemen" and to "stand up and be counted in court." Its source was a Brooklyn desk officer and LEG founder named Leon Laino. A small group from the New Left organization Students for a Democratic Society picketed in support, and fifteen Panthers attended the trial but did not participate in the picketing. The counter-mobilization, however, numbered in the hundreds. "The crowd that gathered to jeer at the pickets was comprised largely of off-duty policemen," Gottehrer recalls, "including members of a particularly conservative splinter group within the PBA," the LEG.

"Many wore sportshirts," he continues, "their shirttails untucked, barely concealing the guns and blackjacks tucked into their belts. Some wore police badges." Abayama Katara, a New York Panther in the courtroom that day, describes the uniformed police trying to provoke the Panthers by poking them with nightsticks. But the fifteen Panthers "weren't fools and were completely outnumbered." Facing an estimated 250 cops in and out of uniform, they attempted to leave in peace, refusing to be baited into a fight they could not win. But as they left the courtroom, a melee ensued. LEG members and other off-duty cops attacked Panthers and their supporters with blackjacks, sending some to the hospital. They chanted "Win with [George] Wallace," "White tigers eat Black Panthers," and "White power!"

When the attack began, uniformed cops dropped their nightsticks for the off-duty cops to pick up and wield against the unarmed Panthers and supporters—some of whom, like Katara, were of high school age. Given the setting, the cops knew there was little chance the people they attacked with clubs had any weapons of their own. Cops chased the Panthers down the street as they attempted to flee and prowled the subways in hot pursuit. LEG affiliates even stole the briefcase of local Panther leader David Brothers, who was beaten viciously and kicked dozens of times while on the ground. Rather than return it, NYPD used its contents for intelligence gathering. Initially they misread an entry for Gottehrer—entered as "Mayor"—as "Major," and placed the Jewish Lindsay aide under surveillance, thinking he secretly held the rank of "Major" in the Black Panther Party.[25]

The attack was widely condemned by polite society. LEG, however, moved forward, renaming itself the Law and Order Society and announcing plans for a formal membership structure. Cassese, who had long pushed the kind of rhetoric LEG now practiced, was forced to pick a side. The following day, without naming the organization, PBA delegate assembly passed a motion condemning groups promoting "unlawful, antisocial, or violent acts" and threatening to expel LEG members from its ranks. LEG denied involvement in the courtroom violence—a claim disproven by the PBA itself, whose leadership announced LEG's direct involvement in the flyer that had circulated before the riot. On the defensive, LEG softened some of its positions, such as the demand for new height standards for cops, widely believed to target Puerto Ricans, and threatened legal action against PBA for excluding them.

It was an empty threat. Under the weight of the union officialdom, LEG faded into obscurity almost as quickly as it had erupted onto the scene. But LEG represented a movement within NYPD that did not go away so easily. An anonymous lieutenant stationed in Manhattan told the *Times* that LEG was the product of "dissident youth on the police force—like around the universities. They're exploding. They're fighting back against what they consider an intolerable situation. Just as there's a New Left on the campuses, there seems to be a New Right among some younger men on the Police Department." As historian Noel Ignatiev later quipped, the rise of LEG was "another victory for unions and dissident youth."[26]

For his part, Cassese quickly found his footing, harnessing the militant energy of NYPD's New Right to push back against anyone who would limit cops' arrogant autonomy in working-class black and brown communities. Under his leadership, PBA ramped up an aggressive contract campaign, demanding significant raises above those received by other municipal unions. "If we're really New York City's finest," one cop remarked after a picket outside City Hall, "how come the city doesn't recognize it? How come the transit police, the housing police, the firemen and the garbage men are getting just about what we get?" Cassese couldn't have said it better. This principle formed the basis for a political offensive by PBA, hinging on the argument that the cops deserved a special place in the city workforce. Simultaneously, "sick-outs" and ticketing slowdowns heralded a new era of workplace militancy that would embolden PBA and other "law and order" unions—including COBA, which would soon bring law-and-order politics to New York City's jails.[27]

10

A City in Itself

A Modern Environmental Approach

Amid this fraught political terrain, Department of Correction commissioner George McGrath attempted, in apparent good faith, to continue the policies of Anna M. Kross. On April 11, 1967, DOC broke ground on the Correctional Institution for Women on Rikers Island. The expansive open space on Rikers made possible a horizontal plan, "predicated on a closed campus design which will offer internal freedom and circulation," as DOC put it. Two wings of chevron-shaped dormitories emanated from a central institutional building. One wing, for sentenced prisoners, featured four buildings, a mixture of dormitories and cells with a capacity of forty women per housing unit. As with the New York City Reception and Classification Center (C-76), two housing units could be monitored by a single guard at the point of the V, connected to the corridor, in the so-called pinwheel design. The other wing featured two buildings for pretrial detainees—one of them two stories tall, the other, three. They followed a similar design, but with a capacity of thirty women per unit. The principles of its design emphasized natural light and free circulation of air, using clerestory windows and window walls. DOC had even consulted with cutting edge "design teams" at Parsons School of Design, culminating in what it dubbed "a modern environmental approach to rehabilitation."[1]

Much of DOC's activities in this period took place on Rikers Island. The opening of C-76 had enabled DOC to close the Hart

Island Workhouse in August 1966, by which point that facility had virtually disintegrated, many of its facilities deemed uninhabitable and requiring costly maintenance just to stay on the right side of fire code. In 1967 DOC added another building, comprised of 496 beds, to the C-71 Adolescent Reformatory facility. DOC established small-scale "specialty clinics" on Rikers in 1966 for "ear, nose and throat, skin, orthopedics, general surgery, and chest disorders," obviating the transfer of prisoners to Bellevue or Kings County Hospitals. A massive bakery opened on Rikers the same year, providing bread for DOC, Department of Education, and the Parks Department, in addition to purported vocational training for prisoners. This infrastructure made Rikers increasingly independent of the broader city system, while constituting it as the new center of DOC activity. All the while, Kross's planned infrastructure overhaul hummed along, as she continued to lay the foundation for a dramatic expansion of DOC's holdings on Rikers Island.[2]

McGrath's administration also continued Kross's policy of involving volunteer organizations in DOC programming, largely to fill the shortfall left by insufficient funding for its penal welfarist vision. Under the auspices of the Pre-Release Orientation Program (PROP), an anti-recidivism initiative for adolescents sponsored by Lindsay, DOC enlisted a broad swath of organizations including the Manpower and Development Administration, the Board of Education, the Harlem YMCA, the City Parole Commission, the Salvation Army, Harlem Youth Opportunities Unlimited, and the Seafarers International Union to offer a variety of job training and post-release services steered by the mantra "If you want help, we'll help you." Another youth program, called BYCEP—an acronym derived from the partnership between the Board of Education, youth programming, corrections, and education and employment programming—provided post-release employment placement in conjunction with the city's major anti-poverty programs and the neighborhood-based Manpower Centers. Conversely, many young people employed by Lindsay's youth jobs program ended up working on the civilian side of DOC programming. The

Summer Youth Work Program put high school–aged students to work in the city jails, filling the gaps left by deficiencies of prisoner labor, in areas like repair and cleaning. The Urban Corps Work-Study Program placed university students from across the country as educators and social workers in the jail system. Most of these students were from New York University, whose School of Social Work continued its partnership with DOC begun during the Kross years. As in the Kross years, however, the efficacy of these projects remained contingent on the expansion of DOC's plant facilities.[3]

On September 1, 1967, the New York City Parole Commission was abolished; and with it, indeterminate sentences. All sentences greater than a year thus became the provenance of the state system. Among DOC administrators, the temporary dip this engendered in the incarcerated population was cause for optimism. "When we contemplate the grim prison fortress of the past and even certain crowded institutions of the present," McGrath wrote, "we find ourselves encouraged at the prospect of the planned Rikers Island Complex." Drawing from criminological tradition of environmentalism, McGrath argued that "the antisocial individual's negative attitude toward the excessive monotony of the city slums—tenements, schools, public buildings"—contributed to "a negative conception of society as a whole." By extension, if monotonous and unpleasant environments caused anti-social behavior, then an "improved environment would tend to change the individual's outlook and attitude."

The new construction projects, which McGrath considered nothing short of the "rebuilding of Rikers Island," were to be "characterized by the use of colors and light." In the place of "prison cells with iron bars, the inmates' quarters feature rooms and doors, with reinforced window dimensioned and placed to let in light and air and a plentiful view of earth and sky." The new facilities taking shape, McGrath boasted, "incorporate the most advanced designs possible in large scale institutions." DOC's ability to construct large, horizontally oriented institutions, McGrath argued, was thanks to the Rikers Island Bridge, which "has made available on the Island almost five hundred acres, sufficient for us to develop new institutional designs," emphasizing a freedom of movement and possibility for classification absent in the high-rise jails DOC was forced to build elsewhere.

"Standards of decent living, essential to human dignity and effective correctional rehabilitative programs," McGrath wrote, echoing Kross, "are difficult to achieve in physical plants that are overcrowded, obsolete, and dominated in their administration by ameliorative emergency measures." And while facilities could be constructed using the most cutting-edge principles, this would be largely for naught if they were allowed to be overcrowded. "When our present Capital Building Program has been completed," McGrath looked "forward to the day of completion of our planned, sound Correctional environment." But if crowding prevented the realization of these facilities' optimum usage, and the influx of prisoners could not be stemmed by chastening NYPD or the courts, much less addressing the political and economic issues driving people to desperate acts, how else could the original intent of DOC's penal welfarist facilities be honored than by simply building more jails?[4]

Uninhibited by such questions, DOC was quite taken with the new real estate possibilities opened by the bridge. The cluster of Rikers Island facilities was christened the "Correctional Institution Complex at Rikers Island," which DOC hailed as "a city in itself." The bridge had enabled five autonomous institutions, constituting a "community" reminiscent of the "island metropolis"; it now boasted not only a power plant and bakery, but a tailor shop, improved classification and segregation, "ready deployment of professional and custodial staff in an emergency," and "centralized control of employees and visitors to the island." This centralization also entailed the increasing concentration of DOC's paramilitary forces on an island the department completely controlled—with one way in and one way out.

"The community" of Rikers facilities, DOC argued, "when completed, will establish for the City of New York one of the finest correctional complexes in the world." McGrath explicitly followed Kross in urging the city to build new facilities, so that the existing ones could realize their penal welfarist potential of turning lawbreakers into docile workers. Absent from this calculation was any number of external factors driving up DOC's census, with which even the most ambitious architectural program could scarcely compete. The year was 1968, and the "city in itself" was, after all, not removed from changes taking place in the world outside.[5]

Urban Action

In the present day, the mention of the year 1968 evokes images of chaos and social turmoil, revolution and anarchy in the streets. It was the year the Tet Offensive rocked the US forces in Vietnam, adding fuel to the conflict over a war that had stratified US society and catalyzed violent clashes in New York's streets, exacerbated by class tensions, racial animosity, revolutionary militancy, and the growing desperation of the city's workers. The student movement bubbled up all over the world, perhaps most memorably in Paris. In Chicago, the Democratic National Convention degenerated into a brutal police riot before the eyes of the world. In New York City, the harmless and goofy "YIP-in" at Grand Central Station, organized by the Youth Internationalist Party's Abbie Hoffman, was violently repressed by an emboldened NYPD. Robert F. Kennedy and Martin Luther King Jr. were gunned down, the latter occasioning riots across the United States and the near imposition of martial law in New York City. After the assassination of King, Barry Gottehrer recalls walking the streets with printed copies of an order declaring a state of emergency in New York City, which placed the National Guard under the command of NYPD.[6]

Then as now, the question of how vigorously the police should uphold the law during protests and riots was a contested political issue. As student protesters and Black Power militants became increasingly confrontational, prone to property destruction, and verbally if not physically aggressive toward the police, the Patrolmen's Benevolent Association demanded a free hand to repress protests by force. By contrast, Mayor Lindsay's administration practiced a pragmatic policy toward urban unrest that enraged some conservatives, going as far as to place known troublemakers, including the Nation of Islam offshoot group the Five Percenters in Harlem, the Yippies in Greenwich Village, and even the Mafia in East New York, on the city payroll.

The Summer Task Force, later rechristened Urban Action Task Force, was premised on building relationships with power brokers on the local level and plying them with resources and access to City Hall in exchange for their cooperation in keeping a lid on unrest. This signaled a new approach to urban management in response to the riots of the mid 1960s. While the Task Force was putatively concerned with collecting grievances, they rarely acted upon them. Instead, theirs was an exercise in intelligence gathering and counterinsurgency. This program was especially notable for its sidestepping of established middle-class leadership, especially in Harlem, who Gottehrer and others wagered had little actual pull. The outcome of these efforts was clear: under Lindsay's Urban Action Task Force, New York City did not experience riots on anywhere near the level of Los Angeles, Detroit, or nearby Newark. Over time, the unstable and politically dangerous alliance with groups like the Five Percenters would be replaced by brick-and-mortar community-based organizations, ushering in a new era of left-wing nonprofits kept flush with cash to prevent discontent from becoming rebellion.[7]

As part of this strategy, Lindsay's office coordinated closely with a growing nexus of nonprofits funded by the juggernaut Ford Foundation. Founded in 1936 by Henry Ford, the organization served as a shelter for his family's wealth against Franklin Delano Roosevelt's New Deal taxation. Following World War II, Ford's grandson, Henry II, began the organization's transformation into a public-facing activist entity. It sought to tackle difficult social problems from a far-sighted ruling-class perspective, and encourage social peace in the interest of healthy markets. Where PBA president Cassese and his cohort saw urban disorder and the rise of black militancy as the cause for violent repression, the Ford Foundation saw these tensions as emblematic of an insufficiently administered working class that lacked "enabling institutions of assimilation."

Such tensions were, they wagered, harmful to optimal market functioning in the short term, and capable of fomenting large-scale public disorder in the long term. Repression alone would not fix the problem; it was one that would require complex social engineering. Unlike Kross, however, the architects of the Ford Foundation endeavored to undertake this engineering outside of the government, spending private—and thereby revocable—money as the ruling-class donors saw fit. This was a marked departure from the New Deal, which had risked redistributing social power, along with its investments, in the US working-class. Such deployment of private capital would make the nonprofits an ideal vehicle for imposing fiscal austerity, as, in contrast to state expenditure, they were positioned to manage social crisis using their own funds. This made them accountable to nobody but their donors.

The Ford Foundation promoted hyper-local investment strategies, empowering pro-business community leaders and organizations on the granular level, with a particular emphasis on improving the value of real estate. The success of these initiatives helped shape the direction of Johnson's Great Society investments, as well as Lindsay's own approach to managing urban unrest by cultivating "indigenous" leadership who spoke to the era's spirit of rebellion but did not challenge capitalism or foment illegal forms of resistance. Thus, in the aftermath of the urban rebellions of the 1960s, the terrain on which Kross's philanthropic Friendly Visitors operated became increasingly populated by professional nonprofit organizations with direct ties to big business. These groups were eager to cultivate local leaders who would sideline black and brown radicals and lead people toward forms of community empowerment agreeable to the finance, insurance, and real estate sectors. Upon meeting one charismatic black preacher from Philadelphia, whose self-empowerment message seemed capable of appealing at once to working-class black people and the pro-business agenda of the

Ford Foundation, Henry Ford II exclaimed: "My God, how do we manufacture more of you?" The preacher replied: "By giving me some money."[8]

Instituting Justice

One of the major "enabling institutions of assimilation" in New York City was its punishment system. A pet project of the Ford Foundation's work to reform the courts and jails was the Vera Institute of Justice. Founded in 1961 by journalist Herb Sturz and philanthropist Louis Schweitzer, Vera began as an effort to maximize pretrial bailouts in the city court system, thus freeing up space in the jails and allowing accused people to navigate the court system from the outside. Through the same kind of cooperative relationship that brought Kross's Friendly Visitors to DOC facilities, Vera worked closely with the city's courts and jails to attempt to rationalize and streamline their functioning. By its own account, Vera has blazed the trail for such public-private cooperation around criminal justice reform, which has grown exponentially in the decades since. While Vera was—and remains—critical of the city's punishment system in sometimes-withering terms, the access on which "criminal justice" nonprofits depend to do their job is purchased with a baseline of loyalty to the legitimacy of that system. In exchange, in ordinary times they provide a veneer of civility to the system, bolstering its legitimacy, while in moments of crisis they offer solutions to the problems of incarceration that do not challenge the social order it upholds.[9]

While Vera has always endeavored to improve the lives of the city's most oppressed and exploited citizens, the organization's true allegiances—and its social position in the city's political landscape—were made clear in the crisis year of 1968. Faced with the specter of black and brown revolt across the United States and the rise of explicit revolutionary movements that threatened to merge with mass movements like the anti-war movement, Vera teamed up with Mayor Lindsay's Committee on the Administration of Justice Under Emergency Situations, which included Herb Sturz. As part of the committee's work, Vera drafted a detailed plan to institute martial law in New York City and to use the city jails as detention facilities for upward of 12,000 arrestees. Rikers would be ground zero. If the city needed to crack down hard on rebellion, it could use the penal colony as a de facto prison camp for anyone challenging the social order.

With unbridled technocratic zeal, Vera generated hundreds of pages of details for how these facilities could be best run as an adjunct to counterinsurgency against black and brown revolt. While these plans never quite proved necessary, the mayor's office, NYPD, and Vera were able to play war games with New York City's student movement during the April 1968 Columbia University occupation. Describing the occupation's violent eviction, which resulted in 700 arrests, Mayor Lindsay's committee reported that "appropriate parts of the plan were invoked with generally successful results during the student demonstrations this spring." When push came to shove, Vera was not only willing, but eager, to be a junior partner in repressing rebellion from below.[10]

The urban rebellions of the mid 1960s, writes scholar Robert L. Allen, "forced white reactionaries and liberals alike to conclude that direct white administration of the black ghettos, at least in some instance, was not longer operating satisfactorily." As schemes for public administration were innovated within the liberal nonprofits funded by Ford, law and order became the touchstone of the 1968 presidential election. Richard Nixon rode the grassroots momentum generated in campaigns like Support Your Local Police, and nourished by militants like John Cassese and PBA, all the way to the White House. This watershed moment in the Republican Party, which had begun with the rise of Barry Goldwater, now culminated with the success of Nixon's ugly campaign. It was a far cry from the Republican progressivism to which Lindsay claimed lineage, which did not survive this new era. The following year, Lindsay would find himself effectively pushed out of the party, defeated in the mayoral primary by Staten Island state senator John Marchi, a right-winger in the vein of Buckley.

Nixon aide Patrick Buchanan celebrated Lindsay's defeat as a "permanent blow to the Dewey-Rockefeller, Eastern Liberal Establishment coalition" within the Republican Party. Lindsay only retained the mayoralty by running on the Liberal Party line. The once-popular mayor, who had staked his candidacy on the hypothesis that the social crisis of New York was governable, was barely hanging on.[11]

Less Humane than Public Zoos

The year 1968 was also of great significance for DOC: it was the first year in the agency's history that its detainee population —meaning prisoners held awaiting trial—exceeded its population of sentenced prisoners. The influx of pretrial detainees put tremendous pressure on DOC, necessitating the move of adolescents—at long last—from the Brooklyn House of Detention. The move was, however, as the old cliché puts it, out of the frying pan and into the fire: their new home was the old Rikers Island Penitentiary. In keeping with the plans for a new facility Commissioner Kross had laid out prior to her retirement, all adolescents were now concentrated in one central location: Rikers Island.

A prisoner from this period, identified as Chick, describes life in the facility: "There they put two people in a cell that's really too small for two people. The cells are about six feet by eight feet by eight feet, something like that. Real small and dirty." As for the daily routine in this facility:

> You don't do too much of anything at Rikers. Some days you might eat at six o'clock in the morning, other days you might eat at eight o'clock in the morning. After you eat you gotta come back to your cell and wait. If they feel like letting you out for some recreation, they let you out around ten-thirty or so. You stay out till around twelve-thirty, then you go to chow. You come back, get locked in again. If they feel like letting you out again,

they let you out. If not, you have to wait until it's time to eat again. It's really what they feel.

It was as if Kross had never come along at all—except for the bridge, the new jails, and plans for still more jail expansion, that she left behind.[12]

The most poignant token of DOC's move away from Kross's vision of Rikers came in 1968, when the so-named New York City Reception and Classification Center (C-76), flagship of Kross's penal welfarist program, was redesignated the new Correctional Institution for Men (CIFM), to take the place of the old penitentiary. Though DOC claimed the facility would still "process" sentenced males and continued to experiment with social work programming at the facility, its revised nomenclature represented a significant revision of the project's original intention, and a move toward inmate warehousing. An ugly incident of racist violence in August 1968 testified to the reality of life in this facility. A gang of at least twenty-three white prisoners viciously attacked six black prisoners, who they claimed had encroached on so-called white terrain, leaving the star pitcher of the Rikers Island Tigers baseball team, an enduring emblem of the island's penal welfarist programming, in a coma.[13]

A rash of suicides in custody—of which there had been forty since 1963 and sixteen in 1968 alone—spurred a 1969 investigation led by jail reformer and state senator John R. Dunne. Dunne's findings documented how "intense overcrowding, inadequate personnel and poorly designed facilities have resulted in turning detention facilities into settings less humane than our public zoos and more fertile breeding grounds for crime than the streets from which they have been taken." Dunne found 2,000 prisoners in the Tombs, meant for 925; 3,100 in the Rikers Adolescent Remand Shelter, meant for 2,100; 1,650 in the Adolescent Reformatory (Penitentiary), meant for 980; and Kross's pet project, CIFM, packed with 2,300 prisoners, far in excess of its 1,457 capacity.

Additionally, the report noted the prevalence of alcoholics in jail custody, estimating that 90 percent of prisoners jailed for public intoxication were in fact alcoholics in need of treatment, who were instead "serving life sentences on the installment plan." While DOC data did not keep track of race—Vera researcher Andrew Schaffer complained at the time of the "dearth of current statistics throughout the criminal justice system in New York City," thanks to which "little is known about the persons who make up the detention population"—one investigative journalist estimated that by this point, 80 to 85 percent of the prisoners on Rikers Island were black or Puerto Rican. The average suicide victim, the report found, was young, nonwhite, and experiencing withdrawal from narcotics in facilities ill-suited for drug treatment. The state report coincided with two high-profile arrests of Rikers guards for brutality and sexual abuse.[14]

As DOC's population climbed, Kross's plans for new infrastructure, including an annex to the CIFM that added 768 beds to the sentenced male facility, were "sorely needed" and well underway. But the grand humanistic theory underlying this design was rapidly becoming at best an afterthought. Kross's Institute of the Behavioral Sciences, which her administration had spent so many hours and so much ink plotting in exhaustive detail, had already been forgotten. Instead, DOC's transportation division, now responsible for 300,000 transfers each year, clamored for a $3.7 million auto shop to be built on Rikers Island to facilitate transfers to court for its growing population of pretrial detainees—for whom there was virtually nothing in the way of programming. Indeed, a *Times* reporter found that overcrowding and insufficient programming and facilities had transformed Rikers into an "island of idleness."[15]

By 1970, only 180 of the estimated 3,000 adolescent prisoners held on Rikers Island could attend school, and preference was given to those who had not dropped out prior to being locked up. Industrial facilities that had been built on the heels of the 1962 Manpower Development and Training Act regularly stood idle, only intermittently activated by the release of much-needed federal funds. Some programming persisted, but as Warden Raymond McAlonan of the Adolescent Reformatory admitted, "If they care for 5 percent of our population, it'll be a lot." A reformatory prisoner named Hector described a crowded and cruel environment marked by violence, fear, distrust, sexual assault, callous disregard for human life, and nothing to do to pass the time. "Night after night after night," Hector recounted, "I'd lay there masturbating—that was all there was for me."[16]

In March of 1970, four students from New York University's Graduate School of Social Work, the lodestone of DOC's Kross-era penal welfarist partnerships, protested the island's conditions by refusing to accept awards recognizing their service to Rikers Island prisoners. The students had previously charged the island's programming as "deforming rather than reforming" young people locked up there. "We would have liked to burn the citations," student Gloria Robertshaw declared, "but we can't, so we just won't accept them."[17] Later that year, Dr. Violet E. Stephenson, DOC's director of psychiatry—and thus head of another Kross pet project—resigned the position in protest, calling its services "disgracefully inadequate" due to short-staffing, disrespect from other DOC staff, and medical standards often below the legal minimum. DOC, she charged, "functions along military and bureaucratic lines, is rigid beyond belief and is phobic about any program which represents change."[18]

Enforce the Laws 100 Percent

Whatever optimism accompanied the temporary decrease in DOC's prisoner population after the 1967 parole reform was soon dashed. In 1969, Vera documented a population explosion with "serious consequences. Already overcrowded institutions have become ever more burdened, resulting in impairment of security, strains on personnel, and destruction of prisoner morale." Moreover, DOC had "been forced to lodge over 2,000 detention cases in facilities on Riker's Island, previously used only for sentenced prisoners. The remoteness of this location hampers the preparation of defenses by lawyers and visiting by families and magnifies the problem of transporting prisoners to court." By 1969, the average daily census in DOC custody was 13,170, up from 10,973 the previous year, a pronounced majority of whom were pretrial detainees. The total capacity of DOC's facilities was 7,993. By 1970, DOC's population would crack 14,000, or 183 percent above capacity. Its facilities were by now synonymous with overcrowding; in Long Island, guards protesting crowding and overwork held signs reading "Keep the Tombs in NYC" and "Don't Bring a Rikers Island to Nassau County."[19]

DOC desperately undertook new hiring to keep up with the surplus, still clinging to the ideology of rehabilitation that was quickly becoming a relic of the past. In hiring 131 guards, twenty-five "trainees" (a second tier of guards aged seventeen to twenty-one, too young to formally take the position), and nine "administrative aides" hired to do administrative work currently done by guards, DOC claimed it was responding to the department's activities having "grown considerably more complex and diversified in response to recent advances in penology." However, such rhetoric was flimsy and by this point perfunctory. As ever, city and state fought to pawn off responsibility for the city's sentenced prisoners on one another. "Governor Rockefeller and Mayor Lindsay," quipped reporter Martin Arnold, "called upon each other yesterday to solve the crisis in the city's jails." But where was this influx of prisoners coming from?[20]

At a July 1968 demonstration outside City Hall, some of the 1,500 young people protesting cuts to city poverty programs departed from the rote playbook for these kind of demonstrations and smashed some parked cars belonging to city workers. The police, who had been prevented by their superiors from aggressively quashing the demonstration, were incensed—especially after one of the demonstration's organizers was revealed to be on Lindsay's payroll, as part of the Urban Action Task Force. In response, Cassese issued a directive to the rank and file: "We're going to enforce the laws 100% … regardless of what orders we may get from any superior officer." The following month came the scandal over the police attack on the Black Panthers in John Furey's courtroom, and the rise and fall of the so-called Law Enforcement Group (LEG) discussed above.[21]

As PBA and LEG loudly clamored that the time had come to "get tough" and "vigorously enforce" the laws "100 percent," outside of street demonstrations, NYPD had largely spent the entire year doing just that. In the first nine months of 1968, arrests in New York City rose by 18.5 percent from the previous year. Felony arrests, however, were down by 0.4 percent. The influx of detainees came not from serious crimes, but from a 36.5 percent increase in misdemeanor arrests, and a staggering 53.8 percent increase in arrests for "violations," in which police have the greatest discretion over whether to make an arrest. These arrests, not felonies, accounted for the influx in the city jail system. One need not dispute the rise in murder and other serious crimes during this period to see that the main engine pushing the thronging of the city's jails was in fact misdemeanor arrests. Far from demanding a new direction for law enforcement, therefore, Cassese and LEG were arguing for the extension to spectacular protest events of police policy that had already been adopted, and which had flooded the city's jails with the lowest level of lawbreakers.[22]

As historian Toussaint Losier has argued, this was consistent with a turn, on the national level, to widespread "preventive detention"—the arrest and incarceration of populations deemed likely to foment disorder—alongside an explicit campaign against the Black Panthers and other Black and Brown Power organizations, led by the Federal Bureau of Investigation. While the young upstarts of LEG wanted to swing blackjacks at the Panthers and their supporters in broad daylight, more responsible agents of the law had a better idea. On April 2, 1969, NYPD had conducted a coordinated raid of five Party houses, arresting twelve of the twenty-one Panthers who had been indicted on a specious conspiracy charge that included a plot to bomb the Bronx Botanical Garden and, of course, police stations. The evidence was flimsy, and all twenty-one defendants, including some already in jail on other charges and some who evaded capture, were eventually acquitted. Nevertheless, in what was surely part of the state's strategy, the trial of the "New York Twenty-One," the longest in city history up to that point, kept some of the core leadership of the New York Panthers in jail for upward of two years. As a result, work on the outside revolved around defending the twenty-one, and recruitment dried up amid suspicion of infiltration.[23]

These were only the most prominent arrestees of the city's black and brown revolutionaries, who by this point were amply represented in the jail system due to NYPD's aggressive crackdown on their presence in the streets. In August of 1970, Tombs prisoner Julio Senidez reflected that a change had come over the jail in the preceding months. "The other times I was in jail," he recalled, "prisoners were sort of conditioned to accept brutality … It's different now. People are not giving in." Senidez attributed this sentiment to the prominence of two groups in the city's jails: the Black Panthers and the Young Lords. Both had been making their presence known in New York City's streets.

That summer, the Young Lords, acting as "representatives of a community fed up with the disgraceful neglect by city government of the health of its citizens," occupied a portion of Lincoln Hospital, an underfunded city hospital in the South Bronx. As with the Panthers, the Lords demonstrated through this action the possibility for broad support among the city's racialized working class. "Although many establishment experts understood that these militant forms of collective struggle were produced by systemic racial oppression and abysmal urban conditions," writes scholar Orisanmi Burton, "the US government moved to restore 'domestic tranquility' by waging war against racialized populations and political dissent."[24]

Soon this struggle would explode into the foreground of the city jail system. Hardly a "city in itself," Rikers Island, and all DOC facilities, were inheriting the brunt of the changing political configuration of New York City. In particular, rank-and-file NYPD cops, strengthened by the public sector recognition of Mayor Wagner's New Deal, bolstered by a national movement of right-wing reaction under the banner of "law and order," and coveting above all else their arrogant autonomy, were now becoming a powerful political actor in their own right.

11

Power to the People

Tinderboxes

"When history is written as it ought to be written," maintains C.L.R. James, "it is the moderation and long patience of the masses at which men will wonder, not their ferocity."[1] In March of 1970, 1,500 prisoners held in Kross's C-76 building, now known as the Correctional Institution for Men, conducted a hunger strike and work stoppage. The stated issues behind the strike were the reduction in the "good time" deducted from one's sentence for good behavior from ten to five days per month and the general conditions of crowding in the facility. The mass action came at a time when oppressed and exploited people worldwide were revolting on both sides of the bars; DOC's director of operations Anthony Principe remarked that the rebellion was the first in memory on the island. Lasting four days, the strike ended only when Commissioner McGrath appeared in person to receive their grievances—the "validity" of which he conceded—and promised to pass along their petition.[2]

As one strike ended, however, another action began. Prisoner workers at the Tombs delayed the service of breakfast in solidarity with the Rikers strike. After breakfast, sixty prisoners refused to be locked back into their cells, three of whom had to be forced back in by guards, causing minor injuries on both sides. Kross had been correct that C-76 would represent the future of DOC; she had been mistaken only about what that future would look like.

If the prisoners' response to these conditions was unprecedented, they weren't alone. Under the direction of President Leo
Zeferetti, the Correction Officers' Benevolent Association had
been conducting slowdowns since February, in direct violation
of state law that prevented workplace actions by public sector
unions. The pugnacious Zeferetti followed in the footsteps of
John Cassese, who had undertaken at least one slowdown since
1968 as head of the Patrolmen's Benevolent Association. Fighting for an increase of 700 guard positions, COBA had been
intermittently slowing down prisoner transportation, thereby
crippling the courts, jail hospital, and prisoner work details. In
fact, when the Rikers prisoners struck in March of 1970, COBA
was still in the waning days of a slowdown. It wasn't so much
COBA's attitude or beliefs that changed during this period as its
ability to act, rooted in the growing political power the organization enjoyed as part of the movement for law and order.[3]

Drastic actions undertaken by prisoners or staff were hardly
a surprise. In early 1970, the Tombs was at 209 percent capacity. Tombs prisoners, "overwhelmingly black and Puerto Rican,"
were packed three or more to a cell, in six-by-eight-foot steel
boxes with one side for bars and no access to fresh air or daylight.
The Tombs library was insulting: it boasted 500 identical copies
of a menu translation book for travelers called *Dining Out in
Any Language*, 200 copies of *Coin Collectors Guide*, and, as the
Board of Correction later noted, not a single Spanish-language
book concerning Puerto Rico. Manhattan congressman Edward
Koch conducted a survey of Tombs prisoners who reported
vermin-infested cells, a shortage of soap, and medical care so
poor that one prisoner had lived there for seven months with a
bullet lodged in his body. Of Koch's respondents, over 40 percent
had witnessed a guard assault a prisoner. Almost all prisoners
reported having no mattress or blanket for days on end, and
those with blankets overwhelmingly reported them to be filthy.[4]

The Tombs became emblematic of the city's jail conditions,
but the facility was not unique. The youngest of the Panther
Twenty-One, Jamal Joseph, was held in the old Rikers Island
Penitentiary, which by this time was being used for adolescent

pretrial detainees. "My cell was cramped and dirty," Joseph recalls, of the protective custody cell where he began his stay, "with a paper-thin mattress on a metal slab passing for a bed. My only bedding was a coarse grey blanket. Mice darted around the floor looking for food like shoppers at a mall ... This was obviously their jail and I was the visitor." General population, he soon discovered, was no better. "The cell block was huge," Joseph recalls.

> Four tiers with two inmates per cell. Four hundred adolescents with hormones raging and anger and frustration pulsing through their veins. The charges ranged from burglary and drug possession to armed robbery and murder. All the teenagers in this section of Rikers were trial prisoners. They either could not afford bail or had been remanded without bail. It was sad to see young men locked up for relatively minor offenses because their family couldn't afford a few hundred dollars to get them out, but that was the case for a lot of the young inmates at Rikers.

These inhumane conditions engendered inhumanity between prisoners. Joseph witnesses a brutal stabbing, with a sharpened bedspring called a figa, over a petty debt involving some cigarettes. It ended in the arrest of the attackers and, it was rumored, the death of the victim.

Soon Joseph experienced firsthand both the brutality meted out between prisoners and the reality that sometimes such ruthlessness was prerequisite for survival. Joseph learned that a "notorious booty bandit" (the colloquial term for a jailhouse rapist), who had befriended him under the guise of learning more about the Panthers, had designs on raping him. Joseph's cellmate, who had previously instructed him in institutional knowledge to his great benefit, described the drastic measures necessary to stave off the common occurrence of rape:

> The only way to back a dude like Lefty off of you is to sneak up on him with a mop ringer or a figa and fuck him up real good in front of everybody. And while he's on the ground bleedin'

you yell at that motherfucker so that everybody can hear you, "I'm a man, motherfucker. I ain't nobody's bitch, motherfucker. Anybody try to take my manhood is getting wasted." The guards are gonna fuck you up and put you in the bing for a couple of months, but when you come out the dudes is gonna know that you ain't to be fucked with.

After repeated entreaties to be left alone, the otherwise thoughtful and cool-headed Joseph ended up beating his would-be rapist with a food tray and stomping him on the ground, breaking the man's nose, for which he served a month in solitary. Upon his release, Joseph learned he was now respected, and he had no more trouble. He had been forced to commit an act of brutality himself and to suffer, in turn, a traumatic punishment, all simply to be left alone.[5]

While life inside these detention facilities was miserable, getting out for the day was possibly worse. Court appearances for pretrial detainees citywide were ordeals of days spent in cramped, garbage-strewn court pens clogged with stale, smoky air reaching temperatures that literally soaked prisoners in sweat. There they were denied medical care, fed barely edible food, and in the cases of recent arrestees, denied food for upward of seventeen hours. Most prisoners in the pens were also deprived of a place to sit. As the final insult, prisoners routinely reached the courtroom to find their case simply postponed to another day—if they even reached the court room at all. The staggering rate of prisoners forced to appear for inconsequential hearings, or not produced from the pens at all, was justified by staffers at the District Attorney's Office as a practice calculated to improve morale by giving the prisoners hope that their case was progressing. Conventional wisdom among prisoners, however, held that this was a tactic meant to bully them into accepting a plea. This theory seems likelier than the official explanation.[6]

Among those subjected to these conditions, on top of being locked up in the first place, anger seems to have been always simmering. One particular Tombs prisoner earned the nickname "the Toilet Breaker." Regularly subjected to fruitless days in the pens, BOC reported, "when the Toilet Breaker is brought to the pens but does not reach the courtroom, he frequently vents his anger at the endless waiting and delay by smashing toilets in the pens. It usually takes four officers to subdue him." This kind of individual frustration is common in carceral facilities. At decisive moments, however, it can become collectivized. And just as people were taking collective action outside the jail in 1970, so too did prisoners find common cause to push back against their captivity, and against the entire social order on which it was propped up.[7]

We Cannot Allow It to Continue

On July 29, prisoners sent a petition to Lindsay and McGrath complaining of these conditions. They received no response. The Tombs was at 212 percent capacity, which meant triple celling. One Tombs prisoner from this period reported quadruple celling. On August 8, David Felder, a black prisoner on the ninth floor of the Tombs, had an altercation with a guard. DOC alleged Felder attacked the guard for bringing him milk in a cup instead of a bowl, as he had requested. Regardless of the veracity of this story, the incident extended far beyond an interpersonal spat between one guard and one prisoner. When Felder was removed by guards, thirty black prisoners, fearing for his safety, held two white prisoners hostage for over an hour until he was returned to his cell. Two days later, at breakfast, prisoners on the same floor took hostage five guards, barricading a housing unit for eight hours while breaking windows. The prisoners declared: "No harm will come to them if we are not attacked. We want to see the mayor and the Press." "The manner in which we chose to express our grievances is dramatic," they wrote in a statement stuck in a paperback book, placed inside a sock, and tossed outside the window to the street below, "but it is not as dramatic and shocking as the conditions under which society has forced us to live."[8]

In their statement of grievances and demands, the prisoners described court proceedings in which they were denied hearings or prevented from speaking, kept waiting in pens all day without ever getting to court, and provided with inadequate counsel who pressured a guilty plea—all the while stuck in the Tombs for upward of a year by excessive bail. There, guards regularly beat prisoners on the slightest pretext, disrespected the women visitors, and evaded accountability, though their behavior was surely known all the way up the chain of command. "Not one leaf of a tree could turn yellow," the prisoners reasoned, "without the silent knowledge and consent of the tree itself." Moreover, the food was deemed "not fit for human consumption," prisoners were denied law books, the facility was infested with vermin, and clothing was inadequate, as was medical care. The prisoners demanded an end to these conditions, and amnesty for all participants. "We do not know how the present system of brutality and dehumanization and injustice has been allowed to be perpetuated in this day of enlightenment," they concluded, "but we are the living proof of its existence, and we cannot allow it to continue."[9]

While racial tension between black and white prisoners had marked the onset of the rebellion, one communication identified the prisoners as the "people of Cuba Puerto Rico Black and whites." Prisoner Julio Senidez later reported that virtually all ninth-floor prisoners were black and Puerto Rican, but "there was one Italian guy, and I give him credit, he was with us all the way." William Hickey, who had been taken hostage and beaten in the original incident, later testified that white and black prisoners were united in the subsequent actions. The discipline that the men showed in keeping their eyes on the common enemy was likely due, in part, to the deliberate political education undertaken by prisoners like Victor Martinez. As a member of Inmates Liberation Front on the Tombs' ninth floor, Martinez had been organizing workshops on politics under the guise of card games, and circulating a private, handwritten newsletter called the *Inmates Forum*.[10]

Meanwhile, at the Adolescent Remand Shelter, Jamal Joseph

had been smuggling Panther propaganda and radical literature into the facility in his legal papers. He had also formed a karate class that became a political cadre; its members were forbidden from participation in "juggling" (usury), sexual assault, hard drug use, and collaboration with guards. The guards broke up their exercises as "unlawful assembly," but they were undaunted and continued practicing martial arts. Joseph's block formed a common fund of commissary items, which were lent out with no interest, and provided basic supplies to new arrivals. "The house gangs and the jugglers didn't like what we were doing," Joseph recalls, "but our cadre was about forty prisoners strong and we knew how to rumble."

As Joseph's cadre began taking root in other blocks, karate replaced basketball, football, and softball in the yard. The guards took notice. Around this time, DOC, which had been fighting Joseph's requests to be housed with the other Panthers, abruptly reversed its position. "We had all been organizing in our various prisons," Joseph recalls. "The authorities now realized it was a greater risk to their security to have Panthers on the loose in the general prison population." Joseph was only one among numerous black and brown radicals, swept off New York's streets by aggressive NYPD policing, who were now bringing explicitly revolutionary politics into the city jails.[11]

The Tombs prisoners released their hostages later that day, after presenting their demands to a City Hall staffer and three reporters. A guard named James Clancey who had been held hostage later reported he had not been harmed, opining, "I believe their grievances are just ... reforms should come. If the reforms are not done, God help the correction officers who are working on the floor."[12]

The following day, while Lindsay met with McGrath at City Hall to discuss the situation, the Tombs exploded once more. Over 800 prisoners on the fourth, fifth, seventh, and eighth floors seized four more hostages, smashing windows, setting fires, and dismantling the facility's tile-and-concrete walls. Three-inch-thick glass tumbled to the street below, followed by burning sheets and the carcasses of dead rats. Meanwhile, members of Youth against the War and Fascism—a front group for the Workers World Party—demonstrated outside, chanting "Bail is ransom" and "Free the prisoners." The rebellious prisoners' comrades on the ninth floor, it turned out, were not so opposed to compromise. McGrath even sent a delegation of ninth-floor prisoners to try to broker a peace deal. Their overtures were rejected. In a matter of days, militancy at the Tombs had grown by leaps and bounds. At stake was an entire way of ordering society, one that increasingly relied on police and jails to repress the lowest tiers of the working class, especially black and brown people. The zeitgeist of struggle within the jails—part of a national movement that had seen a threefold increase in prison rebellions the past four years alone—"terrified the political establishment," writes Orisanmi Burton. "They recognized that if they could not maintain order within the most repressive institutions in society, that society itself was doomed."[13]

When negotiations stalled, tear gas–wielding guards led an assault that quelled some areas of the Tombs, and the hostages were released by the evening. It would, however, take until August 20 for the entire jail to be subdued, with prisoners on the fourth floor holding out for over a week, with no hostages. In the meantime, Tombs prisoners launched a coordinated boycott of court appearances, meant to underscore their demands, intimidating and even attacking those who refused to participate. A small contingent at the House of Detention for Men in Queens also joined in the boycott, and a demonstration outside the Tombs called for the facility's closure. Prisoners at the Bronx House of Detention set small fires and staged a short-lived rebellion of their own. Simultaneously, prisoners at the Correctional Institution for Men staged a small disturbance in the cafeteria. During this time, the many broken windows punctuating the foreboding facade of the Tombs were dotted with episodic flashes of the clenched fist and V sign. A sign draped from the building's fourth floor bore the slogan "Power to the People."[14]

Touchy Subjects

The rebellion sent shockwaves through DOC. After a spirited COBA meeting, President Zeferetti responded by demanding the power to shake down the jail. The city's guards, he argued, must be allowed to "clean up our institutions" by going through each facility, repairing broken locks, returning prisoners to their cells, and searching for contraband. The demand was backed by the threat of a mass resignation. The following day, the guards were allowed to storm the fourth floor of the Tombs, where prisoners had not been successfully locked in their cells since the rebellion began. By threatening to quit en masse, COBA won much more: back overtime pay, paid in-service training, paid orientation, and new riot gear. Additionally, the city worked out a deal to transfer 670 sentenced prisoners to state facilities. The Tombs also took action against prisoner leaders like Victor Martinez, who were transferred to the Branch Queens facility in Long Island City. Adding to the general state of anarchy, Lindsay's announcement of the retaking of the fourth floor was interrupted by a brawl between striking news camera operators and scabs, with "newsmen trading punches and televisions crews swinging their cameras at each other."[15]

It was not only within the city's jail walls that order was disrupted. The disturbances came as city and state politicians and bureaucrats were breaking ranks in a very public way. Even with portions of the Tombs still off limits to guards, McGrath feuded publicly with State Senator John R. Dunne, who demanded Tombs prisoners testify in front of special hearings called by his New York State Committee on Crime and Correction, which had in recent years become sharply critical of the city's jails. Meanwhile, the hearings were disrupted by the striking news camera operators. Placing more blame at the foot of police policy than City Hall or DOC would dare, Dunne proposed all prisoners jailed for nonviolent misdemeanors be released, and that the police begin issuing summonses for misdemeanors. When asked if they considered the Tombs conditions as an outcome of preventative detention, the prisoners responded, "Yes sir! Right on! That's the basics of the thing!" McGrath was subsequently asked by the Board of Correction if he considered bail a form of preventative detention, to which he deferred by citing the issue as a "touchy subject."[16]

The hearings only exacerbated the unfolding feud within New York State politics over who was to blame for the city's jail conditions. "The city's bad, the state's wonderful—that's the kind of thing you heard," complained vice president Kenneth Jackson of the nonprofit Fortune Society, who believed the Tombs prisoners were given false hope by the hearing and were soon going to riot and "tear that garbage can down." Meanwhile in Queens, a judge had publicly ordered that McGrath either produce rebellious prisoners in court or produce himself to explain their absence. The report produced by Dunne's hearings presented a damning account of the Tombs consistent with prior reports and exposés. It painted an equally damning picture of city and, to a lesser extent, state inactivity in the face of crisis conditions. In a remarkable rhetorical flourish, Dunne placed responsibility for the disturbance at the feet of DOC—an agency he claimed "does not correct but further aggravates the problem and spews its pollution in the form of un-rehabilitated angrier men into our streets, bringing forth an even greater pestilence of crime and violence for an already terrified public to endure."[17]

McGrath was singled out for failing to pursue an agreement reached with Dunne in December 1969, in which he had agreed to mitigate overcrowding through shifting some city prisoners to state facilities, work toward a policy consigning all sentenced prisoners to state custody, and undertake "an immediate, intensive search for additional alternative short-term detention facilities within the City." In his testimony before the committee, McGrath was grilled on DOC's monthslong failure to report back to City Hall on an inspection of the Brooklyn Navy Yard Barracks as a potential detention site. The commissioner came up empty. After some breathless speculation about how the report might have been lost in the shuffle of department bureaucracy, McGrath ultimately told the committee, "I don't know any other places, that is all. If you know any, let me know and I'll go down there."

The committee concluded, "McGrath's attitude seemed to be that this ... was somebody else's responsibility, not his, despite the explicit agreement at the December City Hall meeting." The whole affair was "typical of the priority correction matters receive in New York City." The committee also found that key civilian positions in DOC had been left unfilled, central DOC staff had been inaccessible during the rebellion, and a constant rotation of managerial staff had resulted in a low level of institutional knowledge among administrators. What's more, they felt McGrath himself knew little about the institutions, as he had at one point insisted that the Tombs lacked stairs. "Even the inmates knew there was a stairway in the tombs," the report observed, citing one prisoner who told them "mice use the stairway." Moreover, rank-and-file guard morale was discovered to be "very low," which one guard told the committee was due to unheeded warnings from guards, who allegedly had "foreseen" the rebellion and "mentioned it to people in authority many times." In response, their higher-ups "smile—and that's that."

The report also chided the state for moving slowly to mitigate the crisis, and the courts for delays that exacerbated the crowding. The overall picture was bleak. "A man has to be angry," the report concluded, "when he rips an iron leg from the table in his cell and batters through three inches of glass brick—not with the hope of gaining freedom, but of merely transmitting his message of anguish and frustration to the society that imprisoned him." The only thing the city and state bureaucrats could seem to agree on was the need to resist a political interpretation of the rebellion. They took up the view that the prisoners' actions were the logical result of faulty facilities and management, rather than acknowledge the obvious: that they were part of a generalized rebellion against an entire way of life that was unfolding on both sides of the bars, all over the world.[18]

In early September, as the city, state, DOC, and COBA leadership feuded amongst themselves, a new contender announced itself. COBA's rank and file undertook what Zeferetti claimed as a wildcat sick-out on Rikers Island. Zeferetti had long been arguing, and conducting slowdowns, for 700 new guard positions. When the guards took the drastic action of the sick-out, leaving DOC short-staffed and threatening its basic operations, COBA was promised 300 new hires that very day. Zeferetti declared victory. However, many of DOC's rank and file defied him, staying out the following day. Before McGrath knew it, the wildcat had spread to the Women's House of Detention, and only his threat to withhold paychecks brought the action to an end. While guards had always resisted the progressive penology of Anna M. Kross and DOC's authority over them, this kind of organized rank-and-file militancy signaled a qualitative shift in the department's labor politics. This was compounded shortly thereafter, when the nonprofit Legal Aid Society helped file a group of prisoners' class action suit, *Rhem v. McGrath*, calling for the outright closure of the Tombs, on the grounds it violated the First, Sixth, Eighth, and Fourteenth Amendments of the US Constitution. The besieged McGrath, who stubbornly blamed the disturbance on the "doctrine which says the bad guys are the good guys," and society's tendency "to call all criminals political criminals," responded by thanking the litigants, claiming, "I'm very pleased this subject has been brought to a head." It hadn't.[19]

12

Shaping Destiny

Turnabout Day

"The Black man is unique," wrote Stanley Eldridge, imprisoned in the Adolescent Reformatory on Rikers Island in 1968,

> in that his feet are
> perpetually moving toward,
>   around, about, perfect
> rhythm no doubt, tapping,
>   he will eventually, dancing
> get there.
>   The Black hand
> is forever climbing into
>   rings,
> explaining things, fingerprinted,
> pushing brooms, defying grief,
> in shadowy rooms,
>   shaping destiny.[1]

On Thursday, October 1, 1970, the Branch Queens House of Detention for Men in Long Island City, rated for a capacity of 160, held 338 prisoners. Nine of them were Panthers from the New York Twenty-One, having been moved from Manhattan's Tombs to Branch Queens after the August rebellion. Jamal Joseph, who had by now been bailed out, recalls the Panthers' segregation floor at Branch Queens as a place of fierce solidarity buttressed by intensive political education. The group studied

the writings of ancient Chinese general Sun Tzu, military strategy dating back to Hannibal, and the revolutionary texts of Karl
Marx, Mao Zedong, Che Guevara, Patrice Lumumba, Ahmed
Sékou Touré, and Amílcar Cabral. Joseph was assigned to write
position papers, and then arguing them with the other comrades.
"If prison was a university, as Malcolm said," writes Joseph,
"then our Panther wing was grad school." Present elsewhere
in the facility was Young Lord Victor Martinez, who had been
working with comrades from the Tombs since their transfer to
organize another rebellion. In fact, on October 1, around two-
thirds of the Branch Queens population had been at the Tombs
during the August rebellion. [2]

That day, as Branch Queens prisoners were being transported
to lunch, a small group sprang into action, overpowering guards,
confiscating a set of keys, and quickly unlocking nearly every cell
in the jail. Five guards, a captain, and a DOC cook were taken
hostage. Initially, the freed prisoners ran wild through the institution, flooding some floors, setting fires, and smashing almost
every window on the building's east side. But soon the fires were
extinguished, the smoke subsided, and a red, black, and green
flag of black liberation flew from the top floor. It was later joined
with a sign reading: "Equal justice! Stop oppression, exploita-
tion, and persecution. Power to the people." Panther Kuwasi
Balagoon remembers October 1 as "turnabout day," when the
guards "were captured by the people, and put on the right side
of the bars, for a change." "What a beautiful feeling!" he reflects.
"Next to getting out of jail, turnabout day is where it's at ... It
was a religious experience ... It was art and it was life." [3]

The Panthers, sequestered from the rest of the population,
had no direct role in planning the rebellion. But their influence, and that of the Young Lords, was immediately palpable.
Demands included more black people on the Panthers' New
York Twenty-One jury and bail for Afeni Shakur, who was
locked up in Manhattan's House of Detention for Women.
Additionally, the prisoners demanded no reprisals, no transfers, disciplinary actions against certain guards, and an end
to charging prisoners money for basic amenities like soap.

They established a governance system of tier representatives, including Balagoon and fellow Panthers Lumumba Shakur and Kwando Kinshasa, Victor Martinez, as well as unaffiliated prisoners Kenneth Cender, who was white, and Robert Drake, who was black. They delegated responsibilities for guarding the facility, assigned relief duties, and created two roving security teams.

A hostage later described the prisoners' division of labor as "like a guerrilla unit, with an organization staff, lieutenants, and security units." This was no coincidence; in addition to closely studying works by revolutionary guerrillas, Balagoon—and likely other participants—brought prior experience in the US Army to the operation. Stationed in Germany during a stint in the Army before becoming a tenant organizer, Balagoon had formed a clandestine group called De Legislators, "an organization based on fucking up racists," that engaged in a number of carefully planned retaliatory beatings of racist white soldiers. Afterward, he recalls, "we would have critiques, just like at the end of war games." Balagoon had earned the nickname "De Prophet" due to his "prophesying that so-and-so was going to get fucked up in a predetermined amount of time, and then going on and fucking the chump up."[4]

The representatives at Branch Queens requested to meet a variety of public figures, including Mayor Lindsay and famed boxer Muhammad Ali, but settled for visits from Bronx borough president Herman Badillo, Representative Shirley Chisholm, Louis Farrakhan of the Nation of Islam, and Manuel Casiano, the executive director of a city program for Puerto Rican migrants. They also demanded a press conference, which they received, and was widely covered by the city's press. Framing the struggle as waged against "this system, which has oppressed us for 400 years," Victor Martinez declared, "We are ready to die and kill until you pigs give us back our rights." As social anthropologist Orisanmi Burton observes, "Martinez's proclamation reveals the captives' belief that their struggle extended beyond the jail," challenging "the dominant narrative that the rebellion was caused by technocratic inefficiencies such as overcrowding or poor conditions." The representatives also demanded that a bail hearing be held at the Branch Queens facility, or else they would kill the hostages. Meanwhile, 200 police, many armed with shotguns and tear gas, surrounded the jail, erecting barbed wire barricades outside the entrance and inside the underground tunnel connecting the jail to the Queens Court. The takeover became a major news story in New York City, and updates were constantly piped into other jails via local news broadcasts. On Friday, October 2, the Queens prisoners released two hostages in "good faith," to begin negotiations. At 3:00 p.m., as the Queens comrades met with Badillo, Chisholm, and Farrakhan to begin negotiations, prisoners at the Tombs once again rebelled.[5]

A Classic Guerrilla Operation

"The actual take-over of the floor was executed perfectly, like clockwork," recalls Panther Ricardo de Leon, who helped seize the Tombs' eleventh floor that day.

> It was the complete surprise—a classic guerrilla operation. We were coming out of the chapel, where a movie had been shown, toward the elevators to go back to our floor; the advance group split up and seized all the guards on the elevators and herded them toward the chaplain's office. At this, the brothers who were in the chapel had the rest of the guards under control. The gate leading to the elevator was secured with handcuffs and barricaded with furniture; guards were placed. When the policeman who was in charge of the inmate commissary dug the take-over move, he locked the commissary and everybody in there. All we had to do then was post guards so they couldn't get out. Later he gave up the keys voluntarily.

Eighteen hostages were taken, and while the prisoners could secure only the eleventh floor, they did so with precision. They formed a "revolutionary committee," which included prisoners who had participated in the August rebellion. Also present were members of the Young Lords and the Nation of Islam.

They reiterated the demands from August, to which many more had been added, including clothing for prisoners, trained social workers, Spanish interpreters, and a new recreation area. They also pledged full solidarity with the comrades' demands in Queens.[6]

Once more, Tombs prisoners rained debris on the street below, including two guards' hats, shouting, "Power to the people!" They unfurled a banner reading, in part, "We want to see the Mayor and we don't want promises." The mayor, who somewhat sympathetically called the events a barometer of "the tragic state of our criminal justice system and the city's limited power alone to bring relief," refused to meet with either prisoner delegation until all hostages were released.

That evening, upward of 900 prisoners at the Queens House of Detention for Men in Kew Gardens also rebelled, setting fires and smashing windows. They did not take any hostages, but some prisoners briefly attempted escape, until they were beaten back by police smoke bombs. In all likelihood, their lack of hostages was due not to a moral or tactical aversion, but to the rebellion's origins in dayrooms that were guarded from the outside, giving the guards a chance to escape as the prisoners took over.[7]

On the third day of the rebellion, the Branch Queens rebellion was granted one of its most audacious demands: a summary bail hearing, held by a judge, in the ground floor visiting room of the besieged facility. "A precedent was set," reflects Balagoon. "Never before in the history of this racist empire had judges been summoned to a jail by inmates to hold court." The first nine prisoners considered by the judge were paroled outright. Their cases, Herman Badillo recalls, were largely ridiculous: a mixture of frivolous charges and prohibitive bail known all too well to DOC's captives past and present. One prisoner had been held for attempted murder of a police officer—after a cop had asked to see his BB gun, and, complying with the order, he had produced it. The man's low bail signaled to Badillo that this was not a serious charge, and even the courts recognized its frivolity. Nonetheless, the bail had been enough to keep this man locked in a cage awaiting trial. His was a common case of prisoners "in jail simply because they were poor," as Badillo puts it. The judge heard thirteen cases before they refused to continue. By Badillo's reckoning, "had the judges stayed to hear all 460 cases, at least 400 of those men would have been freed on the spot."[8]

In exchange for the thirteen hearings, the Branch Queens prisoners released two hostages. At this point there emerged a conflict over how many hearings had been agreed upon as a condition of releasing the rest. Lindsay aide Barry Gottehrer insists that the Queens prisoners promised to release all their hostages after this bail hearing, thus breaking their word when they proceeded to demand additional bail hearings as a condition for additional releases. By his account, even Farrakhan told the prisoners "they had broken their word and he was very disappointed in them." Sensing loggerheads foreshadowing a violent conclusion, Farrakhan and Badillo departed, on the heels of Chisholm, who had already left, fearing bad press to come. Balagoon recalls that the promise to release all hostages had been made in the heat of the moment by a delegation whose actions did not represent the wishes of all the prisoners—or a sound strategy. "In this writer's opinion," Balagoon reflects, "we should have not given up shit, after giving up those first two captives in some motherfucking 'good faith.' But some members of the team went out there and fucked up, talking about letting all captives go. A general consensus of all inmates, after learning about the fuck-up, was to let two go."[9]

That same day, prisoners rose up at yet another facility, the Brooklyn House of Detention on Atlantic Avenue. Beginning at lunchtime, seven out of nine floors of the facility, packed wall to wall with 1,500 prisoners, were consumed in revolt, during which prisoners took three hostages. The uprising followed the same pattern of freshly liberated prisoners smashing windows and anything breakable, setting fires, and throwing flaming bedding and other debris onto the street below. "Ain't that a rewarding sound," writes Balagoon, on the breaking of glass. "Kids love it. It can't be spelled." It is a sound, Balagoon notes, that cannot be replicated by a human voice: "Some people can sound like cars. Hot rods even. Some can imitate a fire engine. But to hear the sound of glass breaking, glass must be broken."

BHD prisoners also hung signs, including "Power to the People." Thousands of supporters gathered outside, clashing with the cops, who fired their guns at rooftops from which rocks and bottles were being rained down on them. Several arrests were made. Panthers and Young Lords demonstrated in solidarity across the city. By the time it was repressed, more than 2,700 prisoners in city institutions would take part in the rebellion. Like the uprising on Rikers Island, the siege was widely broadcast on television and radio. "The message of revolution," reflected the Young Lords in their publication *Palante*, "gets across all barriers."[10]

Power to the Pigs

Mayor Lindsay promised no reprisals if the Brooklyn prisoners surrendered, but the rebels refused to release their hostages. As the prisoners fought among themselves over strategy, a squadron of guards stormed the facility from the street, firing tear gas canisters. Most of the ill-trained guards had failed to properly secure their gas masks, however, and when a prisoner threw a canister back at them, the guards scattered and ran back into the street, leaving the doors to the jail wide open. Six were hospitalized due to gas exposure. The cops who had held the line outside, not wanting to get involved in what they viewed as a Department of Correction problem, demonstrated for the guards how to put on the masks. Another assault was undertaken, in which all but two floors were retaken. Around midnight, the remaining 450 prisoners were violently subdued, and the three hostages released. Hundreds of prisoners were injured in the process.[11]

Around 3:00 a.m., fifty DOC guards and one hundred cops from NYPD's Tactical Patrol Force stormed the Kew Gardens facility from the roof, cutting their way into the building using acetylene torches. They faced what the warden later called "heavy" resistance, battling floor by floor in hand-to-hand combat on floors made slick with soapy water to slow their advance. The prisoners held out for hours against tear gas and clubs, especially the "hard core" on the fourth floor. It wasn't until 6:00 a.m. that the final prisoner was locked in. Gottehrer toured the facility as the battle raged on and then in its aftermath. "I was stunned by the wreckage," he reflected. "Glass crunched underfoot. Water from firehoses ran ankle deep in the corridors." While much would be made of the wrecked facilities, Gottehrer was certain that "prisoners were responsible for only a fraction of the property damage, much of which could only have been caused by the acetylene torches carried by the guards ... They had injured more than 200 inmates, they had bludgeoned their way through solid walls. They had cut their way through steel doors rather than unlocking them."

In subduing the revolt, "guards had ripped up their own building more vehemently than any gang of rampaging prisoners. One had the feeling, looking at the shattered plaster and falling fixtures, that in the space of an hour or two the guards must have let out violence they had suppressed for years." Even if one sets aside the Lindsay aide's assumption that DOC guards succeed in repressing violence at all, he captures the sheer concentrated violence that played out in the defeat of the jail rebellions.[12]

By this point it was Sunday, October 4, the fourth day of the rebellion, and Lindsay was worried the city was running out of tear gas. He sent an emissary to the manufacturer in rural Pennsylvania, pulled the businessman from his church service, and acquired 1,200 fresh gas grenades. Kew Gardens and the Brooklyn House of Detention had been subdued. Prisoners at a fifth jail—the Adolescent Reformatory at Rikers Island—had briefly erupted, but were quickly put down and their four hostages released. Hostages remained at the Tombs and the Queens House of Detention, the only facilities still holding out.

Facing the possibility of a violent showdown, the political fault lines dividing the self-conscious political militants from the rest of the prisoners began to emerge. From the onset of the takeovers, there had been problems at both jails with some prisoners shirking guard responsibility, eating more than their share of food, taking drugs from the infirmary, and generally causing chaos. The militants were understandably unhappy with this behavior, though Balagoon counted himself among the recreational window smashers. "Some of us had to be restrained by the collective to cut down on the confusion at times," he recalls. "But it was good clean entertainment." Now, with direct conflict on the horizon, both sides understood that their options in the event of a confrontation would be limited.[13]

"If the pigs came in with guns and we fought," Balagoon reasoned, "many of us would die and many of them would die, and we would have guns." In other words, it would be a mixed bag. Alternatively, if the cops "teargassed us and came in with clubs, then the battle would take the form of a medieval war, the Crusades, a gory, bloody, extremely down-to-earth old-fashioned real war, extremely real … how many inside the building would die? Maybe all of us before the shit was over." A particularly acrimonious debate broke out over the release of the remaining hostages, whom the Panthers understood as the source of power—and guarantors of the safety—of the Branch Queens prisoners. While an impressive degree of tactical unity had been achieved in the takeover, broader political, if not existential, questions emerged.

"So many of them that had been right on with the building of barricades, surely they asked themselves, 'What the fuck am I doing?'" Balagoon recalls. "Those of us who wanted to be a man for five days and until death, said, in effect, we ain't giving another inch. We're prepared—and we want to fight anyway!" As time progressed this became a minority sentiment at Branch Queens. One prisoner, upon being told, "This is a revolution," remarked to Balagoon: "You hear that, I've just been drafted into the army."[14]

A similar split was making itself felt in the Tombs. At 9:30 p.m. on Sunday the fifth, Lindsay broadcast a radio message to the Tombs over WINS and WNYC, offering to meet with their representatives upon the release of all hostages. Otherwise, he warned, the facility would be stormed in half an hour. At this, Ricardo de Leon recalls, "all the waverers, fence sitters, and opponents started shouting 'Let them go! Let them go!' Those of us who did not want to give up without getting a commitment on our demands were out maneuvered by the compromisers on the committee, who took over the public address system and steamrollered surrender."

However, Lindsay's threat was not as concrete as it seemed. As the Tombs prisoners debated Lindsay's proposal, DOC chief of operations Anthony Principe revealed his plan—or lack thereof. To Gottehrer's amazement, Principe produced a blank piece of paper and marked it with an X. "Here's the door," he began. "You go up this way." Someone interrupted: "Are you sure the stairway ends up here? I thought it was further over." Debate ensued. In short, Gottehrer quickly surmised, there was no plan; "No one even had a map of the building." Principe further stunned Lindsay's staffers by declaring, "We're just going to have to consider the hostages expendable." City Hall stalled for over two hours, until the prisoners agreed to release the hostages, on the grounds there be no reprisals and Lindsay meet with them as planned. The visiting Lindsay made rhetorical gestures to the validity of the Tombs grievances, and order was restored at the jail.[15]

Meanwhile at Branch Queens, the cops surrounding the jail were having a veritable field day, using their loudspeakers to broadcast the theme song from the television show *Dragnet* interspersed with recordings of machine gun fire. Supporters of the prisoners also rallied. Since the occupation began, Panther Twenty-One codefendants Afeni Shakur, Dhoruba bin Wahad, and Jamal Joseph, now out on bail, had addressed the crowd of supporters gathered outside. Inside, the prisoners' general assembly was consumed by a practical question: whether to kill the hostages if the jail was raided. Positions ranged from "Let's cut their throats, hang them, set them on fire and throw them out the eighth-floor window" to "I think we've gone far enough ... we should call a press conference and give the prisoners up."

The Panthers had consistently disputed accusations, circulating in the media and within the jail itself, that they alone were pulling the strings. When Lindsay broadcast a radio message early Monday morning similar to the one that had quelled the rebellion at the Tombs, the Panthers encouraged a vote on whether to continue fighting. In this ballot, one prisoner elected to represent each tier cast a vote. Initially, they voted to stay and fight. However, the presence of a small army of cops and guards outside, illuminated by floodlights, and an impassioned speech in English and Spanish from DOC Public Affairs director Al Castro urging surrender, apparently occasioned a second vote. The prisoners resolved to turn the hostages loose.[16]

"Listen brothers," Balagoon recalls the Panthers telling the other prisoners, "we'll go along with the majority because we don't want to fight you, but the pigs are gonna fuck you up anyway," regardless of whether they turned the hostages over peaceably. Nonetheless, as in the Tombs, the hostages were quickly released by a faction of prisoners eager to end the standoff. By this point, many of the 300 guards outside—as distinct from the 300 cops—had shed their uniforms and armed themselves with pipes, axe handles, bats, table legs, and trash can lids. NYPD's Emergency Service Division distributed helmets, clubs, and gas masks to the guards, though supplies ran thin. Some guards preferred their makeshift weapons; others were armed with shotguns. Many had come directly from other jails, where they had already engaged in hand-to-hand combat with prisoners. Warned that the guards were restless, Chief of Operations Principe gave a speech ordering the lawful and nonviolent evacuation of the jail. These remarks were met with obscenity-laced heckling by the rank and file. Meanwhile, the Panthers, who had worked with the most militant prisoners to build a cache of weapons to defend the facility, including spears and Molotov cocktails, retreated to the top floor of the facility, where a total of thirty-nine prisoners, Victor Martinez among them, barricaded themselves in.[17]

As Lindsay prepared to meet with the Branch Queens prisoners as promised, Commissioner McGrath argued that the jail should be searched first, which involved herding the prisoners into the yard. Lindsay's aides worried the prisoners would be beaten, in violation of the promise the mayor had made to them.

McGrath assured them he was in control of his men, and that he would personally oversee the operation and ensure nobody was harmed. Under McGrath's leadership, guards began escorting prisoners out of the jail and into the yard. Guards and prisoners alike subsequently testified that the initial evacuation went off peacefully, with over one hundred prisoners taken to the yard. This changed, however, with the appearance of Kenneth Cender, the lone white prisoner representative, who inspired particular loathing among DOC guards.

"It's Cender!" one guard shouted. A ground of more than twenty-five guards began viciously beating him, breaking some of his teeth. As Cender lay on the grass, one guard continued to beat him under the pretext of helping a medic administer first aid. A similar fate befell Robert Drake, identified by one guard who shouted, "That's one of the leaders!" Drake was beaten unconscious with nightsticks in plain sight of Michael Dontzin, a high-ranking City Hall official, as he clutched onto Dontzin for support. They both fell to the ground. According to Gottehrer, the look on Drake's face as he was beaten into unconsciousness shook Dontzin so much he could barely speak about it for months. On the record, most city officials didn't speak about what they saw at all.[18]

From there, the violence became more generalized. A media blackout was thwarted by reporters who, heeding updates on the beatings broadcast over a bullhorn by Victor Martinez, climbed to a nearby roof to behold the violence in progress. They observed prisoners beaten severely, even after they had gone limp, kicked while on the ground, including in the genitals, and denied medical assistance for their injuries. Officials in suits—denoting high rank in DOC or City Hall—whom the reporters could not positively identify, loitered nearby in plain sight of the beatings, doing nothing. When a paramedic requested help from a group of loitering guards to load an injured prisoner into her ambulance, they responded, "Power to the pigs," and walked away.[19]

As their comrades continued to rally outside the jail, the Panthers and other militant prisoners were still barricaded on the top floor with their weapons, prepared to fight. The Panthers' lawyers, including Gerald Lefcourt, worked to negotiate a peaceful surrender. All the while, the prisoners communicated their situation, and the beating they had witnessed, to the crowd below. As guards began to set small fires in the jail to smoke out the holdouts, Lindsay aide Sid Davidoff persuaded McGrath to allow a cherry picker to carry the remaining prisoners out the window, thus avoiding the chance of attack as they made their way through the jail. All parties agreed. As the prisoners' supporters rallied outside, simultaneously bearing witness, the city was forced to demonstrate its commitment to avoiding more bloodshed by removing the holdouts in plain sight and placing them on a bus to Rikers. "The sight of the Panthers 21 members riding down in those cherry pickers with clenched fists," recalls Joseph, "was the equivalent of watching Hannibal enter Rome." As the cherry picker lowered the Panthers to the ground, Lumumba Shakur held up the keys to the Branch Queens House of Detention and threw them to the crowd below.[20]

13

Free Angela Davis!

Empty Diversions

On both sides of the bars, the resistance around New York City's jails continued well after the rebellion. Stonewall riot veteran and trailblazing queer activist Sylvia Rivera came of age in the 1960s, cycling in and out of the wing designated for gay male adolescents at the Adolescent Reformatory at Rikers Island. There, she began using heroin and also learned how to adopt the appearance of insanity to avoid being victimized. As Rivera recalls, she and her friend Bambi L'Amour behaved "like two crazy abnormal bitches," hailing imaginary taxi cabs in the hallways and staying away from the other prisoners. Once Rivera was placed in a holding cell at 100 Centre Street, in Lower Manhattan, with a group of men whom the guard told: "Enjoy yourself boys, have fun." Immediately seized upon as a target for rape, Rivera feigned interest in performing oral sex on them. However, she bit the penis of the first man so hard that it bled, only letting go after being beaten. By the time she got to Rikers Island, Rivera recalled, people said: "'That's the crazy bitch that bit that boy's dick. Leave her alone' … It was always good to play crazy."[1]

Later, alongside fellow activist Marsha P. Johnson, Rivera founded Street Transvestite Action Revolutionaries (STAR), a radical community group for queer and gender nonconforming people who were predominantly young and marginally housed. Based on their own experiences with incarceration, STAR organized around the conditions in city jails, cofounding the Gay Community Prison Committee, picketing the House of Detention for Women on a weekly basis in the early 1970s. Contemporaneously, the Gay Activist Alliance picketed the Tombs over the treatment of queer prisoners, and the Gay Liberation Front routinely bailed out Panthers, Young Lords, and queer liberationists. These regular demonstrations, part of the city's subversive tradition, took on a national dimension when HDW received one of its most famous prisoners.[1]

Less than a week after the October 1970 rebellion ended, Black Power icon and Communist Party member Angela Davis was apprehended in New York City in connection with an ill-fated raid on the Marin County Courthouse in San Rafael, California, meant to free George Jackson and the other Soledad Brothers held at San Quentin State Prison. While awaiting extradition to California, Davis was held in the HDW. Her written account of this time spent in HDW, and the political activity it engendered, provides a window into daily life at the facility at the time of the rebellions in the male facilities, while situating these rebellions in a larger context of everyday resistance born from human caging. Davis found the facility "old, musty, dreary and dim." All women were searched "internally," meaning vaginally and anally, upon admission, despite the scandal provoked by the young activist Andrea Dworkin's testimony years prior. "Just enough activities were provided to distract the prisoners from any prolonged reflection upon their wretched condition," Davis reflects, with regard to the facility's much-vaunted programming—a holdover from the era of Commissioner Kross. "The point was to fill up the day with meaningless activities, empty diversions ... a network of institutions was there to absorb the energies of the prisoner."[2]

While sequestered in a psychiatric unit she dubbed a "maximum security arrangement camouflaged as a therapeutic cellblock," Davis was alarmed at the high doses of Thorazine and other tranquilizers administered to women to keep them quiet. In the general population, Davis discovered, "the prisoners spent most of their time in corridors ... sitting on cold, filthy cement floors." To make matters worse, these cells had no trash receptacles, and garbage was instead tossed through the bars into these corridors. Visits, initially denied Davis, were conducted in twenty-minute intervals through grubby glass, on a telephone prone to breakdown. Women engaged in the nightly ritual of plugging up every crevice in their cell entrances, lest "Mickey"—their name for the facilty's infestation of mice—descend on them in their sleep. One even made it to Davis's top bunk. "Indulging in a flight of fancy," Davis recalls, "I would sometimes imagine that all the preparations that were made at night to ward off those creatures were barricades being erected against that larger enemy"—capitalism—and that "hundreds of women all over the jail, politically conscious, politically committed, were acting in revolutionary unison." If such unity remains elusive to the present day, Davis nonetheless encountered the seeds of solidarity at HDW.

Davis, a prominent member of the Communist Party, had originally been segregated on the pretext that anti-communist prisoners would cause her harm. However, after petitioning successfully to be placed in the general population, Davis found many women receptive to her political ideas. Consequently, she was soon transferred once more, to a makeshift solitary cell in a converted examination room. In protest of being held in solitary, Davis undertook a ten-day hunger strike, in which she was joined by women across the jail. "It was not difficult to go on a hunger strike," Davis recalls. "If the food had looked palatable, it would have been hard; but the unsavory dishes they placed before me actually facilitated the strike." A group of prisoners organized a march by Davis's cell, chanting "Free Angela, free our sister."[3]

On the outside, two Board of Correction members, including a young lawyer named Geraldo Rivera—a future TV star who had been hastily added to the board following the rebellion—filed motions demanding her release into the general population. The duo had pressed for Angela Davis's release from solitary at their first BOC meeting, and had visited Davis before filing the affidavit. On the tenth day of the hunger strike, federal judge Morris Lasker ruled Davis's isolation unconstitutional; she was subsequently released into the general population. "The court was all but saying that Commissioner of Corrections George McGrath and Jessie Behagen, superintendent of the Women's House of D., were so fearful of letting the women in the jail discover what communism was that they preferred to violate my most basic constitutional rights," Davis recalls. The ruling freed Davis only from solitary, not from the jail itself.[4]

Once in the general population, Davis and her comrades on the seventh floor staged multiple direct actions demanding medical attention for their fellow prisoners. One ailing woman had been brushed off repeatedly by the jail's doctor with the advice that she ought to "get a job" in order to feel better. Davis and her comrades refused to return to their cells until this woman received a serious examination. The action worked, and she was rushed to the hospital with tumors in her breasts. At the same time, Davis began leading discussions on white supremacy and communism, finding much interest in her dialogic lectures. Sympathetic guards smuggled in copies of George Jackson's *Soledad Brother*, which became "the most valuable piece of contraband in the jail." Davis corresponded with Jackson, who urged her to inform the women of the HDW he had outgrown his male chauvinist views expressed in the book's early letters. Davis met at least one prisoner who had been locked up with New York Twenty-One defendants Joan Bird and Afeni Shakur, and who wanted to join the movement. Davis conducted karate classes, despite a ban on the practice by frantic administrators, who thought, perhaps rightly, that she was preparing for an insurrection. A few stray books on W.E.B. Du Bois, the Chinese revolution, and the principles of communism lay buried among pulp novels in the jail's library. Davis imagined they had been left behind by Elizabeth Gurley Flynn, Claudia Jones, or other women jailed under the anti-communist Smith Act, thanks to a DOC policy whereby prisoners donated their books to the library upon leaving the institution. When Davis then received ten copies of *Soledad Brother*, however, this policy was revised, just for her.[5]

Free All Our Sisters!

While Davis brought a sophisticated understanding of political praxis to the facility, a culture of subversion and resistance doubtless predated her arrival. After lock-in, she discovered, the prisoners engaged in a nightly ritual of calling to one another by name and saying goodnight, in defiance of the policy of silence. Women used the church services, much heralded by the Kross-era partnerships with the religious organizations celebrated by prison scholar Clarice Feinman, largely as a social gathering where they could see their friends from other floors. Movies served the same purpose, and provided added cover for sex. Davis also discovered elaborate kinship structures modeled on the nuclear family—including marriage, anchored in elaborate wedding ceremonies—and many, though not all, were based on the romantic relationships that crisscrossed the institution. "The gay life," she found, pervaded the entire facility. Davis also encountered prisoners who presented as men and had adopted he/him pronouns. When Davis received notes of support from all over the jail, it was through a well-established and elaborate network of "kites," illegal notes smuggled by fellow prisoners and even guards, with no discernible profit incentive.

This everyday culture of subversion extended, in part, to the guards. "A lot of officers here—the Black officers," one guard told Davis, in confidence, "have been pulling for you," during her period as a fugitive. "We've been hoping all along that you would get to some place that was safe." Davis found several guards who were sympathetic, even politically. "They were a conglomeration of Black women, both young and old, whose political sentiments ranged from 'liberal' to straight-out sympathy with the most militant wings of the Black Liberation Movement." Two had even been dismissed recently for affiliation with the Panthers. These black guards told Davis that "they had been driven by necessity to apply to for this kind of job … it was one of the highest-paying jobs in New York that did not require a college education. In a way," she reflected, "these officers were prisoners themselves, and some of them were keenly aware that they were treading ambiguous waters. Like their predecessors, the Black overseers, they were guarding their sisters in exchange for a few bits of bead." Sympathetic guards smuggled in political literature and hair combs, both of which were contraband, and smuggled prisoners' messages out of the jail. Some even claimed while they were not willing to needlessly sacrifice such lucrative jobs, they would throw down their badges and join the prisoners in a moment of revolt. Davis was skeptical but did not rule out the possibility.[6]

Organizing on the outside had a profound effect on both Davis and the political situation inside HDW. On multiple occasions she heard demonstrations on the street outside, with chants of "Free Angela Davis," and "Free all our sisters!" piercing the jail's walls. Davis was also able to conduct "street visits," a time-honored HDW tradition of shouting out the window to visitors on the sidewalk below. These included a meeting with the Harlem Black Women to Free Angela Davis, which ended with one woman arrested after she ignored the cops' demand to disperse. All the while, Davis fought extradition to California in court.

The threads of outside agitation to free Davis and her own organizing within the facility converged at a final demonstration in December of 1970, organized by the New York Committee to Free Angela Davis. As demonstrators amassed outside on Greenwich Avenue chanting, "One, two, three, four, the House of D has got to go!" and "Free our sisters, free ourselves," Davis and her comrades inside chanted back, in rehearsed unison, from different cells, proclaiming solidarity with the Soledad Brothers, Panthers Erica Huggins and Bobby Seale, and the deceased Jonathan Jackson. Davis attempted to focus the demonstration beyond herself, shouting the names of her HDW comrades to her supporters below: "Free Vernell! Free Helen! Free Amy! Free Joann! Free Laura! Free Minnie!"[7]

As the rally intensified outside, one HDW guard tried to clamp down the chanting of Davis and her comrades, but the women refused to stop. A captain was called to the scene, and she too was rebuffed harshly by Davis's cohort. Soon the HDW administrators gave up altogether on calming the women down, and after lock-in, they demonstrated loudly, banging shoes and chanting: "One, two, three, four. We won't let Angela go! Five, six, seven, eight. We won't let them through the gate!"

Guards responded by loudly beating one of their comrades in the adolescent wing and throwing her in solitary. At this, the women caught the attention of a white couple on the street, who happened to just be passing by. The couple spent the night placing phone calls to whomever they could, and a sizeable demonstration was organized in short order. That very night, Davis was extradited. During the surprise extradition, Davis put up her hands and began fighting with the male riot squad guards, who responded by beating her. Two women guards entered the brawl on Davis's side. They accompanied her until she was turned over to the California authorities.[8]

New York Twenty-One codefendant Joan Bird had similar experiences while in and out of the HDW during their trial, both before and after Davis's stay. In an exhaustive account of the daily life of the facility, Bird corroborates many points of Davis's account while providing rich detail about the facility in what would become its final years of operation. Bird describes a large sign in the receiving room: "You can write Legal Aid for a lawyer after you've been here two weeks." She describes women forced to submit to the internal search, or else locked in isolation until they submitted, or similarly forced to undergo a Pap smear and peppered with "medical" questions that amounted to an interrogation about their sexual history.

Bird and codefendant Afeni Shakur later told their comrade Assata Shakur that the women called this "getting the finger," or "getting finger fucked." It was likely the exact same invasive act Dworkin had described years prior, to great public outcry. The purportedly rehabilitative adolescent school, Bird found, "is actually a game which the adolescents play to get whatever candy, cigarettes, pencils, pens they can con out of the teacher." Like Davis, Bird cites the chapel as a place women go to socialize. It was also a place where, incidentally, there happen to be "a priest and a nun who offer you the forgiveness of the Lord and offer the advice 'Sinner, repent, or to hell you will go,' when actually you are living in hell—jail—called the Women's House of Detention."

In this hell, Bird writes, echoing Davis's account, that many women were doped up with Thorazine or chloral hydrate: "To keep you from shouting out how awful and horrible the place actually is, they just drug you up." Bird claims the Friendly Visitors, the pioneering nonprofit partnership Commissioner Kross had brought to the jails, were just profiteers who sold the clothing women made, in exchange for "nothing but three cigarettes wrapped in foil, deodorant, and candy—and this they expect you to be thankful for." "They say they're now closing the Women's House of Detention on Greenwich Avenue," Bird concludes, "and they're going to have it in a new building." However, "it really isn't going to change things; it's not the building it's the people, the cruel and corrupt people who can treat other human beings in a way they would never in the world think of treating their dogs."[9] Bird was correct that the horrors of jails can scarcely be blamed on the individual physical structures where people are locked up; instead, they are the inevitable consequence of human caging wherever it occurs.

14

Aftermath

Gestapo-Style Lockdown

In the immediate aftermath of the October 1970 jail rebellion, Tombs prisoners found their cells completely wrecked and all their belongings destroyed by guards. They were then kept on twenty-four-hour lockdown. "We have no communications with the outside world," wrote Panther Ricardo de Leon, of the "Gestapo-style" lockdown. There were "no visits, no showers, shaves, haircuts, no opportunity to wash our clothes, no recreation ... Medical attention is non-existent; I have requested a doctor since last Monday and have yet to see one. The guards act as if they were deaf." Commissioner McGrath justified the lockdown, which multiple visitors reported had made conditions worse than before the rebellion, by the claim that keys and a gun were missing. "All this is a lot of B.S.," wrote de Leon. "I was working with the brothers on the security squad and I would have definitely known if any firearms had been available." Besides, he reminded the reader, you can't bring guns into a jail.[1]

The lockdown aggravated conditions of violence and despair in which multiple prisoners were said by the Department of Correction to have taken their own lives—though this claim was controversial among black and brown revolutionaries. Most infamous among these cases would be that of Julio Roldan. Following an October Young Lords demonstration against deteriorating city services, in which uncollected trash had been dragged into the street and set on fire, Roldan was arrested. He was subsequently found dead in his cell. The case fanned the flames kindled by the August and October rebellions. The Young Lords organ *Palante* charged murder, noting that Roldan had been beaten in the court bullpen after calling the judge a "fascist pig," and that he had then been put in a single cell, despite the facility's dire overcrowding. Additionally, they cited prisoners' accounts of him shouting at guards shortly before his death. *Palante* also allowed McGrath and Mayor Lindsay to share its prestigious "Pig of the Week Award," typically only bestowed upon a single pig, for their broken promise of no reprisals to the Queens prisoners and their stonewalling the investigation of Roldan's death.[2]

Appearing before the Board of Correction, McGrath explained that when he promised "no reprisals," he spoke only for DOC. However, he continued, if the district attorney wanted to press charges, that was his prerogative; McGrath could speak for neither the DA nor the mayor. By his account, the seasoned lawyer continued, he had simply promised to meet with the rebellious prisoners in exchange for the release of hostages, which he had done, and had promised no retaliation from DOC, which had not occurred. Progressing from pettifoggery to outright falsehood, McGrath concluded that no physical retaliation had been taken against the rebellious prisoners, and therefore that he had kept all his promises. The broken promise to the Queens prisoners would be compounded by the subsequent indictment of thirty-two of the rebellious prisoners on several charges, including kidnapping. To their ranks was added a guard who allegedly encouraged the rebellion from inside. After drawn-out court proceedings, all but two of the defendants would have their charges dropped, or else were acquitted, and none of them would serve additional time.[3]

By this point, City Hall wasn't looking on McGrath much more favorably than were the Young Lords. Echoing the findings of the prison reformer Senator John R. Dunne, Lindsay aide Barry Gottehrer found that McGrath had little control over DOC or the requisite knowledge to exercise it—especially with regard to the rank-and-file guards who had run wild under his direct command. "Like most bureaucrats," Gottehrer later observed, "McGrath had made it a practice to not probe too deeply into the way his subordinates carried out their duties, and he kept himself above departmental conflict." The staff riot at Branch Queens had revealed how little control he had over his own department. "McGrath's career was ruined," Gottehrer recalls, "and he was eased out after a respectable number of months to make way for a new commissioner," Benjamin Malcolm. When this time came, in November 1971, McGrath was adamant he wasn't being pushed out, though he admitted he felt like "an inmate who's just been given a parole date."[4]

Conversely, the rebellion had a liberalizing effect on the courts. Many judges responded by significantly decreasing, via lower bail, the number of pretrial prisoners remanded to city custody. Lindsay's Criminal Justice Coordinating Council cited this as evidence of more "flexibility" available to judges than was often acknowledged. Less favorable was the impact on the Adolescent Reformatory on Rikers Island. In the wake of the rebellions, DOC shifted hundreds of sentenced adolescents to upstate facilities, to make way for adult detainees. This move to ease crowding in the city system effectively gutted what was left of the reformatory's Kross-era penal welfarist programming—which by this point was already not much.

Despite the facility's mandate to house "reformatory" prisoners, whose indeterminate sentences were purportedly tethered to so-called rehabilitation, out of a random sample of forty-five prisoners, only fifteen had seen a social worker, psychiatrist, or vocational employment counselor. As a testament to this lack of basic oversight, in 1972 BOC received a $7,000 grant to evaluate adolescent prisoners for "mental retardation." After consulting with DOC officials, the board predicted that 30 percent of the adolescent population would be deemed "retarded." They later discovered, however, that these prisoners simply couldn't read. This study also provides data, rare from this period, on the racial composition of the facility's prisoners: 80 percent black, 12 percent Hispanic, 8 percent white.[5]

The Old Way of Doing Things

Upon their arrival at Rikers, the Panthers from Branch Queens were summoned to the office of Warden James A. Thomas, the first black warden in the DOC system. "We are going to take over your institution," one told him, "and when we do, we are going to lop off your head." While this prophecy would never come to pass, the disruption that the August and October uprisings had engendered in DOC would reverberate for years to come.[6]

Three main factors constituted the legacy of the rebellions. The first was the city response to the conditions publicized by them, which spawned a limited yet considerable effort at reforming the city's jails, spearheaded by the revitalized Board of Correction. BOC and its allies constituted a renaissance of the largely discarded Kross-era reforms. The second was *Rhem v. McGrath*, the class action lawsuit filed in September of 1970 over conditions at the Tombs. As DOC struggled to stay on the right side of increasingly activist federal courts, this lawsuit produced others like it and set new precedent for hitherto-unseen judicial intervention in DOC affairs. The third was the continuing tradition of resistance behind bars, which would never again reach the spectacular heights achieved in October 1970, but nonetheless endured. These pressures converged on DOC in the mid 1970s, closing some facilities, hastening the opening of others, and paving the way for further jail expansion on Rikers Island, as the city's massive public sector infrastructure teetered on the brink of fiscal disaster.[7]

"The history of prison riots," writes progressive lawyer William vanden Heuvel in a signed introduction to BOC's 1971 annual report, *Crisis in the Prisons*,

is generally a pattern of immediate concessions to the prisoners to regain control of the facilities with a minimum of violence followed by excited public attention that concerns itself mostly with the noise of the riot explosion rather than the legitimacy of the grievances expressed, a few symbolic gestures of reform—and then a return to the old way of doing things with a few cosmetic touches added to mark the event of the disturbance.

The new BOC intended to buck this trend. Nobody had been appointed to the board since Lindsay took office, and it had gone without a chair for over two years, had multiple vacant positions, and was de facto disbanded by the time of the August rebellion. Testifying before the Dunne Commission, McGrath had remarked that BOC was "just about dead on the vine but nobody has killed it." Following the rebellions, however, Lindsay quickly moved to "reactivate" the board, appointing vanden Heuvel as chair, alongside six newcomers, including William H. Satterfield, the administrator of a Bronx poverty program, and Geraldo Rivera, who had become a media personality due to his work as a lawyer for the Young Lords.[8]

The New York State Committee on Crime and Correction celebrated the new BOC, while recognizing that Lindsay undertook the revitalization only "after initially blaming the entire situation on the judiciary." In 1971 BOC acquired, for the first time, an office and a small staff, funded by a grant from the Federal Law Enforcement Assistance Administration. BOC's $54,283 budget was, vanden Heuvel remarked, a "pittance in terms of the $92 million Department of Correction budget [the board] was obliged to oversee," yet an influx of volunteers reminiscent of the Kross era allowed the board to carry this modest budget quite far. For its part, *Palante* charged that the appointment of vanden Heuvel, a "millionaire, Democratic Party politician," as chair was the precursor to a cover-up, akin to "letting the killers investigate the killing." The board's subsequent report on Roldan's death, for which vanden Heuvel wrote a dramatic introductory letter and Rivera served as co-author, argued this charge to be at least partially unfair. While disputing the Lords' claim that Roldan had been murdered—BOC supported both DOC's and the chief medical examiner's ruling of the death as a suicide—the report held the court system and the prevailing conditions in the Tombs, especially in the lockdown following the uprising, culpable in Roldan's death.[9]

The board handed down an even more blistering assessment in the death of another prisoner, a young gay black man named Raymond Lavon. Vanden Heuvel had met with Lavon shortly before his death. Troubled by inconsistencies in the guards' stories about his final hours, he demanded an immediate report from the board. BOC subsequently recounted how Lavon took his own life after a hellish ten-month ordeal of pointless court delays, wanton guard brutality, disastrously incompetent medical care, and, as the final straw, a fabricated charge of assault on a guard, pressed by guards who had brutalized him in his locked cell—all as his mental and physical health dramatically unraveled and DOC did nothing to help him. The Young Lords interpreted the stridency of BOC's language condemning these conditions, which nonetheless exonerated DOC of Lavon's murder, as "whitewash."[10]

These death reports were only a small part of the revitalized board's mission. Vanden Heuvel released an ambitious program for the board's first hundred days, published in the *Village Voice*—a provocative move in itself—alongside a punchy editorial heralding the board as an activist player in the city's court and jail systems. The fifty-one points of vanden Heuvel's agenda included sweeping reform demands that mirrored, in large part, the demands of the rebellion, including more efficient and equitable court proceedings, bail reform, improved jail facilities and services, more freedom for prisoners to receive mail and visits, work provided for detainees, expanded oversight of guard violence, and of course—what reform program would be complete without it?—"sensitivity training" for uniformed DOC staff.[11]

The Board of Correction also initiated the Clergy Volunteer Program (CVP) in 1971, under which volunteers from local churches labored as de facto social workers. The BOC architects of this program postulated that previous reform efforts had run aground on account of the impossible scale of the jail system. By contrast, they focused on the granular level, the cellblock, each of which would by "adopted" by a local church. In 1972 the CVP acquired its own funding and staff, though the city later assumed a share of its operating costs. The board's Task Force on the Church and Prisons pushed for DOC's waged chaplains to be further professionalized, and to further involve community groups in the jail system. The board also reconstituted ties with the Friendly Visitors, the Ethical Culture Society, the Legal Aid Society, the Women's Prison Association, the Fortune Society, the Vera Institute of Justice, and other legal advocacy and charitable organizations that would increasingly hold aloft the banner of penal welfarism—albeit from outside the DOC seat of power, and dependent on DOC's increasingly conservative leadership for access to the jails.[12]

Similarly, DOC experimented with adding civilian staff to the jails under a program called Correctional Aides that putatively provided employment to working-class black and brown youths as part of Lindsay's youth employment initiative. DOC was, however, driven less by the spirit of social justice than by an influx of federal aid money that allowed it to hire a bottom tier of jail employees to undertake low-level custodial and administrative tasks, in place of the overworked guards. Initially, the president of the Correction Officers' Benevolent Association, Leo Zeferetti, opposed the Correctional Aides, threatening legal action against DOC—though the latter never gained traction. While just about any union president can be expected to oppose the hiring of purportedly unskilled workers to do jobs ordinarily done by union members, Zeferetti couldn't quite put his finger on why he was opposing the program. Therefore, he opted to play the field. The BOC meeting minutes reflect a variety of arguments, offered in rapid succession:

> Mr. Zeferetti stated that one of the major problems with these aides is that there is a conflict with Department of Correction trainees. He stated that aides are permitted in the cellblocks, while trainees are not. He further stated that the Correctional Aide program pays for the aides to go to college while the trainee program does not, and that aides earn more money than do trainees. He added that trainees are checked very carefully as to their background, while aides are not checked as thoroughly.

Mr. Zeferetti stated that one major problem with the program is that institutional personnel have not been briefed or given any sort of guidelines as to what is the responsibility of these aides, or who is to supervise them.

Mr. Zeferetti declared that it is important to determine whether the aides plan to become correction officers upon completion of their program. He further declared that the system of appointment must continue to be based on a competitive examination.

He stated that he had tried to discuss with appropriate Departmental officials, including the Commissioner, ways in which the aide program and the trainee program could be integrated, but was told that since the aide program was federally funded, the Department had no jurisdiction.

Mr. Zeferetti stated that the aides' function so far has only been to assist in making telephone calls.

Ironically, once the aides were situated and began relieving the guards of the more mundane administrative tasks of their day-to-day work, they became an indispensable part of the institution, supported by the guards themselves. When an austerity budget threatened the Correctional Aides' funding several years later, COBA would defend the program. However, this was not due to any shift in the balance of power, or even respect, between civilians and uniformed staff. The volunteers simply did jobs that would otherwise fall to guards, doing their best to stay out of the guards' way.[13]

A Toothless Tiger

Nevertheless, in general terms, DOC under McGrath was far less tolerant of civilians in the jails than it had been under Kross, adding hostility to the upper ranks of the jail administration on top of what had long existed in the lower ones. Speaking with BOC, McGrath said he considered the presence of civilian volunteers in cellblocks, a hallmark Kross policy, "a severe blow to the morale of correction officers." Director of Operations Joseph

D'Elia, "speaking as a former correction officer," told the board: "It is the feeling of correction officers that all 'bad' things are attributed to them." He argued, somewhat perplexingly, "The officers do not always want to be 'repressors,' and having outsiders on the floor makes the officers' job much more difficult, since if a volunteer is more available than a correction officer, the inmate will turn to the volunteer for assistance." George Camp, the assistant commissioner for rehabilitation, agreed with McGrath and D'Elia that the guards would be unhappy with volunteers in cellblocks.

Appearing before the board in 1973, CVP director Greg Harris described a disrespectful guard attitude toward clergy and other volunteers, especially at the Rikers Island control house, which was also extended to BOC staff. This problem would recur; the optimists atop the board's hierarchy, who attributed it to a lack of understanding of the board's role in the jails among uniformed DOC staff, perennially called for reminders to be issued to the guards clarifying the latter. However, the staffers with the most direct experience in the jails reported consistent trouble, ranging from ordinary rudeness to denial of access to DOC facilities on flimsy pretexts.[14]

With McGrath in their corner, and their own power in the city's political landscape rising in the footsteps of the Patrolmen's Benevolent Association, COBA was emboldened to take on the bureaucrats at BOC. Appearing before BOC in February 1971 flanked by two COBA delegates, Zeferetti claimed that since the board's revitalization, guards were afraid to do their jobs, lest a prisoner make an unfounded claim of mistreatment to a board member, who would transmit it to the press without getting the other side of the story. COBA delegate George Smith complained that the board never praised guards but only focused on misconduct. Zeferetti announced COBA would oppose the adoption of subpoena power by the board, advocating instead backroom meetings between DOC, City Hall, COBA, and BOC, to which the board should consent instead of going to the press. Although the board was relatively lacking in its own actionable authority—one staffer complained DOC treated the board as a "toothless tiger"—COBA was certainly correct to distrust the board's ability to call attention to shortcomings in the court and jail system.[15]

Bad press, it turns out, was the board's best weapon. While it might be tempting to echo the Young Lords' claim that the board was simply "whitewashing" the atrocities of the city's jails in the name of the old way of doing things, a more nuanced interpretation of these reports permits us to understand the board's revealing special reports as the outcome of militant struggles within the jails, mediated through a liberal democratic institution. The revitalized board's reports on Roldan's and Lavon's purported suicides were only the most famous of several studies of prisoner deaths that by no means let DOC off the hook. In collaboration with City Hall, DOC, and the Health Services Administration, the board also co-founded the Prison Mortality Review Board to study deaths in custody. It drafted a scathing indictment of the city's court pens, cited in detail above. BOC also presented the plights of mentally ill, indigent, and non-English-speaking detainees, whose experiences in the city's courts and jails were particularly hellish and dehumanizing. The Adolescent Reformatory, a Kross-era innovation, similarly fell under BOC scrutiny. These reports put DOC on the defensive almost constantly, challenging the ability of DOC and COBA to define for the public what was occurring in the city's jails.[16]

BOC's high-profile investigations, coupled with an aggressive public advocacy campaign, resulted in a series of additional early reform victories. The punitive "bread and water" diet and the stripped "bing" cell for solitary confinement at the Tombs were abolished following the Lavon report. Whereas visits had once been limited to family members or else preapproved friends, prisoners were now granted freedom to decide who could visit them. Guards lost the right, formally at least, to screen prisoners' mail. Under board pressure, Lindsay consolidated the disorganized mental health care in the jails under the jurisdiction of the Health Services Administration. Paid work, albeit at DOC's extremely low wages, was offered to pretrial detainees for the first time, including work as "suicide prevention aides," another board innovation. Prisoners were granted the right to know the rules of the institution they were locked up in, a board recommendation backed by a federal judge that resulted in the distribution of a bilingual prisoner handbook. Black entertainers like Harry Belafonte, James Brown, and Odetta were brought to perform for prisoners in the city jails. The board pressured DOC to adopt so-called inmate liaison committees. These were intended as forums for elected prisoners and DOC staff to dialogue about grievances—with the aim of "increased understanding"—in the presence of BOC staff, who would serve as administrators of these meetings.[17]

One enduring figure of this period's reforms is the introduction of methadone into the DOC system. Prior to 1970, the city's addiction policy had effectively been a supervised "cold turkey" withdrawal under grim conditions. The Tombs, for instance, had a small, poorly ventilated block where prisoners experiencing withdrawal, a common symptom of which is vomiting, were crowded two or more into thirty cells set aside for that purpose—this at a facility where some 471 prisoners experienced withdrawal in February of 1970. These wretched conditions made the absolute worst of an already-bad situation. In 1969 the city council, overruling a veto by Lindsay, mandated that DOC establish a methadone program across the jails system. Lindsay and McGrath, however, dragged their feet on initiating the controversial program and had to be continually pressed by counselors. Between the August and October rebellions, Lindsay finally capitulated to the power of rebellious prisoners, announcing a plan to make the program citywide. The new BOC subsequently took up the issue of citywide methadone with determination. Beginning in March of 1971, all prisoners taken into DOC custody had the option of "methadone detoxification," as it was then called.[18]

Another legacy of this period was the abandonment of the direct model of health care in the city's jail system. Prior to the August rebellion, though medical care in all DOC facilities was nominally administered by the Department of Health, it was in fact directly controlled by DOC, whose uniformed staff had considerable power over its day-to-day operations. Lindsay hired an outside consulting firm to evaluate medical care at the Tombs, and its results concurred with the reformers—and the prisoners, who had long denounced care in DOC custody. The city's own Health and Hospitals Corporation undertook an equally damning study of DOC health care, finding it decentralized, "overwhelmed by the influence of the Department of Correction's obsession with custody and discipline," and home to staff deserving of their reputation of "senility and incompetence." In response, Lindsay created the Prison Health Services division of the Department of Health with the mandate to standardize and improve healthcare in DOC custody.[19]

Pushed by vanden Heuvel's board, these reforms were part of what was by all appearances an earnest exercise in addressing the grievances underscored by the 1970 rebellion. As ever, the modest gains made by efforts to work within the system, free from violent repression and permitted minor victories by the ruling powers, came with strict parameters, outside of which the board did not stray. This limit to BOC's capacity was demonstrated in evocative terms by none other than Geraldo Rivera. Soon after joining BOC, Rivera resigned out of impatience with the board's limited oversight capacity and inability to effect dramatic change. In a remarkable letter to the *Times*, he argued with characteristic flair that the board was a "creation of conscience" and as such would "have a lifespan that in terms of effectiveness is very short. For a hesitant moment," he continued, "the lid on the garbage can is lifted. We look inside, see and smell the muck we've probably known was in there all along, experience the appropriate shock, revulsion, and shame, and then move on to the next garbage can ... changing nothing." What was to be done? "After spending hour after hour inside the Tombs and speaking with hundreds of inmates," Rivera concluded, "I've come to the conclusion there is only one meaningful reform: Let them out."[20]

Administration by Administrators

A far cry from his predecessor, Anna M. Kross, DOC commissioner McGrath had openly plotted to abolish the Board of Correction, complaining it "interfered" with his department and calling it "a group of lay people who get involved in matters that are none of their business." His departure would open the door for a commissioner even more hostile to the civilian side of jail administration. By 1972, the prisoners were 90 percent black and brown, as was a majority of Department of Correction staff. To replace McGrath, Lindsay tapped Benjamin J. Malcolm to become DOC's first black commissioner. Malcolm was born in Philadelphia, before moving to Georgia, where he attended college. After a stint in the Army, Malcolm became a New York City parole officer—a position he called the "bottom rung of the criminal justice system," from which he worked his way to the position of deputy chief parole officer. After two decades in Parole, Malcolm served as DOC's deputy commissioner under McGrath, earning a master's in public administration at New York University. Malcolm understood himself as an advocate of "community centered" jail policy, which he took to mean community-sponsored post-release services—not civilian involvement in jails.[21]

"Institutions," Malcolm remarked, "have to be administered by the administrators." And it was not the civilian administrators Malcolm had in mind. For his part, the outgoing McGrath hurled a thinly veiled racial barb at the appointment of a black commissioner, saying, "It helps to have the top man more closely identified with the inmates." By his own account, however, Malcolm's primary identification was with the badge. This was due not only to his professional allegiances, but what he understood as the gravity of the historical moment in which he took over DOC. Malcolm painted a sharp contrast between his tenure and the days of Anna M. Kross. Kross, he said, "was a humane individual, but she was dealing with a docile population of prisoners. Most of them were sentenced inmates, mostly for misdemeanors. We heard nothing of political prisoners then, nothing of riots, militancy." What had changed?

In 1969, Malcolm continued, "the number of detainees began to exceed the number of sentenced prisoners," and subsequently "the unrest in the cities moved to the campuses, and then to the prisons. The year 1970 was critical in New York because you had the emergence of the political prisoners, the emergence of groups who decide they're victims of society. So they're a problem and maybe they'll be even more of one in the future." In a single stroke, Malcolm heralded the abandonment of penal welfarism as a paradigm in the management of DOC, marching in lockstep with the reaction against black and brown revolt that had galvanized the law-and-order movement. This would not have shocked many people; by this point, however, Malcolm's concession was largely platitude. What criminologist David Garland calls the "punitive turn," the move away from penal welfarism and toward naked punishment as the guiding force of carceral policy, was well underway in New York City. In fact, given the daily resistance Kross's policies had engendered among DOC's guards, it would be a mistake to think that penal welfarism ever held unchallenged sway in the first place. Nevertheless, Kross and her cohort had held the line, checking the powers of the guards in a way that future DOC administrators would not. This did not, however, mean conflict between administration and the rank and file over who would rule the facility would subside. But as the jail rebellion of 1970 illustrated, these two sides could almost always find a common enemy in the figure of the prisoner, especially black and brown revolutionaries.[22]

In June of 1972, the board came under heavy fire from DOC guard unions for its willingness to talk to the media instead of meeting behind closed doors and for its continuing insistence on granting jail access to civilian volunteers. The onslaught was also due, in no small part, to a particular incident in which a board member traveled to the C-76 facility on Rikers after a work stoppage and supposedly made comments suggesting that based on the crowding there, violence was to be expected. The board held an emergency meeting with DOC staff representatives, including Francis Buono of the Warden's Association, Gerald Singleman of the Assistant Deputy Wardens' Association, Ray Mandanici of the Captain's Association, and COBA president Zeferetti. The record reflects Zeferetti declaring that "his people saw the Board as a vehicle of sensationalism and as an opportunity for the Chairman to appear in the press. [Zeferetti] declared that the Board was inmate-oriented." Mandanici "declared that his group had 'had it up to here' with its relationship with the Board."

For his part, Singleman offered an olive branch to BOC, suggesting that they could demonstrate "good faith" by issuing a public statement supporting suspended sentences for the Branch Queens guards charged with brutality following the October uprising, which vanden Heuvel granted as a possibility. When the city imposed fines on fourteen of the guards, vanden Heuvel wrote to City Hall requesting the fines be suspended. Yet BOC's obsequiousness did little to improve relations between BOC and DOC. Malcolm subsequently reported widespread sentiments among guards that the board made their jobs more dangerous, while vanden Heuvel complained that COBA actively prevented the board from interfacing with its rank and filers.[23]

Similarly, when Warden Albert Ossakow and ten guards at the Kew Gardens facility were suspended for brutality arising from the handling of the 1970 uprising at their facility, vanden Heuvel continued to defend the guards, taking the position that guards who had not been convicted of a crime should not be suspended without pay. When Ossakow was allowed to plead to diminished charges and retire with his pension intact, vanden Heuvel argued that this leniency should extend to the low-ranking guards as well, spurring a fascinating exchange with Malcolm. "The Chairman declared that he felt that line officers must be treated alike," the minutes reflect. "He stated that the Department cannot treat those who are in subordinate positions more severely than those in command. Malcolm declared that, in that case, the My Lai senior officers should have been punished," referring to the 1968 massacre conducted by American servicemen in Vietnam. "The Chairman responded that he agreed."[24]

Setting aside the hyperbolic rhetoric one can expect from COBA brass, a contemporaneous profile by BOC staffer Sylvia Kronstadt revealed a demoralized and cynical workforce driven to DOC employ as a "last resort" for those with "no place else to go." They understood themselves as serving twenty-year "sentences" while awaiting retirement. The guards Kronstadt profiled hated working for DOC and had no identification with any mission broader than simply securing means of subsistence and material comforts for themselves and their families. They also described a profound stigma attached to their job. "When I ran to tell my mom I was going to be a correction officer," one guard told Kronstadt, "she cried 'Oh my son!' ... like I had just admitted to being a pervert or something."[25]

Rhem v. McGrath

In the months leading up to the 1970 rebellion, the Legal Aid Society of the City of New York planned to file a class action lawsuit around conditions for pretrial detainees in the Tombs. Their inspiration was at once local, stemming from Manhattan congressman Edward Koch's investigation of the Tombs, which had bolstered their own knowledge of the facility's grave condition. It was also national, as a budding prisoners' rights movement had grown alongside a federal judiciary emboldened to take on scandalous conditions in prisons and jails across the nation. This final point is worth emphasis. Prior to the 1960s, the federal judiciary was uniformly reluctant to set any precedent impinging on the ability of prison administrators to run their facilities as they saw fit, deferring to the latter's superior expertise, imperative to enforce order, and their ultimate responsibility to states, not the federal government. Spurred by the Warren Court, the civil rights movement provided impetus for the application of federal authority to constitutional matters once deemed local, and many judges followed suit. Of particular relevance to New

York City, the 1971 case *Hamilton v. Love* found that unconstitutional carceral conditions could not be justified by pleas to state poverty; if the state could not afford to hold prisoners in conditions meeting the minimum constitutional standards, the court reasoned, it could not hold them at all.[26]

The August stage of the rebellion at the Tombs dramatically underscored much of Legal Aid's case against DOC, expediting the filing of *Rhem v. McGrath*. The lawsuit argued that conditions at the Tombs, coupled with lengthy stays spent in these conditions awaiting trial, amounted to violations of the First, Fifth, Sixth, Eighth, and Fourteenth Amendments— constitutional guarantees of free speech, due process, speedy trials, and protection from excessive bail and cruel and unusual punishment. Federal judge Edward McLean approved the case as a class action suit, and, against the protests of the city on account of potential "disruption of prison discipline," mandated that all Tombs prisoners be served notice of the suit. Following the October stage of the rebellion, the plaintiffs sought a preliminary injunction, citing the conditions that Ricardo de Leon described as "Gestapo-style"—including the twenty-four-hour lock-ins, denial of showers, suspension of medical care and practically all programming, and suspension or curtailment of visits—as cause for the court to take immediate action.

Initially, Judge Walter R. Mansfield dealt the plaintiffs a frustrating blow. The conditions, he ruled, did not constitute cruel and unusual punishment sufficient to warrant injunctive relief. Much of these conditions, Mansfield reasoned, were due to the riotous acts of the prisoners, not negligence by the city. Mansfield further cited DOC's good faith efforts to ameliorate these conditions, in part through the construction of three new facilities set to open soon on Rikers Island, and a contract to house thousands of prisoners with the state. Mansfield even noted "new paint ... in pastel colors" set to spruce up the Tombs, in tandem with new windows. Mansfield did, however, issue injunctions ordering DOC to provide private consultation between the plaintiffs and their attorneys, and to post clearly defined rules governing prisoner behavior and a regular schedule structuring institutional

life, to which prisoners could appeal. Despite these minor victories for the plaintiffs, the ruling amounted to a demoralizing
defeat, emboldening the city to continue making a few token
concessions while brazenly flouting the law. The city went so
far as to demand the case be dismissed, though this motion was
denied in December.[27]

The case hung in limbo until the summer of 1972, when
New York State's Southern District instituted a novel assignment system, distributing cases at random to judges who would
assume sole responsibility for carrying them through to completion. To the great fortune of the plaintiffs, *Rhem* fell to the
liberal judge Morris Lasker. Lasker set a November trial date
and began to aggressively pursue a resolution. DOC, by this
point under the control of Malcolm, whose name now adorned
the suit in place of McGrath's, did not wish to defend the city's
deplorable jail conditions in court. Nor did it want the publicity
the case would entail, which would only exacerbate its ongoing
public relations disaster. When negotiations involving Malcolm,
Deputy Mayor Michael Dontzin, prisoner representatives, and
lawyers from both sides failed to produce a settlement in time,
the city's counsel began the hearing by declaring: "The City
finds itself having agreed, at least in principle, to almost every
demand made by the inmates." Testimony proceeded for four
days, during which time the city undertook what was effectively
a media strategy, attempting to impede the inclusion of damaging testimony on the record and generally pushing to wind the
trial down, while emphasizing that the case was unnecessary
due to its willingness to negotiate with the plaintiffs.[28]

In a scathing decision, Judge Lasker ruled that conditions at
the Tombs, which he had twice visited, would "shock the conscience of any citizen who knew of them" and demanded the
city draft a plan for their amelioration. There was, however, no
ambiguity in this ruling about the connection between *Rhem*
and the rebellion. "This suit," Lasker concluded, "constitutes
the effort to secure by law the objectives of the 1970 violence."
But, unlike the militants who had catalyzed this dramatic challenge to DOC, Lasker remained loyal to the social order he

represented. For instance, the case detailed a variety of abuse and degradations meted out on prisoners by guards, ranging from disrespect to the "beating of an inmate chained naked to bars, and the beating of an inmate who was also burned by officers putting out cigars and cigarettes on his body." Though "totally unrefuted by defendants either through cross-examination or by offering evidence in contradiction," Lasker excused the guards' actions as just another manifestation of stress caused by the facility's noise and heat. Nonetheless, the case set an important precedent for prisoners' rights. When Lasker's ruling was discussed by the board, its new chairman, the business lawyer Peter Tufo, astutely "noted that it is the first time the imprimatur of a court had been applied to such broad aspects of prison reform."[29]

From the onset, however, there was ample indication the city was not taking the lawsuit seriously. The case had been set aside pending compliance with an agreement called a consent decree, in which two parties agree to attempt reconciliation provided the defendant meets certain clearly specified conditions. For a time, city officials stymied the plaintiffs by claiming they could not find the consent decree and therefore could not take any action. The city would continue to stall, making it increasingly clear over time that it had no intention of following through on even the most basic step toward compliance: simply writing a comprehensive plan of action. "The history of this case" since January, Lasker wrote in a July 1974 memorandum, "has been one of frustration largely caused by the City defendants' delay and the absence or incompleteness of reports or plans of performance which they were ordered to submit." The city had spent the calendar year first buying time, then submitting an incomplete plan of action, then finally declaring it would not submit a complete plan at all. Running out of patience, Lasker ordered the Tombs closed within thirty days, should the city not submit a plan meeting the specificities of his January ruling.[30]

The city appealed the ruling, to no avail. Adding to the growing cache of poesy lyricizing the wretchedness of life in the city jails, Judge Wilfred Feinberg called Lasker's ruling "a melancholy picture of a fortress in bedlam." The following week, the city attempted to sidestep the case altogether by announcing the closure of the Tombs and the transportation of its prisoners to the House of Detention for Men on Rikers Island. "I didn't realize how much the City was stonewalling," Lasker later told a colleague. "I thought they would comply." Perhaps DOC imagined that upon shuttering the Tombs it was done with *Rhem* and Lasker alike.

When the Tombs closed in December 1974, however, the facility's problems did not disappear. They were simply spread around. A *Times* headline shortly captured the new reality: "Rikers Island Problems," it read, "Now Resemble Tombs's." Moreover, to the chagrin of DOC, these prisoners brought *Rhem* to Rikers with them. The city hadn't seen the last of Lasker yet. Indeed, the federal judiciary would constitute a formidable new power on the increasingly crowded field of contending interests that characterized daily life in DOC facilities. Meanwhile, irrespective of the gains won in federal court, extralegal challenges to DOC continued to flourish.[31]

15

Out of Control

Pandemonium

In the years following the 1970 rebellion, a steady supply of
revolutionary literature streamed into the jail system by mail,
including the English-language Maoist weekly *Peking Review*,
distributed by the Chinese government. Appearing at a meeting
of the Board of Correction, DOC officials noted the prolifera-
tion of study groups, specifically under the leadership of Tombs
prisoner Alfred "Hap" Gary, complaining of "those in the institution who would welcome revolution rather than change."[1]
BOC chairman vanden Heuvel, a dedicated Cold War liberal,
dismissed the Department of Correction's concerns, claiming
that prisoners read such material out of boredom. He therefore proposed DOC arrange for an outside scholar to visit the
jails and talk about another revolutionary who might hold
their interest: Thomas Jefferson. Commissioner Malcolm was
not convinced. In response to Malcolm's argument that revolutionary literature in the jails "causes problems for him and
his staff in administering the prisons," board member Wilbert
Kirby reported that he had read accounts of the 1970 uprising
from a revolutionary perspective—most likely the writing of
Panther Ricardo de Leon in the *Village Voice*—and that while
he didn't agree with the political rhetoric, he could not dispute
the facts.[2]

The board, along with practically every policy document from
this period, hastened to speak of the 1970 rebellion in the past
tense. While nothing quite so spectacular or large-scale would

recur, the legacy of struggle continued, often in the ideological mantle of Black and Brown Power, through a series of rebellions and escapes. Rebels and escapees defied the order imposed on them inside the jail in the most direct sense possible, and in the process, they called into question not just the legitimacy of human caging as a workable social practice, but the social order that relied upon it to function.

On February 1, 1972, prisoners in cellblock seven of the Adolescent Remand Shelter—the facility where Panther Twenty-One defendant Jamal Joseph had built a cadre two years earlier, and that had briefly revolted in October of 1970—smashed up furniture, dismantled toilets, and hurled the debris at guards, at least one of whom they also attacked. Armed with a variety of improvised weapons, the prisoners shouted what DOC officials reported as "revolutionary slogans." Barraged with tear gas, they retreated into their cellblock behind barricades made of broken furniture. The setting was significant. Debriefing on the 1970 rebellions, Malcolm's predecessor, George F. McGrath, had observed that the short-lived uprising at the Adolescent Remand Shelter was handled most deftly—that is, repressed quickly, before the prisoners could organize and develop a strategic advantage. McGrath reasoned that as the clock ticked, DOC forfeited tactical advantage. This had been the city's stated policy since the Attica rebellion the previous September, though the lessons of its own rebellions surely contributed. More importantly, the policy of decisive repressive action reflected the position of the average rank-and-file guard, though it was likely fueled more by testosterone than tactical thinking. When DOC came around to this approach, the guards were all too happy to oblige.

Surrounded in February 1972 by colleagues eager to suit up and repress the rebellion by brute force, career guard Roy Caldwood spurned the gung ho attitude of many of his peers and worked against the clock to broker a deal for the prisoners' surrender. The rebellion's ostensible leader told Caldwood they would desist if assured they wouldn't be beaten, which Caldwood believed to spell the end of the rebellion. "I can't promise them that," the deputy warden had initially told Caldwood, to his shock. Warden James A. Thomas, however, reversed this order, and the standoff between 120 prisoners and forty riot squad guards was defused. Though it was already de facto disallowed, the diplomatic approach Caldwood successfully advocated was subsequently ruled out altogether. After the events of February 1, DOC management officially took clemency off the table as a bargaining chip in prisoner disturbances.[3]

On February 27, the same cellblock, with a capacity of 240, held about 315 prisoners, mostly black and Puerto Rican. Seventy-seven of them had already been convicted and were awaiting sentencing. By Caldwood's telling, the impending transfer of two prisoner leaders set the wheels turning for another rebellion. This time, however, the prisoners were better organized and more defiant. They took five guards hostages, threw up elaborate barricades, and responded to calls for their surrender by announcing their intention to kill their captives. The prisoners demanded to speak with members of the Young Lords, Black Liberation Army, and the Black Muslims. They also demanded to meet with the media, who were not even allowed on the island. This time a captive himself, Caldwood recalls the scene:

> Pandemonium. On fire with energy, the inmates tore at their belongings, carting out bed frames, mattresses, toilet seats and tops, and chairs to build barricades at the cellblock gates. At the gate, they piled it all high, constructing a mountain of prison bric-a-brac and debris. A scaffold used for cleaning the cellblock became the centerpiece of the barricade. The scaffold blocked the gate and gave the prisoners a place to stand, to be up high, ready to swing down on any attacker below.

There was to be no peaceful resolution. DOC devoted less than two hours to negotiations, which simply amounted to a call from Malcolm commanding the prisoners to surrender. Mayor Lindsay, on the campaign trail waging a disastrous presidential run, personally called in a siege to free the hostages just an hour after the rebellion began.[4]

At Malcolm's call, a force of ten guards entered through a side door and fought for upward of ten minutes to open the main gate, through which roughly 140 guards clad in riot gear entered the cellblock in a cloud of tear gas. Prisoners met their clubs with a variety of improvised weapons, including sharpened bedsprings, chair legs, and buckets of hot water. Caldwood recalls the guards "forcing their way into the block, and the prisoners were trying to come out—grunting, screaming, clubs swimming. Pipes, wood, and steel smacked bodies. Inmates threw chunks of metal and toilet tanks and seats—whatever they could rip free." After fifteen minutes of hand-to-hand combat that left a reported seventy-five prisoners and twenty guards injured, the rebellion was quashed. The guards subsequently "had a holiday," one prisoner reported. "Most of the people were beaten up after the prisoners gave up." A staffer from the nonprofit prisoner reentry organization Fortune Society corroborated the same, reporting that after the rebellion was repressed inmates were forced to run between a double line of guards swinging their clubs, commonly called a gauntlet. This was likely not the first appearance of a gauntlet in DOC facilities, and it would not be the last.

Malcolm attributed the rebellion to "a handful of hardcore militants," remarking, "I don't think the inmates have any bona fide grievances. They are making excuses." While not explicitly endorsing the beatings, Correction Officers' Benevolent Association president Zeferetti remarked, "The only thing necessary, is absolute discipline in these overcrowded institutions." The message to his rank and file was clear. Meanwhile, the rebels explicitly linked their activity to revolutionary struggle. Four prisoners—Pedro Yanes, Ernest Hall, Frank Smith, and Stanley Davis, all either twenty or twenty-one—were charged and convicted for their roles in the uprising and given five-year sentences. At their final court appearance, they attempted to flip over their chairs, shouting to their assembled supporters, "All power to the people!"[5]

The Black Liberation Army

One of the groups the rebelling prisoners had requested to meet with would soon become synonymous with black struggle on both sides of the bars: the Black Liberation Army. The BLA emerged at a time when the remnants of the New York Panthers were forced underground by a combination of state repression, FBI subversion, and violent internecine conflict within the crumbling Party. When Panthers Huey P. Newton and Eldridge Cleaver split over the question of whether to engage in immediate armed struggle, New York was the only chapter to side with Cleaver, who supported it. The New York Twenty-One had already been expelled from the Party for penning an open letter that expressed support for the militant Weather Underground (white revolutionaries who carried out a number of bombings, including in support of the Twenty-One), advocated armed struggle, and critiqued the Panthers for not following suit. The remnants of the New York Panthers subsequently drew militants from all over the United States who did not want to wait to undertake revolutionary action. This regrouping spawned the BLA, which included New York Twenty-One defendants like Kuwasi Balagoon, who had participated in the jail rebellion. Cleaver ordained that the BLA have no leadership, operating instead as autonomous cells with no central command structure. After an unplanned shootout between police and four Panthers, including Anthony "Kimu" White, this underground assemblage announced itself as the Black Liberation Army.

Whether through harassment, prosecution, brutality, or outright murder, police across the country had declared war on the Panthers. By 1973, at least fourteen Panther revolutionaries had been killed by police, of whom George Jackson and Fred Hampton were only the most prominent. Moreover, the slain Panthers represented only a tiny fraction of the nearly 1,000 black people shot by US police between 1971 and 1973 alone. These targeted killings were only one part of the state strategy to dismantle the Party, which included the FBI's Counter

Intelligence Program (COINTELPRO) and interminable court cases like the Panther Twenty-One trial. In response, the BLA declared war on the cops.

BLA's inaugural action took place on May 19, Malcolm X's birthday, and resulted in the nonlethal shooting of two cops, Thomas Curry and Nicholas Binetti, who were guarding the house of New York Twenty-One prosecutor Frank Hogan. Two days later, two NYPD cops, Waverly Jones and Anthony Piagentini, were shot dead in an ambush at the Polo Grounds public housing development in Manhattan. The Black Liberation Army took responsibility for both shootings. The group immediately earned the attention of law enforcement all the way up to FBI director J. Edgar Hoover—amid debate, which would long recur, over whether it even existed. BLA thereafter would prove a central ideological figure for NYPD's continuing war on subversion, and the growing militancy of the city's cops.[6]

Calling Their Own Plays

Amid the dramatic rise of the group that had drawn influence from his shootout with NYPD cops, Kimu White sat behind bars in city custody, held on $250,000 bail for attempted murder. In October of 1972, when White was held at the Tombs, a comrade inside named Ronald Johnson received a new pair of size-twelve sneakers from two female visitors. Sewn into the soles were two hacksaw blades. Eleven days later, Johnson, White, and five other prisoners undertook the first escape the Tombs had seen in over thirty years. In preparation, the men had sawed their way out of their housing area and covered the displaced bars with a table. Just after the 6:15 a.m. head count, the group sprang into action. They slipped through the small opening, creeping thirty feet across a gangplank overlaying a disused area still wanting of repair since the rebellion, scaling a sixteen-foot wall to a small window, and, once they had reached it, sawing off its bars. The men then unfurled a rope made of bedsheets, down which they climbed forty feet to the street below.

The entire operation took ten minutes at the most. At 6:25, an employee of the Criminal Court Building spotted one of the prisoners descending the rope and sounded the alarm. Citing no evidence, Malcolm and Zeferetti took turns blaming the escape on the "liberal" policies of BOC-sponsored volunteer initiatives (Malcolm) that, in bringing civilians onto the jail floor, had "allowed everyone and their brother to come and go as they want" (Zeferetti). Only later was the source of the hacksaws revealed as a routine visit.[7]

Upon his premature release, White connected with Assata Shakur, Twymon Meyers, Zayd Shakur, Melvin Kearney, and other BLA cadre whose activity revolved around bank robberies. In early 1973, White perished in a hail of police gunfire alongside his comrade Woody Green. Before the year was out, Meyers and Zayd Shakur would also be dead, felled by police bullets in dramatic shootouts, and both Kearney and Assata Shakur would be in custody. Meyers's demise was particularly grisly. NYPD and FBI agents surrounded him on the street, riddling his body with eighty bullets. As he lay dead, a cop stood over him, firing a single shot into his head, as if to kill him a second time. NYPD subsequently held a rally celebrating his death outside the Forty-Fourth Precinct in the Bronx, while Police Commissioner Donald F. Cawley declared NYPD had "broken the back of the BLA."[8]

That same year, BLA cadre Sha Sha Brown was extradited to New York City from St. Louis, where he had been arrested after a shootout with police. In St. Louis, Brown had been sentenced to twenty-five to life for the shootout, and was alleged to have planned a foiled jailbreak. Wanted in New York for the executions of NYPD cops Rocco Laurie and Gregory Foster, Brown was held at the Brooklyn House of Detention. There, he once again hatched a plan for his premature departure. In July, a sophisticated escape plan well into its final stages was discovered by BHD guards conducting a surprise shakedown. Reminiscent of White's escape from the Tombs, Brown, his cellmate, and two prisoners in an adjacent cell had used carbonite hacksaw blades to saw their way out of their own cells and into the guard catwalk that ringed the floor, thus placing only one more set of bars—and a fifty-five foot climb down a rope they had fashioned from bedsheets—between themselves and freedom.[9]

Two months later, Brown was transported to Kings County Hospital for an X-ray after he complained insistently of stomach pains. In order for Brown to change into his hospital gown, he was uncuffed and shown into a three-square-foot changing booth with no room for either of the two guards escorting him. Brown changed into the gown and received the X-ray. It's likely he was thinking all the while of the curious design of the changing booth: eight feet high, leaving a four-foot gap between the back wall and the ceiling, and fronted with a curtain that extended all the way to the floor. As the guards waited for Brown to change back into his clothing, he hopped onto the booth's bench, scaled the wall and hit the ground running toward an exit eighteen feet away. Hearing the bench clatter beneath Brown's feet, the guards took off after him. They were, as Malcolm later testified, no match for Brown. Based on an informant's tip to NYPD, Brown was recaptured a week later in a BLA safe house in Bushwick, Brooklyn, along with multiple other fugitives.[10]

Though speed and ingenuity had abetted his daring escape, Brown had also been assisted by simple negligence typical of a department stretched to the breaking point. After discussing the escape threat posed by BLA detainees at multiple meetings with NYPD, reviewing the escape record of Brown, and learning a map of Kings County Hospital was captured in a raid of another alleged BLA safe house, DOC had enacted a protocol for monitoring the transfer of BLA prisoners like Brown. It wasn't followed. A defensive Malcolm insisted the accounts of NYPD warnings about Brown had come from "low-level policemen" and there was no forewarning of an escape. Less explicable were the words "escape risk" and "murderer" stamped in red on Brown's prisoner identification card, which had made the trip to Kings County with him. Moreover, DOC denied the map had anything to do with the escape. Ultimately, however, Malcolm conceded: "Any time a Black Liberation Army group wants to release a fellow Black Liberation Army inmate from a hospital they can do it. The Department is planning to establish procedures to make this impossible but the procedures have not yet been created."[11]

Malcolm took the rare step of suspending the guards involved, though they had by all accounts done little wrong. Brown's case came amid a rash of embarrassing escapes, prompting Malcolm to testify "he was personally 'fed up' with reports showing that procedures had broken down without pointing at individuals who are at fault"—or, perhaps more precisely, with those that pointed to him. In all likelihood, the overtaxed DOC simply did not have the capacity to live up to the city's tough talk about BLA and other militant prisoners. One investigator dubbed DOC's uniform staff "Keystone guards," in reference to the comically inept Keystone Cops of the silent film era. While jail administrators plead poverty and under-capacity in the best of times, during this period the New York City system was truly overwhelmed, not just by the throngs of people swept off the streets by NYPD and consigned to jail by the courts, but by the spirit of belligerence and militancy that now drove a critical mass of DOC's captives.[12]

Before fleeing Kings County Hospital, Brown supposedly told guards at BHD, "I will escape, you can't stop me." In December of 1973, Brown had been transferred to the Tombs, along with five other men assumed to be BLA members. At dawn on December 27, a cop patrolling the area spotted two men and two women loitering around an open manhole outside the facility. They included Bernice Jones, a prominent New York Panther and widow of Twymon Meyers, and BLA cadre Ashanti Alston. Jones was alleged to be carrying a list of BLA members in the Tombs, information about their upcoming court appearances, and numerous documents about Brown. Less than two months later, and just weeks after a judge dismissed the final charges against the quartet due to lack of evidence, another group of four—two men and two women, also including Alston—handcuffed a guard in the Tombs visiting area at gunpoint and attempted to cut through the wall with an acetylene torch. Their plan failed only when the torch ran out of oxygen and they had to beat a hasty retreat.[13]

The cadre fled with two guards' guns and a set of keys, the latter of which they mailed to the *New York Times* along with a taunting letter thanking DOC for its "cooperation," thanks to which "you only lost your guns." This was news to the public; an embarrassed DOC, awash in charges of "Keystone guards," had not disclosed the missing guns, downplaying the whole incident. Deputy Commissioner Jack Birnbaum claimed DOC did not mention the missing guns "because nobody asked us." As Public Affairs director Al Castro later complained, despite DOC's efforts to move BLA cadre around the jail system and thwart escape plots, "the trouble is that they can pretty well call their own plays."[14]

In August of 1974, with Brown back at BHD, the facility's brand-new metal detector thwarted an attempt to smuggle hacksaw blades, allegedly intended for him, via the same mechanism that had succeeded at the Tombs: a pair of shoes. The following week, Brown, Kearney, and a third BLA cadre, Pedro Monges, fled a transport van returning them from court to BHD, after the latter stole a key. The unshackled men were able to subdue multiple guards and had begun to climb a thirty-foot fence when Brown was shot in the shoulder by a guard and dropped to the ground. Kearney surrendered, but Monges was able to breach the fence, making it a short distance before a passing police patrol unit drew their guns and recaptured him. The following May, Kearney and Monges sawed an eighteen-by-eleven-inch hole in the back wall of their cell, smashed through a plateglass window, and shimmied through an air vent, all to undertake the 128-foot descent to the ground below. Monges made it safely outside the jail gates but was quickly captured by chance by an off-duty cop. Kearney was even less fortunate. As he descended the makeshift rope, it broke suddenly, and he fell to his death. DOC later alleged that Brown and another BLA cadre, Roderick Pearson, were seen running back to their cells shortly after the rope snapped.[15]

In early 1975 a maximum-security block at Rikers Island's HDM, home to eleven accused BLA cadre, was the scene of another dramatic escape attempt, the failure of which was surely not due to lack of imagination or daring. It began when BLA member Herman Bell, on his second trial for the shooting of NYPD officers Piagentini and Jones, asked a guard to use the phone. When the guard appeared with the phone, DOC officials later claimed, Bell pushed him against a metal-grated wall and held a sharpened stick to his neck. Another prisoner grabbed the guard's keys, and the duo tied him up and placed him in a nearby cell. Next, they lured another guard into the cellblock by complaining of a broken television, and he too was tied up and placed in a cell. Fourteen prisoners, including the eleven BLA cadre, held the block unchallenged for almost an hour while attempting to saw through a barred window with hacksaw blades.

The escape was foiled when a passing guard noticed the men sawing. Evidently deciding on the futility of the effort—and apparently seeing no use in the cellblock occupation tactic as an end in itself—the prisoners surrendered their hostages and returned to their cells. NYPD claimed the escape was part of an elaborate seaborne rescue in which armed BLA cadre set sail in three rafts from the Tiffany Street Pier in the Bronx, at least one clad in scuba gear, headed for the facility. After receiving a report of the flotilla, the harbor patrol had discovered an abandoned raft, which the cops claimed contained ammunition and a map of HDM. The East River current, it seemed, had foiled their mission. Asked at a BOC meeting how hacksaw blades got into HDM, Director of Operations D'Elia replied that a broken window had recently been discovered in a visiting booth. Seeking, as DOC and COBA officials often do, to minimize the role guards play in smuggling contraband into its facilities, D'Elia "declared that these inmates are clever people who can estimate when they will not be searched and thus will be able to sneak contraband into the institution."[16]

It is worth emphasizing that the black and brown revolutionaries of this period by no means held a monopoly on ambitious attempts to free themselves from DOC custody. In fact, some of the civilians proved just as adept at hatching bold escapes as the professional revolutionaries. In 1975, prisoner Joseph James reported to Kings County Hospital for a dental appointment and ducked into the bathroom, where a coconspirator had left him a gun. James opened fire in the crowded hospital, killing guard George Motchan and injuring another guard and a patient. Shortly before Bell's foiled escape, a group of prisoners at HDM discovered that the liquid in the facility's Xerox machine, when ignited, could melt the glass on windows to the outside, allowing it to be noiselessly ruptured using a rag mounted on a stick. Working quickly and quietly, the four were able to create a big enough hole to climb through undetected. Getting off the island, however, proved more difficult, and they were soon recaptured.[17]

In the month of May 1974 alone, at least fourteen prisoners with no established connection to BLA escaped from three different DOC facilities, including Rikers. Among them were four prisoners at BHD who accomplished what had eluded Brown: sawing through the bars of an eighth-floor dayroom, they successfully descended a rope made of blankets and twine. Recaptured prisoners later claimed to have obtained the saw blades from a guard for fifty dollars, as part of an elaborate smuggling operation. This led to the indictment of four civilians and five guards, and a security crackdown that catalyzed a hunger strike at BHD. A mere four days after this BHD escape, nine prisoners at Rikers Island pried open a window and fled into the night. One was apprehended on the island, but three swam to an anchored tugboat and, wielding a knife, obliged the seven-man crew to drop them off on the Tiffany Street Pier in the Bronx. They were captured shortly thereafter, clad in yellow seafarer outfits pilfered from the vessel. Later that month, a prisoner at Branch Queens sawed his way through the bars, climbed down forty feet, then traversed a twenty-foot wall to freedom.[18]

Behind DOC's crumbling walls, in the enforced idleness of captivity, and fueled by the subversive spirit of the age, boundless ingenuity blossomed.

16

Farewell, Anna Kross

Gazing upon the Finished Product

"A current review" of Rikers Island, wrote New York City Department of Public Works engineer Ted K. Raderman in 1972, "reveals a constant upgrading of facilities in a never ending attempt to conform with current penal philosophy, both in new construction and in the rehabilitation of existing buildings." Talk of "penal philosophy," however, was anachronistic at this point and would become only more so. Besieged by escapes and rebellions, the Department of Correction was struggling—and failing—to maintain its facilities at even the absolute-minimum standards provided by law. This account by Raderman, who was responsible for overseeing all construction on Rikers, captures the frenzied activity that accompanied a period otherwise defined by jail uprisings and the *Rhem v. McGrath* lawsuit. Daily operation of DOC facilities was now characterized by the push and pull between not only rebellions prisoners and rank-and-file guards, but union leadership, civilian administration, the Board of Correction, the federal courts, City Hall, and the public opinion on which the jails' legitimacy depended. DOC facilities also constituted a theater of the ongoing conflict between NYPD and the most heavily policed black and brown communities—part of a broader struggle between the city's ruling class and its increasing ranks of workers for whom there was no lasting place in the labor market save the very bottom. This contentious force field overflowed DOC's existing facilities and influenced the planning and implementation of new ones.[1]

Three facilities in particular had been in the works for over a decade. The annex to C-76, planned under the commissionership of Anna Kross, was completed in 1971 but was not immediately operational, due to understaffing. The Correctional Institution for Women (CIFW), designated to replace the scandal-plagued House of Detention for Women, was nearing its opening. So too was the Adolescent Remand and Detention Center (ARDC) designated to replace the Adolescent Remand Shelter in the old penitentiary, where prisoners aged sixteen to twenty had been held since 1968. The viability of these institutions depended largely on a significant expansion of the island's steam system and roadways, including the addition of a four-lane Central Mall underlain with steam lines to power heating, cooking, and cooling in the new facilities. This network of pipes was only the most prominent of a whole series of infrastructural improvements to the island undertaken during this period, which, along with the new facilities, constituted a $100 million capital project. Together, they would lay the foundation for the dramatic expansion of Rikers Island. Raderman later described "the indescribable satisfaction of gazing upon the finished product."[2]

Perhaps the most pressing project was the opening of a new facility for adolescents. "Presumably, the City was induced to place half of its prison facilities and population on [Rikers Island] and to build a $9 million bridge to connect it with the mainland," wrote the Board of Correction in its scathing 1972 indictment of the Adolescent Remand Shelter, "so that prisoners could be kept in safe and rehabilitative confinement secured by geography rather than by steel cages." BOC found the old penitentiary, rechristened the Adolescent Remand Shelter, to be "the worst prison in the City," a "depressing and oppressive physical plant" lacking adequate programming, staffing, and housing, in addition to being a place where, to BOC's incredulity, prisoners were largely kept indoors in a maximum-security institution, despite a majority of its 2,300 adolescent prisoners being held on $500 bail or less.

The Rikers Island location, the board argued, "isolates the prisoners from their families, makes it difficult for them to be in touch with lawyers for the preparation of their cases, and removes the prison from public attention." With DOC in dire need of new facilities for adolescents, the board looked forward to the opening of a new adolescent facility for detention cases—letting it pass unmentioned that this facility too would be on Rikers Island.[3]

If "properly administered," BOC subsequently argued, the new adolescent facility "could be the most innovative institution of its kind in the country. However, if it is left to traditional, unimaginative management and programming, it will stand as a $48 million monument to the past." Again, no mention was made of the drawbacks to a Rikers Island location. The new jail was called C-74, or the Adolescent Remand and Detention Center (ARDC, known today as the Robert N. Davoren Center). It was located on the southeast part of the island, spanning fifty acres that comprised six three-story housing units following the island's now-familiar chevron design. The vast majority of its housing consisted of 1,080 single cells, with the exception of a dormitory built to accommodate sixty sentenced prisoners working in the facility.[4]

The $40 million jail officially opened on June 29, 1973. The ceremony was dour. "I believe very profoundly that we have come to the point where it would be a mistake to continue building large custodial institutions," a defeated Mayor Lindsay told the crowd. "I hope we have struck the last bulldozer in the ground to build a [carceral] institution and that we have turned the corner," remarked Commissioner Malcolm. Anna Kross, too, was in attendance. The former DOC head had cut a slim profile in New York City politics since her departure in 1966, while her vision for making Rikers Island a world-renowned center of progressive penology had since been completely abandoned. While Kross would live until 1979, her dream was already dead. She stood by as Lindsay proclaimed that it was "very difficult to be proud that in an eight-year period we have added to the capacity of incarcerating people by thirty-five percent." The embittered mayor continued: "What a fine commentary that is on the state of affairs in the United States of America that we have to take pride and point with pride to institutions of this kind. It is still a prison." One imagines what Kross was thinking. These were largely facilities she had planned, imagining they would, in fact, become the pride of New York City.[5]

Space Jail

This truly unique opening ceremony stood in stark contrast to the opening of the CIFW on Rikers Island two years prior. Indeed, it signaled the arrival of a remarkably different political environment. By 1971, the ongoing scandal surrounding HDW had congealed a remarkably broad consensus favoring its closure. However, this was not fast in coming. The $24.2 million CIFW facility that took its place covered fifty-five acres. Its horizontal, closed campus was rated to hold 620 adults and adolescents in dormitories and cells, and fifty-eight in the clinic.[6]

"Welcome to New York's newest and perhaps best hotel," then commissioner McGrath had remarked upon CIFW's 1971 opening. While this was surely tongue-in-cheek, it seems to have been a common assessment in the city's official society. Reaffirming its consistent support for new jail construction the *Times* cited the jail as a beacon of progressive carceral architecture, describing the facility in terms perhaps better suited for its real estate section: "With its sleek, two-story chevron design, large windows, and brightly colored interior, it looks more like an Eastern girls' college than a detention facility. The buildings are sprawled across the northern edge of the island, giving the inmates a commanding view of the East River." In fairness, it must have been a great relief for respectable Manhattanites to bid farewell to the spectacle of HDW, which had rubbed their noses in the indignity of incarceration. In 1973, Mayor Lindsay, happy to put that scandal behind the city, led a ceremony celebrating the facility's demolition. Lindsay went so far as to climb a scaffolding and symbolically swing a sledgehammer at the building. Passersby were not impressed; in fact, they booed the mayor. Just about every problem highlighted by the *City in Crisis* series back in 1966 had grown worse under his watch. Accordingly, Lindsay's popularity had cratered, as he proved incapable of resolving the degenerating state of social crisis he had once pinned on the mismanagement of his predecessor Wagner.[7]

The programming at CIFW, reminiscent of the days of Kross, was planned to match its auspicious launch. When HDW prisoners were at last transferred to CIFW, however, it became clear that the effective use of the new facility required a much-larger staff than presently existed. "The place was really colorful," recounts Chris, an early prisoner. "If you had to be in jail, it was nicer than the House of D. It was cleaner anyway. But it was totally boring. There was nothing to do if you were on the detention side except watch television in the Day Room." Moreover, the female guards claimed their grievances about the new facility were not taken as seriously as those of the male guards. Accordingly, they filed a petition with McGrath in the summer of 1971. Visiting the facility, BOC member Rose M. Singer found that pervasive short-staffing among both civilians and guards was exacerbating problems with the physical plant, resulting in a generally demoralized climate of high absenteeism and widespread plans among guards to quit.[8]

The facility also became overcrowded immediately. By the fall, Singer subsequently reported, a crackdown on street-level sex work packed the facility beyond capacity, with forty-two cells in the new building doubled up. This was exacerbated, Singer complained, by the mistaken assumption among judges that there was room to house more prisoners at CIFW. Appearing before the board to discuss medical care at the facility, CIFW warden Essie Murph testified to the scant availability of gynecological services. As Singer subsequently revealed by pressing Deputy Health Commissioner Alan Gibbs, gynecology was considered a "specialty" medical service and therefore inessential to the operation of the jail. In her testimony, Murph "stated that the general attitude of both medical and correction staff is that the inmates are there to be punished and that there are limits to the services to which they are entitled. Some of the medical staff believe chronic medical problems should be treated after inmates leave the institution."[9]

This attitude certainly played a role in the death of prisoner Juanita Robinson. Arrested for disorderly conduct in 1974, Robinson was found dead in CIFW three days later, supposedly from the effects of drug abuse and chronic alcoholism. While Robinson had demonstrated clear symptoms of serious illness and emotional distress, the institution evinced no special urgency in seeing to her care. While the Board of Correction failed to charge criminal negligence in her death, it concluded Robinson's to be "not a story of gross negligence, or deliberate and calculated disregard of a seriously ill human being. Instead, it is an example of how an accretion of rather small and individually almost insignificant failures to do more than the minimum required, to put oneself out on behalf of another, ultimately may help produce a tragic result."[10]

Regardless of CIFW's issues, the primary problem posed by HDW had, in fact, been solved. "The Women's House of Detention ... was a commonly-known [sic] sightseeing spot," reflected Black Panther and Young Lords militant Denise Oliver shortly after its closing.

> They even used to drive a tourist bus by it and point it out: "Oh there's the women's prison." People that lived in the Village area were very used to hearing women that were incarcerated in the prison screaming and yelling "Let me out," and "Let me out, they're beating me in here," and things like that. Finally the City government decided to do something about it. So they moved it, and they put it out on an island so "nice" people outside wouldn't have to be bothered by the noise made from those horrible inmates in there. You see, because as long as the Women's House of Detention was right in the middle of New York City, people couldn't forget it existed.

Oliver simplifies, but not by much. "They have moved women to this place on Riker's Island," she continues, "which they have said it's a much nicer place. The only thing that's nicer is about it is that it's not as old, so there's probably not as much dirt collected in the place. It is still a prison. The conditions are still the same."[11]

The Women's House of Detention in Greenwich Village, circa 1941.

DOC Commissioner Anna M. Kross

The dramatic postwar rise in DOC's total yearly captive population is visualized in 1960.

An aerial view of Rikers Island, 1959.

An aerial view of Rikers Island, 2006.

Adolescent prisoners on Rikers Island, 1959.

A cellblock at the Rikers Island Penitentiary, 1959.

A Rikers prisoner operating a punch card machine as part of DOC's industrial training in the 1960s.

A prisoner reads in his cell at the Adolescent Remand Shelter (the original Rikers Island Penitentiary), 1970.

Eleven defendants in the Panther 21 trial. Standing, from left to right: Abayama Katara, Baba Odinga, Shaba-Um, and Curtis Powell. Seated: Kwando Kinshasa, Sundiata Acoli, Joan Bird, Michael "Cetewayo" Tabor, Ali Bey Hassan, Robert Collier, and Lumumba Shakur.

Cops and protesters clash outside the House of Detention for Women, 1970.

Prisoners at a smashed window of the occupied Branch Queens House of Detention, October 1970.

DOC Commissioner George McGrath meets with prisoners occupying Manhattan's Tombs facility as part of a citywide jail rebellion in October 1970.

Young Lord Victor Martinez addresses reporters, alongside Representative Shirley Chisholm and Black Panther Lumumba Shakur, at the occupied Branch Queens House of Detention in October 1970.

Off-duty and laid-off New York cops storm the Brooklyn Bridge on July 1, 1975, to protest cuts to police during the city's fiscal crisis, menacing motorists and clashing with on-duty cops.

Leo Zeferetti, pictured in 1981 as a US congressman, presided over COBA from 1968 to 1974. He oversaw the union's adoption of militant workplace tactics and its ascendancy to the main stage of New York City politics.

Assata Shakur in police custody, 1976.

Mayor Edward Koch in a 1981 television commercial boasting of the many empty cells at Rikers waiting for anyone caught with a gun. Thanks to Koch's law-and-order policies, there were in fact no empty cells at Rikers.

COBA President Phil Seelig falsely announces the city's repeal of DOC's federally mandated "use of force" protocol to a crowd of guards blocking the Rikers Island Bridge, August 1990.

A Patrolmen's Benevolent Association demonstration in September 1992 turned into a drunken police riot marked by widespread anti-black racism.

The contemporary sign at the entrance to Rikers Island, declaring its guards to be "New York City's Boldest."

The most detailed portrait of the CIFW and its inhabitants in these earliest years comes to us from the Black Liberation Army's Assata Shakur. Captured in 1973 following a shootout on the New Jersey Turnpike that left her comrade Zayd Shakur and a New Jersey state trooper dead, Shakur experienced the new facility firsthand during multiple BLA-related cases between 1974 and 1977. Transferred to Rikers in 1973 to face trial for armed robbery, Shakur recalls, "The car came to a bridge where pigs were stationed, pointing rifles and shotguns." Shakur asked: "Where are we? Where is this place?" A marshal answered: "You are now on Rikers Island. This will be your new home for a while."

"It'll never be my home," Shakur replied.

"When i went in," she recalls, "the door slid shut behind me. It was something out of a science fiction movie. The long halls, the sliding door, the control panel. 'Space jail,' i said to myself." But a familiar scene awaited. "Inside, there was a cot, a dirty sink, a seatless toilet, and a roll of toilet paper." The smell of the jail was similarly familiar. "I don't care what jail i've been in," Shakur recalls, "they all stink. They have a smell unlike any smell on earth. Like blood and sweat and feet and open sores and, if misery has a smell, like misery."[12]

CIFW's state-of-the-art design nonetheless left an impression on Shakur. "Instead of bars," she reflects, "the cells have doors which are painted bright, optimistic colors with slim glass observation panels ... The guards have successfully convinced most of the women that Riker's Island is a country club." However, Shakur argues, this statement is only true "by contrast to the unbelievably barbaric conditions of other prisons." The doctor who initially examined Shakur "was a filthy looking man who looked more like a Bowery bum than a doctor. He coughed all over me without even covering his mouth, and his fingernails looked like he had spent the last five years in a coal mine." The only advantage, Shakur surmised, was that he worked quickly. He "rattled diseases off like he was an auctioneer and asked me if i had them. Then he gave me a one-minute examination, took my blood, and that was it."[13]

Shakur's impression of her fellow prisoners echoes in part the accounts of Joan Bird and Angela Davis from the HDW in Manhattan. "There are no big time gangsters here," Shakur observed,

> no premeditated mass murderers, no godmothers. There are no big time dope dealers, no kidnappers, no Watergate women. There are virtually no women here charged with white collar crimes like embezzling or fraud. Most of the women here have drug related cases. Many are charged as accessories to crimes committed by men. The major crimes women here are charged with are pickpocketing, shop lifting, robbery, and drugs. Women who have prostitution cases or who are doing "fine" time make up a substantial part of the short term population. The women see stealing or hustling as necessary for the survival of themselves or their children because jobs are scarce and welfare is impossible to live on.[14]

Like Davis, Shakur estimates that over 95 percent of the women were black and Puerto Rican. They came largely from New York's majority-black areas: Harlem, South Bronx, South Jamaica, Bedford-Stuyvesant, and Brownsville. Many had suffered abuse as children and at the hands of intimate partners. She estimated that 80 percent used drugs on the street; getting high was the most common activity women looked forward to upon release. Many women also carried scars from self-harm.

Also similar to HDW, over half the women took psychotropic drugs, while "elaborate schemes to obtain contraband are always in the works," constituting a culture Shakur considered pure escapism. The days were packed full of television, love affairs between prisoners, and childish games. Despite the prevalence of romantic relationships, Shakur found no connection between these practices and liberatory politics, noting instead how they replicated the patriarchal couple form of the outside world, including violence and intimidation perpetrated by "butches" against "femmes." Nor did the black liberation movement, nor any kind of anti-capitalist politics, hold any sway. While most women considered "whitey" the source of their oppression, Shakur bemoaned, "They do not want to destroy Rockefella. They want to be just like him."[15]

Shakur found the guards to be similarly hopeless. "I was quickly to find out that the overwhelming majority of guards in the female jail at Rikers are Black," Shakur discovered. "But when they opened their mouths and expressed their opinions, you wondered." To Shakur's chagrin, despite their professed understanding of the white supremacist structure of US society, the guards held unabashedly middle-class values, adhered to the "boot-strap theory," and even considered the legal system "lenient." Additionally, they were possessed of occupational chauvinism, considering themselves superior to the prisoners, even though "their dubious accomplishments are not based on superior intelligence or effort, but only on chance and the civil service list."

Ultimately, however, Shakur discovered that most guards were hemmed in and "hate and feel trapped by their jobs," which were fraught with abuse from coworkers and a punishing work schedule. Yet "no matter how much they hate the military structure, the infighting, the ugliness of their tasks, they are very aware of how close they are to the welfare lines." The guards insisted, Shakur notes, that they were just doing a job like any other. "The more they say that," she concludes, "the more preposterous it seems." Shakur's assessment of the women at CIFW, certainly colored by her experience of increasing isolation in a shrinking vanguard of the black liberation movement, nonetheless speaks to the quickly diminishing horizon for working-class revolution during this period. In the very least, it connotes the death knell of the assumption among many US revolutionaries that the masses were ready to rebel with them. This was not unique to revolutionaries, either; as Mayor Lindsay's remarks at the opening of the new adolescent facility indicate, this was the onset of a protracted period of crushing demoralization for just about anyone who believed in anything besides untrammeled selfishness and the rule of society by force. In other words, it was the city's cops' and guards' time to shine.[16]

17

Burn, City, Burn

Reprivatization

In 1965, candidate Lindsay had denounced then mayor Wagner's spending habits, especially the use of borrowed money based on uncertain assessments of future revenue. However, faced with the immense pressure of holding the city together amid declining revenues and the intensification of the social tension that marred his mayoralty from day one, Lindsay had followed in his predecessor's footsteps. His budgets increasingly relied on speculative borrowing, paying operation costs out of capital funds, and billing one year's expenditures to the budget of the next. Lindsay turned to debt, as historian Kim Phillips-Fein argues, "to evade open struggles about its priorities, and about the limits, disappointments, and failures of the postwar liberal regime."[1]

Amid racially infused struggles over housing desegregation, community control of schools and other social services, and the ongoing state of war between NYPD and many of the communities it policed, Lindsay had hoped to spend his way to social harmony. This strategy could not last forever. By 1973, 21.6 percent of the city's revenue came from federal aid, up from 4.5 percent in 1961. This was due in large part to President Lyndon B. Johnson's Great Society programs—commitments from which Richard Nixon, and then Gerald Ford, were eager to extricate the federal government. State aid to the city also increased fivefold during this time. Meanwhile, New York City lost 257,000 jobs from 1969 to 1973 alone. By 1972, roughly

one in eight New Yorkers were on some form of public assistance. Hiring in city agencies, driven in large part by pressure
from black and brown organizers, continued to balloon, amid
decreasing revenues, until 1974. The social peace Lindsay so
desperately sought to purchase was nowhere to be found.[2]

Lindsay left office at the end of 1973, with his political career
effectively wrecked by the unfolding crisis in New York City.
Taking his place was Abraham D. Beame. It would be difficult
to find a politician who cut a greater contrast to Lindsay in
practically every sense, including stature; standing five feet, two
inches, Beame was known to deliver addresses while standing
atop an attaché case. The child of Jewish Russian immigrants
who fled czarist repression of his father's socialist politics,
Beame hailed from a Lower East Side slum. Educated at City
College, Beame became an accountant and plodded his way
through Democratic Party machine politics. He served as New
York City's comptroller, the top financial manager under both
Wagner and Lindsay, and had unsuccessfully challenged Lindsay
for the mayoralty in 1964.

While Beame's marked divergence from the flashy optimism
of Lindsay was problematic in 1965, it is perhaps what drew a
plurality of city voters, who by 1973 were fed up with everything the Lindsay years represented. Beame had an eclectic base
composed of comfortable working-class white people, labor
unionists, property owners, business owners, the elderly, and
denizens of the so-called outer boroughs. A critical mass of New
York City voters flocked to a mayoral candidate devoid of the
slightest charisma, ideological vision, or grand promises of any
kind save for responsible fiscal management of city affairs and
holding the subway fare at thirty-five cents. Even this promise
would prove impossible to keep.[3]

Beame proved no more adept than Lindsay at finding a way
to keep the city budget afloat, falling back on creative accounting practices on the gray fringes of legality. Each year since the
Wagner era, the city had relied more heavily on creative accounting to keep its budget in the black; Wall Street, meanwhile,
became bolder, more globalized, less invested in the financial

health of New York City, and, above all, had little interest in paying for public infrastructure that rich people do not directly benefit from. The city's finance and real estate elites had long bristled at the redistributive policies of postwar New York, but amid the seemingly boundless plenty the postwar period had facilitated, these policies did not demand drastic and decisive action. However, this changed as the global economic picture soured. The years leading up to Beame's mayoralty were defined by a startling decline in the corporate rate of profit, the loss of tax revenue due to white flight into the surrounding suburbs, and a general sense among the US ruling class that the cities had gone far enough in the wrong direction. As economist William Tabb has argued, "Real elites only enter day-to-day operations of government in periods of crisis; they move to the background as soon as possible, after they have restructured the context of decision-making in ways they find congenial." For New York City, this moment came in 1975.

It was clear in 1974 that the city was having difficulty paying its bills, and City Hall attempted to get in the black by making deep cuts to city departments throughout that year. But events took a crucial turn in early 1975, when Wall Street bankers undertook a coordinated action, refusing to continue funding New York City's expenditures through buying the city's bonds. Emissaries of the finance, insurance, and real estate sector thereby threatened to send the city into bankruptcy, lest New York City's government forfeit immense power over public spending to Wall Street. Washington, DC, refused to intervene. What followed represented nothing less than the seizure of New York City's government by private capital, through the creation of the Emergency Financial Control Board, which took control over city finances.

The crisis provided finance capital the opportunity to dramatically reverse the redistributive trend that had operated under Wagner and Lindsay. In the process, the city government was forced to make deep cuts to its public sector, slashing its total workforce by 15 percent in the first year alone, and upward of 20 percent in sanitation, parks, and schools. New York City thus became a laboratory for policies now commonly known as austerity. This formed one element of a governing strategy relying on the promotion of free market policies, privatization of public services, and the disempowerment of working people—known today as neoliberalism. Tabb sums up the striking contrast between this new era and the preceding decade: "The policies put into practice in the 1960s may be described as redistributive liberalism, and in the 1970s a neoconservative reprivatization." The ruling class had decided that too much of the city's wealth had been poured into the public sector during the postwar years; the time had come to take it back. The effects of this reprivatization hit the city jail system hard.[4]

The Bureau of Budget Takes Charge

In its *1975–1976 Annual Report,* the Board of Correction dedicates the first and last sentence of its introductory paragraph to underscoring, in identical language, how "the City's correction system underwent a series of crises unmatched in its history." The first hint of budget trouble for the board came in May 1974, when City Hall demanded staffing cuts to DOC. BOC executive director John Brickman thought he could eliminate jobs yet to be filled, thereby preserving the existing staff. In an October appearance before BOC, Malcolm was asked about the status of the full-time librarian position the board had been promised. "The Commissioner declared that he recognized the need for a professional librarian position," the minutes reflect. However, "Assistant Commissioner [Alphonso] Ford stated that the coordinating librarian position had been killed by the Bureau of the Budget." And then came the buried lede: "Commissioner Malcolm stated that he will be required to lose an additional sixty civilian employees by the end of this year." To save money, Brickman proposed DOC replace clerical work done by guards with positions held by (lower-paid) civilians, and replace guards who drove buses on Rikers Island with prisoners. Simultaneously, the Correction Aide Program, which provided low-wage workers to perform the clerical tasks that had once fallen to guards, was itself gutted.[5]

BOC fought against cuts to their program, asking DOC to find $700,000 worth of cuts elsewhere. Its demise was emblematic of the rapid changes befalling the New York City public infrastructure. Board member Kirby, for one, framed the cuts as a violation the prisoners' rights as well as the civil rights of the aides, given that they were predominantly nonwhite women. This was an apt observation, which spoke of a broader trend throughout the city: the workers hit hardest by austerity were disproportionately women and nonwhite. The layoff of 15,000 teachers and paraprofessionals, for instance, diminished the share of black and Spanish-surnamed educators in the city's workforce from the already dismal 11 to a mere 3 percent. As Tabb recounts, "Between the fall of 1974 and the winter of 1976, the city workforce lost half its Spanish-surnamed workers, two-fifths of its black male employees, and one-third of its female employees … minorities, who made up 31 percent of the city payroll, suffered 44 percent of the cuts."[6]

For his part, Malcolm claimed that he had defended the Correction Aides program but been told by Deputy Mayor James Cavanagh that it had to go, save for nineteen positions. Commenting that "in his twenty-seven years of working for the City, he has never seen anything like this before," Malcolm shared BOC's frustration with the unilateral cuts. He noted that a permanent civil service job had been effectively eliminated without his consent, and "the Bureau of Budget had taken to running the Department."[7]

Rikers prisoners even circulated a petition supporting the Correction Aides program, which they credited with providing legal advice and helping them communicate with their families on the outside. A ranking officer at the Tombs argued in defense of the program on the grounds that the Aides would wind up on welfare if dismissed. Even the Correction Officers' Benevolent Association, which had opposed the program in strident language some years before, defended the fired aides. BOC courted the intervention of federal judge Morris Lasker, who had proven willing to undertake decisive action in the city jails, hoping to continue the program on legal grounds, but Lasker refused to get involved. Amid the elimination of aides, members of the Clergy Volunteers program were pressured to take on their duties. As the influx of Tombs prisoners doubled the population of that facility amid the mass firing of aides, the HDM Clergy Volunteer coordinator put it thus: "To ask [Clergy Volunteers] to assume what had been a full-time job for a prisoner population half as large is the surest way to the destruction of morale and the general debilitation of the program."[8]

Medical services in the jails, grim as they were to begin with, suffered tremendously. Dr. Lloyd Novick of Prison Health Services told the board that basic services like examination upon intake had become "at best, cursory. Most physicians or physician associates who perform the initial medical exam have not been instructed as to what should be done, he said; at times, the writing on charts is illegible ... Sometimes people who are scheduled for OPD clinics never get to the clinics because of the correction officers' schedules." By March 1975, the jails had lost 10 percent of their medical staff in just three months, and seventy-two positions stood vacant and unlikely to be filled. Novick told the board, "PHS is approaching the point that precludes the minimum medical care needed in the prisons." Even the program's analysts had been cut, so quantification of this diminishing quality of care would be impossible. Novick welcomed the impending takeover of medical care at HDM and CIFM by Montefiore Hospital in the Bronx, in spite of the fact that this would merely shift an impossible burden from one overworked bureaucracy to another.[9]

By the end of 1974, even BOC itself was on the chopping block. In mid December, a round of cuts was announced that would reduce the board to only three city-funded positions. Deputy Commissioner Birnbaum told Chairman Peter Tufo that the cuts were the result of DOC administrators being put on the spot, with only one hour to cut twenty-five "provisional" positions; they were therefore forced to choose, as BOC minutes put it, between "emasculating the staff of the Department or the Board." Board members pushed back against Birnbaum's account, noting that DOC was given more than an hour to make the decision, and many possible jobs to cut, before it decided to gut BOC. Evoking DOC's previous bad faith around guard violence and squalid conditions, Tufo "stated that the Department now has three strikes against it—the Tombs, the Branch Queens House, and the present cutback." For those unaware of the rules of baseball, he clarified: "Three strikes and you're out."

"The rest of the Board was similarly disposed," the minutes report. "The general outlook was that the board can no longer count on the Department of Correction." At this juncture, Tufo got Birnbaum on the phone. Birnbaum assured him that Commisioner Malcolm believed the cuts to BOC to be too severe, and that Malcolm had pledged to call City Hall and advocate for the return of some of the fired staffers. This promise was not kept. Now, questions of the board's future hinged not only on city funding, but on whether Mayor Beame would follow through on a plan to transfer the entirety of DOC to the state, which already had its own Commission of Correction.[10]

The closure of the Tombs had also corresponded with a dramatic rise in the city jail population, which Malcolm attributed to a sharp increase in arrests and a lag in court processing. Moreover, as unemployment mounted and city services unraveled, quantifiable crime had risen precipitously, with the murder rate more than doubling from 653 in 1966 to 1,680 in 1973. Following the closure of the Tombs, the population at HDM shot up from 800 to 1700. "Since Christmas," reported a Clergy Volunteer Program coordinator, "I have begun to see less and less of a possibility of any tasks for the aid and assistance of inmates being completed. It is almost impossible to return to a particular inmate for a follow-up interview. First, you have to find him, then you have to attempt to interview him in the chaos in front of each block." The cuts had only made things worse.[11]

This difficulty was also heightened by the absence of the correctional aides, who were formerly able to relay messages to the clergy volunteers as well as to the proper personnel in social services. Overcrowding became so pressing that DOC considered shifting detainees to buildings for sentenced prisoners, which violated a basic tenet of classification on which much of DOC's infrastructure had been built. Testifying before the board in March of 1975, Malcolm claimed DOC was at 92 percent capacity. Asked if this figure counted total cells or usable cells. Malcolm replied that it reflected the number of usable cells; Deputy Commissioner Birnbaum corrected the commissioner, telling him the figure referred to total cells. The figure, the men agreed, must be higher than 92 percent. Malcolm proceeded to float a hellish plan to partition the CIFM dormitories to accommodate upward of 200 prisoners—more than double their rated capacity—which seems to have amounted to splitting them down the middle with caging and providing an interior catwalk for guards. DOC sought to sidestep the single-cell requirement by building a dormitory facility capable of holding 760 prisoners. This plan would ultimately lead to the construction of the C-95 building, designated for purely custodial incarceration.[12]

By mid 1975, the city was demanding over 800 layoffs from DOC and the closure of the Bronx and Brooklyn Houses of Detention. However, the Bronx House received a stay only after riots at Rikers made the closure impossible for the city to countenance. The Adolescent Remand Shelter was also closed due to cuts in June 1975, and the surplus was foisted on the new Adolescent Remand and Detention Center, where double celling—coupled with a spike in guard brutality and battles between rival factions of black and brown prisoners—became the norm. The violence became so bad that BOC teamed up with COBA to provide anti-violence outreach. By BOC's telling, this promising program was scuttled by DOC administration, which forced itself into the project and ran it aground in bureaucratic red tape before it could gain traction. By September 1975, DOC had lost 209 civilian and 250 guard positions through attrition, and 250 more guards through layoffs. Thanks to the principle of "last hired, first fired," these layoffs skewed disproportionately to nonwhite guards, given the recent adoption of affirmative action policies in hiring.[13]

Malcolm complained that losses by attrition were exacerbated by portended wage cuts, which led to a rush to take advantage of tenuous retirement opportunities. Given that this coincided with both a legal mandate against double celling and a spike in the city jail population, DOC was experiencing pressure from all sides that manifested itself in a redoubled climate of struggle within the jails. Over the July 4 weekend, Rikers guards protesting cuts by staging a sick-out, "crippling" the work shift, as one warden testified, by delaying dinner and keeping the prisoners stuck in their cells. Prisoners responded by setting fires, and order was only restored by imposing further overwork on the guards, some of whom were forced to work shifts in excess of twenty-four hours. In short, the dramaturgy of the New York City fiscal crisis played out in microcosm in the city jail system: even prisoners received a cut in their wages, clothing provisions were diminished, and the number of bread slices per meal was diminished from four to three—while commissary prices went up.[14]

Law and Order Takes the Streets

On July 7, just days after their sick-out crippled operations at HDM, guards undertook another direct action at the mouth of the bridge connecting the island to Queens. Protesting layoffs, COBA rank and filers parked their cars in the middle of Hazen Street, successfully blocking the bridge to Rikers for almost an hour. They dispersed only when police arrived, flanked by tow trucks prepared to impound their vehicles. This would not be the last time guards resorted to this new tactic. Nor was such militancy limited to the city's jail guards: in fact, the action was part of a broader political movement among the organized forces of law and order, operating in tandem with a politicized movement of police and prison guards' unions across the country.

The previous week, a mob of recently laid-off police and their supporters, many visibly intoxicated, had descended on Lower Manhattan for a raucous five-hour demonstration against layoffs within NYPD. The demonstrators blocked the Brooklyn

Bridge, let the air out of car tires, menaced motorists who confronted them, and pelted on-duty cops with beer bottles and invectives. Only when three arrests were made did they disperse. At least one Brooklyn Bridge arrest went awry, when a group of off-duty cops assaulted the arresting officers, thus allowing their comrade to escape. The Patrolmen's Benevolent Association did not immediately demand NYPD and City Hall take action to apprehend these attackers, and no reward was offered for their capture. While the union claimed the entire day of action was "a spontaneous protest," multiple cops told a reporter they had been contacted by the union and encouraged to attend.[15]

Two weeks after the Brooklyn Bridge demonstration, prisoners at Kew Gardens staged an action of their own, beating two guards and throwing a third over a railing to the ground fourteen feet below. Prisoners then seized the fourth floor for almost three hours, smashing chairs, a television, and heating equipment. They also broke into the guards' office, located their own prisoner identification cards, and set them on fire. This rebellion would prove difficult for DOC to attribute to overcrowding caused by city underfunding: the facility was, in fact, under capacity at the time. Moreover, during negotiations, which resulted in prisoners ultimately agreeing to go back to their cells peacefully, no substantive grievances about jail conditions were raised. "They attacked us and we stood up as men," an unidentified prisoner shouted to reporters below. "They have been harassing us ... with penny ante things ... Every damn black man in this institution has a ransom, a bail he can't buy. They harass us because we're Muslims." These events could not be pinned on overcrowding or any other isolated issues; the prisoners took issue with the very social order that had consigned them to jail in the first place.[16]

When the cops picketed City Hall and blockaded the Brooklyn Bridge, one demonstrator's sign said it all: "Burn City Burn." Despite the drunken hooliganry that unfolded in the streets, the politics underlying this nihilistic message were sharper than they might have seemed. The previous month, a group of uniformed unions, including COBA, had authored an ominous pamphlet under the umbrella of the Council for Public Safety. Titled "Welcome to Fear City," the pamphlet was intended for tourists, riffing on Lindsay's oft-ridiculed comment that New York was a "fun city." It warned: "Mayor Beame is going to discharge substantial numbers of firefighters and law enforcement officers of all kinds." Therefore, the reader should "stay away from New York if you possibly can." If this was impossible, the reader could follow the steps taken by those New Yorkers who "manage to survive and even to keep their property intact." This meant vacating the streets after 6 p.m., avoiding walking *anywhere*, staying in Manhattan, guarding their property as if it would be snatched at any moment, and staying mindful of fire hazards —given that there were fewer firefighters to extinguish blazes.

The pamphlet proved immensely controversial; for a time, it was even blocked by a court order sought by City Hall. The cop and guard unions ultimately reneged on their promise to distribute it at airports, bus stations, and Midtown hotels, but the controversy it generated conveyed their message even more effectively. Such theatrics were only the most public expression of a power struggle over who would inherit the spoils of postcrisis New York City. Contrary to the common conservative narrative of years since, the fiscal crisis was not a matter of curbing out-of-control spending. As sociologist Eric Lichten observes, "During crisis periods, the institutional arrangements by which we live, are governed, and produce are open to change by both progressive and reactionary forces." The New York City fiscal crisis was a class conflict over how postcrisis New York City would be run, who it would benefit, and, above all, who would be in control. As such, an important weapon in this struggle would be defining—and enforcing—criteria for which city services were superfluous, and which were essential.[17]

Essential Services

The fiscal crisis was, Lichten argues, "nothing short of a full-scale assault on the liberal agenda that characterized and gave

force to America's social welfare state." Extending far beyond
New York, it represented a turning point in state expenditure
on a national, and then global scale. New York City was the
laboratory of this transformation.[18] The result was, as geographer Ruth Wilson Gilmore demonstrates, the "delegitimation
of programs the state could use to put surpluses"—whether
unemployed people, disused land, surplus tax revenue, or other
means of production—"back to work, while at the same time,
the state retained bureaucratic and fiscal apparatuses from the
golden age." As Gilmore explains, "The state did not disappear
... Rather, what withered was the state's legitimacy to act as
the Keynesian state." As "big government" became a bad word,
the state did not diminish in capacity, but became increasingly
composed of repressive institutions like police and jails, which
replaced public welfare institutions as the latter became ideological untenable.[19] "Meanwhile," writes geographer Samuel
Stein, "stock taxes were dropped, income taxes were halved,
and real estate taxes fell to historic levels. This became a model
for neoliberal governments throughout the country and around
the world." In the 1970s, New York City became an early model
for an international restructuring of capitalism and the nation
states that serve its reproduction.[20]

The pro-austerity coalition that ossified during this period was
based on the alliance between the finance, insurance, and real
estate (FIRE) sector, the cop and guard unions, and the voters
who would elect pro-austerity politicians like future mayor
Edward Koch. The political movement of law and order that
had congealed against black and brown activism now argued
for cuts to the city's expenditures on just about anything besides
police and jails. Simultaneously, large foundations like the Ford
Foundation, representing a farsighted ruling-class response to
social problems, became the socially conscious partners to the
imposition of fiscal austerity and promotion of city policies that
tied public welfare to real estate development. Under this new
regime, the management of the lower tiers of the working class,
disproportionately nonwhite as they were, would be handled
less by welfare state bureaucracies and gainful city employment,

and more by bureaucracies revolving around policing, courts, jails, and prisons, or else nonprofit organizations that were not accountable to taxpayers. As the guiding star of the neoliberal era, the viability of government was tied directly to the profit margins of real estate and finance.

This new vision for New York City life relied on the support of police and guards' unions, who were uniquely positioned to demand a larger share of the city's dwindling pie—in exchange for maintaining order as other municipal agencies were dismantled. To this end, they engaged in political struggle over the definition of what the city considered to be "essential services," carving out in the process what American studies scholar Rebecca Hill calls "the specialness of police and prison guards."[21]

In no eternal register is it carved in stone that a beat cop accosting the homeless, doling out tickets for public urination, or responding to more serious crimes whose perpetrators have long vanished in order to stand around for hours filling out paperwork, is more *essential* to society than a teacher, trash collector, social worker, park ranger, or any other public employee. The definition of "essential" was therefore the result of political struggle. Even a cursory look at NYPD's 1971 wildcat strike makes clear how *inessential* the police can be: the inconvenient fact is that while arrests dropped, there was no great spike in crime. New York did not become Fear City. But if the strike demonstrated the absence of an immediate and clear link between crime and policing, why would the cops undertake a risky and illegal strike in the first place?

First, PBA was leading a campaign against pattern bargaining, the practice by which every city union resolves their contract similarly, ensuring that each gets roughly the same gains. This was a practice the most powerful city unions like the Uniformed Sanitationmen's Association used to set a precedent to be followed by the weaker ones. PBA, which had benefited from pattern bargaining in the past, had grown considerably stronger, and now clamored to end it, in favor of survival of the fittest. Second, in waging the 1971 strike, cops were responding to state investigation of NYPD corruption under the Knapp

Commission—most commonly known for its chief whistle-blower, Frank Serpico, lionized in the 1973 film *Serpico*. Knapp represented not only the dismantling of lucrative corruption rackets, but also the intrusion of civilian authority on the cops' ability to do their jobs as they saw fit. Both motives speak to the rank and file's increasing impatience with their status as one city agency among others, forced to obey the same customs and laws as other city employees.[22]

This was not exactly a new development; since the days of Wagner, the cops had been arguing behind the scenes for a break from pattern bargaining with other city workers, even firefighters and guards. According to PBA's argument, theirs was a uniquely difficult and hazardous job; therefore, they deserved more than everyone else. What they had lacked, up to this point, was a combination of the right opportunity and the sufficient strength to take advantage of it. By 1975, however, they had both. As the fiscal crisis shook out, PBA officially opposed so-called "me-too clauses," by which city unions could demand the city offer similar terms as those won by others. Unsurprisingly, this was met with disgust by other city employees—perhaps especially the sanitation workers, who the cops argued deserved 28 percent less pay than they did. This was doubly insulting, as it was sanitation workers' earlier gains—won through bitter strikes—that had laid the foundation for the success of PBA through the same agreements the cops now opposed. But PBA knew that the power of the cops was no longer rivaled by sanitation, and this was their chance to carve out a unique place for themselves in the city.

Ultimately, PBA's appeal to the *specialness* of the cops worked. While even NYPD was not immune to cuts amid the drastic retrenchment of the early fiscal crisis, its ranks did escape the worst of the layoffs by far, and the cops were poised to dramatically improve their standing in the city in the long term. Steep cuts to addiction treatment programs, disastrously timed to coincide with the implementation of the draconian Rockefeller drug laws, replaced the vestiges of a medical approach to addiction with the carceral solution that still reigns supreme, culminating in the prison boom known today as mass incarceration. Large segments of New York's racialized working class were positively decimated by the transition to come. However, the FIRE sector and the cops weren't the only ones who came out on top of the fiscal crisis. The Correction Officers' Benevolent Association, following in the footsteps of PBA, fared just fine.[23]

COBA would never tire of crying poverty and hardship for its members, or of complaining they were disrespected and denied the benefits given to other city workers, most notably the cops. However, an observer looking solely at the contract COBA won in the heat of the fiscal crisis, during the fall of 1975, would have a hard time believing the city didn't have money to spare. On top of a $17,458 minimum base salary, the guards also received automatic cost-of-living raises pegged to increases in the US Department of Labor price index, an annual "longevity adjustment" of one hundred dollars, upward of $261 per year placed in an annuity fund to be paid upon departure (including termination for any reason), twelve paid leave days per year, and significant medical benefits, combining to provide a comfortable life for those administering captivity in the most uncomfortable quarters in all of New York City. By contrast, $17,450 was the *median* salary for New York City teachers in 1975, with the minimum salary a mere $9,700. John M. Wynne Jr., an MIT-educated management scientist who studied this contract, lauds COBA for "a remarkably effective job of negotiating for economic benefits." One COBA union officer told Wynne that the secret to their success lay in public ignorance of just how good the guards had it.[24]

One of these guards was Eric M. Taylor, a black Bedford-Stuyvesant native whose name today adorns the C-76 building. Taylor was laid off from NYPD in 1975 amid budget cuts, only to find work was available in DOC. Taylor's move was emblematic of an arrangement in which guards fared even better than the cops in avoiding cuts, especially after using a jail rebellion as pretext to force the city to rehire many of the positions that had been lost. On a very basic level, hemmed in by court rulings and already facing dire conditions, there wasn't much to be cut from the jail system without breaking the law. More broadly, however, amid the dramatic reordering of the New York City public sector, the city needed the jails more than ever before. Indeed, they played a key role absorbing the effects of cuts to sundry social services, especially given the simultaneous withdrawal of public sector work that as of late had disproportionately benefited nonwhite New Yorkers. Henceforth the city jails would pick up where other city agencies had left off, housing under squalid and treacherous conditions the same people who would have previously benefited from public housing, public assistance, city employment, or other features of historian Joshua Freeman's "working-class New York," which was effectively vanquished during this time. Ironically, by forswearing solidarity with other unions and pushing their own selfish agendas, to the detriment of much of working-class New York, two major city unions—PBA and COBA—were among its most assiduous gravediggers.[25]

The impact of this new regime of austerity on the city's jail system was palpable. Facilities were so crowded and miserable, and the courts so backlogged, that the number of pretrial prisoners who opted not to go to trial increased. More people were charged and convicted of serious crimes, and received stricter penalties. As chaos proliferated throughout working-class life, the law-and-order regime took hold. Between 1971 and 1980, Tabb notes, "guilty pleas to felonies increased from 47 percent to 66 percent in the criminal courts, the percentage of defendants sent to state prison (excluding city prison sentences) rose from 23 to 54 percent, and the percentage of defendants sentenced to more than three years increased from 26 to 85 percent."

Though there was an uptick in violent crime attendant on this social disorder, these were not all serious criminals. A survey of 300 random city court defendants conducted in 1977 "found only 30 percent to be employed, and of those with jobs over a third took home less than $100 a week; more than 90 percent took home less than $200 ... Many cases involved stealing from supermarkets, not paying for meals, and not paying subway fares." Under the new regime ordering New York City life, DOC helped transfer the greatest burden of the fiscal crisis to those locked unwillingly in its custody. To say that their living conditions went from bad to worse does not do justice to the severity of the situation. Nowhere were the violent implications of law and order's victory in the city's fiscal crisis felt more acutely than inside its jails.[26]

The Real Victims

On November 22, 1975, Peter Tufo paid a visit to HDM after receiving a tip that it was on the brink of rebellion. The BOC chairman found "services to inmates had broken down, food was served cold and late, working conditions had deteriorated to the point where on-duty officers walked off their posts and left the cellblocks unmanned." The facility had absorbed the populations of the Adolescent Remand Center after its closure, due to cuts, on June 19, along with 250 prisoners from the Bronx Detention Center, when it was "half-closed" as part of a planned phase-out. The following evening, Roy Caldwood, now an assistant deputy warden, was on patrol at HDM, when a guard notified him of an "unusual huddle" of prisoners on the opposite end of one cellblock, amid an ominous and thoroughly uncharacteristic quiet. "For the gate officer" guarding these nearly hundred-yard blocks, Caldwood later explained, "it's like trying to figure out what play the other team's quarterback is going to call when you're way down in the opposite end zone." As Caldwood and his colleagues speculated what was afoot, he was called at once to another block, where guards discovered prisoners had been removing bricks from the shower wall. However, this "wasn't the start of an escape hole nipped in the bud. The bricks were ammo for a fight."[27]

No sooner was the plan discovered than the conspirators, packed into two blocks with over 600 prisoners total between them, sprang into action. Malcolm later called the action "a massive force of manpower." Complaining of inadequate medical care, food, and housing, to the point of triple celling, they demanded to speak with Judge Lasker in person. In keeping with its enduring public relations strategy, DOC initially strove to keep the rebellion quiet. The fire department responded to multiple calls reporting fires on the island, only to be turned away and told "everything was under control." Meanwhile, five blocks holding a combined 1,501 prisoners had fallen under prisoner control.

The rebels were also increasingly consolidated; Malcolm soon discovered that "instead of having to attack five different blocks of approximately 300 inmates in each block, the breaching of shower walls between blocks had created two massive forces of inmates," numbering at least 580 and 921 fighters, respectively. The prisoners of Block 7 even electrified its metal gate, of which the guards, anxious to break it down, were unaware. While DOC later tried to explain the rebellion as the logical result of several numerical factors related to crowding and understaffing —which, of course, could be alleviated with more city funds, and still more jails—Malcolm admitted that "it was not clear what their demands were. The spokesmen were making general attacks on the bail system, the courts, inadequate legal representation and the social conditions in this country and its effects on blacks and [H]ispanics." Attempts to cast this action as anything but an assault on the very social order of the United States would inevitably fall short.[28]

Outside the jail, upward of 450 guards, sixty cops, two NYPD helicopters, and two NYPD boats encircled the institution as negotiations dragged on. Judge Lasker made an appearance, as did four journalists, all at the prisoners' request. A lone injury occurred when Warden Louis Greco fumbled a tear gas grenade and it exploded in his hand. Tufo and Malcolm hazarded gas-laden air to enter an occupied cellblock through a hole in the wall, playing an instrumental role in negotiating for a peaceful resolution. In the end, the seventeen-hour revolt concluded with an agreement signed by Malcolm, Tufo, the Bronx district attorney, and a number of prisoner representatives. Against DOC's earlier resolution, it stipulated amnesty for prisoners, promised by both DOC and the DA, to be monitored by BOC. (Recall McGrath's duplicity on this point in 1970, when he promised amnesty to rebellious prisoners and simply shrugged when they were brought up on charges anyway.) No prisoners on the negotiating team would be transferred against their will. Moreover, DOC pledged to address "with all the resources at their command" the problems of overcrowding, bail, prisoner disciplinary procedures, harassment of visitors, and medical care. Finally, DOC agreed to "periodically" admit news media to check up on the institution's progress.

The rebel cellblocks lay in ruin. But unlike three years prior, there had been no great siege of guards. By breaking down the walls between their blocks, the prisoners had created a force that was far too large to be taken on by DOC's guards without considerable injuries or even death on both sides. It was a token of the prisoners' collective power—and not the benevolence of their captors—that at the moment the law-and-order coalition consolidated its control over New York City and US society more broadly, this rebellion was resolved peacefully, with some of their terms met.[29]

This was not happy news for everyone on Rikers. "Scarcely had this crisis ended," recounts Malcolm, "when another crisis developed. Approximately 550 correction officers from all the institutions on Rikers Island [except CIFM] had walked off the job in protest over the settlement and particularly amnesty." In particular, "they were extremely incensed over the presence of outsiders and the role they played in the final decision." No matter that it was the presence of such "outsiders" that had resulted in a peaceful and orderly end to the rebellion. In his first and only visit to Rikers Island as mayor, Beame toured HDM, praising the guards effusively, and as the *Times* reported, "shook his head in disbelief at smashed toilets, broken walls and heaps of make-shift weapons." Malcolm joined him, attempting to appease COBA while defending his position of providing amnesty, on the grounds that "another Attica could have been the outcome" otherwise. But COBA and its rank and file were no longer keen on tolerating any authority on Rikers except their own.[30]

In a prominent show of how the city was to function in the years ahead, as the guards' action escalated, COBA president Harold Brown was not content to meet with Malcolm; he wished to negotiate directly with Mayor Beame. COBA also drafted a telegram to Governor Carey, cosigned by the Correctional Captain's Association, requesting his intervention in DOC's handling of the rebellion, and characterizing the city justice system as "all too quick to make a correction officer a victim and let the inmate go unpunished." This was all announced during a belligerent press conference, at which COBA also addressed the people of New York directly. It was a fitting move, heralding their ascension as an autonomous political entity answerable to virtually nobody.[31]

City Hall, stretched so thin by dictates of austerity that Beame was sometimes brought to tears as he announced the latest cuts, was nonetheless cowed by COBA. Beame "agreed to the correctional officers' demands, for the right to continue carrying guns while off duty, the hiring of 50 more correctional officers for Rikers Island, and the division into quarters of the 355-footlong cell blocks in the Rikers jail to facilitate supervision by the correctional officers," Wynne recounts. "The mayor agreed to these conditions, which entailed great expense, even though other city departments were laying off staff and the city was facing bankruptcy." For its part, DOC responded to this latest rebellion by reducing the prisoner population at HDM by 1,000, achieved by sending prisoners to the infamous Sing Sing Correctional facility in Westchester County, and to a reactivated Bronx House of Detention. New and intense pressure, however, came from Judge Lasker's ruling in the ongoing *Benjamin v. Malcolm* case, finding that all DOC prisoners were entitled to a single cell. What's more, Lasker was just getting started.[32]

Time for Roy to Go

Within DOC, Roy Caldwood was officially recognized as a model guard, and even as a hero. He believed in the principles of penal welfarism and applied them in his daily interactions with prisoners and guards alike. On multiple occasions, Caldwood intervened to stop guard brutality, upholding the rules that he believed kept the institution both honest and functional. By his account, he fought against the culture of brutality within DOC daily, arguing for the fair and dignified treatment of prisoners. Caldwood received an official commendation for his role in ending the November 1975 rebellion, only the latest in a string of accolades spanning his decades of service in DOC. A guard since the days of Kross, Caldwood had climbed the chain of command, despite the fact that he was black during a time DOC was still very much a white boys' club. In this time, he had distinguished himself as a humanist administrator firmly in Kross's mold. But by 1975, Anna Kross was long gone, and avowed loyalists to penal welfarism were an endangered species in DOC.

In the months leading up to the rebellion, Caldwood had noticed a change on Rikers Island. Louis Greco, who had recently taken over HDM, openly ignored Caldwood, refusing to acknowledge him despite the fact that Caldwood was among the highest-ranking officers in the building. At this point, Caldwood began to encounter open insubordination from a guard who had a close relationship with Greco, and who encouraged his fellow "paisanos" to spurn cooperation with Caldwood's attempts to discipline him. One day, Caldwood was summoned to the control room, an unusual occurrence. Once inside, he discovered three prisoners from another building waiting for him—and no other guards in sight. They surrounded him menacingly, before taking leave. There was only one person in the jail who could have arranged such an elaborate scene, he reasoned. "To me, the message was clear," he recalls. "I could be dead at any moment."

That very day, Greco summoned him to his office for the first time, demanding Caldwood post new regulations all over the jail. Though this was surely a task below his rank, Caldwood agreed to do so. "No," Greco replied. "Don't have somebody else post them. I want YOU to do it—throughout the building.

And if any of them come down, I expect you to personally put them back up. I will hold you responsible." Caldwood's next stop was DOC headquarters to fill out retirement papers. There he learned Greco had already called, to inquire if he had enough time to retire. As a vestige of the Kross era, Caldwood was now an anachronism. It was, as he recalls, "time for Roy to go."[33]

18

Law and Order

Death Wish Politics

On Christmas Day 1977, Rikers Island received a special visitor: New York City's mayor-elect, Edward Koch. Abraham Beame's political career had been destroyed by the fiscal crisis and subsequent disclosure of the accounting tricks his office had undertaken to keep the city in the black. In contrast to the hapless Beame, who had buckled under the pressure of imposing austerity on New York City, the incoming mayor was a man uniquely suited for his time and place. Koch was born in 1924 to a working-class Jewish family in the Morrisania section of the Bronx, hit hard by the Depression. Thanks to free tuition at City College, Koch worked his way to New York University Law School, though his time there was punctuated by three years of service in World War II. An unremarkable lawyer handling wills and tort cases, Koch came somewhat late to politics, attracted to the failed 1956 presidential campaign of Democratic reformer Adlai Stevenson. In its course, however, Koch mixed with the reform Democrats of his new home of Greenwich Village and developed a taste for electoral politics. Koch developed a calculated relationship with the Village Independent Democrats, who sought to build power outside the Democratic-machine Tamawa Club, shifting his allegiances between the two with a shrewd eye to his own electoral future. This attention to expediency over ideals would define Koch's impressive political career.

Though opportunistic from the start, in the 1960s Koch had been a staunch liberal. In 1962 he ran for state assembly on a uniquely liberal platform his opponents derided as a "SAD" campaign: the repeal of anti-sodomy laws, better access to abortion, and easier legal avenues to divorce. While Koch lost that race, he reached the city council in 1966, capturing Lindsay's old congressional seat in Manhattan's so-called Silk Stocking district in 1968. At the time, Koch supported Lindsay's 1965 campaign for mayor and his reforms to the Civilian Complaint Review Board. He also opposed the Vietnam War beginning in 1966, backed Robert F. Kennedy's presidential campaign, and advocated for local and even federal rent control regulations. Most notably, at least in hindsight, Koch supported the forced integration of his own district's schools with the use of busing, placing himself on the left side of one of the most divisive issues in urban politics. Koch had also taken a particular interest in jails and prisons, campaigning for improved conditions at the Tombs prior to the 1971 rebellion. As a congressman, he distinguished himself from most other politicians by paying regular visits to the city's jails. By visiting Rikers once on Christmas 1977, Koch had already paid the island as many visits as mayor-elect as his predecessor Beame had during his entire tenure.[1]

Regardless of the sincerity of young Koch's liberal convictions, New York City's political landscape had dramatically transformed since the 1960s. The rise of an organized law-and-order coalition and racial tension typified by the Ocean Hill–Brownsville teacher's strike of 1968, which pitted black residents demanding community control against a white-dominated teachers' union, played out in tandem with diminishing city services and the downfall of Lindsay's vision for postwar New York. Above all, the fiscal crisis had sounded the death knell for the Great Society approach to poverty and race relations. What was left in its place was a cohesive bloc of capitalists bolstered by an equally organized bloc of cops and jail guards. This stubborn fact precipitated a change in Koch. When he campaigned as a moderate liberal, not unlike Lindsay, Koch found little to distinguish himself from a broad field of professional New York City politicians. When he rebranded himself as New York City's very own spokesman for Richard Nixon's so-called silent majority, however, Koch became adept at sounding the racial dog whistles of the city's cruel post-crisis politics. He had found a unique voice at long last.

Koch debuted his new persona in the early 1970s, when he voiced his opposition to a "scatter site" housing development in Forest Hills, which would bring low-income black and brown people to a largely middle-class Jewish neighborhood in Queens. Sensing an opportunity to build a base beyond his Greenwich Village stronghold and capitalize on the racial resentment of outer-borough ethnic whites, Koch joined the coalition against the development, led by an openly racist firebrand named Jerry Birbach, whose followers brandished signs with slogans like "Niggers Go Home." After appearing at one such rally and uncritically encouraging the crowd to keep up the fight, Koch broke with longtime friends and colleagues dismayed by his new alliances and their ostensible root in naked political ambition. Emboldened by his success, Koch turned to embrace two new themes: law and order, and austerity.

As a mayoral candidate in 1977, Koch capitalized on a redoubled popularity for racially tinged law-and-order politics that followed looting amid the July 1977 blackout, turning the race into a referendum on the death penalty—an issue over which New York City's mayor had no power. Koch baited black leaders as "poverty pimps" while maneuvering behind the scenes to get their support, in part by falsely promising to stop using this term. While promising to make dramatic cuts to city agencies, Koch simultaneously staked the position that he would fight the power of city unions, including PBA, even as he pledged to put more cops on the streets. In the end, the same political climate that produced the surprising and enduring popularity of Michael Winner's white vigilante fantasy film *Death Wish*—in which an ordinary man, pushed too far, resorts to extrajudicial violence to cleanse the streets of lawbreakers— also produced a Koch victory. "A *Death Wish* fever," write journalists Jack Newfield and Wayne Barrett, "raced through the hot city during the summer of 1977," culminating with the election of Koch.[2]

Catching the rightward-shifting winds of postcrisis New York, Koch argued government should facilitate private investment, rather than promote public services. It was a position in keeping with the FIRE sector takeover of the city government during the fiscal crisis, dramatically emblematized by the ouster of First Deputy Mayor James Cavanagh. A longtime Beame confidant and public opponent of public sector layoffs amid the crisis, Cavanagh famously declared that a "city is not a business," arguing therefore that city governments could not simply cut services and jobs people needed. Cavanagh was fired and replaced with developer John Zuccotti, who begged to differ. Finding himself at a crossroads, Koch adopted the mantle of Zuccotti: he campaigned openly for the city to be run for the sake of private profits. Koch's calculated political transition, for which he was greatly rewarded, was a sign of the times as potent as any.[3]

As such, Koch's visit to the House of Detention for Men on the eve of his mayoral inauguration constituted at best a dubious act of charity toward those locked up. Koch centered his remarks not on the conditions facing the prisoners, but on the morale of the staff. He pledged to mitigate the jail's problems by expanding DOC's capacity to cage New Yorkers. Koch was sure to emphasize that "the House of Detention for Men currently houses inmates who do"—and he stressed the word "do"—"belong here." However, he continued, so long as the men with whom he broke bread remained locked up "for the protection of the community," they deserved humane treatment. Therefore, Koch would seek $9 million dollars in funds to hire additional guards, to activate disused facilities, and to increase the capacity at Rikers Island by 1,668. Amid massive cuts to the city's public sector, when working-class New Yorkers were in desperate need of relief, Koch aimed to expand the capacities of DOC and, in particular, DOC's holdings on Rikers Island. Such was the cruelty of this era, so formative of our own.[4]

That same year, Benjamin Malcolm argued that while he supported efforts to improve the condition of city jails, "there was no constituency" for DOC. Malcolm predicted there would be no "Stavinsky-Goodman bill for correction," referring to a popular bill ensuring funding of public schools. Instead, he argued, "correction will always receive the crumbs of the criminal justice system." The Koch administration would, in time, prove Malcolm wrong. When the law-and-order coalition met the fiscal crisis, the recipe it devised for spending on police and prisons treated them not only as a mechanism of social control mitigating against movements from below, but as an austerity strategy in themselves. Moreover, politicians like Koch argued that harsh laws and brutal policing represented the only remedy to the social disorder wrought by capitalism in crisis. Many voters agreed. In the end, policing and jails were a less expensive, and thoroughly disempowering, alternative to welfare state spending. Human costs notwithstanding, jails were politically expedient, and a good investment to boot.[5]

Acting deliberately to institutionalize the shift in New York City's political economy introduced by the Emergency Financial Control Board, Koch's mayoralty bridged the gap between the austerity of the fiscal crisis and a return to stability predicated on a new order defined by policing, incarceration, and public governance for the sake of private profits. Accordingly, following political scientist John Hull Mollenkopf, we can divide Koch's mayoralty into two distinct periods. In the first period, Koch enforced austerity sufficient to discipline the city's public sector on behalf of its private sector, and DOC suffered cuts to personnel, alongside most city agencies, as part of deep cuts Koch dubbed the "Program to Eliminate the Gap" (PEG). In the second period, with the city returned to fiscal solvency, Koch undertook an aggressive expansion of DOC unrivaled by any city agency. This led to a considerable enlargement of both its staff and physical plants. The prisoner population throughout the DOC system swelled.[6]

Minimum Standards

Assuming office on January 1, 1978, Koch vowed to bring the jails up to constitutional standards and settle the numerous legal cases pending against DOC. Though Koch was the quintessential law-and-order candidate, it wasn't mere ideology that motivated his plans for jail expansion. The city was under pressure from the federal judiciary to either improve jail conditions or incarcerate fewer people. The 1974 closure of the Tombs had not resulted in the end of *Rhem v. Malcolm*, as DOC had hoped. Judge Lasker had rejected the city's argument that once transferred to the House of Detention for Men on Rikers Island, Tombs prisoners were no longer entitled to the rights they had won at the latter facility. Thus, the *Rhem* defendants at HDM retained certain victories such as one-hour daily recreation and, more importantly, brought the long arm of Judge Lasker to HDM, which now became the subject of judicial oversight. Even as the original *Rhem* defendants dwindled, an additional lawsuit was filed by HDM prisoners not covered by *Rhem*. Called *Benjamin v. Malcolm*, it also fell under Lasker's jurisdiction. The latter effectively subsumed the former. *Rhem* had crossed the river to Rikers, and it was not going away. However, Lasker was quick to point out that the courts' involvements in jails began only where public administration failed. Therefore, it was incumbent on the city to find not just a remedy for the ills of the city jail system, but also for the costly intrusion of federal courts in municipal affairs. Here Koch would have a partner in the Board of Correction.[7]

The year 1977 marked not just the twentieth anniversary of the Board of Correction, but also the beginning of an expansion of the board's role in city affairs. Thanks to a revision of the city's charter, BOC became responsible for establishing "minimum standards for the care, custody, correction, treatment, supervision, and discipline" of all people held in DOC custody, administering a standardized prisoner grievance program and continuing its traditional oversight role as originally defined. The board's new powers were backed by the ability to subpoena, by which the board could now demand documents, examine witnesses under oath, and work in tandem with courts to establish hearings on DOC affairs. Solidifying this independence, in July of 1977 BOC was established as an independent city agency, no longer under the aegis of DOC. BOC's new mandate translated, above all, into bringing DOC facilities into compliance with the federal courts. While the minimum standards were legally distinct from the consent decrees, in practice the two were blurred, due in part to the considerable overlap in their demands.[8]

BOC's minimum standards gained the additional support of the New York State Commission of Correction, a state-level agency with similar watchdog powers. Henceforth DOC would have to answer to BOC directly. More to the point, it would need explicit BOC permission to deviate from minimum standards. The newly empowered BOC did not mask its disdain for how the city had hitherto handled compliance with constitutionality. "The City's adversarial posture continued," the board lamented in 1978, "although courts found that many conditions in New York City Correctional facilities did not meet minimal constitutional requirements. Even when the Federal District Court, as well as the Second Circuit Court of Appeals, had condemned a practice in one institution, the City defended the same practice elsewhere in the system." As John Boston, veteran of the Prisoners' Rights Project of the Legal Aid Society, would remark decades later, "The system does not roll out reform; it quarantines it."[9]

As BOC's new standards—the so-called "Inmates' Bill of Rights"—were tried in the court of public opinion, Malcolm did his best to undercut public confidence in the feasibility of minimum standards, pointing to cost and administrative difficulty as factors that made prisoners' rights impractical. The savvy Malcolm kept BOC on the defensive and otherwise treading softly, even as its powers expanded at the expense of his own. Reflecting the ever-shifting allegiances of DOC politics, COBA initially sided publicly with the board, and against the commissioner, in supporting minimum standards. However, as the reality of an empowered board set in, COBA's new president, Richard Basoa, assailed it, calling for the resignation of Tufo, whom he dubbed "a playboy pseudo-penologist" wielding more knowledge of "the swells of the Upper East Side and [chic Park Avenue discotheque] Regine's than he does about the problems of the city's correction system."[10]

BOC passed its sweeping minimum standards on September 7, 1977. These standards were, in part, the product of compromise, rooted in the practical reality of imposing workable standards on DOC's crumbling facilities and its belligerent guards. They stipulated minimum requirements governing hygiene, clean clothing and bedding allowances, regular laundry service, protection against racial and religious discrimination, limited lock-in time (with an option to lock in during lock-out), access to daily recreation, access to lawyers and legal material, regular contact visits, telephone access, written correspondence with the outside world (including the receipt of packages and publications), and access to journalists. Of greatest consequence to the DOC administration were stipulations that limited involuntary guard overtime (albeit worded to allow significant managerial discretion); the promise of seventy-five square feet per pretrial prisoner; and a guarantee of single celling for every prisoner.

A final item, however—an allowance for temporary "variances" that would exempt DOC from compliance with individual sections or terms of the minimum standards—provided a considerable opening for noncompliance. Jails could violate the standards, provided they were issued a variance by the board. Regardless of this wiggle room, however, when Koch pledged to implement constitutionally sound jail conditions at his Christmas dinner at Rikers Island, he effected a sincere departure from the evasive and defensive posture of the prior administration. The city was ready to follow the law, Koch proclaimed. It was just going to need more time... and more jails.[11]

True to Koch's word, City Hall further assisted the effort by allocating $16 million dollars to DOC for the year 1979 to assist it in coming into compliance. For its part, BOC leaned on the private sector. Nonprofit organizations like the Ford Foundation, the New York Community Trust, the Burden Foundation, and the New York Foundation supplied BOC with added revenue. Simultaneously, these organizations abetted the city's abrogation of its most basic responsibilities to its people by allowing City Hall to shift its responsibilities to the private sector, which was ultimately not beholden to anyone. By providing for public services through private and revocable means, these organizations made themselves the underside of neoliberal governance: social goods funded by unaccountable private interests serving an explicitly private sector agenda.

Beginning in 1978, Koch's deputy mayor for criminal justice was Vera Institute founder Herb Sturz, who had long-standing ties to the Ford Foundation. Sturz's appointment was representative of the porous boundaries between City Hall and the city's elite nonprofits, which were called upon to govern for the sake of private profits amid the withdrawal of public services. Indeed, after leaving the Koch administration, Sturz was subsequently appointed the head of the City Planning Board, where he oversaw substantial real estate development in Midtown Manhattan and Long Island City. "What Sturz ... had in the way of planning background has never been clear," writes organizer and journalist Robert Fitch, "but Ford [Foundation] functioned as a kind of Triple A farm team for the Koch Administration (or was it the other way around?)." Sturz subsequently became a developer, moving seamlessly between the nonprofit world, city government, and the FIRE sector—in Fitch's words, "enabling him to appropriate in private life in the nineties the plans he developed in the eighties in the public sector." Sturz was emblematic of the role Ford and other ruling-class nonprofits played in the new face of New York City politics, thinly veiled by the pretense of benevolence.[12]

Back in 1978, BOC's power to set minimum standards was safe under Koch. However, DOC's willingness, or ability, to follow them was another matter altogether. In November 1979, with the minimum standards formally in effect across the jail system, the city signed several consent decrees with the Legal Aid Society, covering most of its ongoing litigation. This meant that litigation would be paused pending the city's willful compliance with standards set by the court. The influence of BOC and its sister agencies was palpable. "These agreements," the board reflected, "many of which reflect the language of the Board's minimum standards, saved the City the considerable time and resources which would otherwise have been expensed in costly litigation." *Benjamin v. Malcolm* was only the most famous of these. Bronx House of Detention for Men was embroiled in *Ambrose et al. v. Malcolm*, Brooklyn House of Detention in *Moctezuma et al. v. Malcolm*, Queens House of Detention for Men in *Webb et al. v. Malcolm*, Adolescent Remand and Detention Center in *Maldono et al. v. Ciuros*, Correctional Institute for Women in *Forts et al. v. Malcolm*. All were supported by the indefatigable Legal Aid Society. Settling these cases and bringing DOC into compliance with BOC and constitutional standards were Koch's primary managerial objectives. They were also part of a broader approach to manage the city and render it governable on the new terrain of an explicit austerity regime based around support for private capital and the dismantling of the noncarceral public sector.[13]

Management and Responsibility

As a candidate, Koch had courted not just disaffected ethnic whites in the outer boroughs, but also the increasingly powerful FIRE sector, which had emerged from the fiscal crisis in the driver's seat of New York City politics. As mayor, Koch set about restoring New York's credit rating by marketing himself in Washington, DC, as an agent of austerity. Appearing before Congress, Koch boasted of his 20 percent cut to the city workforce, forcible removal of hundreds of thousands of people from the welfare rolls, closure of day cares and fire stations, fare hikes on the subway, and the imposition of tuition at the City University of New York. Until this time, the university had been largely tuition free; pushed by student militancy, it had also recently adopted a policy of open admissions that precipitated an influx of working-class black and brown students. Cutting expenditures like free CUNY, Koch increased investment in spending that encouraged private development, along with spending on the managerial side of governance. Koch even assigned John Zuccotti to oversee monthly meetings reviewing departmental compliance with austerity, including DOC. BOC called this placement of DOC under the scrutiny of Zuccotti— its chairman Peter Tufo's law partner—an "extremely positive development."[14]

Koch's neoliberal ethos was reflected in the leadership of DOC in his first term. When Benjamin Malcolm vacated the commissioner's chair in November of 1977, he declared, "Free at last! Free at last!" and dedicated his emergency pager to "whoever has the guts, the intestinal fortitude, and the stupidity to succeed me." For a short time, that someone was twenty-five-year DOC veteran Joseph D'Elia, who served as acting commissioner under Beame and for whom DOC uniformed staff lobbied Mayor-elect Koch to appoint as commissioner. Koch opted instead for the deputy commissioner of DOC, forty-four-year-old William Ciuros. Hailing from the upstate prison town of Elmira, Ciuros had dropped out of high school to become a prison guard and worked his way up the ranks of the state system. Despite his correctional lineage, Ciuros would prove far less popular than Malcolm in DOC, thanks to policies that included a ban on informal coffee breaks, encouragement of civilian inspectors to monitor guard activities, the replacement of elective with mandatory overtime and, most controversially, restrictions on guards' use of force against prisoners.[15]

In a way reminiscent of the commissionership of Anna Kross, Ciuros undertook an extensive shake-up of uniformed brass. Dubbed the "Monday Morning Massacre," the shuffle applied to some seventy of DOC's highest-ranking officials; some were promoted, others demoted, but all were reassigned. Unlike Kross, however, Ciuros's motives were largely pecuniary. In most cases, those demoted had failed to prevent staff from taking excessive overtime and sick leave. This raised the hackles of COBA president Basoa, who called for Ciuros's removal, declaring: "Let's stop all the bull about him being out to improve the system. He wants to create a public-relations image of a reformer who can cut costs." Ciuros responded to the controversy his management inspired by accusing his detractors of resisting the reform of systematic abuses of power. "Good correction officers," he insisted, "are not frightened by me." An investigation by the *Times*, however, found Ciuros widely unpopular among the rank and file. Tufo, by contrast, praised Ciuros as a reformer.[16]

Ciuros was not acting on his own. At the onset of his mayoralty, Koch imposed a corporate management style on all his department commissioners. He demanded that they institute a complex evaluation system for their subordinates, with the option of assistance from private consultants, and that they submit biweekly progress reports. In a practice dating back to Lindsay that seemed to become more popular under Koch's austerity regime, unforeseen budgetary requests, such as a replacement generator for the Adolescent Remand and Detention Center totaling a mere $12,000, were made directly to the mayor using "declarations of emergency." At Koch's insistence, Ciuros also undertook "management and responsibility" trainings for ranking uniformed staff. While these trainings were couched in the patronizing frozen smile of corporate governance, inviting attendees to "enrich your careers as corrections professionals," Ciuros made their real intent clear.[17]

"No longer will I tolerate the imagined or conceptual Table of Organization that separates you from Central Office and aligns you with Correction Officers, Captains and Assistant Deputy Wardens," wrote Ciuros in an invitation to a mandatory training addressed to wardens and deputy wardens. "It is this misperception that has caused some of you to view your primary role as that of advocate for your subordinates. In fact, you are responsible for and are paid substantial salaries to help develop and then to carry out policy rather than defend others' failure of it." This was a bold assertion of civilian power, albeit in the name of austerity, not penal welfarism; the city was torn between the need to respect the newfound power it was giving its cops and guards, and the imperative to manage their agencies using the principles of fiscal austerity. In a letter to Koch outlining DOC's budgetary priorities in imposing the PEG austerity program, Ciuros argued that cutting his "analytics" staff of management specialists would constitute "the gravest of sacrifices for [the city's] financial security." Ciuros invested considerably in a scientific approach to management of staff and prisoners, spending $350,000 on a single computer as part of DOC's Management Information System. Moreover, Koch contracted a private firm to evaluate Ciuros's progress and to make recommendations for the more efficient management of the department.[18]

This attempt to foist more rational management on DOC was met by increasingly powerful guard unions, led by COBA, who brought their pursuit of arrogant autonomy to a new level. Phil Seelig, elected president of COBA in 1979, was a highly intelligent, manipulative, and belligerent fighter for untrammeled guard power. In 1980, a subset of unions representing housing police, NYPD, the fire department, DOC, and other "uniformed" unions undertook a move that further normalized the break with pattern bargaining. Bargaining as part of the Uniformed Forces Coalition, they effectively separated their negotiations from those of non-uniformed city unions. The leaders of these unions represented a new crop of combative law-and-order unionists produced by the mean and lean times of the late 1960s and early '70s. This new breed understood both the stakes of their historical moment and the ferocity required to win. While their alliance was originally disdained as amateurism by the city and long-standing municipal union politicians, such doubts were quickly put to rest. As it transpired, Uniformed Forces had claimed better contracts than even the representative of New York City's largest public employee union, Victor Gotbaum of DC37. Gotbaum was an avatar of professionalized municipal union politics who had bent over backward to accommodate the imposition of austerity during the fiscal crisis, but who now saw PBA, COBA, and other uniformed unions reaping the spoils.[19]

COBA made no secret of the violence at the root of their newfound power in city government, conducting intimidating street demonstrations reminiscent of those that took place at the height of the fiscal crisis, including a belligerent march on City Hall. Their bargaining team even displayed their guns during negotiations, as one negotiator conspicuously cleaned his fingernails with a knife. An anonymous city official complained to the *Times* that city guards tended to bring to negotiations "a sourness of outlook [and] a tendency to intimidate" that were the hallmark of their workplace. COBA's unapologetic showings of force were paired with emotional appeals to deaths in the line of duty, which these law-and-order unions falsely argued set them apart from all other city unions. Doubling down on arguments made in the late 1970s, the Uniformed Forces Coalition argued for a greater share than non-uniformed unions. They even endorsed the unabashed union buster Ronald Reagan for president in 1980—and again in 1984, after four devastating years for much of the non-uniformed US labor movement. As the old cliché runs, "I'm safe on board; pull up the life rope."[20]

No More Sweetheart Deals

While Koch and COBA were both part of the same compact with the FIRE sector, COBA feuded with Ciuros throughout his troubled commissionership, most vehemently over Koch's citywide policy to limit overtime for senior employees who were soon to retire. Pushed by Koch, Ciuros sought to end the common practice by which outgoing guards could inflate their pension considerably by taking on copious overtime in their final years, the salaries of which would determine their retirement rate. The new plan amounted to a limitation of overtime for these employees, and compulsory overtime across the board. As matters escalated, COBA took out a half-page advertisement in the *Daily News* threatening a slowdown action if Ciuros was not fired. An agreement was struck in advance of any further action, adding the possibility for guards to opt out of this imposed overtime. "I hope this signals a new era of cooperation with the union," Ciuros wrote to Koch, in a scrupulous recounting of the conflict, "but one in which they realized we will not be intimidated into making any more 'sweetheart' deals to keep labor happy at the expense of the future of this City." "You're absolutely right," Koch replied, "that there cannot be any more 'sweetheart deals to keep labor happy at the expense of the future of this City.'"[21]

The feud signaled a contradiction at the heart of Koch's governance. On the one hand, the mayor was beholden to reduce city expenditures across the board as part of an austerity regime conducted at the behest of the FIRE sector and politicians, locally and nationally, who looked upon New York as a decisive victory for the forces of neoliberalism. On the other, accomplishing such a rapid transformation of city institutions and working-class life required the cooperation of PBA, COBA, and other uniformed unions, who demanded compensation for the outsized role they now played in the city. To straddle this widening chasm, Koch essentially hid behind his commissioners and allowed them to take the heat for whatever austerity he had to visit on the cops and guards. In a letter to Ciuros praising his elimination of the "chronically ill" from DOC payroll, Koch declared: "Malingerers where identified should be removed forthwith wherever possible in accordance with departmental regulations. Keep it up!" By contrast, when Koch attempted to weaken the power of public sector workers by introducing at-will positions in a number of city agencies that were outside the purview of civil service law and thus far easier to manage, Ciuros wrote to Koch complaining that DOC was exempt; his power as commissioner would not be enhanced along with other commissioners, because DOC was not just any municipal workforce.[22]

Similarly, to eliminate waste and prevent lawsuits, Commissioner Ciuros was tasked with corporatizing a uniformed workforce that functioned like a cross between a branch of the armed services and a Cosa Nostra family. In a highly provocative move, he pressed charges against two assistant deputy wardens and a captain for negligence precipitating a suicide—the first time in DOC history that charges related to a suicide had been filed against a ranking officer. In what Ciuros claimed as retaliation for this, along with the earlier "shake-up," an anonymous group calling itself the "Coalition of Concerned Correction Personnel" drafted a statement denouncing Ciuros for a variety of offenses, including allegiance to "upstate political cronies," hiring unqualified staff, ethnic favoritism, throwing lavish parties and picnics, and even lying about his New York City residence. Ciuros addressed these charges in detail in a rebuttal addressed to Koch, except for one. "I stand by my exceptionally well-qualified Executive Staff," he wrote. "I also will not dignify the allegation that it is 'loaded with alcoholics' with an answer."[23]

Aware of their centrality to the new order in New York City, the rank and file of COBA became ever bolder and more confrontational. In response to the new overtime policy, for instance, the union slowed down prisoner transit. In turn, Koch and Ciuros floated the possibility that New York's anti-strike Taylor Law had been violated, but ultimately they gave up; escalation to that degree was not worth the trouble, just yet. COBA also picketed City Hall against what it considered the wrongful dismissal of probationary officers. In its most dramatic move to date, in July 1979 guards staged what COBA insisted was a wildcat walkout, bringing hundreds to the Queens side of the Rikers Island Bridge and blocking the bridge from prisoner transfer and other traffic as part of a fifteen-hour strike. Their principal demands concerned the guards' right to place prisoners under arrest and COBA's control over staffing matters pertaining to seniority. This time, Ciuros and Koch quickly invoked the Taylor Law, suspending a total of 856 guards, though the move was later reversed as part of a settlement. While the action was called a wildcat, it nonetheless had the full support of COBA president Phil Seelig. In the summer of 1980, another wildcat blocked the bridge to Rikers—a picket line solid enough that civilian employees had to board a ferry to get to work. The action was eventually halted by Seelig, who was at the bargaining table discussing the overtime policy.[24]

As non-uniformed unions were settling in for the long retrenchment ahead, COBA was flexing its muscles even more than it had before the fiscal crisis. Notably, the Rikers Island Bridge, a strategic chokepoint from which the functioning of city courts and jails could be brought to a virtual halt, was emerging as a strong tactical position from which COBA could bargain with the city. Of course, it was Koch, not Ciuros, who was the mastermind of the hated overtime restriction and other policies fueling their ire. But when it came to one pet COBA issue—guards' ability to resist alleged violence committed by prisoners—Koch was perhaps even more zealous than COBA. In all likelihood, Koch was simply pandering to the powerful union, offering them a victory at the expense not of the city coffers but the far more disposable rights of prisoners. Regardless, this matter brought Koch into conflict with Ciuros, whose managerial approach to DOC treated guard violence against prisoners as yet another facet of their power to be limited by administration.

Case in point, when Koch pressed Ciuros to promptly and indiscriminately arrest prisoners charged with assault on staff, Ciuros pushed back, arguing, "Sometimes the case in which the Union is most demanding is also the case in which the inmate is the victim and not the villain." In other words, Ciuros knew that often, the prisoner being painted as the aggressor had in fact been beaten up by guards, then charged with assault as a cover-up. Striking a position tailored to Koch's budgetary sensitivities, Ciuros continued, "If we arrest an inmate who assaults an officer while the inmate is awaiting shipment upstate, we must now house the inmate for an additional six months to a year in our facilities," thus constituting an undue expense. In this case, however, Koch was willing to foot the extra bill for the imposition of law and order.[25]

In a telling exchange, Koch even instructed Deputy Mayor Sturz to press the matter with Judge David Ross, and to "take whatever other steps are appropriate to see to it that we heighten the consciousness of judges on the need for consecutive sentencing in these matters." Koch's pressure campaign sheds light not simply on City Hall's treatment of a pet issue to the mayor, but, more broadly, on the kind of extrajuridical pressures placed on the city's judges during a period of rising political conservatism, when sentences were getting tougher. Beyond this particular disagreement, Ciuros found himself learning a lesson many city administrators had already grasped: Koch was a great friend—until he wasn't. Since taking office in 1978, Sturz had pushed a jail-reform agenda centered around the sale of Rikers Island to the state and its replacement with borough-based jails. Sturz deemed Ciuros insufficiently supportive of this plan and wanted him out. In the summer of 1979, he got his way.[26]

When Koch rearranged his deputies, he eliminated Sturz's title, demoting him to coordinator of criminal justice; as a consolation, however, Koch offered him the power to fire Ciuros. Sturz leapt at the chance, doing so within two days. There was just one problem. "We were worried about him," Sturz recalls.

At Rikers Island he held ceremonies and would march through the audience—the audience was largely comprised of convicts— in full dress regalia, literally with a sash. God knows where he found it. He was so proud. Upon learning of his ouster, he made one demand: he wanted to see the Mayor, who hired him. He felt that was his right. Later that afternoon we arranged this.

But one thing that we worried about was that Ciuros wore a gun in his ankle holster. [Corporation Counsel] Allen [Schwartz] and I were afraid he might take it out and try to shoot someone. This was after the Harvey Milk shooting in San Francisco. And yet we couldn't ask him, we felt, to disarm. I remember speaking to Koch's security guards, placing them at a slightly open door with a direct view of our meeting. Now, you might think this was melodramatic, but it was Ciuros's life. He'd suddenly been stripped of his job; caught in a power fight. It was tough.[27]

Ciuros didn't shoot anybody, resolving instead to remain outside the city's jails. Upon leaving office, he even echoed a choice expression of Kross's, declaring DOC to be "no longer a stepchild of the criminal justice system; rather, it is a professional, efficient, responsible municipal agency." Simultaneously, Sturz's plan to replace him with a more loyal commissioner proceeded. "Not only did I move on Ciuros," Sturz recalls, still savoring his victory years later, "but I immediately called Ben Ward and offered him the job of Commissioner of Corrections."[28]

Good Guys and Bad Guys

Benjamin Ward was born in a Central Brooklyn neighborhood he continued to refer to as Weeksville, after the community founded there by free black professionals in the mid nineteenth century. Ward's white father and black mother worked in show business. Early in his career, Ward served in the military police, drove a truck, and collected garbage; later, he became a cop, and earned a law degree through Brooklyn College. Ward subsequently chaired the Civilian Complaint Review Board in the contentious year of 1966, served as commissioner of the state prison system, and briefly worked at the Vera Institute, where he met and befriended Sturz. Though regarded by at least one DOC union as a welcome change from Ciuros, Ward had left DOC under acrimonious terms, declaring he was moving to a job with the housing police, "where one can tell the good guys from the bad guys, at least with more certainty than corrections."[29]

Upon his return to corrections, however, Ward swore allegiance to Sturz's plan to sell Rikers and build borough-based facilities. Yet Ward simultaneously carved out a position skeptical of bail reform—among the only possible means of lowering the prisoner population, short of taking on the sacred cow of NYPD autonomy. "One of the great weaknesses in American jurisprudence," he once argued, "is that judges do not pay enough attention to public safety in bail decisions." Ward later recalled that he was leery of Koch's racial politics, especially his language denouncing the Great Society "Model Cities" Program, and the notorious remarks about "poverty pimps." While conceding that neither Model Cities nor community-based anti-poverty programs were above reproach, Ward recalls, "The way he said some of the statements, you know, it made you a little nervous about it ... I didn't think I'd ever work for him."[30]

Tension around race was an undeniable aspect of Ward's commissionership. Ward was happy not to have to deal with the Ku Klux Klan, as he did as commissioner of the state correction system, when he felt the need to issue a directive forbidding employees from belonging to the Ku Klux Klan. But he nonetheless encountered malicious white chauvinism from some uniformed DOC staff, including members of a DOC branch of the Columbia Association, an advocacy group for Italian Americans. In a letter to Koch, whom it sized up to be a potential ally, the organization charged Ward had "wrongfully singled out many Italian Americans with years of dedicated service in correction and made them seem inept. On the other hand, he has promoted and/or elevated others with horrendous records, simply because they are ethnically acceptable." Columbia Association president Frank Bruni wrote Koch charging, with clear racial implications, that the mayor found it "Politically Expedient to have him as your Commissioner." Bruni forwarded to Koch a letter addressed to Ward (also forwarded to "every Italian American Politician" in the city) denouncing Ward for his pernicious discrimination against Italians, noting that the "history and dedication of Italian Americans in this department ... is a rich one and has not yet been topped by any other ethnic group." Citing Italians' "hereditary trait of being a proud people," Bruni informed Ward he was not welcome at the Columbus Day Parade.[31]

Ward pursued, at least outwardly, the controversial Koch policy of "civilianization" of DOC. This was operated under the auspices of PEG cuts, which amounted to the creation of lower-waged civilian roles to replace uniformed guards in functions like staffing DOC mailrooms. However, retention proved difficult in these positions, due in part to COBA hostility to these nonunion jobs, as rank-and-file guards made them very unpleasant on the day-to-day level. Moreover, Ward continued to enforce Koch's overtime policy, which was sure to draw COBA's ire. Well into Ward's tenure, COBA president Seelig declared, in his characteristic idiom, that "most orders that come out [from DOC administration] are promulgated for one of two reasons—either to have a Damoclean sword hanging over every officer's head as a means of social control, or to find scapegoats."

Seelig was hardly reinventing the wheel with his criticisms of Ward's administration, which echoed COBA's line stretching back decades. On the other hand, it is impossible to overstate the amount time spent by DOC management, operating in tandem with Koch's City Hall, to cut costs, while lower-level managers were made to feel less secure in their own positions should they fail. The model DOC and other agencies followed during this period is undeniably corporate, from its elaborate charts and data sets to its euphemistic managerial jargon. More importantly, city management emphasized not just short-term cost savings, but a long-term realignment of the balance of power that Seelig aptly termed "social control." By expanding managerial capacities to impose austerity, planners sought not simply to save money in the coming fiscal year, but also to advance their long-term interest of disempowering the workforce. This placed the civilian administration at odds with the city's guards once more, not in the name of anything as lofty as penal welfarism, but in accordance with the dictates of neoliberal governance.[32]

Most importantly, Ward also oversaw the continuing expansion of DOC capacities on Rikers Island. The flagship of Koch's plan for a revitalized Rikers Island was meant to accommodate the influx of New Yorkers swept off the streets under the new regime of law and order. Designated for basic custodial incarceration, the facility bore an ironic name: Anna M. Kross Center. Technically known as C-95, AMKC was conceived as a "support building" for C-71, the facility Kross herself had opened as the Adolescent Reformatory back in 1962 as an adjunct to the Penitentiary. C-71 thus lacked administrative space, a dining area, or any other amenities enabling it to function as an independent facility. By design, the three-story C-95 structure added these support facilities and space for 768 dormitory beds. Despite the facility's name, there was no space for prisoner programming. Though the building was dedicated on November 12, 1977, as Kross-era BOC member Rose M. Singer stood by, it could not open immediately, due to short staffing.[33]

It was this very lack of staffing that Koch meant to remedy with his $9 million promise in 1977. But AMKC had bigger problems than short staffing. Just three years after its opening, with AMKC still not fully operational, DOC found the facility already in need of significant infrastructural repair, with water leaking onto electrical equipment, no smoke detection or sprinkler system, and basic amenities like toilets and sinks in disrepair. This was in addition to a host of other oversights, including a lack of industry-standard security functions like reinforced ceilings and walls. AMKC, DOC concluded, was "a monument to the folly of cutting development budgets ... and to the poor quality of construction which results when there is inadequate involvement in the development process by the user/client." The only defensible use of the building, the department argued, was to repurpose it to include no housing at all. In sum, the problems nagging DOC's newest facility were emblematic of a citywide failure of DOC institutions and programming to stay on the right side of minimum standards and the law.[34]

They Could Have Done a Lot Less

As early as the end of 1977, Peter Tufo had observed that DOC lacked a long-term plan for bringing its institutions into compliance with BOC's minimum standards. "It is, I believe, the desire and intent of the City of New York to implement the standards at the earliest possible date," Ciuros wrote to Koch in October of 1978. "However, lack of personnel in many instances, will lead to partial, and even total non-implementation." In the city's 1979 budget, Koch set aside an additional $16 million to support compliance with the standards. By early 1979, just months after the minimum standards had taken effect systemwide, BOC was beset with several variance requests, to which it typically granted stays of four and six months to delay compliance. Tufo told DOC leadership, as BOC minutes paraphrase: "Disagreement in costs or means of implementation was acceptable, but disagreement on principle was not." Despite intermittent tough talk from Tufo, this formula provided considerable wiggle room for claims to no-fault noncompliance, for which DOC simply needed to prove its variances were filed "not because of negligence" but due to some external factors, of which there was no shortage. For instance, DOC officials cited the prevalence of cell vandalism, which, by no fault of its own, necessitated double celling. Moreover, DOC claimed the hiring of additional guards to be a necessary step toward compliance, without which noncompliance was to be expected. Tufo confronted DOC general counsel Larry Finnegan with a letter from the Legal Aid Society asserting, "The history of the Department's response over the years to the Minimum Standards, as well as to court orders, is that it will move only so fast as it is absolutely required to move." Finnegan begged to differ. In response, he cited DOC's adolescent recreation program, insisting, "We could have done a lot less."[35]

Ward's own position on the consent decrees illuminates DOC's attitude under his tenure as commissioner. During Beame's mayoralty, Ward recounts, he had "stonewalled the federal courts, which is not too smart, not too swift. Those federal judges served for life, and they're tough as hell, and they're not going to take stonewalling, and promises to do things, and then you don't do them." Ward reasoned that Koch was correct in wanting to work with the courts rather than against them. However, to Ward's mind, Koch bent the stick too far in the opposite direction by entering into consent decrees that actually exceeded the constitutional requirements for incarceration. Ward made his feelings known to Koch, going so far as to refuse to sign any of the decrees himself, insisting instead that the corporate counsel handle it, since he was the city's attorney. Thus, while Ward did not publicly oppose the consent decrees, a position that likely would have put him at odds with Sturz on the city stage, he nonetheless privately doubted their wisdom.

By contrast, Ward believed prisoners were only entitled to the legal minimum outlined in the US Constitution, which could be a lot less than what DOC was on the hook for providing. "Just because you built a gym," Ward later argued, "doesn't say you have to play basketball. When we signed the consent decree we not only had to play basketball in the gym, we had to build more gyms." Ward contrasted this with the federal prison system, which evaded consent decrees altogether, retaining considerable freedom to deal with crowding on the basis of need alone. "What the Feds did was turn [gymnasiums] into dormitories. They didn't like basketball. Play ping pong. Play checkers. Because we need this space to make beds."[36]

As Ward's DOC fell consistently short of compliance, Tufo's BOC remained committed to mediation over litigation and provided DOC with a wide berth to consistently violate the prisoner rights BOC was supposed to be enforcing. "If we believe we are not being stonewalled," Tufo told a skeptical Clay Hines, of Legal Aid's Prisoners' Rights Project, "and if we have seen reasonable efforts to show that what can be done administratively is being done, then we believe taking the Department of Correction to court would not be helpful." When COBA attacked BOC for mandatory overtime pursuant to the minimum standards, however, Tufo traveled to Rikers Island to explain to guards that it was the consent decrees, and not the minimum standards, that they should blame. On another occasion, Tufo advised his fellow board members to remember that "the compliance report only shows where there is not compliance and not where there is compliance." In a February 1980 BOC meeting, following considerable new hiring, board member Wilbert Kirby pointedly asked Commissioner Ward for an update on just how many guards it would take for minimum standards to be met. "Mr. Ward," the minutes reflect, "replied that it was impossible to give such a number and that it was unrealistic to state that by some magical date in the future the Department would be in compliance."[37]

Austerity bore down on DOC, as it did on just about all agencies, save City Hall management during the early Koch years. However, it was the noncustodial aspects of DOC administration that suffered the most during this period. Classification protocol proved faulty and ill applied, or else nonexistent, across the system—most surprisingly at the Correctional Institute for Women, the penal welfarist flagship of Rikers Island. There, prisoners were admitted without even speaking to a mental health professional unless their file specified a prior record of mental health issues or unusual behavior. Upon hearing this, BOC member David Schulte "commented that if a classification system could not be made to work at the CIFW, it would never work anywhere." Fifty-one doctors working for Prison Health Services were laid off in 1979. Mental health services were among the worst impacted, emblematizing the generalized apathy toward noncustodial programming of any kind.

"The frustrations of working to improve prison mental health services," BOC wrote in 1979, "are compounded in times like these and easily give way to the norm which says: 'we're doing the best we can with these inadequate resources.' Defeating that attitude becomes an important part of the change process." BOC was not, however, naive in its assessment of the city terrain. Tellingly, they remarked: "These same resource stringencies require that we alter the nature of our response. Ten years ago, one could have discussed mounting a political effort to generate money for new programs and staff. That simply won't work today. Instead our activities must be geared to finding solutions within the limited dollars available."[38]

19

Lines of Flight

Escape from Rikers Island

In this period of grim austerity, with the Department of Correction hemmed in on all sides by the twin scourges of neoliberalism and law and order, one radical option remained: evacuation of Rikers Island. Deputy Mayor Herb Sturz's proposal for the sale of Rikers Island to the state, and the opening of "cost-effective, modern decentralized facilities," not only provided an alternative to DOC's growing penal colony on Rikers, but also allowed DOC to defer improvements on Rikers pending the outcome of the deal. In September of 1979, the city entered into an agreement that postponed further action on *Benjamin v. Malcolm*, contingent on the sale. According to this plan, a phased process of transfer from city to state would culminate in the reopening of the Tombs, the erection of similar facilities located near borough courts, and the final transfer of Rikers to the state for use as a prison for prisoners approaching release from the state system. The renovated Tombs, based on the most cutting-edge principles of environmental design, would be the prototype for eight borough facilities, including another Manhattan jail nearby.

It seemed simple enough—on paper. However, New York City and New York State proved ruthless negotiators. By DOC's account, as negotiations advanced, the state threw the city a curveball in early 1979 by demanding the handover of the Correctional Institution for Women and C-74, "the two best facilities on Rikers," during the first phase of the transfer; it subsequently rejected all proposed compromises. In the summer of 1979, both parties agreed to a ninety-nine-year lease, but the terms of the transfer continued to be hotly contested. The proposals included a plan to split the island in half, which of course implied questions over which facilities would fall on whose half, in addition to countless financial logistics surrounding this intricate deal.[1]

An initial memorandum of understanding specified September 1979 as the beginning of the transfer, with CIFW the first facility to change hands. By late June, however, many details remained up in the air, most ominously those of cost. As crunch time approached, the long-term savings associated with extricating the city from consent decrees, in addition to the far more abstract moral rewards of housing prisoners in adequate facilities, increasingly paled, in the city's eyes, in comparison to the estimated $15 million in added operations costs it would assume by staffing new facilities in compliance with the decrees. For instance, the new Tombs would require a staff of 350 guards and one hundred civilian employees, all to administer 450 prisoners. By 1980 standards, it would be an astronomical jump in ratio. The city's Office of Management and Budget and Board of Estimate made clear to DOC that they would simply not finance such a rise in operation costs.

Though BOC was an enthusiastic proponent of the deal, it soon defaulted to the passive voice, claiming that "interim arrangements have to be made." Meanwhile, Phil Seelig's Correction Officers Benevolent Association opposed the plan on the grounds that it was too costly and threatened the communities in which the new jails would be built. The advantage of Rikers, Seelig argued, was that it boasted a river between any escaping prisoners and the nearest New York neighborhood. The penal colony was, in his words, "cheap and safe." COBA simultaneously found common ground with Queens residents opposing the state facility on Rikers, which to them was apparently the greater of two evils. The union joined forces with so-called NIMBY ("not in my backyard") activists for a thousand-strong march through Queens. Waving American flags, the demonstrators rallied once more at the foot of the Rikers Island Bridge.[2]

While the NIMBY forces cited the greater security threat purportedly posed by prisoners convicted of serious crimes—regardless of the fact many would have to pass through Rikers anyway en route upstate—COBA's opposition was more complicated. The group had for decades taken issue with DOC's inadequate plant facilities, which at the Brooklyn House of Detention for Men, in particular, had become indefensible from any angle. Moreover, the new facilities would require more guards, another perennial demand. Against these benefits of new jails, however, COBA had to weigh the possession of a fortified paramilitary island under the control of a powerful and centralized uniformed force of guards who were increasingly comfortable taking militant direct action. As a base of operations, Rikers was simply too strong a position for COBA to give up without a fight. As time wore on, the date of transfer continued to change, with numerous logistical loose ends left untied. Disputes over the logistics of the transfer increasingly spelled doom for the project.

The Board of Correction held out hope until the end, holding a series of public hearings and drafting an elaborate set of recommendations in support of the transfer. Shortly after the recommendations were released, Mayor Koch summarily killed the plan, citing the high costs of building new facilities. When reporters asked Koch if the plan was truly dead, the ordinarily verbose mayor responded with one word in the affirmative. Asked if negotiations would resume, Koch provided one word in the negative. "Did you ever get such short answers?" he teased his interlocutors. As an alternative, Koch pledged $40 million to get the existing city jails up to compliance.[3]

The expenditure of $40 million, and likely more, would be necessary almost immediately; the city was at once back on the hook with Judge Morris Lasker. Finding "the lease has failed of consummation," Lasker proceeded with enforcement of the consent decrees. He responded to the plaintiff's demand for a cap of 1,000 on the population at HDM—at the time home to 1,500 prisoners—by mandating a population cap of 1,200. Lasker also underscored to DOC that all decrees were back in full effect. Koch instructed DOC to produce a capital construction program capable of bringing the existing facilities up to compliance with minimum standards and the consent decrees, which it did in September, titled *Jails for the 80s*. The study is a damning assessment of DOC's holdings on Rikers. "It is today hard to believe that a facility intended for adolescents would be built with dropped metal pan ceilings in areas accessible to inmates," DOC wrote, of ARDC, where "inmates routinely remove the supporting metal struts, sharpen them, and use them as weapons." HDM was found to have "outlived its useful life" and stood in need of closure and replacement. In short, to solve the problems of its old jails, DOC needed new ones.[4]

"Rikers Island," the report sourly notes, "conceived originally as a complex for sentenced inmates, has been forced to become a detention center." This was a bitter pill to swallow. But plans to vacate Rikers were off the table for the time being, and DOC would therefore have to make do with that it had. DOC's new capital plan called for upgrading the Correctional Institution for Men, C-71, and the Adolescent Remand and Detention Center, while working toward the closure of HDM. The Rikers Island Hospital would be closed and replaced with a new Rikers facility, and the Tombs was to be reopened as quickly as possible, along with a new maximum-security detention facility with 500 beds, also in Lower Manhattan. The other borough facilities were to remain operational, amid modifications to recreation and programming areas, and basic physical plants, to bring them to compliance with consent decrees. The new construction emphasized maximum-security cells over dormitories, though there was to be a new dormitory at the Brooklyn House of Detention for the one hundred or more sentenced prisoners forced to work there. The plan was based in part on shifting DOC's center of gravity away from Rikers Island, where pretrial detainees were never meant to live. DOC was, however, shoveling against the tide.[5]

"It continues to be our position," BOC chairman Tufo wrote Koch in response to the new capital plan, "that Rikers Island is unsuitable for the housing of pre-trial detainees, and that the only rational correction system is one in which those awaiting trial are housed in jails located close to the borough court houses."[6] Nonetheless, BOC continued to provide variances that allowed Rikers facilities to continue functioning—and, in fact, to proliferate. BOC's continuing complicity in the expansion of Rikers was a testament to the dour pragmatism that prevailed in this period. "In a time of shrinking resources," BOC itself lamented, "'improvements' are often in fact the avoidance of decline; 'success,' is the absence of failure." Asked later if Koch had a particular agenda for DOC, Commissioner Ward replied that "he had the same agenda as every other chief executive officer has. Sit on the lid of the can and keep the garbage inside. Don't let it rise. Don't let them get out." Even this purely custodial task, however bluntly Ward described it, would prove impossible.[7]

Patron Saint of Prison Breaks

The bureaucrats were not alone in plotting a dramatic exit from Rikers. The spirit of resistance among DOC's captive population continued unabated in this period, aided by the corrosion of DOC facilities and an overtaxed workforce. These factors would catalyze a new wave of impressive jailbreaks. Looking back on 1977, BOC recalled ruefully that the year "will be remembered as a year of many escapes from Rikers Island," totaling thirty-five successes, to say nothing of attempts. These pushed the total of escapes from DOC custody since 1974 to 153. A steady stream of hacksaws winnowed its way into Rikers jails, enabling multiple exoduses, including from the maximum-security area of HDM reserved for prisoners deemed escape risks. According to DOC, in one case blades were smuggled into the jail concealed inside fully functional ink pens, which family members had given prisoners in court. Purportedly, these pens were capable of passing a basic contraband test, by which the prisoner was made to uncap the pen and write with it, to prove it contained an ink cartridge. For reasons that will soon be clear, however, it is a story to be taken with a grain of salt.

As DOC facilities crumbled and teemed, prisoners increasingly escaped in large groups, sometimes as many as eight at a time, by cutting their way out of HDM and other facilities. As in the early 1970s, these escapes demonstrated not only familiar patterns, but also featured a recurring cast of prisoners who at once rejected the authority of DOC and undertook ingenious attempts to proactively free themselves from its custody. Their efforts challenged not just the power of the jail system, but the authority derived from politicians, like Koch, who based their fiscal austerity on their supposed ability to keep lawbreakers behind bars.[8]

In 1977 three adolescents locked up at ARDC broke free, crept to the guards' parking lot, commandeered a guard's car, and successfully drove straight off the island, past multiple checkpoints, to the freedom of suburban Queens. In response to this embarrassing breach of security, DOC hastily claimed the young men had undertaken a sophisticated—and highly cinematic—jailbreak, complete with meticulous timing of guards' comings and goings, and even counterfeit badges to get past the checkpoints. It was a compelling story. But there was one problem.

"There was no evidence to sustain that story," BOC concluded. "What was known at the time the Department was being quoted [in the press, about its imaginative version of the escape], is that the inmates took advantage of two inattentive correction officers who simply weren't doing their jobs." Three years later a trio of prisoners pulled off a "carbon copy" of this escape, leaving a hapless guard's car at John F. Kennedy Airport for investigators to discover the following day. Less successful but no less bold were a group of twenty-four prisoners who took over a transport bus moving them between Rikers facilities and attempted to drive it off the island. Their plot was foiled when the driver crashed the bus. Foregoing the bridge altogether, a quartet of prisoners inflated trash bags into makeshift rafts, greasing themselves and the bags with Vaseline to stay afloat. The bags proved insufficient to the task and burst, but one of the four nonetheless made it across. Subsequently, a pair of Rikers prisoners concealed themselves in a truck delivering stale bread to the Flushing Meadows Zoo. The duo's disappearance was only detected by the driver, whom they startled by hopping off the back of the truck on Grand Central Parkway and vanishing into the freedom of the Queens night.[9]

Rikers was not the only place DOC prisoners deemed worthy of escape. In 1980, a famed horse trainer and Upper East Side socialite named Howard "Buddy" Jacobson, held at the Brooklyn House of Detention following a murder conviction, received a visit in the facility's counsel room from a man purporting to be his lawyer. During this visit, the men swapped clothing and identification. Jacobson then tapped on the door, announced the visit had ended, flashed his supposed lawyer's credentials, and strode out the front gate of BHD to freedom, leaving the latter, apparently well-compensated for the ruse, to face charges for abetting escape.

In early 1982, a group of six prisoners in the south wing of the sixth floor of the Bronx House of Detention overpowered the two guards overseeing their cellblock, bound them, and placed them in the dayroom while attempting to saw through a window with hacksaw blades. One guard managed to set off his emergency alarm before being overpowered, but when the control room called, a prisoner answered, posing as a guard, and reported a false alarm. A third guard appeared shortly thereafter; welcomed inside by a prisoner dressed in a captured guard's uniform, he was also taken hostage. The plot was at last detected when the guards on duty did not respond to calls for a coffee delivery. The tour commander responded in haste, flanked by a small squadron of guards who foreswore riot gear, rushing to the scene so quickly they forgot the keys to the tier's gate. Once inside, they fought the prisoners with their clubs, viciously beating the rebels in a manner BOC found "completely disproportionate to the circumstances." There were no consequences for the guards.[10]

This wasn't the most spectacular escape attempt that year—
or even that month. Less than two weeks later, ten prisoners in
transit at the Brooklyn Supreme Court escaped leg irons and
handcuffs to overpower three guards, one of whom provided
them with a gun that a fleeing prisoner used to carjack a motorist,
shooting the motorist in the process. In a scathing 1982 report to
the mayor and city council, BOC concluded: "Despite the image
of prisoners furtively digging tunnels or quietly sawing through
bars to escape, prisoners are more likely to escape by recognizing and taking advantage of lax or poorly trained personnel
and inadequate or loosely enforced security procedures." For his
part, the studious Ward attributed the rash of escapes to several
factors. The erection of the Rikers Island Bridge, he reasoned,
had slowed the East River current; the extension of the LaGuardia Airport runway provided an attainable goal for swimmers;
and an increase in detainees meant an increase in smuggling,
since they had more visits than sentenced prisoners. Moreover,
technology had advanced, bequeathing better jailbreak tools
such as smaller and more powerful saw blades. DOC's Joseph
D'Elia was markedly more defensive, telling BOC, "An escape is
made on an officer, not on a system."[11]

One escape of this storied period stands out so spectacularly
that it prompted artist David Wojnarowicz to immortalize its
protagonist as "William Morales, Patron of Prison Breaks." Part
of the diminished, but by no means vanquished, revolutionary
underground, William Guillermo Morales manufactured bombs
for the Puerto Rican Armed Forces of National Liberation
(FALN), who fought for an autonomous Puerto Rico. Morales
and his comrades in FALN had operated under the radar for
years, detonating over one hundred explosive devices throughout the mid to late 1970s, without a single member being
arrested. On July 12, 1978, a bomb Morales was manufacturing
in a house not far from Rikers Island detonated prematurely.
The blast destroyed Morales's hands and mutilated his face.
Badly burned, maimed, bleeding profusely, missing one eye, and
virtually blind in the other, Morales managed nonetheless to

flush a number of incriminating FALN documents down the toilet before the police arrived. He then filled the apartment with gas, hoping to blow himself up along with the cops. Instead, Morales was captured. Despite his grave condition, he managed shortly thereafter to tell a NYPD detective, from beneath layers of bandages, "Fuck you. Fuck yourself."[12]

In April of 1979, after Morales had been held for over a year at the prison ward of Bellevue Hospital, he was convicted of weapons charges and sentenced to twenty-nine to eighty-nine years behind bars. Prior to sentencing, Morales remarked, "They're not going to hold me forever." One month later, this prediction was borne out. Morales managed to get hold of a pair of fourteen-inch wire cutters, which NYPD suspected his attorney smuggled to him, though she was never formally charged. With the help of a fellow prisoner, Morales subsequently affixed these cutters around his waist using shoelaces, so that they dangled beneath his bathrobe. Over the course of the next two nights, despite having lost his hands and much of his sight, Morales cut a small hole in the metal grating covering his window. He then punched through the outside screen, produced a rope made of bandages, and began his descent from his third-floor room, some forty feet in the air.

Waiting on the ground below were more than a dozen cadre from the remnants of the Black Liberation Army and the Weather Underground. The bandage rope apparently failed, sending Morales tumbling to an air conditioner unit that broke his fall, and then onto the grass below. His comrades whisked him away to a New Jersey safe house, from which he later made his way to Mexico, then Cuba, where he lives today as a free man. A mortified and enraged Ciuros, ridiculed for the escape of a handless man from DOC custody, pursued a slew of administrative charges against sixteen guards and captains responsible for every conceivable failure leading to the escape. The story became less about the tenacity of the enduring revolutionary underground and more about the latest fiasco for DOC's Keystone guards.[13]

Doubling Up, Doubling Down

These escapes demonstrated considerable prisoner ingenuity, but they were also symptomatic of a jail system that remained stretched to the breaking point. In the aftermath of the fiscal crisis, as the social crisis attendant to austerity politics was met with the brute force of law and order, the sheer number of people being hauled off the streets and crammed into DOC's teeming facilities was overwhelming. For the city, the situation was increasingly dire as their own plan to escape Rikers Island fell apart. While career guard Eric M. Taylor, whose name today adorns the C-76 building, made the move to DOC after being laid off from NYPD, many police in similar circumstances resumed their old jobs as quickly as the latter would have them back. Indeed, NYPD quickly recuperated the modest staffing losses it suffered at the height of the city's budget cuts, leaving DOC facilities like the Adolescent Remand and Detention Center suddenly short staffed. Compounding inadequate staffing, Lasker affirmed a previous ruling by Judge Orrin Judd demanding the end of double celling for pretrial detainees, who constituted the vast majority of prisoners in facilities with cells. While BOC's minimum standards were negotiable, this was not. This joined Lasker's cap of 1,200 at HDM, and a fifty-prisoner cap on the dormitory population at the Anna M. Kross Center, which proved ever more difficult to observe as the population rose.

By early 1981, DOC had opened a fifth quad at C-71 and four new dormitories for newly admitted prisoners at C-95, and had shifted sentenced prisoners to the C-95 dormitories. These solutions, however, served only to spread HDM's problems across the island, as C-71 now became the site of double celling and C-95's dormitories exceeded standard capacity. In what had become a matter of course, DOC sought a variance from a sympathetic BOC, and received it. Simultaneously, the practices of housing prisoners in nonhousing areas such as gymnasiums became standard across the system. Through the early 1980s, DOC's pretrial prisoner population would climb steadily, while crowding in the upstate jails would increase the backlog of sentenced prisoners awaiting transfer into the state system.[14]

The racialized law-and-order ideology that Mayor Koch relied on to retain legitimacy and power prevented the reining in of NYPD, to say nothing of proposals to mitigate overcrowding by setting prisoners free. Instead, as part of an eight-point plan to reduce crowding, Koch favored the erection of temporary modular units on Rikers Island, akin to the mobile homes provided in the wake of major disasters—which wasn't far off the mark. In March 1981, the Board of Estimates voted to purchase modular units that would add 300 beds to Rikers Island. Judge Lasker tentatively approved the units, while clarifying that they too fell under court jurisdiction. Construction of the first batch was completed by early August. Simultaneously, the city, with increasing tenacity, began to campaign against the seventy-five-square-foot-per-prisoner requirement BOC had imposed on dormitories. Regardless, BOC was typically amenable to crowding variances, allowing DOC to rely on their routine provision to keep its facilities running. By the end of 1981, sentenced prisoners, not covered by the square footage mandated by BOC, were given an estimated thirty-five to forty square feet of space—roughly half the board's requirement for pretrial detainees. BOC kept the variances coming as DOC made a mockery of its minimum standards throughout the system.[15]

BOC also supported, at a pivotal juncture of New York State's carceral history, the Security through the Development of Correctional Facilities Bond Act of 1981. It was a massive prison expansion plan, put to statewide ballot initiative, that would net $50 million for DOC facilities and allocate a staggering $450 million for new beds in the state system. By Tufo's estimation, the city's share would allow DOC to comply with minimum standards at long last. The board was therefore willing to throw in its lot with nascent mass incarceration in New York State, in the name of jail reform in New York City. The consensus was not unanimous. Board member Wilbert Kirby disputed the notion that locking more people up would somehow reduce crime. Echoing the cynical pragmatism of the era, vice-chairman John Horan responded that not only would the act enable compliance with minimum standards, but "it was utopian to presume that other approaches such as alternatives to incarceration would stand a better chance of succeeding if the Bond Issue were defeated." State Commission of Correction chairman Kevin McNiff had previously argued to the board that the city, in particular, ought to support the measure, given that the state could get its desired funding by other means should the measure be defeated—a feat not so easy for the localities. This prediction proved prescient: the initiative was, in fact, defeated in the polls, and New York State subsequently circumvented the wishes of its voters, digging up the money for prison expansion through clever state budgetary tricks that DOC was unable to replicate on the municipal level.[16]

While the plan to leave Rikers had fallen through, construction for the Tombs proceeded. The Tombs had been reactivated for a short period, in response to large-scale arrests during the July 1977 citywide electricity blackout. Upward of a dozen detainees had been crammed into each tiny cell, where they were chained together and deprived of mattresses and phone calls for up to a week. Defending the arrests, then-mayor Beame had told the board his options were "to overload our prisons or to overload our morgues." The elaborate plan concocted by the Vera Institute less than a decade earlier for the orderly management of mass arrests during emergency conditions was ignored. In assessing DOC's response to the blackout, Tufo had remarked, "The Department of Correction responds better to emergencies than it does to normal demands."

By the early 1980s, the Tombs was being remodeled with the aid of sentenced prisoners. The notorious facility received a considerable facelift thanks to the collaboration of social scientists in the tradition of Anna Kross, who supported the construction of a new Tombs as an opportunity to test their theories of progressive human caging. Gone were the days when this sort of expert coveted leadership of the department; by the 1980s they were happy to just design its cages.[17]

The result was a structure combining three "mini-jails," each three stories tall and self contained. They featured all the support services of a jail facility, with the addition of computer technology that controlled even the locks. The renovated Tombs was hailed by its new warden as "a state-of-the-art jail, the most modern jail in the city of New York." COBA's Seelig argued against the amenities offered in the Tombs, predicting that the prisoners would simply fashion anything they could get their hands on into lethal weapons. "The more you give them," Seelig claimed, "the more aggressive they'll become." The Tombs' reopening in autumn of 1983 generated some positive press for the modicum of penal welfarism left over from Deputy Mayor Sturz's failed attempt to build borough facilities in place of Rikers. But such fanfare was soon replaced with a new headline: "Koch Says He May Have to Free Some Inmates in City's Overcrowded Jails."[18]

Severe Fiscal Constraints

Ever since taking charge of the 1972 *Rhem v. McGrath* suit, Judge Morris Lasker had assumed a heightened role in DOC affairs. This evolution was, in fact, part of a national trend of jail and prison reform promoted by federal courts. In December 1981 a judge ordered 350 state prisoners in Alabama freed on early parole, in order to accommodate a mandatory cap on crowding. After the December 1981 release, Alabama attorney general Charles Graddick responded with derision. "Parents should not tell their children that Prancer and Dancer are on the roof," he remarked, "because it's going to be a bunch of thugs and criminals released from our prisons." New York City was similarly taxed to the breaking point. But in 1980, Koch had literally advertised the city's empty jail space on television, to await anyone found in possession of an unlicensed firearm. A TV commercial depicted the mayor strolling through an empty Rikers Island cellblock and declaring sternly: "No plea bargaining. No judges feeling sorry for you ... if you've got the gun, we've got the room." This was a misrepresentation; in reality, the cellblock was empty because DOC could not afford necessary repairs to get it up to compliance. Elsewhere in the facility, the city was packing prisoners together in considerable excess of its lawful jail capacity, part of an upward trend that would not subside for many years, even as the federal judiciary cracked down.[19]

A much-abused concept, "crime" is difficult to quantify, due to the high degree of variance in how illegal acts are discovered and prosecuted; this was especially true amid the rise of draconian policing and prosecutorial strategies that accompanied law-and-order politics. Over the four years since Koch had taken office in 1978, however, the rate of indictment had grown 75 percent. That year, the average daily census in DOC custody had been 6,993, a degree of crowding that was already significantly overtaxing the department's aging facilities. By 1982, however, the average had climbed to 9,279. "At the Correctional Institution for Men," Tufo wrote Koch in October 1982, "we see conditions which are strikingly similar to those at the House of Detention for men in the period preceding the 1975 riot." The facility, Tufo continued, "which once housed only sentenced adult males, is now the repository for system overflow," including almost 700 pretrial detainees. Since the summer, the population had soared from 1,700 to 2,600.

The following week, Ward wrote to Koch aghast at still more austerity requests made of DOC amid these conditions. "At a time when I am sleeping inmates in thirty square feet of space in converted warehouses and classrooms," Ward bemoaned, "I should be increasing services, not cutting them." Echoing Tufo, Ward argued CIFM was particularly hard hit. Prisoners without immediate life-threatening injuries were given only two chances per week to visit the clinic, and four social workers administered a population of 2,600 in the facility once designated as a Reception and Classification Center. By DOC's own account, the facility did "little more than 'warehouse' sentenced prisoners who work elsewhere during the day."[20]

DOC fought regulation on multiple fronts. First Deputy Commissioner Richard Koehler, appearing before BOC, adopted language all too familiar to city officials under Koch, arguing that requests for noncompliance "must be viewed in the context of the severe fiscal constraints facing the City." DOC also appealed to Lasker, who had ruled that the DOC population should not exceed 10,250, and who resisted DOC's numerous attempts to raise this figure. DOC's repeated variance requests around the seventy-five-square-foot requirement were only an overture to the request for its outright reduction to sixty. The Legal Aid Society pushed back, reminding DOC that not only was this requirement part of BOC standards, it was also built into a number of consent decrees. Further, Ted Katz of Legal Aid argued that DOC's appeal to the fiscal crisis were increasingly anachronistic, as the city was in fact in significantly better economic shape. A rebounding city, Katz argued, could no longer flout minimum standards with appeals to financial insolvency. Still, this did not stop DOC from pleading poverty as a means of consistently violating minimum standards. By 1983, an exasperated Tufo "stated that it appeared to be Department policy to not cooperate with the Board," adding, "It would be a mistaken policy for the Department to continue to ignore and not provide information to the Board, which is established by local statute."[21]

Over and over again, DOC stalled at implementing minimum standards, and BOC balked, issuing variances that bought the department more time. By 1983, however, Judge Lasker, pushed by Legal Aid, was demanding action. As rising population outpaced DOC's infrastructure expansion, the department demonstrated time and again it was clearly unwilling to following the law. To Lasker's mind, the only feasible alternative to noncompliance was the release of prisoners, following the precedent set in Alabama. The city pleaded, with the usual entreaties, for Lasker to raise the population caps in place of a mass release. Lasker's reply was a damning indictment of life in HDM and AMKC. Writing of squalid and dangerous conditions in which daily medical care was unavailable, the judge noted that sanitation had degenerated to a disgusting state, including a dehumanizing shortage of toilet paper, while prisoners were forced to fight each other for chairs, space, access to telephones, and even food. DOC, Lasker found, lacked an adequate plan to address these dire conditions. Therefore, the department had no legal basis for holding prisoners in its custody. A mass release, like that in Alabama, was all but assured.[22]

Judge Lasker's Federal Jailbreak

In February 1983, a visibly intoxicated Benjamin Ward stumbled into night court for no discernible reason, and began berating the judge for not working hard enough. The district attorney, Commissioner Ward argued, belonged in the holding pens alongside the prisoners. As for Legal Aid, he demanded they be held in contempt of court for taking a dinner break. Ward was flanked by a female companion who remained unidentified; the married commissioner would later run into trouble for using his private boat to spirit a "girlfriend" to his office on Rikers Island for a series of late-night trysts. The following month, a more subdued Ward told the board it was "unacceptable to release prisoners after the police have risked their lives apprehending them and after the anguish that victims have suffered." Ward affirmed his commitment to "everything possible to find or create space to house as many prisoners as necessary in order to avoid the indiscriminate release of prisoners," this being the city's uncharitable characterization of the plan to release prisoners with low bail. This would, however, prove impossible to achieve.[23]

In late October, Koch wrote to seventy-seven judges, urging the expedition of sentencing in felony cases, in order to make room in the city system presently taken up by prisoners bound for upstate prisons. Koch claimed a mass release was eminent. One high-ranking state judge responded by reminding Koch that the mayor could always make more space available in jails. Others claimed that Koch was trying to scapegoat the judiciary, which was already working as quickly as it could.

While Lasker was clear that the prisoners released would be those with the lowest bail who had been held for the longest time, for the most minor offenses, this nuance did not translate into the public discourse. For instance, Ward had long warned that in any release, literal rapists and murderers would walk free—an argument that appears to have seeped into the public imagination. Lasker had originally planned to simply release prisoners outright, without the payment of any bail. After negotiating with the city, however, the ultimate plan amounted to a reduced-bail policy, by which any prisoner with $1,500 or less in bail and no administrative holds or open warrants could be freed on just 10 percent of their bail. On November 1, 1983, the releases began. The most serious charges included robbery and assault. When a dozen prisoners charged with murder and sexual assault successfully met the financial criteria, the policy was hastily modified to exclude them. When the city ran out of prisoners fitting its limited criteria, it began to release misdemeanants with bail less than $1,000. Indicative of the temperature of the debate, Ward would later claim, falsely, that the first prisoner released was charged with raping a ten-year-old.[24]

Ward called the move "Judge Lasker's federal jailbreak." When the dust had settled, 613 prisoners had been freed. While Koch predicted a crime wave, a study one month later showed nothing of the sort. Only a tiny fraction of the released prisoners failed to appear for their court proceedings, while a small handful were subsequently arrested for charges ranging from felony burglary, larceny, and drug possession to two instances of robbery and one of rape. The rate of failure to reappear in court was within the average of 10 to 15 percent, skewing dramatically toward those charged with minor offenses. As for the prisoner charged with rape, he was later acquitted on all counts, and the judge criticized the role the case played in the media following his arrest. *Times* reporter Philip Shenon noted that while City Hall and the judiciary were quick to exchange charges of blame, nobody seemed interested in discussing the cops and prosecutors who had in fact increased arrest and indictment rates considerably, thereby flooding the jails.[25]

Regardless of who was to blame, Lasker's actions had a lasting effect on the jail system. Koch had staked his entire career on fidelity to law and order, basing the legitimacy of the new social order in New York City on the ability of cops and jail guards to control the city's working-class black and brown populations by any means they deemed necessary. Around this time, for example, the city's Human Resources Administration, tasked with overseeing homeless shelters, noticed that sheets on the shelter's beds were deteriorating far more quickly than they should. An investigation revealed that the sheets were being laundered at Rikers Island—where guards jabbed the bales of freshly laundered clothing with bayonets to stop prisoners from escaping the island by hiding in the laundry. Such was the tenor of Koch's approach to law and order.[26]

Accordingly, Lasker's large-scale prisoner release posed an existential threat to Koch's entire political mythology. It would not be tolerated. "I am faced with a choice," Koch somberly announced one month after the mass release, "of releasing prisoners onto city streets, or taking scarce capital dollars from other programs to build more jails." Unsurprisingly, Koch's decision was to pursue an aggressive jail expansion plan that would add 2,200 beds to the city system—1,620 of which would be on Rikers Island. Seven hundred of the latter would be modular dormitories, to be constructed as quickly as possible.

In December, Koch wrote to Benjamin Ward to compliment an interview he had given in *New York State Association of Counties News*. "You summed up the issue," Koch wrote, "when you said, 'The issue is not: Do we build more jails or let people go free? The issue is not: Do we spend many millions more or run illegal inferior jails? The issue is: Do we make the courts accountable in a very real or literal sense or risk the collapse of our local criminal justice apparatus?'" Koch continued: "I suspect the answer ultimately will be more jails and more relevancy by the courts." To protect the legitimacy of the social order he was forging in New York City, Koch would need yet more jails. And these jails would largely be constructed on Rikers Island.[27]

20

Show This Motherfucker Who Is Running the Jail

No More Doubts

In a poignant scene from Tom Wolfe's 1987 novel *Bonfire of the Vanities*, Bronx prosecutor Larry Kramer beholds a blue and orange DOC bus unloading its daily cargo into the Bronx County Supreme Court. "Kramer had reached that low point in the life of an assistant district attorney in the Bronx," writes Wolfe,

> when he is assailed by the Doubts. Every year forty thousand people, forty thousand incompetents, dimwits, alcoholics, psychopaths, knockabouts, good souls driven to some terrible terminal anger, and people who could only be described as stone evil, were arrested in the Bronx. Seven thousand of them were indicted and arraigned, and then they entered the maw of the criminal justice system—right here through the gateway into Gibraltar, where the vans were lined up. That was about 150 new cases, 150 more pumping hearts and morose glares, every week that the courts and the Bronx County District Attorney's Office were open. And to what end? The same stupid, dismal, pathetic, horrifying crimes were committed day in and day out, all the same. What was accomplished by assistant D.A.'s, by any of

them, through all this relentless stirring of the muck? The Bronx crumbled and decayed a little more, and a little more blood dried in the cracks. The Doubts! One thing was accomplished for sure. The system was fed, and those vans brought in the chow. Fifty judges, thirty-five law clerks, 245 assistant district attorneys, one D.A. ... and Christ knew how many criminal lawyers, Legal Aid lawyers, court reporters, court clerks, court officers, correction officers, probation officers, social workers, bail bondsmen, special investigators, case clerks, court psychiatrists—what a vast swarm had to be fed! And every morning the chow came in, the chow and the Doubts.[1]

The historical moment that produced Wolfe's masterful satire was characterized by the emergence of New York City from fiscal crisis and the beginning of its rebirth as a vibrant center of finance, insurance, and real estate. The first half of Ed Koch's mayoralty, from 1978 to 1983, represented the imposition of austerity on the city government and realignment toward private interests. In the second half, the city began to spend lavishly, but not in the same way that it had under Wagner, Lindsay, and Beame. Alongside extravagant giveaways to private developers (chief among them a young Donald J. Trump), a somewhat unlikely force in city politics enjoyed an immense reversal of fortune in this period: the Department of Correction. While surely some of Kramer's doubts persisted, these were allayed in short order, along with the final obstacles to the development of Rikers Island as we know it today.[2]

Koch had every intention of keeping his promise to dramatically expand the city's carceral capacity in the wake of Judge Lasker's mass release. In effect, his plan would amount to a doubling of the jail expansion plans that had been proposed in 1980. At Koch's behest, the city proposed the creation of 3,876 new beds at a total cost of $277 million. The only serious obstacle lay in the timetable of approximately five years from conception to ribbon cutting—one that reflected the standard for carceral facilities at that time. This included not just the sundry logistical considerations inherent in any construction project, especially one that was publicly funded, but also the added factor of community opposition, arising both from NIMBY considerations and anti-prison political sensibilities. In a city with such precious little land to spare, this made site selection and construction particularly fraught. The bridge to Rikers Island, however, had opened up hundreds of acres of land where most of this red tape could be avoided. "The opposition of community groups to jail facilities in residential areas and the necessary delays incidental to the Uniform Land Use Review Procedure," admitted a reluctant Board of Correction in 1983, "cause Rikers Island to become the primary site by default."[3]

In the early days of the 1980s crowding crisis, DOC's solution to the logistical problems of jail construction largely hinged on a combination of temporary "modular" units and the expedited construction of new jails on Rikers. BOC supported Koch's latest expansion plan as part of a "three-part strategy," which also included "more rigorous management of the State court system" to expedite legal cases, and "a conscientious search for prudent alternatives to pretrial detention." On the second point, the board was concerned that the state would interpret the city's carceral expansion as an effort "to build its way out of the overcrowding crisis" and therefore not take seriously the concomitant need for court reform. Above all, BOC emphasized that "this plan must be viewed as a short-term solution only," en route to a citywide jail topography concentrating detention facilities around borough courthouses. For its part, the city took BOC's consent to expand Rikers Island jail construction far more seriously than it did the caveats BOC attached to it.[4]

The Completion of Rikers Island

At the end of 1983, Benjamin Ward left DOC to become NYPD's first black commissioner. To take his place, Koch appointed a Ward protégée, Jacqueline McMickens. She became not only the first black woman to serve as commissioner of DOC, but perhaps more significantly—as McMickens herself was quick to point out—the first career New York City jail guard to attain this post. McMickens was born in Birmingham, Alabama, the daughter of the first black conductor on the Railway Express transportation line. She became a New York City guard in 1964, working her way through the ranks while obtaining her bachelor's in criminal justice and a master's in public administration at John Jay College of Criminal Justice. As incoming commissioner, McMickens cited Koch's jail construction program as a top priority. In fact, McMickens's own plan would soon make the mayor's 1983 proposals seem modest.[5]

In early 1985, McMickens presented the Rikers Island Development Plan, an impressive expansion of Koch's proposal that called for the replacement of temporary facilities with permanent jails that would not simply meet existing departmental needs but prepare for large population surges in the future. Contrary to BOC's wishes, this move represented not just the normalization of DOC's emergency capacity limits, but the location of new facilities for pretrial detention on Rikers Island. "Commissioner Jacqueline McMickens," wrote Ward to Koch in early 1986, "has developed the best and perhaps first comprehensive plan for the completion of Rikers Island in the history of Rikers Island as a Correction Facility." Ward added, by contrast: "All of my plans were crisis initiatives." Now, as city finances recovered and Koch looked to establish lasting stability, the perennial capacity expansion of the city jails built into Ward's crisis management was to become status quo.[6]

There is much to be gleaned from the rhetoric of "completion" that framed this aggressive jail-expansion initiative, suggesting as it does that to cover Rikers Island's entire surface with jails was DOC's inevitable task since time immemorial. Despite BOC's entreaties throughout the years against the concentration of detention facilities on Rikers, by 1985 DOC was treating any available surface on Rikers as *lacking a jail*, including a site on the far east side of the island that was home to an active city tree nursery. Thus began the most dramatic expansionary program in the history of Rikers Island, a breakneck race toward its *completion* as a penal colony packed with overcrowded jails composed largely of pretrial detainees.[7]

It had become common practice under Koch's mayoralty, during years of crisis budgets, to issue declarations of emergency to divert additional funds to meet DOC's needs. However, this practice expanded considerably after 1983, leading to the expedition of several infrastructure projects in accordance with McMickens's Rikers Island Development Plan. These included modular units appended to existing facilities like the Correctional Institute for Men, Correctional Institute for Women, and the Anna M. Kross Center. Additional modular units comprised the Interim North Command, known at the time as the "Arthur Dorms," after their assigned contractor, Arthur Industries. These facilities were crowded into the island's northernmost tip in anticipation of a permanent structure, which would itself be expedited using emergency declarations. The structure would be called the North Facility, known today as the Otis Bantum Correctional Center (OBCC). The rapid pace of this work demonstrated that DOC under McMickens had the full attention of City Hall.[8]

Mayor Koch cut the ribbon for the North Facility on July 1, 1985, a mere thirteen months after construction began. This staggering timeline was partly an exaggeration: the facility's 800 beds would not be fully operational until the fall. Nevertheless, such political theatrics still indicate the seriousness with which Koch was pursuing jail expansion in the wake of Lasker's jailbreak, using capital projects that allowed investors to profit by fronting the money the city needed to construct them. The North Facility was part of a new generation of jails built using pre-engineered components subsequently assembled on Rikers, a system that cut down construction time considerably. In its original incarnation, prior to a 1989 annex, the building stood two stories tall and comprised sixteen rectangular dormitory units, emanating at ninety-degree angles from a central corridor. In contrast to the sprawling chevron design of CIFM, CIFW, and ARDC, the North Facility's design crowds an extensive jail into a comparatively small space, with little room between housing

units. Its presence on the map is a tiny block, scarcely notice-
able next to the other facilities stretched luxuriantly across the
once-spacious island. Its architecture is a spatial representation
of DOC's discovery, in the mid 1980s, of the very real limits to
what Anna Kross had once referred to as the island's "practically unlimited land."[9]

The opening of North Facility in June of 1985 was part of a
1,500-bed increase that took place over the span of one year. The
lion's share of these new facilities, completed in April 1986, were
modular units. Along with this construction, DOC proceeded
with renovations to existing facilities like CIFW and CIFM,
planning for a minimum of not seventy-five, but sixty square
feet per prisoner. These designs indicated in no uncertain terms
that DOC intended to lower the bar to this figure permanently.
Koch and McMickens argued against the imposition of population caps on the new facilities, claiming quite bluntly that they
did not want to support rules that they might, at a future date,
be unable to follow. These new units, and McMickens's plan in
general, were not prepared in advance of an anticipated spike
in sentenced prisoners. Instead, they were intended for pretrial
detainees. One way or another, the capacity of the system had
to be enlarged to make way for prisoners swept off the streets,
denied bail or unable to afford it, and awaiting trial in congested
courts. Virtually all of them would be held on Rikers Island.

When Tufo tendered his resignation from BOC in January of
1986, he commended Koch for stewardship over the city "during
a period that crime control became a primary concern of City
government, the inmate population doubled to over 12,000,
the correction budget grew to over 600 million dollars and the
City undertook the largest prison construction and modernization program in its history." Thanks to their liberal distribution
of variances at moments when they could have stemmed the
growth of the city's jail population by refusing to comply, Tufo
and BOC also deserved credit for their role in the dramatic
expansion.[10]

A smaller part of this plan took place not on Rikers but several
miles away, in the Brooklyn Navy Yard. As part of Koch's original

1983 expansion plan, DOC had taken control of a disused Navy brig that had been a detention facility for the Immigration and Naturalization Service since its abandonment by the Navy in 1966. Under DOC's stewardship, the jail was dubbed the Brooklyn Correctional Facility, nicknamed "the Brig." Originally intended to house 600 prisoners, the Brig presented one logistical problem after another, demonstrating how difficult it was to build jails off of Rikers Island. Foremost among these was a strenuous community opposition, organized under the banner of the Committee against the Navy Yard Prison. Their grievances included typical NIMBY concerns, but also broader complaints about the expedited process demanded by the city. Despite such protests, the facility opened in May 1984. However, it would house only about 200 sentenced prisoners, all of whom had less than ninety days remaining on their sentences.[11]

While Commissioner McMickens had foregrounded prisoners' short sentences in her marketing of the facility to the community, she later claimed, "This is not an absolute requirement and we are not bound by it." The facility was, however, bound by the same BOC standards that bedeviled the rest of the city system, and DOC found it logistically difficult to recognize even these basic rights. The provision of adequate outdoor recreation, for instance, required prisoners to be ferried daily to Rikers from the Navy Yard. Moreover, the community-impact assessment that DOC had effectively railroaded during the renovation of the Brig eventually caught up with the city, necessitating millions of dollars in costs and ongoing engagement with the activists and the Fort Greene Community Review Board. Though it remained open until 1994, the Brig never became a major focus of DOC expansion. Similar community opposition awaited the White Street Jail, planned in the early 1980s to open next door to the Tombs in Lower Manhattan. Organized under the banner of the Citizens' Coalition for Lower Manhattan, the Chinatown community managed, in one instance, to draw over 12,000 people to a 1982 demonstration in Foley Square. The activists ultimately succeeded in stopping the plan in its tracks. Simultaneously, the coalition's strident opposition produced several conciliatory suggestions from City Hall, most notably a proposal to construct a mixed-use jail, which would also feature space for day care facilities, offices, and retail.[12]

No Alternative

Though a former rank and filer, McMickens was, practically by necessity, no longer a friend to the Correction Officers' Benevolent Association. In fact, she quickly became embroiled in its unrelenting war with civilian administration for control of the jail system. In 1984, when McMickens introduced a tougher policy limiting sick leave, the union took out a full-page ad in the *Chief-Leader* lambasting the commissioner as "ANTI-OFFICER," regardless of the fact she "claims to be one of us." On top of DOC's new sick leave policy, which made it easier for City Hall to label guards' "chronic" absentees liable to loss of benefits, COBA also bemoaned the imposition of mandatory overtime and a policy that limited time spent out of the house by guards on maternity leave. While McMickens took the heat, the austerity policies bore all the fingerprints of Koch. Meanwhile, the mayor enjoyed the continuing support of COBA and other uniformed unions, McMickens forwarded the *Chief-Leader* article to Deputy Mayor Stanley Brezenoff, with a note: "This is what happens when I try to reduce sick leave. What do you think?" Illustrating City Hall's convenient relationship with McMickens and other commissioners who served as the face of austerity to their angry subordinates, Brezenoff replied by scrawling on the memo, "What I've always thought: you're the best!"[13]

In 1985 COBA sued unsuccessfully to block a new policy mandating guards wear nameplates that would clearly identify them to prisoners. That same year, McMickens courted an annual conference of the American Correctional Association by pledging the participation of guards as volunteer guides. COBA took this opportunity to escalate an increasingly ugly feud. Calling McMickens a "lousy administrator," its president, Phil Seelig, publicly opposed this agreement. COBA further embarrassed McMickens by staging a picket outside the conference demanding her ouster. "The inmates harass us, abuse us, and murder us," Seeling declared. "If we fight back, McMickens charges us with brutality."[14] This complaint was only a token of what was to come. Fueled by circumstances outside both DOC and COBA's control, the escalating row would ultimately raise the stakes of the brutal contest for supremacy in the city's jails.

In the wake of the 1970 Knapp Commission's revelations of police involvement in the illicit drug trade, NYPD had virtually abandoned street-level policing. This accounted, in part, for a dip in the city's jail population in the 1970s. By the early 1980s, a widespread, often blatant culture of drug sale and use had flourished in many working-class New York City neighborhoods. A cheap and highly addictive new cocaine by-product—crack—became popular in communities hit hardest by deindustrialization, the fiscal crisis, and the city's subsequent restructuring away from non-security public spending. While addiction was, and remains, a serious social problem, focusing myopically on substances like crack cocaine became, as criminologist Travis Linnemann argues, a way for politicians and media figures to explain social disorder without talking about its root causes in protracted capitalist crisis, deindustrialization, and the new regime of austerity. Instead, the so-called War on Drugs crystalized the myriad hardships of late twentieth-century American life into a cartoonish military foe, to be defeated with whatever violence police and prisons could muster.[15]

Beginning in 1984, New York cops undertook frequent mass arrests of drug users and low-level dealers on inflated charges, meant to destabilize the drug market by levying felony charges in what would usually be considered low-level possession. These sweeps were undertaken with greatest frequency in neighborhoods like the Lower East Side, which the finance, insurance, and real estate sector was busily gentrifying, using NYPD cops as its shock troops. After arrestees had languished for a time in the city's overcrowded jails, the charges would eventually be reduced or dismissed. Indeed, the point was not to secure convictions, or to end drug addictions, which draconian drug enforcement has never succeeded in doing. Instead, this new approach to policing some of the city's poorest people functioned to perform toughness to Koch's base, while clearing designated areas of the city for development. DOC facilities, which absorbed the human beings who became the collateral damage of this dirty business, thus became ground zero of the city's disastrous War on Drugs.[16]

At the beginning of 1980, the average daily population in DOC custody was under 7,000. In early 1984, even prior to NYPD's turn toward aggressive street-level policing, that number hung just below 10,000. By October of 1986, the population in city jails was over 13,000. Many of these were technically state prisoners awaiting transfer following sentencing, while others were state parole violators. Though an August 1986 agreement between city and state over the contentious issue of their custody limited the stay of state prisoners to fourteen days, their presence nonetheless presented a strain on the city system. Simultaneously, DOC's use of the precedent set by a landmark Connecticut district court lawsuit, *LaReau v. Manson*, enabled DOC to temporarily house prisoners in dormitories with as little as *forty* square feet per prisoner—barely more than half the amount specified by the city's minimum standards.

"As you know, I have reservations about the addition of more modular [units]," Deputy Commissioner Koehler wrote Koch in a 1986 request for yet another emergency order to expand facilities on Rikers—this time to the tune of six new dormitories. "Unfortunately, there is no alternative given the surge in new admissions. The need for these beds is inescapable." Overseeing these precarious conditions was a workforce of guards that had grown considerably in the previous five years, from 4,523 to 7,008. It was, accordingly, a younger force, ever more emboldened by the confrontational mien of their leader, Seelig, who was truly a man for his time and place.[17]

In August of 1986, City Hall removed McMickens from her post at DOC and transferred her to a position at the Housing Authority. This lower-paying job was widely viewed as a demotion, imposed on account of her failure to minimize overtime and mitigate the chaotic effects of crowding. The following day, DOC attempted to move twenty-five bunk beds into a dormitory already packed with ninety-four state parole violators. The prisoners decided immediate action had to be taken. Barricading their dormitory with broken furniture, they armed themselves with makeshift weapons. Seelig, an unlikely spokesman for the action, declared the prisoners "serious about their intentions to not be overcrowded." He demanded DOC take immediate action to expand its facilities and staff. In response to mounting bad press, and the stubborn fact of dire overcrowding that lay beneath it, the Koch administration unveiled a plan to construct to two city facilities near the Canadian border, and to convert a disused Staten Island ferry boat into a floating jail. Asked by reporters how he could countenance exposing prisoners to seasickness, Koch replied: "We'll give them Dramomine."[18]

We're Going to Get You

To take McMickens's place, Koch appointed Richard Koehler, a career cop serving as NYPD's chief of personnel, who had been DOC's deputy commissioner under Ward from 1981 to 1983. Not only would DOC prioritize the interests of its uniformed force above all else; it would now be run by a prominent city cop. Despite the semblance of order his appointment was meant to convey, however, Koehler's return to DOC could not prevent disorder of a historic magnitude. On October 11, less than three weeks after Koehler took office, 161 state prisoners held at AMKC were moved to two dormitories at CIFM, known as 5 and 6 Main. There, they were deprived of their street clothes and placed in double-bunked cells. Two days later, these prisoners refused to leave their beds for the 8:00 a.m. count.

The morning count was loathed by many prisoners, as it typically entailed guards waking up sleeping prisoners, who were made to stand beside their bed and be counted. Worse yet, this could involve a guard placing their hands on a sleeping prisoner, or even slapping them. The guards' touch represented the transgression of even the barest minimum of privacy, making the morning count a particularly onerous instance of the countless daily degradations of jail life. Such rituals of subordination, however, cut both ways: they produce compliance, alongside simmering resentment. When the opportunity presents itself, many prisoners readily channel this well of collective resentment into acts of resistance. October 13, 1986, was one such day.

After the newly arrived prisoners refused to stand for count, tensions escalated rapidly, forcing the guards to beat a hasty retreat from both dormitories. Following a familiar pattern, the prisoners then erected barricades made from bed frames and other furniture and fabricated weapons with which to defend themselves. Appointing delegates to meet with the jail administration, the rebels presented a collectively signed list of eleven demands. These included access to a law library; the cessation of guards' disrespectful behavior toward visitors; receipt of cosmetic products from the outside; access to jobs throughout the facility (as opposed to roles within house gangs, who clean only their own dormitory); more telephones; regular meal schedules; better food (including Halal food); a meeting with prisoners who had been removed from the house and placed in segregation; the removal of a particularly reviled guard from the dormitory staff; and an end to both standing counts in the morning and the practice of waking prisoners up by touching them.[19]

Negotiations between the rebel prisoners and DOC administrators, including the CIFM warden and DOC chief of operations, lasted from 9:25 a.m. until 3 p.m. During that time, the prisoners held down their barricades, some breaking windows. One prisoner who attempted to distance himself from the occupation was beaten over the head with a broken bed leg and later required twenty-one sutures to his scalp. Meanwhile, at the negotiating table, DOC officials conceded to virtually all the prisoners' demands, including non-retaliation, more telephones, the cessation of the morning standing count, and even the reassignment of the despised officer. It was a breathtaking victory for the CIFM prisoners and a monument to the efficacy of direct action. Simultaneously, the outcome was a startling affront to the arrogant autonomy of the guards, and of COBA. Though they had threatened guards and destroyed DOC property, prisoners had won significant concessions, including the end of the standing count. In one instance, the prisoners had literally been allowed to dictate staffing protocol. Such contumacy would not be tolerated.[20]

In response to DOC's peaceful settlement with prisoners, virtually all CIFM guards assigned to the next shift refused to assume their posts. Instead, they marched to the facility's chapel, meeting with COBA and DOC representatives from 3:30 until about 11:30 p.m. This job action, a violation of the anti-strike Taylor Law, itself produced several demands, ranging from renovations to DOC facilities to new emergency equipment, more guard assignments with overlapping shifts, relaxed disciplinary standards for guards, increased legal consequences against prisoners assaulting guards, and the right to carry handcuffs. Finally, as a clear line in the sand illustrating the power struggle at CIFM, guards demanded the return of standing count in the morning. This token of prisoners' deference to their authority had to be restored. As DOC management fumbled to balance these contending forces, the issues were largely deferred for future discussion, and the guards returned to work. Koehler commanded his wardens to read a statement declaring that DOC had done nothing to endanger their safety. They all refused. That very day, the DOC population reached 14,264, its highest census since the early 1970s.[21]

At 9:30 a.m. on October 16, sixty-six supposed parole violators at CIFM staged a similar action to that of the thirteenth. The New York State Commission of Correction (NYSCOC) later described it as a deliberate and premeditated imitation of the prisoners' victory, which by this point had become known across the facility. Their demands included long-distance telephone calls, receipt of basic amenities like underwear and cosmetics from the outside (or else provided by the institution), shorter waits for visitors, regular mealtimes, a daily opportunity to see a doctor, and a hastier transfer into the state system, and no reprisals. This penultimate point was likely not a hard sell, especially after the rebellion on the thirteenth. This time, however, the warden demanded the removal of the barricades as a condition for negotiations, to which the prisoners agreed. Talks lasted for almost four hours, concluding when the prisoners decided DOC would meet enough of its demands. The department also kept its promise and did not retaliate against the prisoners.[22]

The following day, October 17, prisoners from 5 and 6 Main were lined up for lunch in the CIFM cafeteria when a prisoner named Bebe Wise allegedly demanded an extra cup of juice. A guard named Angel Almanzar instructed Wise he could not have the juice, but Wise picked it up anyway. Almanzar then blocked Wise's path to the dining area, commanding that he return the juice. At this, Wise threw the juice at Almanzar, proclaiming, "Take your fucking juice!" As Wise was escorted out of the cafeteria, some fellow prisoners encouraged him to fight back. Wise turned around and a fight broke out, with dozens of people, prisoners and guards, quickly entering the fray. In the fracas that ensued, two guards were knocked unconscious. Following the brief scuffle, eleven guards (including two captains) and five prisoners reported injuries, though it was likely prisoners concealed additional injuries to avoid culpability for the fight.

In a telling indication of the institution's atmosphere, at the sounding of the alarm, two responding guards from elsewhere in CIFM showed up armed with guns; a third was in such a hurry to get to the scene that when a gatekeeper took too long to open a locked door, he picked up a heavy standing ashtray and attempted to smash through the reinforced glass. As the subdued prisoners were escorted out of the dining hall, unsupervised rank-and-file guards taunted and physically menaced them. One guard got "almost nose to nose" with a prisoner, declaring, "We're going to get you."[23]

This provocation was part of an escalating series of encounters "marked by increasing tension and attempts at intimidation from both sides," as monitors later reported. One side, of course, had considerable weaponry, endless backup, and the legal monopoly on the use of violence, for which they had seized a wide berth through decades of activism. Nonetheless, the guards considered themselves an aggrieved party on par with those they guarded, whose insults and provocations must be met in kind—as if the jail system amounted to one big, rowdy proletarian barroom. Following the brawl in the dining hall, guards were talking openly among themselves about "breaking heads and kicking ass" in retribution. Two false alarms were triggered in the afternoon, to which response teams promptly mobilized without any orders from superiors, as the chain of command required. "We are on the verge of a riot," Seelig predicted—or threatened. "The whole jail system is out of control."[24]

Use of Force

As the day wore on, DOC's Inspector General staffers, also on hand as monitors, resisted repeated attempts from a deputy warden to move them away from sites of guard–prisoner interaction. As dinner began at 4:15 p.m., Inspector General Judith Schultz later recorded, "Deputy Warden Brooks kept trying to steer the IG staff into the chapel where the top brass was assembled, but they resisted and remained in the corridor near the mess hall." Something was up. Beginning in the early evening, CIFM officials began the planned transport of the 5 and 6 Main prisoners to the House of Detention for Men. Despite the fact that these facilities were only a short walk apart, protocol required a complex transport operation, involving seven DOC buses. DOC's elite Correctional Emergency Response Team (CERT), a unit of self-styled warrior guards, also showed up to oversee the transfer.

Before departure, multiple prisoners relayed their fears to IG observers that guards were planning retribution, along with protestations that DOC was violating its promise to not transfer any of them without forty-eight hours' notice. Handcuffed together in pairs, the prisoners were allowed only one free hand to carry their belongings in plastic bags. As they exited CIFM for the buses at 8:10 p.m., IG observers later reported, the assembled CERT team formed a gauntlet-like formation, edging toward the prisoners menacingly. "Tensions," they recorded, "were at the near breaking point." Nevertheless, the prisoners were loaded into the buses peacefully, likely thanks to the presence of the civilian observers.[25]

The HDM receiving area was nearly pitch dark when the buses arrived. A light rain spattered the stone facade of the gloomy old jail. The first bus, containing two prisoners and a squadron of CERT guards, emptied without incident, and the prisoners were dispatched into the HDM receiving area. However, the arrival of the second bus was quickly embroiled in chaos. Accounts of what happened next differ. Guards later claimed that some prisoners refused to exit the bus and subsequently tussled with guards in a conflict that spilled off the bus. Prisoners claimed a small group of guards simply boarded the vehicle and began violently ejecting them, on the pretext that they were not exiting quickly enough. The latter version is more likely, since, as IG observed, various details of the guards' accounts were suspicious and contradictory.

Regardless, nobody disputes what happened next. Heavily armored guards, brandishing clubs, tore the handcuffed prisoners off the transport bus and beat them wantonly. The guards ran prisoners through a gauntlet, raining down baton blows on their heads and torsos as they struggled to protect themselves with their bags of belongings. Some of these bags were dropped or split open, strewing prisoners' precious few personal effects on the wet ground to be trampled underfoot or stumbled over in the encroaching dark. HDM warden Dante Albertie stood watching as the beatings unfolded and did nothing. Only when prisoners began to enter the facility bloody and screaming did BOC and NYSCOC staffers, joined by ranking DOC officials, rush out to demand order. When the dust had settled, thirty-four prisoners were injured, including several with head injuries. BOC staffer Brenda Lloyd described the impact of clubs on prisoners' heads and bodies as sounding like "someone was beating a rug."[26]

The chaos did not end there. At approximately 8:45 p.m., prisoners in the 1 Top dormitory of AMKC erected a barricade at their front gate. It is unclear whether they knew about the brutality outside nearby HDM, but it is quite possible, given the impressive information grapevine at Rikers. The immediate trigger, however, seems to have been the removal of prisoner Sammy Mercano for placement in administrative segregation—a formal punishment to follow the beating he had received from guards earlier that day unrelated to the conflict at CIFM. As two guards attempted to remove him, an argument ensued between 1 Top prisoners and a handful of guards. AMKC's probe team responded promptly; at the sight of the armored probe team, who extract prisoners from cells and dormitories with whatever violence they see fit, the prisoners threw up barricades and tried to take the two guards hostage. The guards escaped, but the barricades remained.

Shortly after the barricades went up, Assistant Deputy Warden John King initiated DOC's emergency response Mutual Assistance Plan, meant to call specially trained guards from across the island. He was joined by Deputy Warden Brian Conroy and Supervising Warden Quaslim Inham, who began negotiating with the prisoners. Simultaneously, these ranking officials attempted to prevent a squadron of roughly thirty guards, agitated and itching for a fight, from entering AMKC and bringing a violent conclusion to the standoff. This tension was only exacerbated when a captain overseeing the negotiations was struck by a boot thrown from inside the dormitory. Many CERT guards who had beaten prisoners outside HDM had been ordered to leave the vicinity, on account of their acts of brutality, and to report to CIFM for a meal. However, when they reached CIFM, they learned of the alarm at AMKC and were promptly dispatched there.[27]

Once CERT was at AMKC, the commanding officer of the operation, Deputy Warden Clarence Brooks, called for an assault on the rebellious dormitory. He did so without consulting the delegation of ranking facility commanders presently inside that very dormitory attempting to broker peace. Because the main gate was blocked by prisoners' barricades, angry AMKC guards, and the ranking officials sandwiched between them, Brooks planned to lead his men through the dormitory's fire escape. To reach it, they had to pass through the dorm below, 1 Upper. The plan was to use the dormitory as a passageway, and not to engage with the prisoners on the floor. Once inside 1 Upper, however, CERT guards began beating prisoners at random. Amid the torrent of flying batons, one of the guards yelled, "Wrong dorm!" This fact, it seems, mattered little to the CERT team, many of whom had participated in the earlier gauntlet outside HDM and seemed content to brutalize any prisoner they could get their hands on.[28]

Meanwhile, guards amassed outside 1 Top at AMKC, agitated and armored for a confrontation. Some demanded to their superiors: "Let us at them! Let us at those motherfuckers!" Deputy Warden Conroy, who was inside the calm dormitory attempting to negotiate, observed the rogue CERT teams barreling through the back exit. He instructed CERT team commander Guillermo Velez to "hold it." This was an order rooted not only in Conroy's authority over the building, but also in the chain of command, which required CERT assaults to be cleared by DOC higher-ups. Nevertheless, just as the CERT guards had ignored protocol in removing prisoners from the bus prior to the beating outside HDM, Velez ignored both protocol and Conroy's order. CERT entered the 1 Top with clubs swinging. They rained blows down with abandon on the prisoners, including one Craig Singleton, who was beaten by multiple guards while on the ground. All the while, ranking officers ran around trying to restore order, outnumbered and ignored. Singleton was helped to his feet by of these officers and took off running out of the dormitory and down the stairs. By one captain's account, he soon thereafter found Singleton surrounded by club-wielding guards, ready to beat him more. The captain ordered they desist, and even then, one guard refused to stand down until the captain physically restrained him. Singleton's ordeal was only one instance of a grisly scene that left thirty 1 Upper and 1 Top prisoners injured, including numerous serious wounds to the head.[29]

They'll Kill You

Simultaneously, perhaps the most politically significant event of this tumultuous week was unfolding below, in AMKC's administrative corridor. As NYSCOC monitors arrived, they stumbled on a diabolical scene. Gathered were upward of forty guards, the four highest-ranking COBA officials—Phil Seelig, Frank Ayala, Stanley Israel, and Fred Wilson—Supervising Warden Joseph D'Elia, Captain Ralph Mierzejewski, and monitors from BOC and the Inspector General. They looked on as a guard clad in riot gear beat a prisoner in the head with his club, while the guards designated to escort the prisoner restrained him, including by the hair. One guard banged the prisoner's head repeatedly against the wall.

Seelig, flanked by his subordinates and a squadron of rank and filers, cheered on the beating, encouraging the guards to keep it up, in between giving speeches. This was only one of multiple documented beatings that unfolded in the same manner under the leadership of COBA's top brass. "Show them who is running the jail!" Seelig implored guard Steven Knutson, as he battered one defenseless prisoner with his club. "Show this motherfucker who is running the jail!" repeated Wilson, as a group of guards, including Knutson, beat another prisoner on the ground. As Singleton was taken to the receiving room, he was also taken through this hallway and similarly beaten by his escorts. When D'Elia tried to intercede, he was shoved by an unidentified guard who said, "You can indict me." At least five prisoners sustained serious injuries in this hallway, far removed from the action in the dormitories.[30]

When NYSCOC monitor Joseph Patron entered the hallway, he was immediately surrounded by the COBA brass and serenaded with a chorus of "'What the fuck are you looking down the hall for,' 'what do you think you're doing,' 'what are you doing here,' 'we don't want you here,' and 'get him out of here.'" Like D'Elia, Patron attempted to halt a beating in progress, but the bloodthirsty guards under Seelig's command prevented him. Patron then attempted to leave the corridor to summon help, to which Seelig ordered the hallway locked, making Patron his prisoner. An unidentified guard stepped forward and physically restrained Patron as the COBA brass shouted curses and threats. Seelig began to issue commands to D'Elia, insisting that Patron was from IG. "Get him out of there," Seelig barked to the supervising warden. "He is IG and all they want to do is burn officers." Wilson joined in, attempting to attack Patron while shouting, "Get these fucking IG out of here!" A flummoxed D'Elia placed himself between Wilson and Patron, at once explaining that Patron was not in fact IG, and insisting to Patron and other civilians, including BOC and NYSCOC monitors, that they had better leave. "They'll kill you if you don't back off and shut up," D'Elia told the civilians.[31]

For a short time, DOC successfully covered up the greatest excesses of this wild week of prisoner revolt and guard riots. For his part, Mayor Koch insistently blamed the presence of state prisoners, "the toughest inmates in the system," for the disturbances. Details slowly trickled out, however, including the beating of handcuffed prisoners as ranking DOC officials stood watching. Koehler was forced to take action. Three wardens— Supervisory Warden Kathleen Cera, CIFM's Dennis Cowan, and HDM's Albertie—were given the choice of demotion or resignation. They chose the latter. Koehler also brought departmental charges against two CERT commanders, CIFM deputy warden Clarence Brooks and assistant deputy warden Robert N. Davoren, whose name today adorns the Adolescent Remand and Detention Center.

Hearing that disciplinary charges were being announced, Seelig hastily organized a press conference—only to cancel it when it was revealed, to his surprise, that no COBA members were charged. There would only be a few token sacrifices at the top; no serious challenge would be posed to Rikers guards. Nonetheless, in response to Koehler's mere suggestion that prisoners had been beaten, one hundred CERT guards resigned from the team. It was apparently insufficient that not a single guard suffered any consequences for their actions—including those referred to by name in IG reports, with multiple witnesses to their abuses. Nor was it sufficient that Koehler's official response to the guards, distributed and read at every roll call, emphasized his compliance with the demands of the CIFM guards' illegal job action, downplayed the brutality, and issued a pledge of support, concluding with the words: "Keep up the good work." On the contrary, the emboldened rank-and-file guards of the New York City Department of Correction, with Phil Seelig at their head, demanded that reality itself bend to their unquestioned command. And if reality wouldn't, at least Rikers Island would.[32]

21

A Bridge to the
Twenty-First Century

Never Again

Unable to contain or spin the story of the bloody events of October 17 forever, City Hall and the Department of Correction adopted a familiar stance: they chalked up the violence as the mathematical outcome of overcrowding, the remedy for which was even more new jails. Mayor Koch quickly announced the addition of 70,000 square feet of additional modular units to its existing facilities, as well as locker rooms, clinic space, prisoner intake facilities, and a barbershop. The project would add 600 beds to the island's capacity. More dramatically, the city converted a disused Staten Island ferryboat into a jail barge, to be docked off the northern tip of Rikers Island. While the floating jail was widely criticized for its unorthodoxy and overruns of cost and time, Deputy Mayor Robert Esnard defended the project on the grounds that "no one in modern times has built a prison ship. It's something you couldn't figure out until you did it ... Now we're experts." In fact, Esnard declared, DOC would replicate the plan with a second ferry, which it did.

Using its newfound expertise, DOC subsequently opened two more floating jails, on redesigned troop barges left over from the Falkland Islands War. These vessels, the *Bibby Venture* and the *Bibby Resolution*, raised considerable logistical problems due to their mazelike layout and design meant to facilitate privacy.

Noting these deficiencies, and expressing its hesitation about normalizing the practice of prison barges in New York City, the Board of Correction nonetheless cooperated with the plan, stipulating several modifications be made to the vessels. They opened in 1987 and 1988, respectively, in the East River near Greenwich Village and the Lower East Side.[1]

In June of 1988, DOC opened a new 800-bed women's facility on Rikers, named for veteran BOC member Rose M. Singer. The new jail was sited just to the southeast of the Correctional Institution for Women—close enough to connect to the latter's modules, which in turn became part of the new women's facility. CIFW was subsequently converted into a men's facility and renamed the George Motchan Detention Center, after the guard killed by Joseph James in his 1975 escape from Kings County Hospital. The main building of the Rose M. Singer Center originally included 798 beds, most of them in dormitories, though there was also a twenty-five-bed nursery for expectant mothers. Including the modules, the capacity for RSMC was roughly 1,150.

Rehearsing a ritual by now familiar to generations of DOC officials, Koch oversaw the ribbon cutting at the new facility, flanked by Singer. He was also joined by former commissioners Ward and McMickens, whose administrations had proven so vital in the so-called completion of Rikers Island. Koch's embrace of redoubled construction was also in keeping with what Koch aides called his "never again" policy, formulated in the wake of the Lasker releases of 1983. Koch was willing to do whatever it took to make sure no such event would ever again tarnish his law-and-order credentials. That same year, the island-wide Central Punitive Segregation Unit (CPSU) solitary confinement facility opened at the House of Detention for Men. The $1.5 million investment was supported by Koch and lauded by DOC officials on the grounds that the threat of moving prisoners to the notorious penitentiary would itself be a deterrent to misbehavior. (This deterrent would ultimately fail to take effect, prompting a successful DOC campaign to extend the maximum length of sentences served inside CPSU from thirty to ninety days.)[2]

By this point, DOC had jail construction down to something of a science. The winning technique was a cooperative effort by developers, designers, and politicians that aimed to deliver new jails in less time than the customary three to five years. The process, as one team of jail designers describes it, hinged upon the consolidation of design and construction into one streamlined process, along with the use of prefabricated materials amounting to "something like an erector set"—including prefabricated furniture built into premade cells assembled off site. Simultaneously, the city provided ample emergency declarations, "onboard" management and review protocol, and "quick response" directives conducted on the fly, in order to eliminate red tape at every juncture and fast-track a new jail from the drawing board to completion. It was this kind of hybrid "design/build" team that the city contracted to construct a 300-bed addition to the Otis Bantum Correctional Center in 1987. "Pile driving for the building foundation began the same week the team received the 'go-ahead' for the projects," the designers reflect, "even though the building design had not been completed." Throughout this building spree, DOC continued to rely heavily on variances from BOC, and BOC continued to dispense them, despite episodic performances of opposition—and the consistent DOC violation of minimum standards.[3]

Some of this new construction addressed a new problem in the city jail system: the AIDS epidemic. DOC recorded its first AIDS-related death in 1982, followed by three in 1983, and seven in 1984 and 1985. The state system, composed largely of prisoners who had passed through city custody, experienced an explosion of deaths during this time, from two in 1981, to three in 1982, eighteen in 1983, fifty-seven in 1984, and seventy-six in 1985. By 1984, AIDS was the leading cause of death in state custody. Virtually all the prisoners who died in city, state, or county custody during this time had previously lived in New York City. One-third had been born in Puerto Rico, and 46 percent were classified as Hispanic, compared to 39 percent black, and 15 percent white. Over 90 percent identified themselves as past intravenous drug users. In 1986 black revolutionary and New

York Twenty-One defendant Kuwasi Balagoon, who had fought in the 1970 jail rebellion, died of AIDS-related complications in state custody, where he was serving time on charges related to his revolutionary activities. Significant cuts to the public health infrastructure during the fiscal crisis—including to addiction services, which had gone unremedied even as Koch ramped up city spending once more—considerably exacerbated the impact of the AIDS epidemic.[4]

In July of 1985, DOC reported twenty AIDS cases in its custody. By 1987, the number was forty. In accordance with a state penal law dictating the isolation of prisoners with a communicable disease, prisoners diagnosed with AIDS were initially held in the Rikers Island hospital. That year, as DOC moved to renovate the hospital in response to the litigation of *Vega v. Koehler*, these prisoners were moved to module dormitory 18 E at the North Facility, pending the completion of a purpose-built module. Assembled from prefabricated components, the specially designed sixty-six-bed modular clinic, the first of its kind in the United States, was opened in May of 1989—just eighteen weeks after the city issued final approval for its construction. "There ought to be something done," remarked a prisoner forced to live out his final days in the North Facility dormitory, "so AIDS patients could die outside, not in prison. If I had a choice, I'd rather die in the East River, not in here." Several days later, he was dead.[5]

Fisher v. Koehler

Speaking at a DOC medal ceremony in 1989, Mayor Koch looked back on the immense expansion of the department he had overseen in the previous decade. Its consummation had come in tandem with the growth of a program of aggressive policing, prosecution, and incarceration that had taken the place of social service expenditure and employment in the public sector for the lowest tiers of New York City's working class. Disorder in working-class life, including violence and other predation, would not be treated as symptomatic of underlying social causes, as the postwar liberals had done. Instead, it was the occasion for stricter laws, more cops, and more jails. The results were stunning. "In 1978," Koch reflected,

> there were approximately 7,000 inmates in 17 prison facilities. Today, the prison population—on any given day—is in excess of 19,000. Today, there are 25 prison facilities fully operative or planned for completion by 1990 ... In 1978, as I took office, the Department of Correction [had] a total of 4,800 uniformed and civilian employees. Today there are slightly under 11,800. In 1978, there were approximately 570,00 arrests through the city in the categories known as "the seven major crimes" [murder, manslaughter, rape, assault, arson, burglary, larceny]. Last year NYPD figures show over 718,00 arrests in these major categories. And apart from those arrests, there were 90,000 drug arrests.[6]

Of DOC's guards in this period, 54 percent were black. The ranks of DOC, among the city's least-desirable civil service jobs, accounted for the highest rates of nonwhite growth in city employment during this period. As the fiscal crisis had foreclosed employment opportunities for black workers in other city sectors, they could find work in DOC, guarding a majority-black population of prisoners which they were encouraged by their peers, their union, and their daily experiences at work to view as the enemy. DOC's guard workforce became less white throughout the 1980s. However, with some notable exceptions, high-ranking positions in DOC were disproportionately held by whites.[7]

The expansion of the city jail system during the Koch years was staggering. Between 1980 and 1988, the capital budget allocated to DOC increased over 3,000 percent, from $5.2 million to $169.1 million—some $370 million in today's dollars. Simultaneously, direct public assistance was curtailed, and funding that had once put cash assistance in people's hands was increasingly allocated to nongovernmental organizations overseeing the basic needs of the city's poorest people—with far more strings attached than had come with direct material assistance. What New Yorkers got instead were more jails, and particularly miserable ones at that. Daily life in the city system was riven with violent conflicts, among prisoners and between prisoners and guards, of which the incidents of October 1986 were only the most extreme. In fact, during that tumultuous week, at least three other instances of violence flared up between prisoners that were later deemed unrelated to the central conflict between prisoners and guards at the Correctional Institution for Men. Meanwhile, Rikers Island was at the center of yet another lawsuit, *Fisher v. Koehler*, which argued that violence among prisoners and visited upon prisoners by guards at this facility violated the Eight Amendment, which prohibits cruel and unusual punishment. The trial was set to begin in Judge Lasker's court on October 23, 1986, and as Lasker himself admitted, the unfolding events on Rikers lent weight to the plaintiff's key arguments, as well as a sense of urgency to the case.[8]

The testimony of CIFM prisoners Roy Hartley and Rene Lisojo, the latter just eighteen years old, capture the fear and brutality that characterized life in this facility:

> On February 22, 1986, Hartley was assigned to night sanitation duty. While he was working outside the dormitory the inmates in his dormitory, 5 Lower, were warned that if the inmates continued to make noise, the riot squad would be called. Hartley arrived back at 5 Lower at about 3:10 a.m. and went to bed. Almost immediately, he felt the covers being pulled off him, and saw Captain Chesaniuk, Assistant Deputy Warden DeCanditis and ten correction officers in the dormitory, throwing inmates out of bed and ordering them to the front of the dormitory. As Hartley walked to the front, Officer Henry hit him in the face, Officer Bland grabbed him from the back, and Officer Fisher punched him in the back of the head and kicked him. Fisher also hit two other inmates. When Hartley got to the front of the dormitory, he asked Captain Chesaniuk if he could go to the infirmary. Chesaniuk said that if Hartley would state that he received his injury from a fall, he would not get an infraction. Hartley refused to do

this and was given an infraction for disobeying a direct order to stop talking after lights out.

...

First, in June or July 1986, an inmate chased [Rene Lisojo] with a broomstick when Lisojo refused to give him his sneakers, tried to extort money and commissary items from him and scraped him with a razor. Second, on the night of June 20, 1986, Lisojo woke up to discover that someone had wrapped burning toilet paper around his hand. He suffered second degree burns. Third, on another occasion, an inmate punched Lisojo in the face in the bathroom, allegedly in the presence of a correction officer. Lisojo required five stitches in the mouth. Lisojo testified that the inmate and his friends threatened to slash him if he reported the incident to the authorities, so he told the officer to report that he received his injuries by falling down in the bathroom.[9]

However extreme, Lasker found these cases to be representative of daily life in the treacherous facility, designed so assiduously by Kross to be a penological milestone. In a perverse way, it was.

In a 1988 ruling, Lasker paints a damning picture not just of the daily violence of the facility but of the degrading conditions of life in its dormitories, even for those who escaped being victimized by a guard or fellow prisoner. The result of *Fisher* was the entry of the city into still more consent decrees, requiring still more oversight of dormitory capacity, prisoner classification, and the handing of "use of force" incidents. As the trial was underway, Mayor Koch issued Executive Order 105. Handed down less than two months after the 1986 events at Rikers Island, the order limited the scope of the Inspector General of each city agency to corruption and outright illegality, leaving the rest the sole provenance of the civilian leadership of each department. This made "use of force" investigations an in-house matter for DOC leadership unless they were deemed overtly criminal. In the long term, this meant the Correction Officers' Benevolent Association could largely get its earlier wish, to *get these fucking IG out of here.*

As long as the *Fisher* consent decree continued, however,

DOC was required by Lasker to develop both stricter and more actionable criteria for wrongful use of force against prisoners, and to demonstrate the enforcement of these new rules by investigating guard violence. DOC's new standards required intensive and well-documented investigations for all violent episodes involving guards, thus eliminating the ability of the latter to classify violent acts as mere "unusual incidents" and therefore avoid investigation. While the plaintiffs argued that considerable ambiguity persisted in the new classification system, which could still allow both guards and DOC administration to erase violence through bureaucratic word magic, Lasker intended to oversee the development and application of these new criteria to make sure the city followed through and applied it in good faith. In short, the arrogant autonomy of DOC's guards was under attack. The department's adoption of basic Eighth Amendment rights for New York City's captive population would soon be rejected by DOC's rank-and-file guards in the most spectacular fashion.[10]

The Game Is On

Conditions of crowding and brutality presented opportunities for resistance, through both escape and mass struggle. Following the 1981 installation of elaborate perimeter security, with multiple layers of razor wire–tipped fencing and motion-sensor technology, escapes from the island dropped off dramatically. However, as conditions at Rikers deteriorated, new options presented themselves for prisoners seeking self-activated early release from custody. In 1987 a trio of prisoners held at the Hospital—George Konstantides, Joseph Anzalone, and Emmanuel Rivera—acquired a hacksaw blade, sawed through a window frame, and removed its protective glass. They proceeded to climb down five stories on a fire hose, aided in part by a first-floor corridor connecting the infirmary to the House of Detention for Men. Two of the men had been hospitalized for leg injuries, including one with a broken leg. Undaunted, he left the leg cast behind, protruding from a bed stuffed with clothing in the shape of a human form. The trio covered their tracks by pinning a centerfold over the dislocated window and concealing the fire hose cabinet with a towel. They made it out of the much-vaunted security perimeter and off the island.[11]

As is often the case with escapes, this successful attempt followed two the previous week. Two men fled the second floor of the Anna M. Kross Center by similar means, although they did not make it off the island. Meanwhile, a few miles away in Long Island City, prisoner Sal Lupo successfully freed himself from his handcuffs while in transit to court. Upon arriving at the court's sally port, Lupo broke free of the guards, climbed onto the roof of a nearby shack, and leapt to freedom over a wall topped with barbed wire. Guards took chase, pursuing him down Jackson Avenue until he hopped a turnstile at Twenty-First Street and vanished into the New York subway system. These were only the most notable of a series of escapes that bedeviled DOC as it battled crowding, violence, and the ascendance of a brutal movement of rank-and-file guards bent on running the city's facilities as they saw fit, with the full approval of the mayor.[12]

In August of 1987, over 500 prisoners at AMKC staged a hunger strike, purportedly against unsanitary conditions and bad food. The action also came amid a wave of violence among prisoners and meted out on prisoners by guards. Among the most provocative issues was the guards' shakedowns of prisoners' living quarters. These invasive and sometimes violent shakedowns amounted to an act of tremendous cruelty, as prisoners were threatened, insulted, and made to watch as their meager belongings were tossed around carelessly by guards, many of whom are itching for a confrontation. In February of 1988, a large-scale guard shakedown of AMKC pushed a critical mass of prisoners to the breaking point.

On the evening of a particularly forceful shakedown, rebellion broke out among prisoners in twelve different AMKC dormitories, most of whom were already awaiting transport to state facility. They threw up barricades, burnt mattresses, smashed the television and multiple windows, and armed themselves with broken furniture and shards of glass. This time, Commissioner Koehler spent scant time negotiating before calling in a squadron of 200 guards. They proceeded to violently repress one of the rebelling dormitories using clubs and gas, prompting the others to surrender rather than face a similar fate. COBA president Seelig argued this outcome demonstrated that rebellious prisoners had been treated too well in the past. As if summarizing DOC leadership's approach to the spiraling violence on Rikers Island, Supervising Warden James T. Garvey, appearing alongside Koehler and other ranking DOC officials at an emergency press conference, opened his coat to reveal a T-shirt reading, "Don't bother me now, the game is on."[13]

In September of 1989, AMKC was the site of a similar scene, spurred by the removal of two prisoners who had fought with a guard over use of the phone. Prisoners of the 4 Top dormitory once more erected blockades, smashed glass, broke furniture, and set fires. Three surrounding dormitories also joined in. Initially, the prisoners claimed their action was in response to the removal of the two combatants, one of whom they claimed was beaten. In response, DOC administrators produced the prisoner, ostensibly unharmed. But the issue, as the old saying goes, was not the issue. Like many jailhouse rebels before them, they were striking back against the entire social order that incarcerated them, not any singular disagreeable aspect of that incarceration.

"When the other inmates saw that he was unharmed," Koehler later complained, "the inmates focused their complaints on general living conditions. During negotiations, the inmates change their reasons for the disturbance several times." Deputy Warden John Bedron, attempting to negotiate with the prisoners, was hit with scalding water. At this, Bedron lost his temper. In defiance of DOC policy—according to which prisoners had to be warned prior to the use of gas—he order an immediate attack. In the chaotic scene that followed, twenty guards and six prisoners were reported injured. Seelig denounced the raid as the product of a "personal, rather than a professional" handling by Bedron, arguing the prisoners should have been given a chance to surrender. Any temptation to consider Seelig's sentiments as stemming from sympathy for prisoners' rights, and not simply the fact that guards were injured in the fracas, can be safely allayed by the events of the following summer.[14]

Cause for Alarm

By the late 1980s, Mayor Koch's aura of invincibility had dissipated amid a rising tide of corruption scandals that eroded even his long-standing base and destroyed any chance of a fourth term. In 1989 he was defeated in the Democratic primary by Manhattan borough president David Dinkins, a measured and understated clubhouse politician from Harlem. Whereas Koch had stoked racial animosity for over a decade, perhaps most markedly by openly race-baiting 1988 presidential candidate Jesse Jackson, Dinkins presented himself as a figure capable of bridging the city's divide in the wake of high-profile racially charged incidents like the Central Park Five case (in which five black and Latino teens were falsely accused in the assault and rape of a white women) and the death of a black man fleeing a white mob in Howard Beach, Queens. His Republican challenger, Rudolph Giuliani, walked a fine line, mining the racial chauvinism Koch had courted so successfully, while avoiding the rhetorical excesses that characterized the latter's approach.[15]

In particular, Giuliani appealed directly to white voters in his oft-stated refusal to allow the election to become a referendum on the need to repair race relations. Dinkins correctly observed that in so doing Giuliani was, in fact, centering the election around race, under the guise of doing the opposite. As a former prosecutor with no formal political experience, Giuliani accomplished this rhetorical sleight of hand by falling back on a classic New York City racial shibboleth: "law and order." Giuliani positioned himself as uniquely suited to put the bad guys behind bars and return peace to the city's streets, through the liberal deployment of the policeman's truncheon. As one of his supporters argued, the answer to crime was not to promote healing, as supposedly Dinkins intended, "but effective law enforcement and more jails." In reality, Dinkins's line was scarcely a departure from this logic; at this juncture in US politics, just about every political candidate was a law-and-order candidate. Even in the primary season, disagreement on the issue in both major parties centered on *how* to fund a dramatic increase in the number of cops. In the end, Dinkins was sufficiently hawkish on policing and jails to earn even COBA's endorsement. Despite a bitter campaign, he triumphed in the polls, subsequently defeating Giuliani in the general election to become New York City's first black mayor.[16]

To lead DOC, Dinkins tapped Allyn Sielaff, an attorney who had run state prison systems in four states before managing juvenile justice and probation programs for the Cleveland court system. Sielaff distinguished himself as both a pragmatic manager and an advocate of "alternatives to incarceration" and "community-based" punishment, which Dinkins hoped would lower a jail population that by early 1990 had exceeded 21,000. In the months prior to Sielaff's March appointment, two separate *shootings* among prisoners had occurred inside Rikers facilities, using firearms smuggled in from the outside. This was a new high-water mark for disorder, even at Rikers. "The system is in total chaos," Seelig claimed. While variations of this statement had been uttered by COBA brass for decades, it nonetheless rang true; DOC had documented over 1,000 stabbings and slashings between prisoners the previous year alone—and, unmentioned, almost twice that number of instances of guards using force against prisoners. Despite the routine violence by guards against prisoners, Seelig argued that "inmates are running wild ... They are going around stabbing and slashing one another. Staff morale is at an all-time low. There is an emergency and no one is showing a willingness to bring the situation under control." Seelig's tirade was, at root, an appeal to push back against the regulation of use of force by Lasker.[17]

Despite such calls for control, Seelig opposed searches of guards for contraband, blaming its presence in the jail solely on prisoners. Contrary to evidence that drugs—to say nothing of the alarming appearance of guns inside jail walls—were coming into the facilities at least in part through the guards' entrances, COBA's solution was the end of contact between visitors and prisoners, more invasive searches conducted on prisoners, and additional jail time for prisoners caught with drugs. In short, COBA members' carte blanche remained the organization's bottom line, for which it was willing to trade away not only the dignity and well-being of the city's prisoners, but also the safety of its own members.[18]

On July 12, 1990, OBCC administrators imposed a six-minute limit on phone calls. In response, prisoners in at least one housing area rebelled, taking control of their dormitory. The administrators capitulated, agreeing to longer phone calls. Perceiving this as a betrayal, rank-and-file guards took issue with the decision, and tension between guards and prisoners remained heightened for the coming month. On August 7, three prisoners held in the annex of OBCC isolated guard Steven Narby in a secluded staircase, where they punched and kicked him, cut him with a shank, and pushed him down a flight of stairs, where he fell unconscious. In the process, they robbed Narby of his jewelry, leaving him with a fractured skull, a broken jaw, a broken palate, and multiple teeth missing.

The brazen attack in an already-polarized climate electrified DOC's rank and file, who quickly connected it to a recent cut in guard posts, DOC's turn toward "alternatives to incarceration," and, above all, the new, more explicit "use of force" directives required by Judge Lasker as part of the *Fisher* negotiations. These new standards were despised on account of their clarity and insistence that "all reasonable alternatives must be exhausted before force is employed." While it was still the same guard-friendly administration that would be determining what constituted "reasonable," it was widespread consensus among the guards that the new standards had to be relaxed. Meanwhile, word spread that DOC administrators had blamed Narby for wearing jewelry, an insensitive assertion made more inflammatory by Lasker's insistence that pretrial detainees possessed a right to wear jewelry in the city jails. This coincidence bolstered the common contention, propounded by COBA and ostensibly believed in earnest by a critical mass of DOC rank and filers, that the prisoners had more rights than the guards. To DOC's uniformed staff, it was a situation that could not stand.[19]

The final straw in the minds of the city's guards came when the Bronx district attorney announced the charges against Narby's assailants. Contrary to what DOC had promised its guards, they did not include attempted murder. In response, rank and filers representing every jail in the DOC system banded together, ostensibly outside the official channels of COBA, to form the ad hoc group Friends of Officer Narby. They drafted a belligerent open letter to Sielaff. "One of your mandates," they wrote in the statement, dated August 10,

> is to develop and implement alternatives to incarceration and detention for so called eligible offenders. These alternatives are suspose [*sic*] to provide more effective types of specialized program options for inmates. Program options that are connected with the Community, where these inmates will ultimately return. Commissioner, this is not good Community relations. The People of the City of New York would like to rid the City of Crime and Criminals from their local communities. They do not want to have Homecomings for Criminals in their own neighborhoods ... There are no alternatives [*sic*] programs that will change inmates for a return to society.

As for the treatment of these prisoners, who—irredeemable one and all—must remain kept behind bars, the Friends of Officer Narby concluded the letter by informing the commissioner that if it were up to them, he'd be replaced by athlete Bo Jackson. " 'Bo' knows baseball," they remarked of the Kansas City Royals left fielder adept at swinging his bat, "and that is all you have to know to be Commissioner of Correction's [*sic*]."[20]

The letter was drafted on a Friday, as talk of a job action the following Monday began to circulate around OBCC. The next day, literature circulated among rank and filers calling for a "meeting" at the mainland side of the bridge, which guards had blocked in protest on multiple occasions dating back to the

1970s. Simultaneously, Seelig and fellow COBA official Stanley Israel attempted to initiate an emergency meeting with Mayor Dinkins, Commissioner Sielaff, and other ranking DOC and City Hall officials to warn the city of the possibility of an impending wildcat job action. The meeting included Sielaff, DOC director of labor relations Richard Yates, Office of Labor Relations deputy commissioner James Hanley, DOC chief Gerald Mitchell, and New York City Office of Labor Relations commissioner Eric Schmertz. Seelig was visibly disappointed when Dinkins did not appear.

Seelig and Israel were adamant they had nothing to do with the hypothetical action; in fact, they claimed, they wanted to prevent it from happening. Hanley, for one, did not believe them. It was his position that either COBA was using the threat of a wildcat as a bargaining chip, or else it had a hand in whatever job action was coming down the pike. Regardless, the union leaders did in fact claim to have the power to stop the action. In a dizzying sequence, Seelig and Israel assured the city officials there would be no action Monday and scheduled a follow-up meeting for Tuesday; simultaneously, they continued to claim that while the threat of a job action was real, they had nothing to do with it. Seelig even rebuffed the city's request to make it known to COBA members that he and Israel were engaged in talks around the grievances animating the rank-and-file campaign. In short, Seelig and Israel were anxious to portray themselves as in total control of a situation that was quickly escaping their grasp.[21]

Direct Action

Around five thirty the following morning, Monday, August 13, roughly twenty off-duty guards assembled near Eightieth Street, one of two access roads from East Elmhurst, Queens, to the Rikers Island Bridge. The other, Hazen Street, was blocked due to construction, making Eightieth Street the sole access point to the island. They carried signs with messages like "Stop cutting posts," "No more assaults on officers," and "An assault on a prison guard is like a cop being shot." The guards requested that drivers slow down traffic and honk their horns while driving across the bridge. As the Department of Investigation later noted, this suggested there was not a plan to block the bridge entirely. "Slow down. Slow down," they chanted to their colleagues driving by, "What happened to Narby could happen to you." If it was in fact the organizers' intention to merely slow traffic, the situation soon escalated organically. One guard laid flares across Eightieth Street, blocking it entirely. At this, some of his comrades removed them. Soon, arriving guards were stopping their cars altogether, blocking the intersection and feigning that their vehicles had stalled. With traffic backed up for nearly a mile, guards began to simply exit their cars and join the demonstration. The parked cars and growing mob effectively jammed traffic in both directions. Buses attempting to leave Rikers to transport prisoners to court were made to turn around. By 9:00 a.m., DOC had canceled all outgoing court trips. The bridge was blocked.[22]

Shortly after, Yates called Israel to inform him that the bridge was impassible and that buses were unable to make it off the island. "Oh my God," he replied. "Let me get to Phil [Seelig]; I'll get back to you." After this consultation, however, Seelig and Israel were defiant; they refused the overtures of DOC management to intercede, reiterating that COBA had nothing to do with the action and disclaiming responsibility for its resolution. In response, Chief Gerald Mitchell invited a delegation of representatives, two from each institution, to meet with him and various other DOC brass in Commissioner Sielaff's conference room on the island. As a condition, these rank-and-file delegates were to instruct their comrades to cease their bridge blockade for the duration of negotiations. The delegates agreed, but the blockade did not cease for a single second, either due to bad faith negotiations by the representatives, or, more likely, because nobody was in charge anymore.

Nevertheless, the delegation of guard representatives was allowed to cross the picket line to Rikers, where Mitchell heard their grievances. He later claimed, somewhat improbably, that after a mere twenty minutes, the meeting was working toward a resolution. However, at that moment—and this part seems to be fact—Israel burst through the door, demanding the negotiations cease. Mitchell, he warned the rank and filers, was a skilled negotiator, and they stood no chance, in contrast to professional union politicians like himself and Seelig. In the process, Israel argued that the guards should not listen to Mitchell, who he noted was a "black man." The comment enraged his own members, most of whom were black. A shouting match erupted, and Israel, vice president of COBA, was run out of the room by his own members for his failed attempt to race-bait management. A desperate Seelig stepped into the vacuum and convinced the guards to allow COBA to take over negotiations on their behalf, thus terminating their talks with Mitchell. Shortly thereafter, however, when Sielaff attempted to drive through the demonstration, his car was stopped by guards, who refused to let him pass. "Meet with us," they commanded Sielaff, "not the union." The picketers blocking the bridge were not answering to anyone.[23]

City cops were initially slow to respond. One NYPD mobile-command vehicle arrived, at last, around 11 a.m., as protestors were already lined up at least twenty deep across the street. Misidentifying the vehicle, one guard shouted, "Paddy wagon!" and the demonstrators immediately ceased marching and sat down. DOC captain James Grillo attempted to convince the cop in charge that the presence of this vehicle was a provocation. "In a very rude, uncaring, and disrespectful manner," Grillo reflects, "he stated it would be placed as close as possible to the guard shack" near the center of the action. This enraged the crowd and seemingly steeled their resolve to keep the bridge blocked. As the massive police vehicle approached, a guard operating a DOC dump truck pulled across Hazen Street, blocking it entirely and preventing the command center from advancing. Amid fevered shouts from the cops, the guard driving the truck claimed he was simply trying to turn around and got stuck. The police commander on the scene demanded his arrest. Grillo interceded and escorted the dump truck driver away, after the path was cleared.[24]

As the police presence increased, rumors swirled among guards that the cops planned to open fire on them to clear the bridge. Unbeknownst to the guards, NYPD brass had, in fact, determined that a direct confrontation with the guards, many of whom openly carried guns and, in Sielaff's words, engaged in "considerable drinking," could very possibly degenerate into a firefight. Sielaff shared this assessment, as did Mayor Dinkins, who later spoke of a possible confrontation "that could have been very, very nasty." Corroborating this account, Ted Katz of the Legal Aid Society subsequently described the guards as "flashing their guns on the bridge."[25]

At roughly 4:30 p.m., an ambulance arrived at the picket line, responding to a call of a seizure on Rikers. The assembled guards refused to let the paramedics through, surrounding the vehicle, smashing its windshield, denting its side panels, attacking the paramedics, and attempting to drag them off the ambulance. In the melee, the driver hit the gas and the vehicle lurched forth, striking three guards. The guards then came to blows with each other over whether to further beat the bloodied EMTs, who put out a "10-13" call for police assistance and issued another call for help from their supervisors. When ranking supervisors from Emergency Medical Services responded, their vehicle too was surrounded and attacked. These supervisors then put out a call for additional backup, and at least six ambulances responded. At the sight of the emergency caravan, a wild brawl erupted between paramedics and guards. Paramedics fought each other and the guards, who continued to fight among themselves, while keeping an eye on the cops—with whom they might also end up doing battle at any moment. DOC officials who tried to intervene were punched and kicked from all sides. By the time cops were able to break up the fight, eight paramedics had been injured. Ultimately, criminal complaints were lodged against fifteen guards. One paramedic even claimed a guard had stabbed him. (He was later charged with inflicting this wound himself, but his lawyer claimed the accusation was an attempt by the city to sweep the ugly incident under the rug.)[26]

By evening, there were anywhere from 600 to 1,000 guards blocking the bridge and assembling in the street around it, drinking openly and loitering on people's lawns, sometimes to relieve themselves. Even when it began to rain, the picketers were not discouraged, in part due to the distribution of plastic ponchos by on-duty guards.

Meanwhile on the island, Seelig and Israel were locked in negotiations to end the picketing. COBA insisted that only the elimination of the use-of-force restrictions stipulated by *Fisher* would bring the action to an end. At one point Seelig declared that he would refuse to calm down the rank and filers until the EMS workers who had rumbled with the guards were arrested. COBA's thirty-some demands included more staffing (including double coverage for guards sent on hospital runs), an end to mandatory overtime, harsher penalties for prisoners who assaulted guards, more regular searches, the lodging of "attempted murder" charges against the prisoners who attacked Narby, amnesty for all participants in the action (including the nullification of parking summonses for those whose vehicles blocked the street and the cancelation of towing fines), no invocation of the Taylor Law against the guards undertaking the blockade, and—most importantly—the repeal of the use-of-force protocol stipulated by *Fisher*.

This final demand had become the central issue of the entire wildcat: the guards were demanding an end to stringent oversight of how and why they chose to inflict violence in the maintenance of order in DOC jails. It was the logical outcome of decades of right-wing activism, beginning with the movement against the Warren Court, through the triumph of law and order, the restructuring of the city amid the fiscal crisis, and the solidification of this new order under the Koch administration. The power to use violence indiscriminately was not a demand for better wages or material comforts of any kind. It was, rather, a demand for unquestioned power. It is no exaggeration to say that the issue of use of force, which catalyzed the wildcat in the first place, was as important to the rank and filers as all the rest of the demands put together. This was an explosion, in spectacular form, of long-standing struggles over control of New York City's jails and, by extension, the city itself. This demand made cops and guards junior partners in the neoliberal restructuring of New York City, which they enforced with great alacrity—provided, of course, that nobody told them how to do their jobs.[27]

Overwhelmed DOC administrators were happy to concede most of COBA's demands almost immediately, but they had no jurisdiction over the use-of-force rules imposed by Judge Lasker. Commissioner Sielaff, who had to access the island by boat after being denied entry to the bridge by the picketers, emphasized this fact throughout negotiations. In response, Seelig demanded to see Lasker. The judge was not produced. The city, for its part, was hesitant to invoke the Taylor Law, reasoning, as DOC later explained, that "a Taylor Law injunction is not self-executing and does not automatically impose a settlement. Officers may not have returned to work in spite of an injunction." This made a conclusion "even more difficult to reach." In other words, invocation of the anti-strike Taylor Law was no guarantee the action would end—or that the guards would lose in the end.

As the for the use-of-force issue, compliance with the federal courts prevented the city from changing the existing policy, and DOC could only promise to present a modified use-of-force agreement to Lasker. In reality, Lasker's guidelines only covered CIFM, the subject of *Fisher*, but DOC had adopted them throughout the system and, apparently, wished to continue tethering the entire department's use-of-force protocol to the most restrictive version. The final resolution with COBA, therefore, produced a nonbinding agreement to work toward replacing the hated protocol with a less restrictive one, while keeping the existing language in place in the meantime. The agreement was struck at 6:30 p.m. on Tuesday, over thirty-six hours after the action had begun.[28]

Seelig quickly took to the bridge to announce the supposed victory to his ranks. "With the swagger of a conquering hero," recounted *Village Voice* reporter Annette Fuentes, "Seelig jumped on a van, bullhorn in hand, and told the crowd what it wanted to hear: that the use-of-force rules had been eliminated." The announcement was met with great celebration. The only problem was that it was not true. Seelig later claimed he had qualified his declaration with a more technical explanation of how the rules were to be amended at Lasker's discretion, but that the crowd was cheering too loudly to hear him. DOI, however, unearthed a video of Seelig's proclamation that, prior to cutting out, shows him standing for nine seconds after the initial announcement, basking in the adulation of the crowd, and making no such statement. Nobody seemed to believe Seelig's protestations of innocence. "Your false statements," labor relations commissioner Schmertz later wrote to the COBA president, "may have constituted incitement to riot." This was not hyperbole.[29]

Set It Off

Conditions inside the Rikers jails deteriorated considerably over the course of the blockade. The guards on duty were kept on for five consecutive shifts, totaling more than forty hours. Simultaneously, many prisoners bound for court, seventy of whom from CIFM alone were scheduled for release, were prohibited from leaving the island. Visitation was canceled. Movement through the jails was restricted to emergency situations, constituting a de facto lockdown. Medication ran out. Food service deteriorated to the point where many prisoners missed breakfast. Conditions were particularly poor at OBCC, where tensions had been heightened since the Narby incident. On Tuesday morning, a brawl between black and Latino prisoners erupted. Later that day, prisoners broke into the commissary, where one prisoner's attempt to take an extra carton of milk in the cafeteria was met with a squadron of guards in riot gear, followed by the retaliatory beatings of several unrelated prisoners. Still more violent guard retaliation followed a group of prisoners' telephone call to local news to report on conditions at OBCC. This repression came not from a position of strength, but of weakness—something the prisoners likely sensed. Guards were exhausted and in short supply, leaving all facilities understaffed in order to take breaks. By Tuesday afternoon, prisoners across the facility were organizing to "set it off" that night—slang for staging a riot.[30] The prisoners' subsequent organizing to set it off was a fascinating analogue to the events unfolding across the East River. Soon, a letter circulated between the dormitories calling for a unified action. Its organizers intended to initiate a building-wide rebellion at a designated hour in the mid to late evening— accounts differ as to the time, placing it variously at 9:00 p.m. and midnight—beginning with noisemaking and barricades, then leading to coordinated dormitory occupations. In the early evening, guards, some of whom had overheard references to prisoners planning to "set shit off," began observing prisoners "padding up" their bodies with extra clothing, blankets, and other cloth items, which they took to mean preparation for a violent encounter.

In response, a probe team entered the 6 Upper dormitory, demanded prisoners remove excessive clothing, and confiscated their blankets. When prisoners in nearby 4 Upper saw the probe team entering 6 Upper, they too began padding up, and a second, smaller probe team was dispatched there. Initially, the 4 Upper prisoners complied with orders to remove their excessive clothing. One prisoner, however, seated on his bed, refused to remove his winter jacket or to stand. The guards moved on him. Unbeknownst to them, in the climate of violence since the Narby attack, the 4 Upper prisoners had decided in advance that to prevent assault during transport, they would not let anyone be taken out without a representative providing oversight. When confronted with the harassment of their comrade, however, this resolution turned into a refusal to let anyone be taken at all.

Prisoners armed with shanks or their bare hands squared off against riot gear and batons. Multiple guards were slashed. A handful lost their batons and shields to the prisoners, who picked them up and used them in the melee. Some guards were choked and beaten, as they sprayed tear gas wildly into the air. Reinforcements soon arrived, laying siege to the rebellious prisoners. Guards commanded all prisoners abstaining from the rebellion to sit on their beds, and then to huddle in the front of the dormitory, while the rebels held down the back. Still more guard reinforcements arrived and lobbed one, then another tear gas canister into the back of the dormitory.

At this, all remaining prisoners surrendered. They were herded into the dayroom, all the while being beaten with batons. Once in the dayroom, many were beaten again and sprayed in the face with more caustic chemicals. By this point, word had spread throughout the facility that it was going down in 4 Upper. Barricades sprang up across OBCC as prisoners padded up and prepared for battle. Prisoners breeched a security station and unlocked the doors of multiple dormitories on the lower floor, setting fires and smashing windows. One prisoner attempted escape out a broken window, but he was quickly captured outside the facility.[31]

Faced with a facility-wide rebellion, DOC administrators made the curious decision to evacuate every dormitory into the facility's receiving area and dining hall. During the first evacuation, that of 4 Upper, prisoners were lined up, ordered to place their palms on the hallway wall, and then pummeled from behind with clubs. Guards made little distinction between those who had resisted and those who had obeyed their commands. They also stripped some prisoners of their jewelry and explicitly told them this was retribution for the assault and robbery of Steven Narby. Twenty-three prisoners from 4 Upper sustained injuries, nineteen of which required hospitalization. By the time the prisoners had been transported to the receiving area, the hallway floor and walls were streaked with blood. There would be more still.[32]

As Seelig stood atop a parked van issuing his spurious victory speech, the rebellion in 4 Upper was already underway. The guards—who by now had been drinking heavily, fighting other city workers and one another, and brandishing firearms for two straight days—cheered as the firebrand COBA president proclaimed the end of policies restricting their ability to mete out violence on prisoners. Shortly after Seelig's speech, word reached mainland Queens of the prisoner rebellion at OBCC. The assembled guards packed onto DOC buses, which ferried them directly to that facility's parking lot.

Once at OBCC, the guards attempted to join the hundreds of their comrades already mobilizing inside to quash the prisoner rebellion. DOC director of labor relations Richard Yates, who witnessed this chaotic scene outside OBCC, later testified he beheld "150–250 people [from the bridge] outside in civilian clothes; 35 to 40 people were trying to get in through the left door, but Chief Mitchell pushed them back." As they battled to get inside and make use of their newly relaxed policies on violence, he also saw a "hysterical correction officer and was advised the officer had been hit by his fellow officers," as well as another guard "overwrought with hysteria." A number of guards inside were openly carrying firearms; lacking holsters, some had tucked the guns in their waistbands.[33]

Most DOC officials later testified that none of the guards from the bridge demonstration made it into OBCC. Commissioner Sielaff, for his part, claimed that Division Chief Garvey and his own personal driver stood guard and prevented their entry. However, Garvey himself admitted that some OBCC guards had let the guards into the facility, and that "many appeared to be drunk." A DOI report found that some guards fresh from the bridge made it into OBCC, evidenced by multiple sightings of guards clad in riot gear overlaying T-shirts and shorts. The rest refused orders to return to the buses. The mob chanted: "Don't let the fucking IG in!" In response, Garvey advised against letting in civilian monitors, on the grounds it would only worsen the riot.[34]

By all accounts, the building-wide evacuation was a brutal affair, even as the prisoners' resistance crumbled. Most dormitories surrendered peacefully, even according to DOC's unreliable narrative. Nonetheless, hundreds of prisoners were subjected to the same treatment as those from 4 Upper: placed against the wall, they were stripped of jewelry and other personal effects, including glasses—which were either thrown on the floor and stomped on or, in the case of gold, pocketed—and beaten from behind while being taunted with references to the Narby assault. Some were stripped completely naked. Prisoners were thrown down stairs, kicked in the genitals, beaten with handcuffs, and clubbed so hard that one nearly lost an ear and another almost lost a finger from baton blows. One prisoner was asked if he was bleeding, and when he replied in the negative, he was beaten with a club. Another had his Walkman broken over his head. There was an unevenness to who received violence, which seems to have been determined more by the absence of supervisors than any particular wrongdoing, imagined or actual, on the part of any of the individual prisoners.

Some prisoners, most notably those in 6 Upper, resisted eviction until they were gassed into submission. Once outside, many were viciously beaten according to the same pattern. Numerous prisoners describe guards issuing conflicting orders, then striking them for failing to obey the impossible commands. Meanwhile, guards had ceased to follow any protocol of their own, with the exception that they sometimes refrained from beating prisoners in the presence of their superiors—other times, not. During the eviction of 6 Upper, a group of guards were awaiting a captain's orders to proceed through a barricade when a large group of their workmates stormed in, pushing them out of the way, and attempted to lay siege on their own initiative. "When you come to our jail," one prisoner was told, "we run things."[35]

At the end of this grisly procession, prisoners were packed into either the receiving area or the dining hall. Many were denied medical assistance for serious injuries stemming from the beatings. They were made to sit with their hands on their heads and heads on the tables, or else to kneel against the wall. If they moved, they were struck with batons. One prisoner's head was grabbed and bounced off the table by a guard. Prisoners were beaten for requesting water while detained for hours in the stifling August heat. Another was punched and kicked as he suffered an asthma attack, on the grounds he was faking it. Guards walked around asking prisoners which dormitory they were from, striking each one with a baton if they did not answer or answered too slowly. From beginning to end of this surreal and macabre sequence of events, the press was denied access to the island. "It is a berserk irony," Ted Katz later remarked, "that Ted Koppel is in Baghdad and Sam Donaldson is in Saudi Arabia and no reporter is permitted on the island and none was permitted during the riots and ensuing violence."[36]

There were 120 prisoner injuries serious enough to record, including eighty-one head injuries. Of these, only fifty-one came from dormitories that were said to have put up any fight at all, and even many of those accounts were spurious. DOI issued a scathing report finding widespread inappropriate use of deadly force, and a systematic effort on the part of DOC staff to dissemble the facts. "In negotiating to resolve the job action that led to the closing of the Rikers Island bridge," the report concluded bitterly, "representatives of the correction officers union said that their members were in large part protesting the lack of respect they believe they were given. In this Department's opinion, public servants earn the respect of the public and others in public service by the competence and integrity they demonstrate in doing their jobs." Following their ordeal, many prisoners returned to dormitories to find their personal effects smashed and strewn about, and even more of their jewelry stolen.[37]

Always the Worst

The fallout from this spectacular week was largely dominated by open feuding between Dinkins and Seelig. "The Mayor is a minority mayor," the COBA president told reporters, "and the largest number of inmates, as the Mayor well knows, are minority." Dinkins, he argued, was afraid to side with the guards against the prisoners. Seelig caused further problems for himself by claiming that the prisoners had "threatened to riot, take women and rape them"—a statement some women guards took to imply they could not handle themselves and had to be protected by the men. Seelig even attempted to stoke a lasting feud between guards and EMTs by suing to put an end to the police escorts that EMTs had requested for trips to Rikers, following the brawl at the foot of the bridge. It was Seelig's remarks about Dinkins, however, that became the primary focus of the controversy that ensued.

"His logic escapes me," Dinkins replied, "given that the overwhelming number of correction officers also come from Latino and African American communities." The logic was, however, plain. In his desperation, losing control of his own rank and file and battling for political survival, Seelig had played an old tune that sounded hopelessly tone deaf to the new generation of black leaders emerging in the DOC rank and file. In response to Seelig's comments, an organization of black guards called the Guardian Association called for his resignation.[38]

Seelig's loss of control of COBA, and the clumsy steps he and Stanley Israel had taken to reassert it, were evidence both of the changing racial composition of DOC's uniformed workforce, and of its unchanging desire, by no means lessened by the guards' racial makeup, to wantonly mete out violence on the black and brown prisoners who constituted the vast majority of the city's jail population. Perhaps more offensive to the guards than Seelig's race-baiting of Dinkins was his implication that racial solidarity could weaken black guards' resolve to run Rikers by brute force. In reality, DOC's gradual evolution into a majority-black workforce had not translated into increased compassion for prisoners. If anything, the wildcat nature of the action, its emphasis on slackening the use-of-force protocol, and the brutality at OBCC, most of which occurred outside COBA's control, demonstrated that Seelig wasn't militant enough in his opposition to even a modicum of human rights for prisoners in city custody. As COBA resolved the final wording of the new use-of-force protocol that would replace Lasker's standard, a lawyer for the union attempted—albeit unsuccessfully—to sneak in a clause providing immunity for *any force whatsoever* used in "altercations with inmates."[39]

As with the staff riot of 1986, in the months following the bloody August events, special reports abounded. Fingers pointed in every direction, but ultimately, nobody in DOC or COBA faced any consequences. When Deputy Mayor Norman Steisel contacted DOI, in the 1990s riot's aftermath, for all available papers on the October 1986 staff riot, he was provided with a modest cache of internal documents and told that no trial or grand jury transcripts could be found. That was because they didn't exist. Nor would they for the events of 1990. In the end, as in 1986, no guards faced criminal charges.

Propelled by a militant rank and file, the city's guards had capitalized on the law-and-order coalition and the shake-up of the fiscal crisis to craft a powerful niche in city politics that was answerable to practically nobody. Their base of operations was a militarized compound in the East River called Rikers Island. Their union, the Correction Officers' Benevolent Association, had emerged as a power on the city stage unmatched by any its size. Built by jail reformers to be a world-renowned hub of penal welfarism, Rikers Island was now the domain of a violent custodial force that demanded—and won—almost-untrammeled city recognition of their freedom to dispose of the city's prisoners however they saw fit. Reached for comment following the bridge blockade and riot at OBCC, Ed Koch, now several months into his retirement, recounted his own experiences dealing with COBA. "Their threats are always the worst," he told a reporter. "Their rhetoric is always maniacal. They are the most irresponsible of all the unions." Considering the source, it was a high compliment.[40]

Afterword:
Miracles Aren't Real

The central events of this book conclude with the chaos of August 14, 1990. The East River outpost of Rikers Island was now crisscrossed with teeming jails that warehoused, in brutal and dehumanizing conditions, some of the city's poorest people —who were disproportionately black and brown, and the vast majority of whom had not been convicted of any crime. Control of the island, along with New York City itself, had decisively fallen to the organized coalition of law and order, a pact unifying the city's cops and jails with the finance, insurance, and real estate sector against just about everyone else. Rank-and-file guards were now accountable to virtually no one—neither their bosses, nor even the mayor. In exchange for maintaining the social order in New York City, Department of Correction guards could engage in rampant illegality and brutality without explanation and without appealing to any ideal higher than dominion by brute force. These conditions inside the city's jails only mirrored conditions on New York City's streets, which belonged, without question, to NYPD's cops.

It is a bitter and instructive irony, no doubt familiar to the reader by now, that the decisive battle for control of DOC was fought over a piece of infrastructure that Anna Kross envisioned as an avatar of penal welfarism—one ruled by civilian experts, and on which the custodial power of guards would be made extinct. Instead, Kross had laid the foundation for a fortress of that very custodial power. By 1990, Rikers Island was emblematic of the unvarnished violence that held together the new order in New York City, following the repression of the crisis of postwar New York through the twin figures of neoliberal governance and law and order. "Perhaps the 1980s and 1990s secured a punitive cultural hegemony," writes historian Naomi Murakawa, "but the carceral state developed over decades, 'unaware' that it would serve conservative ends."[1]

But history does not end in 1990. What follows attempts to bridge this moment of great decision to the present day. The decades that followed that year's bloodshed are deserving of their own sustained study, just as those who suffered in the city jails during this period deserve more space for their stories to be told. Therefore, omissions do not signify that event as unimportant. Rather, they have been made, at great pains, for the sake of brevity and coherence in an overview of the period connecting the events of 1990 with a political moment that just might see the closure of Rikers Island.

A Dark and Dirty Tunnel

COBA president Phil Seelig's remarks in the wake of the 1990 wildcat were the type of white male chauvinism that would not have raised an eyebrow in public institutions for most of the city's history. However, the DOC workforce was no longer a white boys' club. An influx of women and African Americans, the latter by this point constituting the majority of the ranks of the Correction Officers' Benevolent Association, represented a new constituency to which Seelig's entreaties to white power were unable to appeal. Facing public outcry and dissent among his own members, Seelig left COBA and DOC in 1993 to work as an attorney. Stanley Israel, his handpicked and unelected successor, was dogged from the start by claims of illegitimacy and was soon challenged by a young upstart named Norman Seabrook, a black Muslim who had worked as a guard since 1985 and had been present on the bridge in those fateful days of August 1990.

Seabrook campaigned on the claim that COBA's leadership was "dictatorial" and its funds were mismanaged. Further, Seabrook argued, Seelig had retired and bequeathed the position to Israel on the pretext that Seelig would be retained as COBA's counsel for $150,000 per year. This arrangement, Seabrook claimed, had been scuttled only upon its discovery by membership. When Israel passed away in 1999, Seabrook's claims of impropriety were lent considerable weight by the discovery of $2 million in a safe at his modest residence in Flatbush, Brooklyn, along with nearly $1 million spread across multiple bank accounts and stocks. Seabrook claimed the funds had been embezzled through benefits paid out to 2,200 "phantom members." Israel's wife remarked, "That son of a bitch never took me to a movie."[2]

Beyond such claims of financial impropriety—to which Seabrook himself would later succumb, forfeiting his presidency of COBA amid prosecution for corruption—the most basic demands animating Seabrook's campaign were old ones: the jails needed more guards, with more control over how Rikers Island would be run. It was a fight Seabrook would prove capable of winning time and again, while continuing COBA's decades-long project to tail the successes of the Patrolmen's Benevolent Association by demanding parity of pay and benefits with the city's powerful and politically organized cops.

Thus, while Seelig's high-profile, racially tinged spats with Mayor Dinkins and COBA dissidents augured the demise of his tenure as president, after 1990, the average rank-and-filer was secure in their arrogant autonomy. Moreover, while the composition of the city's jail system—prisoners and guards alike—was now overwhelmingly nonwhite, the increasingly nonwhite guards showed as little sympathy with their captives as had the majority-white workforce in the preceding decades. In fact, with Seabrook now at the helm of COBA and willing to defend any and all acts of violence and dehumanization visited on prisoners, Rikers guards were arguably more brutal than ever. When Seabrook claimed his candidacy symbolized "a rainbow at the end of this dark and dirty tunnel," he was not speaking about improvements to the lives of DOC's prisoners. His concerns were more narrowly cast, for the city's jail guards and their own self-interest.[3]

War on Fear

Facing down hard-line policing hawks Ed Koch and Rudy Giuliani in the 1989 mayoral campaign, David Dinkins had promised tirelessly to be "the toughest mayor on crime this city has ever seen." Once elected, he was dogged by stubborn media portrayals, in the vein of Seelig's race-baiting, painting the city's first black mayor as soft on crime and even secretly on the side "criminals." Perennially placed on the defensive, Dinkins declared a "War on Fear" and was careful to appear framed by flags and flanked by high-ranking cops. "We will flood the streets with an army of police officers," he pledged. Accordingly, Dinkins announced the renewal and redoubling of an aggressive NYPD street presence under the banner of "community policing," meant to take the cops out of the station house, and out of their cars, and put them to work walking the beat—and making street-level arrests.

"Our war against fear will return peace to our communities," Dinkins promised, leaving no buzzword unspoken, "leaving us with safe streets, in a safe city." With this, Dinkins unveiled an ambitious plan to expand the city's carceral net—including more jails, prosecutors, probation officers, and cops—in tandem with gestures toward the expansion of public services like after-school programs, summer jobs, and teen-pregnancy counseling. Despite these latter welfare state trappings, the proverbial stick far outweighed the carrot, and they ultimately became part of a quasi-militarized campaign against the city's black and brown neighborhoods. Tellingly, Dinkins referred to the spending plan as "an assault on all fronts."[4]

The explicitly punitive portion of the "War on Fear" fell under the umbrella of a get-tough initiative called "Safe Streets." This sweeping investment in the city's carceral net would continue

the militarization of New York begun under the Koch administration, promising the largest municipal police department
in history, with a particular emphasis on the kind of aggressive street-level policing often credited to Dinkins's successor,
Giuliani. To keep the pace with an anticipated spike in arrests,
Dinkins promised to expand DOC's capacity by 2,950 beds by
July of 1993. Thus, in the years following the 1990 staff riot,
Rikers added several crucial pieces of infrastructure to absorb
and manage a jail population that was taxing the existing facilities to their absolute limit. In the process, administrators effected
the further "completion" of the island. This effort culminated in
the all-time-high city jail census of 21,449 people in 1992, the
vast majority of whom were held on Rikers.

Commissioner Sielaff, whose reputation suffered greatly
from his handling of the 1990 staff riot, stepped aside in late
1991 following another controversy, in which a suspicious
$1.9 million bid for electronic monitoring equipment had been
issued noncompetitively to à firm close to Dinkins. To replace
him, Dinkins tapped Commissioner of Probation Catherine M.
Abate, a human rights lawyer dogged by claims that her father
had until recently been a high-ranking member of the Lucchese
crime family. Abate insisted the allegation was simply anti-
Italian discrimination.[5]

Set in Stone

Among the noteworthy construction feats of the late 1980s,
Rikers boasted the first two-story modular jail in the United
States. Though penal welfarism was nowhere to be found, DOC
became famous for its innovations in rapid carceral expansion
across the island's ever-receding acreage of undeveloped land.
In 1991 DOC hastily erected twenty framed fabric structures
at four sites on the island to act as auxiliary facilities to existing jails. These large tent-like structures, manufactured by the
Sprung corporation, provided sixteen dormitory units and four
support buildings, debuting alongside fifty additional modular

units reserved for administration space. The Petracca & Sons construction firm, which won the contract less than two weeks before work was scheduled to begin, boasted: "Despite harsh winter working conditions, three of the sites were completed on time, with the fourth finished [two] days ahead of schedule." Later that year, the firm was again contracted on an emergency basis to construct a veritable Sprung village called the West Facility, comprised of sixteen Sprung dormitories and seven Sprung support units, along with seventy-five modular administrative units. Using the streamlined "design-build" approach that unified design and construction under a single contract, the firm met its daunting emergency deadline of seventy-five calendar days to add an additional 800 beds, and ancillary support facilities, to Rikers Island's carceral infrastructure.[6]

During this period, DOC also opened the George R. Vierno Center (GRVC), named after a DOC veteran who had recently suffered a fatal heart attack off duty. Its name serves as another reminder that, despite COBA's rhetoric that its members risk their lives, very few DOC guards have ever died on duty. GVRC added 850 maximum-security cells to a portion of the island once home to the city's tree nursery and a radio beacon for LaGuardia Airport, earning the facility the nickname Nursery-Beacon, shortened over time to the notorious appellation "the Beacon." Even this was not sufficient; to meet the Safe Streets mandate for additional jail beds, and the broader zeitgeist of militarizing incarceration in tandem with the rest of the city, the GVRC had to be expanded almost immediately. "The directive, you might say, was set in stone," quips construction journalist John Gregerson. "New York City's Department of General Services was ordered to add 500 inmate cells to [GVRC] ... And quickly."

The stone in question was poured concrete, and the additional cellblocks were to comprise two towers, one four-story and one six-story, of maximum-security cells, home to 200 and 300 cells respectively. In order to meet the perhaps-unprecedented time window of twenty-two months to design and construct the facility, contractors introduced modular concrete units to Rikers

Island. Much like the modular trailers that increasingly littered the island's landscape in various states of repair, these buildings arrived on Rikers in large prefabricated parts, including cells furnished with completed interiors, and were simply stacked together at breakneck pace. Whereas the city, under pressure from construction unions, had once balked at plans to use concrete modular units, these objections were overridden by the imperative to cover Rikers Island's surface with as many cells as possible. DOC proved the design-build process could accomplish this imperative quickly; the addition to GVRC finished twenty-six days ahead of schedule.[7]

In 1992 community opposition to Koch's jail barges *Bibby Venture* and *Bibby Resolution*, along with their continuing unfitness for even the most rudimentary of carceral purposes, and pressure from the Army Corp of Engineers, resulted in the removal of these vessels from their Lower Manhattan moorings. Undaunted, DOC anchored a third vessel in its fleet, previously disused and docked at Riker Island, to the South Bronx shore, not far from the original dock from which prisoners were ferried to Rikers before Anna Kross built the bridge. In 1987 Deputy Mayor Robert Esnard had claimed the city had learned its lesson from the over-budget and over-time fabrication of the previous two floating jails and become "experts" in the process. However, New York City's carceral history offers scant examples of learning from past mistakes, and this was no exception. Ultimately DOC commissioned a boat from scratch—a 625-foot jail barge, christened the Vernon C. Bain Center after a former DOC warden. Today, the uncannily cubist structure is known simply as "the Boat." When it opened its 800 beds, the project was $35 million over budget and eighteen months behind schedule. The Boat's staggering $161 million price tag made it the most expensive jail facility in New York City history. It was also supposed to be temporary, though it proved anything but.[8]

Finally, in order to handle a precipitous rise of prisoner writs claiming civil rights violations during this period—which climbed, disproportionate even to the island's rapid expansion, from thirty or forty per week in 1988 to roughly 200 per week by 1991—DOC constructed its own courthouses inside a pair of two-story triple-sized trailers previously used for administration. The spartan interiors of the twenty-eight-by-seventeen-foot courtrooms fashioned out of modular trailers would have been immediately recognizable to prisoners who, for the previous decade, had been packed into similar prefabricated units across the island. It is doubtful this setting made them any more optimistic about their prospects for receiving a fair hearing.[9]

Utmost Disrespect

None of Mayor Dinkins's tough-on-crime measures—or the decreases in quantifiable murder, rape, and robbery during his mayoralty—could shake the insistence among representatives of the law-and-order coalition that the city's first black mayor was on the criminals' side. Prominent critics pushing this narrative included PBA president Phil Caruso and Dinkins's electoral rival, Rudolph Giuliani. As political scientist Wilbur C. Rich argues, Dinkins may have been able to lower the crime rate, but he "could not rely on law and order rhetoric that would have been regarded by some as code for cracking down on black criminals." Instead, Dinkins had to strike a delicate balance, courting law-and-order voters while avoiding alienating his base among black and brown New Yorkers.

Dinkins was constantly pressed by a police force that had abided black leadership before, but was far less tolerant of any measures to limit the unchecked power of the cops. Following the disclosure of a staggering level of police corruption in Brooklyn, including armed robbery, drug dealing, and systematic brutality among a small cadre of arch-criminal cops, Dinkins appointed the Mollen Commission to probe NYPD. Simultaneously, and fatefully, he also pressed for an independent civilian review board to oversee the department. This move proved just as unpopular for Dinkins as it had for Mayor Lindsay twenty-six years prior. Given the determining role of race throughout his tenure—thanks in part to the 1991 Crown Heights riots that pitted black New Yorkers against ultra-orthodox Jews—this time around, the backlash was a whole lot worse.[10]

The growing tension between Dinkins and the city's cops came to a head the following month, around the police killing of José "Kiko" García in Manhattan's Washington Heights neighborhood. On July 3, 1992, the twenty-three-year-old Dominican national was shot and killed by white undercover cop Michael O'Keefe. While NYPD insisted García had brandished a weapon, many in the community disputed this story, including witnesses who claimed García was unarmed and had been beaten and shot with little to no provocation. One witness in particular beheld O'Keefe firing into García's prone body as the latter lay seemingly unconscious from a beating O'Keefe had inflicted with his police radio. Moreover, the loaded .38 Smith & Wesson revolver that O'Keefe claimed to have taken from García following the shooting had been stripped of its serial number, consistent with the common cop practice of carrying untraceable "drop guns" to plant on suspects in order for a shooting to seem justified.

It was a New York story all too common. This time, however, the neighborhood wasn't going to suffer in silence. Disbelieving the police version of events, and having plenty of grievances of their own against NYPD, hundreds of García's outraged neighbors rebelled. Over the course of five raucous days marked by street skirmishes that engulfed upward of forty blocks. Washington Heights residents threw garbage, pelted cops with bricks and bottles, shattered windows, and set cars ablaze. By the time the city had restored order, over one hundred people had been arrested, fifteen injured, and one killed.[11]

With both Crown Heights and recent anti-police riots in Los Angeles surely at the front of his mind, Dinkins attempted conciliation. He denounced the rioters while attempting to broker peace by paying respect to the Washington Heights community. Dinkins visited the area multiple times alongside local politicians, including a meeting with García's family, and paid for García's funeral costs with city funds. The response from PBA was predictable: any semblance of sympathy with García or his family was unacceptable. The union and its allies tirelessly touted a coroner's report that found cocaine in García's system—as if to say cocaine use warranted a summary execution. According to President Caruso, Dinkins had "callously ignored the traumatic plight of the police officer" and "transform[ed] a drug villain into a martyr." Tellingly, Caruso complained that Dinkins had "done nothing to uplift the morale of the troops in the area," meaning the cops who increasingly resembled an occupying army in Washington Heights.[12]

Soon thereafter, this army went on the offensive against the mayor's plan for independent civilian oversight. On September 16, 1992, PBA called for a massive demonstration outside City Hall to protest the proposed board. It was widely understood as simultaneously opposing Dinkins's impaneling of the Mollen Commission and, perhaps most of all, the mayor's ostensible sympathies with José García and other victims of police violence in Washington Heights. What followed harkened back to the height of the fiscal crisis. A crowd approaching 6,000 off-duty cops descended on City Hall, many openly intoxicated and discarding bottles at their feet. The crowd was worked up by firebrand speeches from Caruso, Giuliani, and even García's killer, Michael O'Keefe, who had himself become a martyr to the cause of the autonomous policeman.

The paltry detail of cops assigned to manage the demonstration stood back as the rowdy mob overturned barricades, menaced journalists, and reveled in what one reporter called "a beer-swilling, epithet-hurling melee that stretched from the Brooklyn Bridge to Murray Street." Echoing the days of Fear City, a large contingent broke from the main rally to block the Brooklyn Bridge for an hour, as off-duty cops bounced on occupied vehicles, denting their hoods and threatening the people inside. For their part, many on-duty cops cheered the spectacle on. Senior NYPD brass arrived on the scene to observe, only to be taunted by chants of: "Empty suits, empty suits!" When one motorist hopelessly snarled in the logjam emerged from her vehicle to plead with the crowd that her infant was imperiled by the heat, she was told: "Hey, why don't you call a cop."

While NYPD was by this point 22 percent nonwhite, the turnout for this rally was almost entirely white cops. Explicitly racist signs held by revelers included "The mayor's on crack," "Dinkins, we know your true color—yellow bellied," a placard comparing Dinkins to a "washroom attendant," and another depicting the mayor with an afro hairstyle and enlarged lips. At least one cop chanted "Daryl Gates for mayor," in reference to the white supremacist Los Angeles police chief known for sanctioning brutality and the shootings of black Angelenos, and for his intolerance of civilian oversight. The crowd also appropriated a popular anti-racism slogan that arose in the 1980s by chanting: "No justice, no police!" Darker still, taunts and chants of "nigger" were directed at black city council member Una Clarke and a black journalist. Numerous claims of widespread racial epithets were later verified by Dinkins, who understandably considered himself the target. Even one on-duty cop, assigned to control the crowd, was subsequently suspended when it was proven he had shouted this slur, in uniform.[13]

In a sad irony, Dinkins later complained that the cops' hatred, and their charges he was "anti-cop," were unfair and unwarranted, given his faithful upholding of law-and-order austerity in New York City. Indeed, he had made sweeping cuts to public services while promoting the largest expansion of NYPD in city history. "Now we're cutting a lot of social-service areas—health, education, all kinds of horrendous, difficult choices," he remarked. Instead of the cops and their allies showing appreciation, he continued, "I get called a nigger and treated with the utmost disrespect and it is all but sanctioned by the PBA and Rudy Giuliani." The *Times* editorial board echoed this sentiment, while simultaneously expressing support for the hard work Dinkins had done to promote the neoliberal governing paradigm established during the fiscal crisis. "Angry police officers," they wrote, "still fail to accord [Dinkins] the monumental credit he deserves for expanding the police force even while squeezing other city services."[14]

Righteous Anger

In the aftermath of the police riot, Caruso walked a tightrope, offering a tenuous apology for his role in organizing the demonstration, while excusing the cops' behavior as "righteous anger." The PBA president taunted Dinkins and the city's liberals, accusing them of generously searching for the "root causes" of urban disorder in all cases—except when this disorder was caused by the cops. Beyond the obvious racial chauvinism that came to define the conflict between PBA and Dinkins, as it had that between Dinkins and COBA, Caruso offered a more basic explanation for the vehemence of his ranks to defy City Hall. They were, above all, violently opposed to civilian review, which threatened the power of the cops to dispose of those under their power as they saw fit. It conjured the specter of the cops' ultimate nightmare: "There is nothing more humiliating or demoralizing to a police officer," Caruso told the city council, "than in the pressures of making an arrest, they then have to answer to charges made by the person they arrested."[15]

Giuliani, for his part, had even less interest in denouncing the miniature race riot in which he had taken part, the stakes of which would soon be revealed in ballot boxes across the city. The 1993 mayoral rematch between Giuliani and Dinkins was in many ways a referendum on the state of race relations in New York City since the 1989 election. Giuliani's ultimate victory in 1993 revealed a meaner city than the one that had elected Dinkins. This was an evolution due, in part, to a renewed economic depression that called to mind the bad old days of the fiscal crisis, itself heavily steeped in a racialized mythology that blamed black and brown New Yorkers for capitalism's latest self-inflicted calamity.

This downturn also dovetailed with the long-term effects of disinvestment in services for these working-class New Yorkers, dating back to at least 1974. The fiscal crisis had marked the beginning of a dramatic trend of downward mobility, which forced many of the city's most vulnerable people to subsist off anti-social, dangerous, and illegal activities. Finally, the sour economy, crumbling standards of living across much of the city, and other effects of enduring capitalist crisis and the austerity regime meant to steady it spurred throughout the city a generalized state of nagging anxiety, for which the ideological figures of racialized crime served as ready scapegoats.

This zeitgeist, which geographer Neil Smith dubbed "revanchism," was a cruel form of vengeance seeking that expressed itself in the desire to reconquer the city in the name of the white power structure of old. It came at the precise moment that finance capital was returning to the city, in large amounts, from its adventures in the suburbs. The combination of right-wing populism and FIRE sector capital in search of a productive outlet produced an aggressive campaign to take back New York City's streets, supposedly from the racialized figure of the criminal terrorizing innocent New Yorkers. In actuality, this campaign acted on behalf of Wall Street investors, who were rediscovering the immense value that could be gleaned from the development of neighborhoods that had been largely abandoned by capital for decades—and where nonwhite New Yorkers had taken up residence in large numbers.[16]

The imprimatur "Giuliani Time" was stamped on this epoch during the grisly 1997 abduction of Haitian immigrant Abner Louima by four white cops who brutally beat him in NYPD custody and raped him with a broken broomstick, nearly ending his life. "It's Giuliani Time," the cops supposedly informed Louima in the midst of his ordeal, "not Dinkins time." Spearheaded by NYPD commissioner William Bratton under the banner of "quality of life," Mayor Giuliani pursued an aggressive and racialized campaign against the city's poor. This cruel offensive had two prongs. One redoubled attacks on the social safety net preventing people from becoming homeless, while the other viciously punished the homeless and hounded them to the far reaches of the city. The result was a spate of freezing deaths and untold acts of callous violence and degradation carried out by cops and ordinary citizens, including a rash of incidents in which homeless people were set on fire as they slept. This

campaign was carried out in tandem with the further militarization of city space, as an influx of militaristic police equipment
and ground troops marked the expanding terrain of gentrifying neighborhoods reconquered from working-class black and
brown communities in the name of FIRE sector profits.[17]

A crucial window dressing for this strategy of brutal expro-
priation was provided, as ever, by the field of criminology.
NYPD draped its violence in a convoluted and anecdotal screed
penned for *The Atlantic* by criminologists George L. Kelling and
James Q. Wilson called "Broken Windows." In it, Kelling and
Wilson lend the legitimacy of their prestigious academic expertise to the preverbal imperative to force unwanted people out
of space one intends to claim as one's own. "Broken Windows"
begins with an observation of street-level policing conducted in
Newark, New Jersey, in which a majority-black neighborhood is
patrolled by a paternalistic white cop named "Kelly." Kelly, we
are told, uses police authority in response not to transgressions
of law, but of order. Steered by the philosophy of "order maintenance," he ignores certain illegalities, like public drinking in
designated areas, while simultaneously applying the extralegal
power to force unwanted people to vacate public space in areas
reserved for more respectable citizens.

"Sometimes what Kelly did could be described as 'enforcing
the law,'" the authors write, "but just as often it involved taking
informal or extralegal steps to help protect what the neighborhood [property and business owners] had decided was the
appropriate level of public order." While Kelling and Wilson
note that "some of the things he did probably would not with-
stand a legal challenge," the written law was largely beside the
point. As policing scholars David Correia and Tyler Wall note,
"The courts might throw out the arrest, but the arrest would
clear the street." Nor did it matter, according to the twisted logic
of "Broken Windows," that quantifiable crime was not even
reduced by Kelly's policing. Supremacy over space had been
attained, in the interest of local property owners and business
interests. This practice had an obvious impact on Rikers Island,
increasing the number of street-level arrests, and thus thronging

the city's jail population to an all-time high. The pseudoscientific praxis of Broken Windows would also make its way across the East River, to DOC administration.[18]

Let Them Eat Corn Dogs

The incoming Giuliani administration wasted no time in ousting Commissioner Abate from DOC and tapped as her replacement Anthony Schembri, the police commissioner of Rye, New York. Schembri was "a regular 'dese,' 'dem,' and 'dose,' Brooklyn guy," on whom the television show *The Commish* was based. Schembri boasted of his Hollywood connections often, and it became something of a joke around DOC. Reminiscent of the days of Koch, Commissioner Schembri was propped up by City Hall as the face of unpopular budget cuts that would have eliminated more than 1,300 guard positions alongside civilian positions in education and drug rehabilitation, at the exact time the city jail population had reached record heights. While the cuts to guard positions were largely spared at the expense of widespread cuts to prisoner programming and civilian staff, Schembri would not live down his image as hatchet man. "Tony Schembri made a pact with the Devil when he took the job," a well-placed informant told journalist Craig Horowitz. "The reason the mayor couldn't get a quality person to fill that post was because anybody of quality would not go along with the things Schembri had agreed to go along with."[19]

As Bernard Kerik, a former jail warden turned decorated NYPD detective, recalls, "In early 1994, at the same time he was threatening to lock up every criminal in New York, Mayor Giuliani wanted the budget to the jails further trimmed." Schembri took considerable heat on behalf of Giuliani, who, like Koch years before, relied on the support of the city's law-and-order coalition as an important part of his base at the same time as he imposed austerity. Of course, this regime of austerity at Rikers only mirrored what Giuliani was imposing on the streets of New York. At Rikers, Schembri was ultimately forced out in less than a year over scandal that amounted to paid speaking engagement undertaken on city time, the use of a city driver for personal errands, and his failure to keep a New York City address—transgressions for which a more popular commissioner would likely have been forgiven.[20]

With Schembri out, Giuliani needed a DOC leadership capable of bringing law and order to Rikers Island that would match the spirit of cruel revanchism from which he drew his governing mandate. This was especially urgent given that the specter of prisoner revolt was once more rearing its head. As word spread of coming budget cuts, thousands of prisoners across Rikers went on episodic meal and work strikes, in signs of organized revolt that troubled administrators. These strikes came alongside an uptick of coordinated violence, which similarly demonstrated a heightened degree of organization among the numerous street gangs increasingly concentrated on Rikers, thanks to NYPD's law-and-order policing. Schembri's replacement would need to be a special kind of manager: one who could fulfill the demands of austerity governance while simultaneously swearing allegiance to the autonomy of the guards, which they had so decisively won in 1990. The ideal manager could impose the facade of effective civilian management on Rikers, while allowing the guards to more or less run the island, on the basis of their own de facto rules, with as much violence as they desired. This would be civilian leadership in name only. Giuliani found what he needed in the duo of Michael Jacobson and Bernard Kerik.[21]

All the credit William Bratton has earned for imposing Broken Windows policing on New York's streets is due in equal portion to Jacobson and Kerik for bringing it to New York City's jails. Michael Jacobson earned a doctorate in sociology at the CUNY Graduate Center before becoming a city budget bureaucrat, and then commissioner of probation, both under the mayoralty of Dinkins. Jacobson entered DOC with the explicit mandate to cut costs while imposing order, all the while maintaining the absolute bare minimum of constitutionally permissible conditions for the city's prisoners. Asked if he would violate prisoners' rights in the pursuit of austerity, Jacobson quipped: "We're not saying that's it, we're just going to feed them corn dogs." COBA's Norman Seabrook hailed the new commissioner as "trustworthy and honest." At his side was Kerik, the former warden and NYPD detective who subsequently worked as DOC's director of investigations before becoming Jacobson's deputy commissioner. Though Jacobson has since become the public face of the management style the duo brought to DOC in the mid 1990s, Kerik was the one running the show. This became official in 1998, when Jacobson left DOC and Kerik officially took over.[22]

Emergency Services

Rudy Giuliani's aggressive campaign to take back land on which the FIRE sector could capitalize, and its growing workforce could safely reclaim for yuppie neighborhoods, went hand in hand with NYPD's crackdown on so-called gangs like the Latin Kings. Giuliani took office vowing aggressive crackdowns on the "hardened criminals" in gangs, along with street-level drug sales and use. Despite his tough rhetoric, this was in large part a continuation of the policies of Dinkins—and for that matter, Koch. As NYPD targeted accused gang members, the population explosion in Rikers in the late 1980s and early 1990s brought high numbers of gang members to the island, as the jails had been filled with black and brown revolutionaries in the late 1960s. Gangs became the principal form in which prisoners organized themselves, in part dictated by associations on the outside, but also driven by the inability of DOC to provide safety for its captive population. For instance, the United Blood Nation, also known as the East Coast Bloods, were formed at Otis Bantum Correctional Center by black prisoners who federated several smaller gangs, as a defensive maneuver, in response to the power wielded by the more organized Latin Kings and Ñeta street families.[23]

In response to a reported influx of organized gang activity, Kerik and Jacobson made sure the guards remained the top gang on the island. They accomplished this by reconfiguring the Emergency Services Unit into an elite squadron with no purpose other than meting out violence against prisoners. Kerik recalls that before he came to Rikers, ESU "had consisted of eighteen officers, who only worked day shifts, when the jail was at its calmest ... But Mike and I had talked the mayor into increasing the funding, allowing the ESU to employ 150 members who would work around the clock to improve their training, preparation, and equipment." The duo expanded and militarized the unit from a small band of volunteers into a "huge SWAT team," as one *Times* reporter put it, with the capacity to roam the island 24/7, perpetrating random shakedowns and responding to alarms, all the while meting out violence with pepper spray, electrified shields, and their clubs, fists, and feet.

If your only tool is a hammer, everything looks like a nail. DOC's hammer was ESU. No longer were guards responsible for blocks or dormitories required to engage with conflict. They could simply call in a heavily armored band of warriors, accountable to nobody, who could mete out violence to whatever degree they pleased. The professionalized violence ESU represented had the full sanction of DOC leadership, who counted on the fear they instilled in prisoners to keep order on Rikers. "The minute we got intelligence that inmates were becoming restless," recalls Kerik, "I'd load up the streets with Emergency Services vehicles and send out the ESU teams in full body armor to march and do drills, to test-drive the armored vehicles and run the dogs. When the inmates came out into the yard for recreation, they'd see this army training," and understand that this violence awaited them if they stepped out of line.

This shift was part of a broader crackdown at Rikers that resembled the activities of Giuliani's NYPD on the outside. DOC monitored prisoners in order to build up a database of the city's growing list of "gang members." Collected by DOC's Gang Intelligence Unit, this information was shared with NYPD, who used it, as now, to target individuals by inference and association. The brutality of ESU was also matched by increases in the frequency and duration of time prisoners were forced to spend in solitary confinement, itself a form of violence. Solitary was originally used for supposedly extreme disciplinary cases, but as the solitary confinement infrastructure expanded on Rikers, it came to be used casually against anyone who crossed a guard. Steep criminal charges replaced administrative charges for assault. Drug possession also became a criminal matter. This meant that prisoners held in the dangerous confines of Rikers against their will while they awaited trial could face additional charges for how they navigated this setting, regardless of the outcome of their cases. "In a number of cases, in fact," Kerik gloated, "inmates have been acquitted of the charges they were brought to jail for, only to find themselves serving years in state prison for violent crimes they were convicted of committing while in jail."[24]

Around this time, the guards began calling themselves "New York's Boldest," which was subsequently adopted as the official motto of DOC. Both the phrase and its appropriation for official use were emblematic of how Kerik and Jacobson struck the balance between running a significantly tighter ship at Rikers and staying on the right side of the guards. The "zero tolerance" "pro-arrest" policy promoted by Kerik was particularly popular with COBA, whose members could be reasonably certain whatever version of events they offered of a given assault would be treated as the truth in court. This meant that a prisoner who found themselves on the receiving end of an unprovoked beating from a guard, and was subsequently cast as the aggressor, could now expect criminal charges on top of the violence and institutional discipline they had already suffered. However, the real genius of this new totalitarian order at Rikers Island, for which the duo would become famous, was the mantle of corporate managerialism in which it was cloaked. Kerik was to thank for this accomplishment; along with the Broken Windows praxis he brought to DOC from NYPD, Kerik also provided the firmament upon which one could gaze as the violence of order maintenance unfolded beneath. This system originated in the NYPD, where it was called "CompStat."[25]

The Firmament

CompStat's name is often cited by proponents as a portmanteau of "computer statistics," "computerized statistics," or "computer comparison statistics." In actuality, the name "CompStat" derives from "compare statistics." The term refers to the ordinary practice of comparing crime statistics to one another to identify places where certain crimes are more likely to be committed, how the rate of reported crimes has changed, and other obvious police uses of even the most rudimentary data. "This distinction is not trivial," write policing scholars John A. Eterno and Eli B. Silverman, "since the 'computer statistics' interpretation frequently suggests that an advanced statistical computer program is synonymous with effective crime control," whereas the program instead has its origins in extremely simple computer software and blunt analysis ancillary to the deployment of Broken Windows policing.

The obfuscatory mist that ensconces CompStat, elevating its data to a fetish object, is no accident. Nor is it coincidence that CompStat's measurements are presented in theatrical meetings of the kind familiar to viewers of the television program *The Wire*. At these meetings, police brass call middle managers to account for their numbers in dramatic and often humiliating scenes, while polished PowerPoint slides bearing colorful graphs and charts flash, wipe, and dissolve across a big screen. Outside observers, write Eterno and Silverman, "often become mesmerized by the flashy overhead display of multiple crime maps synchronized with technologically advanced portrayals of computerized crime statistics." What is taking place is, in fact, much simpler.[26]

CompStat's scientific, quasi-mystical aura conceals what is at root the deployment of aggressive street-level policing, focused on generating higher arrest statistics and reducing reports of crime in targeted neighborhoods. The areas selected are usually designated for gentrification by local developers. The result of CompStat's supposedly complex calculations is plain old head-cracking policing, conducted against unwanted people, with little concern for their rights, in the service of FIRE sector profits.

In the first two years CompStat was deployed in New York City, civilian complaints for illegal searches grew 135 percent, illegal vehicle searches 108 percent, and illegal apartment searches 179 percent.

CompStat practitioners ceaselessly sound the neoliberal watchword of "accountability." But accountability, in the form of professional consequences, is largely reserved for mid-level bureaucrats who could not make the appropriate statistics appear on the screen, or else for those arrested or otherwise harassed on the street level, often for no good reason. Accountability, however, is not a problem for the rank-and-file cops who carry out the dirty business of "stop and frisk" street harassment, and other integral strategies of order-maintenance policing, with however much violence they see fit. If anything, CompStat pushes accountability for low-level cops' behavior further up the chain of command, toward a vanishing point where nobody has to answer for anything. The result is the symbiosis between street cops who desire to do whatever they want in their daily dealings, and commanders who ask themselves simply: "How can I get by the next CompStat meeting?"[27]

This question suggests an obvious flaw in the system, what PBA recording secretary Robert Zink called "the fudge factor." "In the early days," Zink writes, "it was easy for a precinct commander to benefit from CompStat. He or she had crime-ridden neighborhoods where rudimentary policing techniques could bring crime down. Add the increased resources [i.e., more cops] from the Safe Streets/Safe City program, and just paying attention to patterns and putting cops where crime was happening caused stats to fall dramatically." Once the presence of aggressive street-level cops had suppressed quantifiable crime, however, the demands continued for ever-decreasing stats, and commanders had to present themselves at CompStat meetings to face the music. "So how do you fake a crime decrease?" Zink writes. "It's pretty simple. Don't file reports, misclassify crimes from felonies to misdemeanors, under-value the property lost to crime so it's not a felony, and report a series of crimes as a single event." Thus, the fetishism of data works both ways:

while numbers can conceal the reality of what amounts to ordinary head-cracking policing, so too can crimes committed by civilians be made to disappear. All the while, the spectator is left gazing at the firmament above, believing they are witnessing something truly novel.[28]

You Don't Want to Know

Kerik and Jacobson brought their own firmament to the order-maintenance protocol of Rikers Island. They called it TEAMS, a corporatese acronym standing for "Total Efficiency Accountability Management System." As ESU tore through Rikers Island dressed like Robocop, and prisoners suddenly faced steep penalties either in the dreaded "bing" or in the court system, TEAMS provided a managerial face for the whole operation. As Kerik put it, TEAMS "was essentially taking the business principles that Rudolph Giuliani preached and applying them to our jails." As with CompStat, the program presented detailed graphs and charts, and proponents of TEAMS emphasized the novelty of the management style attendant to letting rank-and-file guards loose on some of New York City's most vulnerable people.

"The TEAMS theory," writes Kerik, in characteristic HR argot, "is that every unit within the department affects how the agency performs as a whole, that managers must be agency-focused, not narrowly orientated, and that they be aware of and participate in realizing the department's goals and objectives." Accordingly, TEAMS furnishes a fount of graphs and charts quantifying everything from violence to the cleanliness of showers at Rikers, while performing corporate management in the same data spectacle pioneered by CompStat. In institutional circles, TEAMS is credited with a dramatic decrease in violence at Rikers Island. However, TEAMS had a "fudge factor" of its own. This fudge factor was to play a key role in obscuring the full character of Kerik and Jacobson's legacy at Rikers Island, and exactly what lay beneath the firmament overarching the East River penal colony.[29]

It is difficult to gauge whether the Kerik-Jacobson regime accomplished a reduction in violence at Rikers, as they so often claimed. By DOC's numbers, stabbings and slashings, used as a measure of violence due to the difficulty of concealing them, dropped precipitously, from 1,093 in 1995 to 229 in 1998. A 2014 internal investigation into violence at the Adolescent Remand and Detention Center, renamed the Robert N. Davoren Complex (RNDC) in 2006, however, discovered that a similar feat at that facility—a two-thirds drop in violence, almost overnight—had been achieved exclusively on paper, by simply omitting hundreds of violent incidents from the official tally. This report echoed concerns, voiced by *Fisher* plaintiffs in the 1980s, and BOC long before Kerik and Jacobson took over, that DOC was engaging in the creative accounting of violence to suit its public relations needs.

As discussed above, the *Fisher* plaintiffs had balked at the ambiguity and wiggle room in DOC's court-ordered force protocol, even while the latter was violently resisted by guards in the 1990 staff riot. Similarly, a board member had argued in 1991 that DOC's violence reporting system functioned to distinguish between two types of violent incident: those that would make it onto the final tally, and those that would not. This decision was highly subjective and allowed for the creative accounting of violence. A similar observation would be made almost twenty-five years later, in a 2014 US Department of Justice investigation into conditions at RNDC. The DOJ investigators found that statistics on violence at the facility were manipulated daily by a number of practices running up and down the chain of command. These included the fabrication of paperwork and the destruction of evidence and, notably, the imperative for assaulted prisoners to "hold it down"—that is, to refrain from reporting what had happened to them, under threat of violence.

Regardless of whether violence truly went down, in the early days of TEAMS, invasive searches increased 74 percent, while arrests of prisoners in DOC custody exploded by 400 percent. Mental health clinician Mary Buser learned another dirty secret of how DOC calculated its application of punishment during this period. As one guard told her in 1999, "The way they're loading up the island, they're scrambling for beds. With five hundred beds in the Bing, they can't afford to let one of them sit empty. Every time somebody goes into the hole, a [general population] bed opens up. We have our orders: 'Write 'em up! Write 'em up!' Let me go find some poor schmo." Alternatively, Kerik recalls a conversation between Jacobson and Giuliani in 1997, when the two discussed Jacobson's retirement from DOC. Jacobson recounted to Giuliani the success Kerik had in forcing his subordinates to make their numbers. "Now, I don't know what he does in there," Jacobson remarked. "I'm not sure I want to know. And you know what, Mayor? You don't want to know either." At that, Jacobson recommended Kerik to take his place as DOC commissioner. Giuliani agreed.[30]

Ground Zero

In early September 2001, rapper China Mac was incarcerated on Rikers Island. "I looked out the window," he recalls,

> and there was like smoke coming out of the tower—like yo crazy smoke, it was looking crazy! You could see the part where [the plane] crashed 'cause there was mad smoke coming out of it … I went to grab my headphones, so I'm listening to the news, also listening to Hot 97, listening to the music … Then I walked back to the window, and I'm talking to my bro Gangster Lou … while we're talking, somebody's like 'Yo, look! It's another plane!' I look up and a plane is coming … and I'm like 'Oh Hell no is this real? Another plane is about to crash?' And it just goes slow motion … BOOM!

At this, Mac's entire cellblock erupted in excited shouting.

"While everybody was making all that noise," he continues, "I remember thinking to myself: 'Damn, if something serious is happening now, and we're locked down, what the hell is gonna happen to us?'" He instantly recalled rumors among prisoners about what would happen during martial law: "Because we're prisoners they would just kill us first ... so we don't go with the opposition." At once, all prisoners were ordered to return to their cells for lockdown, where they were kept for upward of five hours. "I was just thinking about the worst," Mac recalls. "I couldn't close my eyes. What if they start coming in here and opening up the cells and just shooting us? ... I didn't know what to think, and I did not wanna die in jail bro, I did not wanna die on no Rikers Island."³¹

It was the beginning of a new era of US politics and culture, defined by the migration of extralegal order-maintenance praxis from the vanguard of crime fighting in New York City to a central organizing principle of American society. The principles of order maintenance, soon to be typified by "stop and frisk" policing, openly trumped both the US Constitution and international law. This is not to say they hadn't before, but now it was official. The belligerent brutality that marked the era of Giuliani—dubbed "America's mayor," and even "mayor of the world," due to the historical accident of a major terrorist attack occurring on his watch—was now thoroughly incorporated into the fabric of polite civil society and afforded all the pomp and respectability attendant to bipartisan political support.

The victory of the FIRE sector in the postwar period had also raised the curious specter of declining rate of incarceration in New York City, attendant to a slide in quantifiable crime. This was a new era; the aggressive crackdowns under Koch, Dinkins, and Giuliani were less necessary when much of New York had been decisively gentrified, and sufficient land reconquered by the ruling class to turn the city into a playground for the rich. The working-class New Yorkers, who had provided a vital base of support for law-and-order politics and the rise of the FIRE sector, were thus rewarded by the upending of their neighborhoods to accommodate a new breed of yuppie New Yorker—one who had much more in common with John Lindsay than John Cassese. None of this, of course, translated into the shrinking of either NYPD or DOC, or their decline in ferocity, as the War on

Terror ideology that animated this period saw a redoubled commitment to so-called security agencies.[32]

Flush with cash from private capital, nonprofit organizations like the Center for Court Innovation, following in the footsteps of the Vera Institute, became highly specialized partners to the administration of punishment and surveillance. For example, to manage the influx of misdemeanor arrests under Giuliani, CCI opened Midtown Community Court near Times Square, abetting the prosecution of Broken Windows cases, and preventing these arrests from overwhelming the courts. The porous boundaries between nonprofits, city government, and the private sector also endured. Jacobson served as Vera's president from 2005 to 2013, after which he founded the CUNY Institute for State and Local Governance. Based in a historically working-class institution presently besieged by austerity, ISLG applies the principles of neoliberal managerialism to public–private partnerships, seeking to ameliorate social problems within terms acceptable to capital, and otherwise promote development. Recently, ISLG teamed up with CCI to oversee electronic monitoring and other "community supervision" programs that have turned the entire city into an open-air jail. Post-9/11 New York was a period uniquely suited for Jacobson, who had experience dressing the violence of Giuliani's order-maintenance practices in respectable business attire. And nobody donned this attire better than Michael Bloomberg, a political novice whose claim to succeed Giuliani as New York City's mayor rested on his private sector bona fides and the same technocratic, post-ideological ethos that defined the regime of CompStat and TEAMS.[33]

All the while, hushed-up stories of brutality, sexual violence, and neglect continued their steady trickle out of Rikers Island. The 2014 case of Bradley Ballard called particular attention to the plight of prisoners suffering from mental illness, suggesting things had not changed since the BOC investigations of the 1970s—or had even become worse. For the trifling offense of offending a female guard, Ballard was left in a stifling cell for six days and denied medication or medical care as his mental health unraveled. He ultimately perished. In spite of such grave offenses, DOC had consistently avoided crippling scandal, largely by touting the accomplishments of the mid 1990s. A characteristic op-ed from the *New York Times*, chronicling a beating death under the heading "Rikers Horror Story," nonetheless began: "New York City correctional officials have done a commendable job reducing the number of beatings, stabbings, and other violent acts that have long plagued city jails." The Kerik-Jacobson system, taken over in 2002 by devotee Martin Horn, could not eliminate such horror stories, but it could limit them to an amount largely acceptable to polite society, while simultaneously burying the violence that held it all together beneath mountains of flashy graphs and managerial data.[34]

This period also represented a golden age for COBA, under the leadership of Norman Seabrook. Before his 2016 indictment for fraudulent handling of union funds, Seabrook had built up COBA into an immensely powerful and influential union in New York City, second only to PBA, despite having a small fraction of the membership. A feared power broker adorned with a pistol at his hip, Seabrook flexed COBA's muscle spectacularly, including a 2013 incident in which he brought transit between Rikers and the city courts to a halt for an entire day—just to prevent a single prisoner from giving testimony against guards who had beaten him.

The specific issue of so-called use of force remained a central figure of COBA's workplace militancy. Seabrook proved himself adept at defending guards accused of assaults, no matter how brazen, while pushing back against the civilians' ability to punish or even oversee the actions of his rank and file. The cruel contempt for the dignity of prisoners and civilians that continued to animate COBA during this time was best captured in a 2014 incident, in which prisoners completing an intensive group therapy program were rewarded with a pizza party. In response, guards staged a small wildcat work stoppage. Seabrook supported them, saying, "You want to eat pizza, stay home." His successor, Elias Husamudeen, has largely followed in his footsteps.[35]

In 1998, medical care was taken over by St. Barnabas Hospital, followed by the private corporation Prison Health Services (subsequently renamed Corizon Health, Inc.) in 2000. Neither organization demonstrated much alacrity beyond following the imperative to cut costs—which was why they got the contracts in the first place. While firmly anchoring the austerity regime that ruled New York City in the twenty-first century, DOC was able to achieve a tenuous holding pattern in which prisoner revolt was repressed, labor peace was maintained, and, above all else, the legitimacy of DOC and its penal colony on Rikers Island were not substantively challenged, either in the streets of New York City or in the pages of its respectable publications.[36]

Still, this is not to say there wasn't community opposition during this time. When Commissioner Horn attempted to expand the Brooklyn House of Detention and construct a women's facility in the South Bronx as part of a plan to phase out the use of Rikers by constructing new jails, he met vociferous community opposition from both NIMBY and prison abolitionists. Abolitionist Pilar Maschi, a member of the Community in Unity (CIU) coalition against the new jail in the South Bronx, describes how the city tried to break the ranks of the anti-jail resistance by setting up meetings with individual groups that seemed less radical and more amenable to cooptation. Some agreed to meet. But when the city delegation arrived at the meeting, the "office was packed. We had signs displaying fifty alternatives to jail, and we made them listen to each one. We also made sure that when Martin Horn came into the office, he was positioned in the back, unable to leave. We cornered him." Ultimately, fierce community opposition defeated both new jails. Another activist victory came in 2014, when a coalition of immigrant rights groups successfully evicted an Immigration and Customs Enforcement office from Rikers Island, on the basis of New York City's new policy, however incomplete, of noncooperation with the agency.[37]

"We work in settings that are designed and operated to keep the truth hidden," writes Homer Venters, who served in several high-ranking medical positions in the city jails between 2008 and 2017. "Detainees are beaten and threatened to prevent them from telling the truth about how they are injured, health staff are pressured to lie or omit details in their own documentation, and families experience systematic abuse and humiliation during the visitation process." As a new century dawned, the power configuration established by Kerik and Jacobson constituted a marriage of convenience between a neoliberal political regime and the managerial science by which it was making the public sector resemble the private. A powerful rank-and-file workforce of guards kept it all under wraps, in exchange for being given a wide berth to do the job with as much violence as they deemed necessary. The truth, however, would not stay hidden forever.[38]

The Collapse of Consensus

"Among the most common ways to describe a bad cop," write Correia and Wall, "is to call him or her a 'bad apple.' This is not an innocent phrase. The bad apple metaphor of police violence condemns the individual bad cop and preserves the perceived righteousness of policing as a whole." In early 2009, three guards at RNDC were indicted for their role in an organized ring called "the Program," an extortion racket in which hand-picked adolescent prisoners had been deputized to administer the jail. These guards encouraged violence between prisoners and erased it from the institutional record, as part of de facto management of RNDC by specially selected prisoners made to do the dirty work on the institution's behalf. It took the beating death of eighteen-year-old Christopher Robinson, an RNDC prisoner who refused to go along with the Program, for this arrangement to come to light. COBA insisted, against mounting evidence, that the Program had simply been made up out of thin air by opportunistic prisoners. Horn, who was criticized for knowing about the Program long before its revelation, was quick to chalk the incident up to the proverbial bad apples.[39]

Beyond the obvious need to deflect bad press, Horn understood the need to defend not just the character of his guards, but also the TEAMS management system, of which he was a firm proponent. "I don't think the performance management system failed," he argued shortly after the revelations.

> As we focused on stabbings and slashings, the inmates learned these kind of attacks would be prevented. We were taking firm preemptive actions, searching for weapons and aggressively isolating those inmates who showed a proclivity for using them. So they changed their tactics. When they began administering beatings instead of cuttings we began to investigate every broken nose, every fractured orbital, every black eye. So they responded by moving to beatings about the mid body, where the injuries would not show and where clothing concealed the injury.

What was needed, therefore, were more variables, and more data. "In this instance, at least," Horn concluded, "performance management was not sufficiently granular to reveal what was happening inside individual cell blocks in a single jail." In short, he quipped, "If we had a princess, perhaps we would have felt the pea under the mattress."[40]

It did not take a princess to generate the most comprehensive portrait to date of the widespread and systematic fudge factors obscuring guard violence beneath the magic of data. This was accomplished by the US Justice Department. Acting in response to the class action lawsuit *Nunez v. City of New York et al.*, which DOJ subsequently joined as a plaintiff, DOJ's 2014 investigation into the management of RNDC details a climate defined in equal parts by brutal violence and an Orwellian lexicon meant to obscure it from the data altogether. Both of these appeared to have been sanctioned by the top officials in the prison. The *Nunez* case, and subsequent DOJ investigation, were significant for two reasons. The first is that, whereas Mayor Bloomberg had refrained from entering into the kind of consent decrees Lasker had enforced in the 1980s, his successor, Bill de Blasio, announced his intention to work with the plaintiff and allow the judiciary a foothold in the city jails. The second is that the findings of DOJ, and subsequent investigations under *Nunez*, reveal a pattern of brutality, erased from the official record, beneath the veneer of the Kerik-Jacobson regime.

DOJ found that when a guard punched a prisoner, which is not permitted, this was written up as a "control hold." When the prisoner was beaten to the floor, this became "guiding" the prisoner to the floor. Guards who instigated physical altercations with prisoners routinely wrote that they were attacked "out of nowhere." Guards also cynically uttered the phrase "Stop resisting" while committing violence against prisoners, even if the prisoner was not resisting, as a means of justifying violence. Video evidence routinely disappeared. Moreover, even when it was uncovered, it could be successfully contradicted by the mere testimony of guards, with blessings extending all the way to the top of the chain of command. DOJ found widespread cooperation between guards to cover up unsanctioned violence. Prisoners who were assaulted or witnessed assaults were, once more, systematically instructed to "hold it down," with injured prisoners aggressively pressured to avoid medical care and thereby keep the violence out of the department's data. When this was impossible, they became victims of "slip and fall" accidents in official paperwork, which would not be registered as violence. "Slip and fall" accidents, DOJ found, were an epidemic at Rikers Island.

Even in the rare case when a guard was found to have used unsanctioned violence, and was not abetted in covering it up by colleagues and superiors, DOJ found the penalty typically amounted to a slap on the wrist. Above all, the practices of fabricating reports and erasing violence were no secret, but were conducted openly, and sanctioned up and down the chain of command. While DOJ limited its investigation to RNDC and the adolescent houses at the Eric M. Taylor Center (the C-76 facility, previously known as the Correctional Institution for Men), they stated with reasonable certainty that the findings could be generalized to all of Rikers. Official DOC policy had thus created two distinct worlds: the data, where violence was under control thanks to the practices of technocratic management; and the real world of life at Rikers, where widespread violence reigned supreme.

The DOJ report was part of an incipient sea change in the city's understanding of the penal colony in its backyard, a long-overdue reassessment of Rikers that had been purchased with untold misery and death. The significance of the investigation was heightened by the difficulty prisoners now had filing lawsuits against carceral facilities. While the *Nunez* case can be credited with bringing much-needed attention to the dark underbelly of Kerik and Jacobson's rule of order, the suit faced the considerable obstacles laid down by the 1996 Prison Litigation Reform Act. This bipartisan legislation made it considerably more difficult for US prisoners to sue for their civil rights, and made lawsuits like *Benjamin v. Malcolm, Fisher v. Koehler,* and even *Nunez v. City of New York* nearly impossible to file. Indeed, it is clear that far more cases would have made it before a judge under the old rules. The facade of the Kerik-Jacobson regime was falling apart.[41]

Shut Down Rikers

In the spring of 2010, sixteen-year-old Kalief Browder was arrested near his home in the Bronx. He was charged with robbery under a flimsy pretext, which eventually fell apart. Initially unable to make bail, and subsequently held on a probation violation, Browder would spend nearly three years on Rikers Island, two of which were in solitary confinement. At Rikers, Browder was the victim of brutality from his fellow prisoners and guards alike, including a vicious assault from a guard that Browder did not report at the time. During this ordeal, Browder was pressured to plea to the charge, for which he would receive time served and go home—a common tactic of New York prosecutors who instrumentalize the horror of life on Rikers to force people to take pleas. Browder refused, however, professing his innocence. By the time the Bronx District Attorney's Office admitted their case against Browder had long disintegrated, and was forced to release him, the young man had attempted suicide multiple times. Upon his release, Browder became a vital voice for the suffering that takes place at Rikers Island day in, day out. But the trauma he endured in his hellish ordeal ultimately foreclosed a bright future. In 2015, Browder took his own life.[42]

Kalief Browder's ordeal was by no means the first such tragedy associated with DOC or Rikers Island. But it came amid a national watershed around the figure of mass incarceration and, in particular, the structural racism of the US punishment system. DOJ's interest in taking on conditions at Rikers, Mayor Bill de Blasio's willingness to cooperate with the courts by entering into consent decree with *Nunez* plaintiffs, and the rise of cultural touchstones like Michelle Alexander's 2010 bestseller *The New Jim Crow* augured a changing political consciousness around questions of race and punishment in the US. The 2014 Ferguson Rebellion and the emergence of the Black Lives Matter movement further pushed an anti-prison, anti-policing sensibility into the nation's streets, popularizing radical critiques of incarceration like prison abolitionism. Even among political moderates, the failure of the War on Drugs became common knowledge. For the first time since the days of penal welfarism, judges and prosecutors were under organized public pressure to apply *less* punishment.[43]

Amid this new moment, the spirit of refusal that had defined Kalief Browder's short life—the refusal to be bullied by his fellow prisoners, sadistic Rikers guards, or judges and prosecutors who waste lives like Browder's for a living—did not die with him. Following his death, the name Kalief Browder became the watchword of a redoubled movement against Rikers Island, bolstered by revelations of the Program, the *Nunez* lawsuit, the DOJ report, and countless victims of Rikers Island emboldened by Browder's stance to speak out. Finally, outside the working-class black and brown communities where the horrors of Rikers are known all too well, people were listening.

As a critical mass of New Yorkers began to reject the grim reality unfolding beneath the firmament of managerial science, Rikers Island became a liability to the legitimacy of the city's social order. The spirit of this new era was captured by the name of a prison abolitionist organization begun in the wake of Browder's death: "Shut Down Rikers." The group demanded the penal colony be closed, and replaced with nothing. It was an issue whose time had come, and the city's elites could not ignore it. To this demand, however, emissaries of the city's non-profit sector—including the Ford Foundation, the Vera Institute of Justice, the Center for Court Innovation, Michael Jacobson, and even Herb Sturz—would append another. The city should shut down Rikers, they argued, and replace it with new, state-of-the-art penal welfarist jails, guided by the latest innovations in the social sciences, and managed by trained experts—all in the name of social justice for the communities hit hardest by the *last* jail buildup. This time around, they assured the public, the city would get it right.[44]

Archives Consulted

Board of Correction Archive (BOCA)
Oral History Archive at Columbia University (OHCU)
LaGuardia / Wagner Archive at LaGuardia Community College
   (LWA)
New York City Public Library, Special Collections
New York City Municipal Library
Yale University Library, Manuscripts and Archives
Smith College Library, Special Collections
John Jay College of Criminal Justice Library, Special Collections

Notes

Introduction

1 See the introduction.

2 Shouting back and forth with pedestrians below was an everyday feature of life in HDW, leading essayist Tom Wolfe to speculate "there is probably not another large prison in the country that is in such intimate contact with the outside world." Tom Wolfe, "The Voices of Village Square," in *The Kandy-Kolored Tangerine-Flake Streamline Baby* (New York: Farrar, Strauss, & Giroux, 1965), 309.

3 "Women Prisoners Here in 2-Hour Uproar; Protest Disciplining of One for a Remark," *New York Times*, September 25, 1954; DOC, *Annual Report for 1954* (New York: DOC, 1955), 70; Wolfe, "Voices of Village Square," 309.

4 Orisanmi Burton, "Organized Disorder: The New York City Jail Rebellion of 1970," *Black Scholar* 48: 4 (2018), 4, 28.

5 DOC, *1954*, 70; Claire Feinman, *Imprisoned Women: A History of the Treatment of Women Incarcerated in New York City (NY), 1932–1975*, PhD Diss., New York University, 1976, 95–7; "City to Improve Prison Program," *New York Times*, January 28, 1955; David Wise, "City Spurs Plan to Move Women's Jail to Island," *New York Herald Tribune*, September 26, 1954; Burton, "Organized Disorder," 28.

6 DOC, *1954*, Appendix, xvi–xvii; Feinman, *Imprisoned Women*, 150; Malcolm X, "The Ballot or the Bullet," in *Say It Loud: Great Speeches on Civil Rights and African American Identity*, Catherine Ellis and Stephen Drury Smith, eds. (New York: The New Press, 2010), 12.

7 Wolfe, "Voices of Village Square," 309.

8 Feinman, *Imprisoned Women*, 54–83; Wolfe, "Voices of Village Square," 309; Jarrod Shanahan and Nadja Eisenberg-Guyot, "All Jails Fit to Build," *Brooklyn Rail*, February 2020.

9 Angela Davis, *An Autobiography* (New York: International Publishers, 1988), 18.

10 Russell Porter, "City Jails Called Schools of Crime, Crowding Blamed," *New York Times,* December 27, 1954; DOC, *1954,* 110–112, 115; DOC, *Saga of the Women's House of Detention,* n.d., 2, Anna M. Kross Archives, Box 4, Folders 6–7, Smith College; Max Wylie, *400 Miles from Harlem: Courts, Crime, and Correction* (New York: MacMillan, 1972), 2.

11 Russell Porter, "City Prison Head Fights Crowding," *New York Times,* December 28, 1954; DOC, *1954,* 12, 72; Charles Dickens, *American Notes for General Circulation* (London: Chapman & Hall, 1842), 219; DOC, *1954,* 76–88. Today, prisoners with sentences longer than a year are transferred to the custody of the state. From 1915 to 1967, sentenced prisoners could serve up to three years in the city system on an indeterminate sentence.

12 DOC, *1954,* 13, 92–3, 96–7, 107–8; Dario Melossi and Massimo Pavarini, *The Factory and the Prison: Origins of the Penitentiary System* (New York: MacMillan, 1981), 33–47.

13 DOC, *Annual Report for 1953* (New York: DOC, 1954), iii; David J. Rothman, *Conscience and Convenience* (Boston: Little, Brown, & Company, 1980); Dorothy Schneider, *American Women in the Progressive Era* (New York: Anchor, 1994); Robert H. Wiebe, *The Search for Order: 1877–1920* (New York: Macmillan, 1967), 113–17.

14 David Garland, *The Culture of Control: Crime and Social Order in Contemporary Society* (Chicago: University of Chicago Press, 2001), 27.

15 James Forman, Jr., *Locking Up Our Own: Crime and Punishment in Black America* (New York: Farrar, Straus & Giroux, 2017), 229.

16 Thomas J. Sugrue, *The Origins of the Urban Crisis: Race and Inequality in Postwar Detroit* (Princeton: Princeton University Press, 2006), 11.

17 Joshua Freeman, *Working-Class New York: Life and Labor Since World War II* (New York: The New Press, 2000).

18 Ralph Ellison, *Invisible Man* (New York: Penguin, 1965), 7.

19 Georg Rusch and Otto Kirchheimer, *Punishment and Social Structure* (Piscataway: Transaction Publishers, 2003); Dario Melossi and Massimo Pavarini, *The Prison and the Factory: Origins of the Penitentiary System* (London: Macmillan, 1981); John Irwin, *The Jail: Managing the Underclass in American Society* (Berkeley: University of California Press, 1985); Ruth Wilson Gilmore, *Golden Gulag: Prisons, Surplus, Crisis, and Opposition in Globalizing California* (Berkeley: University of California Press, 2007).

20 James Rikers, *A Brief History of the Riker Family, from Their*

Emigration to This Country in 1638, to the Present Time (New York: D. Fanshaw, 1851), 9; Tom McCarthy, "Rikers—The Unwanted Island of the Unwanted?," Presentation to the Greater Astoria Historical Society, June 25, 2017; Eric Foner, *Gateway to Freedom: The Hidden History of America's Fugitive Slaves* (Oxford: Oxford University Press, 2015); Brentin Mock, "The Dark 'Fugitive Slave' History of Rikers Island," *Bloomberg City Lab*, July 23, 2015, bloomberg.com; "Riker's Island's Stenches," *New York Times*, August 14, 1880.

21 "To Build a Bigger Jail," *New York Times*, September 20, 1886; "Plan for Separation," *New York Times*, September 28, 1896; *A Pickpocket's Tale: The Underworld of Nineteenth-Century New York* (New York: Norton, 2007), 98–109; Jarrod Shanahan and Jack Norton, "A Jail to End All Jails," *Urban Omnibus*, December 16, 2017, urbanomnibus.net; Rosalie Butler, "Separation of Charities and Correction," *Charities Review* 2: 1 (1892), 164–70; Josephine Shaw Lowell, "Extracts from a Paper Read at the Women's Conference, New York, April 25 1887," *Lend a Hand*, 2:1 (1877), 548–52.

22 Nellie Bly, *Ten Days in a Mad-House* (New York: Ian L. Munro, 1887); "A Grand Jury's Suggestions," *New York Times*, December 1, 1883; "The Grand Jury Discharged," *New York Times*, April 4, 1886; "To Build a Bigger Jail"; "Adopts $47m Water Supply Plan, New Prison Blocked," *New York Times*, June 27, 1908; "Reclaiming Rikers Island," *New York Times*, November 25, 1900.

23 "Leper Dies Alone in a Hut," *New York Tribune*, November 4, 1900; Jarrod Shanahan and Jayne Mooney, "New York City's Captive Work Force: Remembering the Prisoners Who Built Rikers Island," *International Journal of Law, Crime, and Justice* 56 (2019), 13–26.

24 Julie Schneyer, "Riker's Island: The Penitentiary That Almost Never Was," unpublished paper, 2008; Prison Association of New York and the Association of Grand Jurors, New York County, Prison Association of New York and the Association of Grand Jurors, New York County, *A Study of the Conditions Which Have Accumulated under Many Administrations and Now Exist in the Prisons on Welfare Island New York City, and a Plan for the Erection and Economical Financing of a New Penitentiary Elsewhere* (New York, 1924).

25 "First to Flee New Jail," *New York Times*, December 11, 1935; Jayne Mooney and Jarrod Shanahan, "Rikers Island: The Failure of a 'Model' Penitentiary," *Prison Journal* 100: 6 (2020), 687–708; DOC, *1954*, 96–100.

26 Lil Wayne, *Gone 'Til November* (New York: Random House, 2016), 77.

27 Jarrod Shanahan and Tyler Wall, "'Fight the Reds, Support the Blue': Blue Lives Matter and the US Counter-Subversive Tradition," *Race and Class* 63: 1 (July 2021), 70–90; Karen Ferguson, "The Perils of Liberal Philanthropy," *Jacobin*, November 28, 2018, jacobinmag.com.

28 Raven Rakia and Ashoka Jegroo, "How the Push to Close Rikers Went from No Jails to New Jails," *The Appeal*, May 29, 2018, theappeal.org.

29 Van Alen Institute and Lippman Commission, *Justice in Design: Toward a Healthier and More Just New York City Jail System* (New York: Lippman Commission, 2017), 9. See also Lippman Commission, *A More Just City* (New York: Lippman Commission, 2017); Lippman Commission, *A More Just City: One Year Forward* (New York: Lippman Commission, 2018); Michael Jacobson, Elizabeth DeWolf, Margaret Egan, and David Hafetz, "Beyond the Island: Changing the Culture of New York City Jails," *Fordham Urban Law Journal* 45: 2 (2018), 373–436; Janos Marton "#CLOSErikers: The Campaign to Transform New York City's Criminal Justice System," *Fordham Urban Law Journal* 45: 2 (2018), 499–570. Zhandarka Kurti and I critique this plan in detail in "Rebranding Mass Incarceration: The Lippman Commission and 'Carceral Devolution' in New York City," *Social Justice* 25: 2–3 (2018), 25–50. Judah Schept, *Progressive Punishment: Job Loss, Jail Growth, and the Neoliberal Logic of Carceral Expansion* (New York: New York University Press, 2015), 11.

30 Shanahan and Norton, "A Jail to End All Jails."

1. The Era of Horse and Buggy

1 DOC, *Annual Report for 1957* (New York: DOC, 1958), 14; DOC, *Annual Report for 1954* (New York: DOC, 1955), 77, 83, 86, 89, 93, 105, 112; Warden Edward Dros, "Critical Conditions at the Workhouse Division, Rikers Island," July 14, 1954, Robert F. Wagner Papers, Box 26, Folder 366, LaGuardia Wagner Archive, at LaGuardia Community College (henceforth LWA).

2 Office of the Mayor (Division of Administration), *Department of Correction Institutional Needs*, April 1958, 8, Wagner Papers, Box 26, Folder 373, LWA, my emphasis.

3 DOC, *1954*, 10, 11; DOC, *Annual Report for 1953* (New York: DOC, 1954), v; Joseph Batka, "Commission of Adolescent

Remand Shelter, 1955 Capital Outlay Program," October 13, 1954, 3, Wagner Papers, Box 26, Folder 368, LWA. In 1959 the total census was 111,091, or an increase of roughly 26 percent. See DOC, *Annual Report for 1959* (New York: DOC, 1960), 63.

4 Dros, "Critical Conditions," 1–3; COBA, "Resolution Urging Immediate Correction of Living Conditions in the Dormitories of the Workhouse Division, Riker's Island," June 15, 1954, Wagner Papers, Box 26, Folder 366, LWA.

5 Meyer Berger, "Leaders of Tammany Admit Close Links to Racketeers as State Opens Crime Study," *New York Times,* November 14, 1952; Charles Grutzner, "Court Bids Mayor Bare Final Report," *New York Times,* October 7, 1953; Richard M. Flanagan, *Robert Wagner and the Rise of New York City's Plebiscitary Mayoralty: The Tamer of the Tammany Tiger* (New York: Palgrave, 2015), 19–20.

6 Robert F. Wagner, Oral History Archive at Columbia University, 357–8; Flanagan, *Wagner,* 23.

7 "Commissioner Kross," *New York Times,* January 5, 1954; *Rikers Review* 2: 15 (Winter 1954), NYPL Special Collections; Max Wylie, *400 Miles from Harlem: Courts, Crime, and Correction* (New York: MacMillan, 1972), 22, 47, 61; Farnsworth Fowle, "Wagner Names 2 Women to Cabinet," *New York Times,* January 1, 1954; Joan Cook, "Anna M. Kross Dies; An Ex-City Official," *New York Times,* August 29, 1979; DOC, "Biographical Sketch," 1964, 5, Kross Papers, Box 1, Folder 1, Smith College. This text was certainly drafted in cooperation with Kross, if not by Kross herself.

8 Wylie, *400 Miles,* 18–19; DOC, "Biographical Sketch," 5–6; Alfred Grunberg, "Interesting People: Anna Moscowitz," *The American Magazine* (May 1917), 55–6.

9 Wylie, *400 Miles,* 27–42; Robert Caro, *The Power Broker: Robert Moses and the Fall of New York* (New York: Vintage, 1974), 96–111.

10 Anna M. Kross, appearing on *Ladies of the Press,* January 21, 1964, Kross Papers, Box 5, Folder 3, Smith College, my transcription; DOC, "Sketch," 6–8; Flanagan, *Wagner,* 23; DOC, "Biographical Sketch," 6–8; "Kross Decries Judges with 'Pull,'" *New York Times,* May 18, 1954.

11 William K. Tabb, *The Long Default: New York City and the Urban Fiscal Crisis* (New York: Monthly Review, 1982), 11–12; Eric C. Schneider, *Vampires, Dragons, and Egyptian Kings: Youth Gangs in Postwar New York* (Princeton: Princeton University Press, 2001), 29, 42–5, 50, 55, 71, 192; Stuart Hall, Chas Critcher, Tony Jefferson, et al., *Policing the Crisis: Mugging,*

the State, and Law and Order (London: Macmillan, 1978), 389.

12 Schneider, *Vampires*, 50.

13 Kevin McCloskey, "The Day They Barred Behan from the Parade," *New York Times*, March 14, 1982. Schneider, *Vampires*, 50; Marilyn S. Johnson, *Street Justice A History of Police Violence in New York City* (New York: Beacon Press, 2003), 205; Schneider, *Smack: Heroin and the American City* (Princeton: Princeton University Press, 2008), 138. DOC, *1953*, iv; DOC, *1954*, 3.

14 Johnson, *Street Justice*, 203–28.

15 "Youth Crime Rises in City," *New York Times*, September 16, 1954; Schneider, *Vampires*, 57, 75–7; Lucy Freeman, "Youth Delinquency Growing Rapidly over the Country," *New York Times*, April 20, 1952; Johnson, *Street Justice*, 192; Elizabeth Hinton, *From the War on Poverty to the War on Crime: The Making of Mass Incarceration in America* (Cambridge, MA: Harvard University Press, 2016), 30–3.

16 Mayor's Task Force on Youth and Work, *Youth in New York City: Out-of-School and Out-of-Work* (New York: City Hall, 1962), 1–11.

17 DOC, *Annual Report for 1958* (New York: DOC, 1959), 20–1.

18 Raymond A. Mohl, "Race and Housing in the Postwar City: An Explosive History," *Journal of the Illinois State Historical Society (1998-)* 94: 1 (2001), 8–30; Joshua Freeman, *Working-Class New York: Life and Labor Since World War II* (New York: The New Press, 2001), 14–17.

19 Anna M. Kross, "Municipal Corrections Department and Crime Control," *Proceedings of the Annual Congress of Correction of the American Correctional Association* (Washington, DC: American Correctional Association, 1954), 28–9; Anna M. Kross, appearing on *This Is New York*, November 5, 1958, Kross Papers, Box 7, Tape 7, Smith College, my transcription.

20 "Kross Blasts Prison for Socially Sick," *New York Post*, August 12, 1959; Rose C. Boyer, "Report of Medical Activities 1954–1960," *Progress through Crisis, 1954–1966*, ed. DOC (New York: DOC, 1956), 78–9, my emphasis.

21 DOC, *Annual Reports, 1911–1913*; New York University Research Center of Graduate School of Public Administration and Social Service and DOC, *Pilot Statistical Study of 10,924 Youthful Offenders (Sixteen to Twenty Years) Held in Detention New York City Department of Correction January 1 to December 31, 1956*, 10–19, 32, Kross Papers, Box 4, Folder 2, Smith College.

22 Sundiata Acoli (Clark Squire), *Look for Me in the Whirlwind: From the Panther 21 to 21st Century Revolutions* (Los Angeles: PM Press, 2017), 336. This work is collectively authored, hence notes below will cite different contributors. Freeman, *Working-Class New York*, 55; Roy Caldwood, *Making the Right Moves: Rikers Island and NYC Corrections: Being Calm in the Storm* (New York: Creative Space, 2015).

2. The Chasm

1 DOC, *Annual Report for 1954* (New York: DOC, 1955), 25; DOC, "Statement Supporting Supplemental Budget of the Department of Correction of the City of New York," 1954, 3, Wagner Papers, Box 26, Folder 366, LWA; DOC, *Annual Report for 1953* (New York: DOC, 1954), v.

2 Max Wylie, *400 Miles from Harlem: Courts, Crime, and Correction* (New York: MacMillan, 1972), 16; DOC, *1954*, 21; DOC, "Supplemental Budget," 12; DOC, *1954*, 11; DOC, *Progress through Crisis*, 32, 122.

3 Anna M. Kross, "Municipal Corrections Department and Crime Control," *Proceedings of the Annual Congress of Correction of the American Correctional Association* (Washington, DC: American Correctional Association, 1954), 35; DOC, *1953*, iii.

4 Rose C. Boyer, "Report of Medical Activities 1954–1960," *Progress through Crisis, 1954–1966*, ed. DOC (New York: DOC, 1956), 66–8.

5 Committee on Public Health, New York Academy of Medicine, "Report on the Survey of Medical Care in New York City Prisons," *Progress through Crisis*, 54.

6 DOC, *1954*, 17–18.

7 Anna M. Kross, appearing on *This Is New York*, November 5, 1958, Kross Papers, Box 7, Tape 7, Smith College, my transcription.

8 Boyer, "Report of Medical Activities," 81.

9 Jarrod Shanahan, "Solidarity Behind Bars: New York City's Correction Officers' Benevolent Association," *Brooklyn Rail*, September, 2017.

10 Albert Williams to Deputy Mayor Charles Horowitz, August 24, 1953, Vincent R. Impellitteri Papers, Box 26, Folder 354, LWA; Office of the Commissioner (DOC) to Deputy Mayor Charles Horowitz, October 21, 1953, Impellitteri Papers, Box 26, Folder 354, LWA; Frank J. Prial II to Commissioner Albert Williams, September 21 1953, Impellitteri Papers Box 26, Folder 354, LWA; Albert Williams, "Letter Dated September 21, 1953,

from Mr. Frank J. Prial II, Concerning Manhattan Court Pen Grievance," October 16, 1953, Vincent R. Impellitteri, Box 26, Folder 354, LWA; Morris Kaplan, "Correction Guards Stripped of Badges to Stop 'Abuses,'" *New York Times*, November 25, 1953; Abe Peskoff to Mayor Vincent R. Impellitteri, November 28, 1953, Impellitteri Papers, Box 26, Folder 354, LWA; "Time for the Axe!" *The Chief*, n.d., Impellitteri Papers, Box 26, Folder 354, LWA.

11 Kross, "Municipal Corrections," 32.

12 C. L. R. James, *American Civilization* (Cambridge, MA: Blackwell, 1993), 166.

13 *Rikers Review* 2: 20 (n.d.), 7, NYPL Special Collections; DOC, *1954*, iv, 8, 100, 16.

14 "Badges Worn Again by Correction Aides," *New York Times*, March 5, 1954; DOC, *1954*, 105, 24, 26.

15 DOC, "Statement Supporting Supplemental Budget 1954–1955 of the Department of Correction of the City of New York," 1, Wagner Papers, Box 26, Folder 366, LWA.

16 DOC, *Progress through Crisis, 1954–1966* (New York: DOC, 1966), 25; Anna Kross, *This Is New York*; Wylie, *400 Miles*, 73.

3. War of Position

1 "Scotch Sold at $35 in Racket at Tombs," *New York Times*, December 1, 1955; Don Hogan, "Jail Favors Sold Here; Guards Held," *New York Herald Tribune*, December 1, 1955. In a contemporary advertisement, a fifth of scotch is advertised for $5.63 ("Tallyho! for the Happiest of Holidays," *New York Herald Tribune*, December 13, 1955); Charles F. Kiley, "3 Seized Jail Guards Had Arrest Records," *New York Herald Tribune*, December 2, 1955; Jack Roth, "Three Prison Guards Arrested," *New York Times*, December 2, 1955; Charles F. Kiley, "All of City's Prisons and Staffs Are Probed," *New York Herald Tribune*, December 3, 1955; Robert A. Poteete, "Dope, Too, Sold in Jail, Mrs. Kross Discloses," *New York Herald Tribune*, December 5, 1955; "Mayor Absolves Correction Chief," *New York Times*, December 13, 1955.

2 Poteete, "Dope, Too, Sold in Jail"; "Shake-up Begun in City's Prisons," *New York Times*, December 6, 1955; Judith Crist, "Mrs. Kross Shifts 25, Gets Mayor's Support," *New York Herald Tribune*, December 6, 1955; "Mrs. Kross Defies Employee Groups," *New York Times*, March 16, 1956.

3 Richard M. Flanagan, *Robert Wagner and the Rise of New York*

City's Plebiscitary Mayoralty: The Tamer of the Tammany Tiger (New York: Palgrave, 2015), 23–4; Robert A. Poteete, "Kross Aides Complain to Wagner," *New York Herald Tribune*, March 14, 1956; "Mrs. Kross Facing Revolt of Guards," *New York Times*, March 15, 1956; "Mayor to Discuss Correction Case," *New York Times*, March 19, 1956. While there are three uniformed staff unions, I focus largely on COBA, which is by far the largest and most politically active, and blazes the trail in which the others follow.

4 "Juror Criticizes Correction Head," *New York Times*, May 16, 1956; Charles G. Bennett, "Jury Unit Protests Kross Rule as 'Bad,'" *New York Times*, June 7, 1956; "Mrs. Kross to Head Own Bureau's Study," *New York Times*, May 20, 1956. If the excerpts of the grand jury that survive in the subsequent *Preusse Report* are indicative of its findings, Kross was scarcely exaggerating. The jury called for immediate relief of overcrowding, new facilities, better classification and segregation, better medical care, higher standards for staff hires and better training. Above all it concurred with Kross's program of rehabilitation and called for better funding. See Mayor's Committee on the Department of Correction, *Organization and Management of the Department of Correction* (New York: City Hall, 1956), 92–103.

5 "Conference of Heads of Institutions and Warden Eligibles, Held on May 22, 1956, at the House of Detention for Women," May 23, 1956, Wagner Papers, Box 26, Folder 368, LWA; Jack Roth, "Mrs. Kross Shifts Twelve City Wardens; Denies Shakeup," *New York Times*, May 26, 1956; Robert F. Wagner, "Statement by Mayor Wagner on Proposed Plan for 40 Hour Week for Uniformed Forces of Department of Police, Fire and Correction," August 8, 1956, Wagner Papers, Box 26, Folder 368, LWA; "Police, Firemen to Get Extra Pay," *New York Herald Tribune*, August 9, 1956.

6 COBA, "Resolution Unanimously Adopted by Correction Officers Benevolent Association Feb. 15, 1958 Urging Creation of Additional Facilities for Inmates and Appointment of 150 More Correction Officers," Wagner Papers, Box 26, Folder 373, LWA; *Correction Sidelights* 2: 1, 1. Kross Papers, Box 4, Folder 3, Smith College; DOC, *Annual Report for 1954 Digest* (New York: DOC, 1955), 14–15.

7 "Women Create Uproar at House of Detention," *New York Times*, April 27, 1958; Jack Roth, "Mrs. Kross Accused by One of Top Aides on Outbreak in Jail," *New York Times*, May 2, 1958; Richard C. Wald, "Mrs. Kross Quizzed on Jail Fight," *New York Herald Tribune*, May 3, 1958.

8   Jack Roth, "Mrs. Kross Shifts 111 on Jail Staff," *New York Times*, June 21, 1958; Charles G. Bennett, "City Prison Heads See 'Powder Keg,'" *New York Times*, May 22, 1958; Edith Evans Asbury, "City to Restore Jail Funds to Keep Guard Roster Up," *New York Times*, June 7, 1958.

9   C.L.R. James, *American Civilization* (Cambridge, MA: Blackwell, 1993), 168.

10 J. Rogers, "Rehabilitation in Action," *Rikers Review*, July 1958, 12–15, NYPL Special Collections. Rogers says "the people here" but means guards. Rogers does not provide an explicit time frame situating these remarks—a rare criticism of staff to appear in the pages of the *Review*—but they almost certainly refer to the beginning of the Kross administration.

11 "Mrs. Kross Sure Job Is Safe," *New York Times*, June 20, 1956; "Mrs. Kross to Head Own Bureau's Study," *New York Times*, May 20, 1956; "Kross Agency Study Headed by Preusse," *New York Times*, May 22, 1956.

12 "The 'Kross Report,'" *New York Times*, December 8, 1956; Paul Crowell, "Mayor Is Advised Correction Unit Needs a Shakeup," *New York Times*, December 7, 1956; Mayor's Committee, *Organization and Management*, 9.

13 Mayor's Committee, *Organization and Management*, 12–15; DOC, *Annual Report for 1957* (New York: DOC, 1958), 27; Paul Crowell, "Mayor Is Advised Correction Unit Needs a Shakeup," *New York Times*, December 7, 1956; "The 'Kross Report.'"

4. The Lesser of two Evils

1   Robert F. Wagner, "At Brooklyn House of Detention for Men," December 4, 1956, Wagner Papers, Box 26, Folder 368, LWA.

2   DOC, *Annual Report for 1956* (New York: DOC, 1957), 34, 39.

3   DOC, *1956*, 40, 42, 45; Emmanuel Perlmutter, "New Jail to Open in Brooklyn Soon," *New York Times*, August 15, 1956.

4   DOC, *1956*; "Young Offenders Go into New Jail," *New York Times*, February 7, 1957.

5   "$3,000,000 City Prison Proposed by Patterson," *New York Herald Tribune*, September 8, 1930; Robert Moses to Anna Kross, August 16, 1956, Wagner Papers, Box 26, Folder 371, LWA; Office of the Mayor (Division of Administration), *Department of Correction Institutional Needs*, April 1958, 12, Wagner Papers, Box 26, Folder 373, LWA; Anna M. Kross, "Re: Approval of Site for C-74 Adolescent Remand Shelter," October 18, 1957, Wagner Papers, Box 26, Folder 371, LWA.

6   DOC, *Capital Budget Project C-74, Adolescent Remand Shelters (Detention Cases)* (New York: DOC, 1956), 1, Wagner Papers, Box 26, Folder 368, LWA; Anna M. Kross, "Municipal Corrections Department and Crime Control," *Proceedings of the Annual Congress of Correction of the American Correctional Association* (Washington, DC: American Correctional Association, 1954), 34.

7   Mayor's Committee on the Department of Correction, *Organization and Management of the Department of Correction* (New York: City Hall, 1956), 40; DOC, *Annual Report for 1957* (New York: DOC, 1958), 20; Larry Ellis, "What's Happening in Construction?," *Rikers Review*, July 1958, 54, NYPL Special Collections; M. Jones, "The Operation of P.S. 616," *Rikers Review*, Summer 1962, 23, NYPL Special Collections; DOC, "Prisoner Education," in *Progress through Crisis, 1954–1966* (New York: DOC, 1966), 122–3; Robert H. Terte, "Theobold Praises School at Prison," *New York Times*, March 22, 1960; Ellis, "What's Happening in Construction?," 54.

8   DOC, *Annual Report for 1959* (New York: DOC, 1960), 37; DOC, *Annual Report for 1962* (New York: DOC, 1963), 24; DOC, *Jails for the 80s: Five Year Capital Development Program for Corrections* (New York: DOC, 1980), 42–3; DOC, *Annual Report for 1961* (New York: DOC, 1962), 16; "Raymond Street Jail, in Use since 1880, to Close Tomorrow," *New York Times*, June 20, 1963; DOC, *Saga of the Women's House of Detention*, n.d., 2, Anna M. Kross Archives, Box 4, Folders 6–7, Smith College.

9   DOC, *1956*, 11; DOC, "Volunteers," in *Progress through Crisis*, 143; DOC, "Prisoner Education," 123.

10 DOC, *Saga*, 31–3; Claire Feinman, *Imprisoned Women: A History of the Treatment of Women Incarcerated in New York City (NY), 1932–1975*, PhD Diss., New York University, 1976, 191–233, 279–80; Max Wylie, *400 Miles from Harlem: Courts, Crime, and Correction* (New York: MacMillan, 1972); DOC, *Saga*, 33; DOC, *1957*, 17.

11 DOC, *1956*, 23–4.

12 William E. Farrell, "Inquiry Ordered at Women's Jail," *New York Times*, March 6, 1965; Sara Harris, *Hellhole: The Shocking Story of Inmates and Life in New York City's House of Detention for Women* (New York: E.P. Dutton & Co., 1967).

13 Feinman, *Imprisoned Women*, 134; "A Letter to City Editors," *Correction Sidelights* 9, no. 1: 1–2, Kross Papers, Box 4, Folder 3, Smith College.

14 Ruth Wilson Gilmore, "In the Shadow of the Shadow State," in *The Revolution Will Not Be Funded*, ed. INCITE! Women

of Color Against Violence (Durham: Duke University Press, 2017), 41–52; Zhandarka Kurti and Jarrod Shanahan, "Carceral Non-profits and the Limits of Prison Reform," *ACME: An International Journal for Critical Geographies* 20: 6 (2021), 597–617.

15 Harris, *Hellhole*, 24–34.

16 Harris, *Hellhole*, 59; Chris, in *To My Brother Who Did a Crime*, ed. Barbara Habenstreit (New York: Doubleday & Co., 1973), 152–3; Marlene Nadle, "Superintendent Says: Women's Jail: Prison Reflects What Public Wants," *Village Voice*, April 15, 1965; Andrea Dworkin, "Answering Mrs. Lindsay," *Village Voice*, April 22, 1965. Harris anonymizes the names of her informants.

17 Harris, *Hellhole*, 102–3, 110, 175; Ella Baker and Marvel Cooke, "The Bronx Slave Market," *The Crisis* 42: 11, 1935. Chapters 4, 5, and 6, of *Hellhole* trace three generations of HDW prisoners within the same family, whose lives revolve quite literally around the facility.

18 Harris, *Hellhole*, 50, 233–4; Chris, *To My Brother*, 153. Harris examines HDW's queer subcultures in detail, especially in Chapters 9, 10, and 11.

19 Sidney H. Schanberg, "Women Here Tells of 'Snake-Pit' Jail," *New York Times*, April 14, 1965; William E. Farrell, "Inquiry Ordered at Women's Jail," *New York Times*, March 6, 1965; Harris, *Hellhole*, 17–18; Douglas Robinson, "City Seeking End of Jail Crowding," *New York Times*, March 20, 1965; Harris, *Hellhole*, 278–9; Office of the Mayor, *Department of Correction Institutional Needs*, 19–21; DOC, *Saga*, 15–16; Wylie, *400 Miles*, 74.

20 Anna Kross to James Felt, October 18, 1957, 1–2, Wagner Papers, Box 26, Folder 271, LWA; DOC, *1959*, 26.

5. An Island Metropolis

1 DOC, *Annual Report for 1960* (New York: DOC, 1961); "Island Metropolis," *Rikers Review*, n.d. 1961, 14, NYPL Special Collections.

2 DOC, *1959*, xliv; "Help Wanted," *Rikers Review*, Summer 1962, 20, NYPL Special Collections; DOC, "Prisoner Education," in *Progress through Crisis, 1954–1966* (New York: DOC, 1966), 124–9; Roberta Rovner-Pieczenik, *A Review of Manpower R&D Projects in the Correctional Field (1963–1973)* (Washington, DC: United States Department of Labor, 1973), 3; DOC, "Prisoner Education," 124–9.

3 Clyde E. Sullivan and Wallace Mandell, quoted in Rovner-

Pieczenik, *Review of Manpower R&D Projects*, 6; DOC, *Progress through Crisis*, 42; Thomas J. Sugrue, *The Origins of the Urban Crisis: Race and Inequality in Postwar Detroit* (Princeton: Princeton University Press, 2006), 7; Claire Feinman, *Imprisoned Women: A History of the Treatment of Women Incarcerated in New York City (NY), 1932–1975*, PhD Diss., New York University, 1976, 134; Rovner-Pieczenik provides evidence for the limited success of this program in placing prisoners in jobs post-release, as well as a collection of similar studies. See also Candace Marie Johnson, *The Effects of Prison Labor Programs on Post-Release Employment and Recidivism*, PhD diss., Florida State University School of Criminology, 1984; Feinman, *Imprisoned Women*, 228–9.

4   "Rikers," n.d., Kross Papers, Box 7, Tape 24, Smith College, my transcription

5   DOC, *Annual Report for 1954 Digest* (New York: DOC, 1955), 13.

6   DOC, "Curricular Handbook for Correctional Academy," in *Progress through Crisis*, 222; DOC, *Annual Report for 1957* (New York: DOC, 1958), 23–4; DOC, *Annual Report for 1958* (New York: DOC, 1959), 78; DOC, "College Affiliations," *Progress through Crisis*, 180–1.

7   DOC, *Progress through Crisis*, 31–2, 35; Boyer, "Report of Medical Activities," 80.

8   Rose C. Boyer, "Report of Medical Activities 1954–1960," in *Progress through Crisis*, 66; Lawrence O'Kane, "Jail Doctors Ask Apology by Chief," *New York Times*, January 27, 1962; DOC, *Progress through Crisis*, 50.

9   DOC, *1954 Digest*, 33.

10 W. David Lewis, *From Newgate to Dannemora: The Rise of the Penitentiary in New York, 1796–1848* (Ithaca: Cornell University Press, 1965), Chapter 2.

11 DOC, *1959*, 27–9, 88–9; Brown & Guenther, DOC and DPW, "Capital Project No. C-76: Workhouse of the City of New York, Rikers Island, New York City," 4, NYC Municipal Library.

12 Brown & Guenther et al., "C-76," 4–5; DOC, *1959*, 29; DOC, "A Penological Milestone," *Correction Sidelights* 9: 10, 7, Wagner Papers, Box 27, Folder 380, LWA.

13 DOC, "A Penological Milestone."

14 "Proposed Plan for Reception and Classification Center Operations," *Correction Sidelights*, 8: 2, 10, Kross Papers, Box 4, Folder 3, Smith College; DOC, "Penological Milestone," 7; DOC, *Progress through Crisis*, 18.

15 "Rikers," n.d., Kross Papers, Box 7, Tape 24, Smith College, my transcription.

16 DOC, *Progress through Crisis*, 26; "T.V.iew," *Rikers Review*, Fall
1962, 4, 25, NYPL Special Collections. An anonymous editor of
Rikers Review leapt to Kross's defense, noting skepticism that
the program "facilitated matters at all." He claimed it "was not
able to capture the average inmate's peeves," due in part to Rigby
being known for having a "split personality." Above all, he complained, the show was not aired at a time most prisoners could
have even seen it. ("Block-Busters!," *Rikers Review*, Fall 1962, 6,
NYPL Special Collections)

6. Build, Build, Build

1 Henry J. Noble, "Warden's Page," *Rikers Review*, June–July
1960, NYPL Special Collections; "Renovation for Rehabilitation," *Rikers Review*, Winter 1962, 7, NYPL Special Collections.
2 David Ruskin, "Rehabilitation Build-Up Hits Rikers Island,"
Rikers Review, Fall 1964, 4, NYPL Special Collections.
3 DOC, *Progress through Crisis*, 1954–1966 (New York: DOC,
1966), 32, 40–2, 164.
4 DOC, "Proposal for the Institute of Behavioral Sciences," *Progress through Crisis*, 271–85.
5 DOC, *Annual Report for 1954* (New York: DOC, 1955), 57;
DOC, "Proposal for the Institute of Behavioral Sciences," 271;
Andrew T. Scull, *Decarceration: Community Treatment and the
Deviant—A Radical View* (Englewood Cliffs: Prentice Hall),
1977; Anna M. Kross, "The Role of the Municipal Prison Systems
in the Administration of Criminal Justice," address delivered to
the Third Italian Congress of Forensic Medicine, New York City,
September 25, 1963, in *Progress through Crisis*, 437.
6 DOC, *1960*, 23; For a first-hand account of the plane crash
written by a prisoner participant, see Rubin Rosario, "Current
Events," *Rikers Review*, Spring 1957, 14–15, NYPL Special
Collections.
7 DOC, *Annual Report for 1960* (New York: DOC, 1961), 28;
DOC, *Annual Report for 1961* (New York: DOC, 1962), 11–16;
DOC, *Saga of the Women's House of Detention*, n.d., 2, Anna M.
Kross Archives, Box 4, Folders 6–7, Smith College, 21.
8 Quoted in DOC, *Saga*, 24–5; DOC, *1961*, 12; "Island Actions,"
Rikers Review, Fall 1961, 13, NYPL Special Collections; DOC,
Saga, 25–26.
9 Henry J. Noble, "The Warden Says," *Rikers Review*, n.d. 1961,
3–4, NYPL Special Collections; "Hot Line News," *Rikers Review*,
Spring 1964, 6, NYPL Special Collections; Max Wylie, *400 Miles*

from Harlem: Courts, Crime, and Correction (New York: Mac-Millan, 1972), 73.

10 DOC, *Progress through Crisis*, 29; DOC, *Annual Report for 1954 Digest* (New York: DOC, 1955), 13.

11 *New York Times*, "Inmates Rise 2,971 in Year; Total in City Passes 12,000," March 8, 1964; Christopher Hayes, "Decline in an Era of Triumph: Black Workers in 1960s New York City," *Labor History* 61: 5–6 (2020), 486–502; Robert F. Wagner, Oral History Archive at Columbia University, 649.

12 Muhammad Zahir, "The Concept of Human Brotherhood in Islam," *Rikers Review*, December 1957, 23–5, NYPL Special Collections; J. "Trip" Davis, "The Tiger and I," *Rikers Review*, September 1957, 8–9, NYPL Special Collections.

7. The End of an Era

1 These articles were edited and collected in a volume that became something of an unofficial campaign platform for John V. Lindsay. See Barry Gottehrer, ed., *New York City in Crisis* (New York: Pocket Books, 1965), 76–83, 194–205.

2 M. Grice, "Something for Nothing," *Rikers Review*, n.d. 1961, 24, NYPL Special Collections; *Rikers Review*, Spring 1964, NYPL Special Collections.

3 Joshua Freeman, *Working-Class New York: Life and Labor Since World War II* (New York: The New Press, 2001), 166, 201.

4 Richard M. Flanagan, *Robert Wagner and the Rise of New York City's Plebiscitary Mayoralty: The Tamer of the Tammany Tiger* (New York: Palgrave, 2015), 21; Freeman, *Working-Class New York*, 202–203; Jarrod Shanahan and Andy Battle, "The Velvet Glove and the Iron Fist," *Jacobin*, July 26, 2018, jacobinmag.com.

5 Flanagan, *Wagner*, 23; DOC, *Progress through Crisis, 1954–1966* (New York: DOC, 1966), 49; Freeman, *Working-Class New York*, 182.

6 Flanagan, *Wagner*, 37, 39, 60–7; 77–9.

7 Mark Maier, *City Unions: Managing Discontent in New York City* (New Brunswick: Rutgers University Press, 1987), 18–19; Robert Brenner, *The Economics of Global Turbulence* (London and New York: Verso, 2006), 44–56.

8 Karl Marx, *Capital*, Volume III, David Fernbach, trans. (New York: Penguin, 1991), 253; Eric C. Schneider, *Smack: Heroin and the American City* (Princeton: Princeton University Press, 2008), 102.

9 Francis J. Bloustein, quoted in Gottehrer, *City in Crisis*, 92; Freeman, *Working-Class New York*, 181, 103–4.

10 James Boggs, *The American Revolution: Notes from a Negro Worker's Notebook* (New York: Monthly Review Press, 1963), 37.

11 Flanagan, *Wagner*, 80; Joseph P. Viteritti, "Times a-Changin'," in *Summer in the City: John Lindsay, New York, and the American Dream*, ed. Joseph P. Viteritti (Baltimore: Johns Hopkins University Press, 2014), 7–8; Gottehrer, *City in Crisis*, 17.

8. Battle Lines

1 Marilyn S. Johnson, *Street Justice A History of Police Violence in New York City* (New York: Beacon Press, 2003), 234–5.

2 Abayama Katara, in *Look for Me in the Whirlwind: From the Panther 21 to 21st-Century Revolutions* (Los Angeles: PM Press, 2017), 180–1.

3 Barry Gottehrer, ed., *New York City in Crisis* (New York: Pocket Books, 1965), 10.

4 Langston Hughes, "Death in Yorkville," in *The Collected Works of Langston Hughes: The Poems, 1951–1967*, Vol. 3, ed. Dolan Hubbard (Columbia, MO: University of Missouri Press, 146).

5 Joshua Freeman, *Working-Class New York: Life and Labor Since World War II* (New York: The New Press, 2001), 192; Daniel Perlstein, "The Dead End of Despair: Bayard Rustin, the 1968 New York School Crisis and the Struggle for Racial Justice," in *Civil Rights in New York City*, ed. Clarence Taylor (New York: Fordham University Press, 2011), 101; Peniel E. Joseph, *Waiting 'til the Midnight Hour: A Narrative History of Black Power in America* (New York: Henry Holt & Company, 2006), 110; Barry Goldwater, "Transcript of Goldwater's Speech Accepting Republican Presidential Nomination," *New York Times*, July 17, 1964.

6 Mark Maier, *City Unions: Managing Discontent in New York City* (New Brunswick: Rutgers University Press, 1987), 94–5.

7 Johnson, *Street Justice*, 227; Jarrod Shanahan, "Solidarity Behind Bars: New York City's Correction Officers' Benevolent Association," *Brooklyn Rail*, September, 2017.

8 Jordan Camp, *Incarcerating the Crisis: Freedom Struggles and the Rise of the Neoliberal State* (Berkeley: University of California Press, 2016); Chip Berlet and Matthew N. Lyons, *Right Wing Populism in America: Too Close for Comfort* (New York: Guilford Press, 2000), 176–81; Johnson, *Street Justice*, 233–4; "Pickets Oppose Civil Review of Complaints against Police,"

New York Times, May 17, 1964; Jarrod Shanahan and Tyler Wall, "'Fight the Reds, Support the Blue': Blue Lives Matter and the US Counter-Subversive Tradition," *Race and Class* 63: 1 (July 2021).

9 Rebecca Hill, "'The Common Enemy Is the Boss and the Inmate': Police and Prison Guard Unions in New York in the 1970s–1980s," *Labor: Studies in Working Class History of the Americas* 8: 3 (2011), 65–96; James Baldwin, "A Report from Occupied Territory," *The Nation*, July 11, 1966. Tyler Wall and I discuss the "arrogant autonomy" of the US police in detail in "'Fight the Reds, Support the Blue.'"

10 Charles G. Bennett, "Police Decry Bill for Review Panel," *New York Times*, June 17, 1964. Barry Gottehrer, the series' architect, who went on to become a key player in the Lindsay campaign, and then the Lindsay administration, credits the series with Wagner's stepping aside. (Barry Gottehrer, *The Mayor's Man* [New York: Doubleday, 1975], 125; Vincent Cannato, *The Ungovernable City: John Lindsay and His Struggle to Save New York* [New York: Basic Books, 2001], 23–4).

11 Johnson, *Street Justice*, 231–232, 238–240.

12 William F. Buckley, "Remarks to the New York Police Department Holy Name Society, April 4, 1965," in *The Unmaking of a Mayor* (New York: National Review, 2016), 431–4; *New York Times*, "Buckley Praises Police of Selma," April 5, 1965. 433. In the course of a humorous anecdote, Buckley likens his own support for NYPD, for which he felt publicly besieged, to that of a Franco supporter in Spain.

13 Buckley, *The Unmaking of a Mayor*, 145; Cannato, *Ungovernable City*, 40.

14 Neal B. Freeman, "William F. Buckley's Run for Mayor: Fifty Years Later," *National Review*, October 2015; Cannato, *Ungovernable City*, 53; John Leo, "Very Dark Horse in New York," *New York Times*, September 5, 1965.

15 Freeman, *Working-Class New York*, 196–200; Hill, "Common Enemy," 76–8.

16 George Rawick, "The American Negro Movement," in *Listening to Revolt: Selected Writings* (Chicago: Charles H. Kerr Press, 2010), 16; Michael Javen Fortner, *Black Silent Majority: The Rockefeller Drug Laws and the Politics of Punishment* (Cambridge, MA: Harvard University Press, 2015).

17 Gottehrer, *Crisis*, 193.

9. Crossing the Rubicon

1 DOC, "The Rikers Island Bridge," John V. Lindsay Papers, Box 65, Folder 237, Yale University; "Rikers Island Bridge: Background Material," John V. Lindsay Papers, Box 65, Folder 237, Yale University; John C. Devlin, "'Bridge of Hope' to Rikers Island Is Dedicated Here," *New York Times*, November 23, 1966; EMR, "Fact Sheet for Mayor Lindsay Public Appearance," November 17, 1966, John V. Lindsay, Box 65, Folder 237, Yale University; DOC.

2 Eric Pace, "New City Prisons Chief Sworn In," *New York Times*, March 31, 1966; "Firm Prison Hand," *New York Times*, March 31, 1966.

3 John B. Martin, ed., *New York City Charter, Adopted at the General Election Held November 7, 1961, Effective January 1, 1963, as Amended January 1 1965* (New York: The City Record, 1965); DOC, *1966 Annual Report* (New York: DOC, 1967), 3; George F. McGrath, "Is Our Investment in Prisons Justified?," in DOC, *1966 Annual Report* (New York: DOC, 1967), 6–7.

4 McGrath, "Prisons Justified?," 7; DOC, *1966*, 8, 12.

5 Task Force on Corrections, "Report to Mayor John V. Lindsay," April 30, 1966, 7–8, Lindsay Papers, Box 18, Folder 212, LWA; Task Force on Corrections, "Report," 3.

6 Task Force on Corrections, "Report," 5–6, my emphasis.

7 Task Force on Corrections, "Report," 5–10; Barry Gottehrer, *The Mayor's Man* (New York: Doubleday, 1975), 262; David A. Schulte Jr. to Ethel H. Wise, January 20, 1966, Lindsay Papers, Box 18, Folder 12, LWA.

8 BOC to Mayor John V. Lindsay, June 7, 1966, Lindsay Papers, Box 18, Folder 212, LWA; Letter to BOC Members, Lindsay Papers, Box 18, Folder 12, LWA.

9 Geoffrey Kabaservice, "On Principle: A Progressive Republican," in *Summer in the City: John Lindsay, New York, and the American Dream*, ed. Joseph P. Viteritti (Baltimore: Johns Hopkins University Press, 2014), 27–33; Vincent Cannato, *The Ungovernable City: John Lindsay and His Struggle to Save New York* (New York: Basic Books, 2001), 11–12.

10 National Advisory Commission on Civil Disorders (Kerner Commission), *Report* (New York: Bantam, 1968), 1–2.

11 Kerner Commission, *Report*, 1; Dick Schaap, "The Fun City," *New York Herald Tribune*, January 6, 1966.

12 Pete Hamill, "The Revolt of the White Lower Middle Class," *New York Magazine*, April 14, 1969.

13 Charles Grutzner, "Monaghan Ouster Sought in 'Deal' over

Brutality Cases," *New York Times,* February 20, 1953; Marilyn S. Johnson, *Street Justice: A History of Police Violence in New York City* (New York: Beacon Press, 2003), 229–36; Joshua Freeman, *Working-Class New York: Life and Labor since World War II* (New York: The New Press, 2001), 189–195; Sara Harris, *Hellhole: The Shocking Story of Inmates and Life in New York City's House of Detention for Women* (New York: E.P. Dutton & Co., 1967), 24; Peniel E. Joseph, *Waiting 'til the Midnight Hour: A Narrative History of Black Power in America* (New York: Henry Holt & Company, 2006), 1–34, 41–3; James Baldwin, "A Negro Assays the Negro Mood," *New York Times Magazine,* March 12, 1961, 25.

14 *New York Times,* "Texts of Statements and Preamble of Order on Police Review Board," May 3, 1966; Gottehrer, *Mayor's Man,* 51.

15 Edward Kirkman, "PBA Chief Says Commies Battle for Review Board," *New York Daily News,* September 20, 1966; William J. Bopp, "The New York City Referendum on Civilian Review," in *The Police Rebellion: The Quest for Blue Power,* ed. William J. Bopp (New York: Charles C. Thomas, 1971), 120–2, 129–30.

16 University Heights Civic Improvement Association, "Which Side Are You On?, " Lindsay Papers, Box 242, Folder 33, Yale University; FAIR, "Where Do You Stand on the Civilian Review Board?," Lindsay Papers, Box 242, Folder 33, Yale University. Inconveniently, the voter had to vote "no" to support the board, but there's no indication anyone wasn't sure what their vote meant.

17 Rebecca Hill, "'The Common Enemy Is the Boss and the Inmate': Police and Prison Guard Unions in New York in the 1970s–1980s," *Labor: Studies in Working Class History of the Americas* 8: 3 (2011), 65–96; Gottehrer, *Mayor's Man,* 128. John Garvey compellingly critiques the political failures of the CCRB campaign, in which he was a participant, in an unpublished manuscript from the early 1980s that he was gracious enough to share with me.

18 Mariame Kaba, "An (Abridged) History of Resistance to Police Violence in Harlem," *Historical Moments of Policing and Violence* 3: 9 (2012); "400 March to Score Police in Harlem," *New York Times,* April 29, 1957; Malcolm X, *The Autobiography of Malcolm X* (New York: Ballantine Books, 1992), 255–6.

19 Portions of this section appeared on the Gotham Center for New York History blog. See Jarrod Shanahan, "'White Tigers Eat Black Panthers:' New York City's Law Enforcement Group," *Gotham Center for New York City History* (blog), March 21, 2019, gothamcenter.org.

20 Joshua Bloom and Waldo E. Martin Jr., *Black against Empire: The History and Politics of the Black Panther Party* (Berkeley: University of California Press, 2013), 30–47, 70–3; Lumumba Shakur, in *Look for Me in the Whirlwind: From the Panther 21 to 21st-Century Revolutions* (Los Angeles: PM Press, 2017), 408–14; Bloom and Martin, *Black against Empire*, 70–3. Bloom and Martin emphasize that the Panthers' ten points were influenced greatly by Malcolm X's ten points, albeit in secularized form.

21 Afeni Shakur, in *Whirlwind*, 307–8, 405–7, 455–8.

22 Kuwasi Balagoon, in *Whirlwind*, 426–8; Kuwasi Balagoon, "Brink's Trial Opening Statement," in *Kuwasi Balagoon: A Soldier's Story: Writings by a Revolutionary New Afrikan Anarchist* (Montreal: Kersplebedeb, 2013), 28; David Gilbert, "In Memory of Kuwasi Balagoon, New Afrikan Freedom Fighter," in *A Soldier's Story*, 9; George Jackson, *Soledad Brother: The Prison Letters of George Jackson* (Chicago: Lawrence Hill, 1994), 225.

23 Bloom and Martin, *Black against Empire*, 149–54, 290–3; Irving Spiegel, "P.B.A. Will Issue 'Get Tough' Advice," *New York Times*, August 12, 1968.

24 Joseph Novitski, "Brooklyn Police Set Up Group to Back 'Vigorous' Enforcement," *New York Times*, August 8, 1968; Sidney E. Zion, "Rights Groups Assail Demands of New Police Unit," *New York Times*, August 9, 1968; James P. Gifford, "Dissent in Municipal Employee Organizations," *Proceedings of the Academy of Political Science* 30: 2 (December 1970), 159–72.

25 David Burnham, "Off-Duty Police Here Join in Beating Black Panthers," *New York Times*, September 5, 1968; Carl J. Pelleck and Helen Dudar, "Leary to Act in Panther Attack," *New York Post*, September 5, 1968; John Murphy, "Probe Cops' Roles in Attack on Panthers in Courthouse," *New York Daily News*, September 5, 1968; Katara, *Whirlwind*, 443–5; Barry Gottehrer, *The Mayor's Man* (New York: Doubleday, 1975), 222.

26 David Burnham, "New Police Group Maintains Stand," *New York Times*, September 14, 1968; David Burnham, "PBA Condemns New Police Group," *New York Times*, September 13, 1968; Charles Grutzner, "New Police Group Is Incorporated," *New York Times*, September 12, 1968; Sylvan Fox, "Many Police in City Leaning to the Right," *New York Times*, September 6, 1968; Noel Ignatiev, personal correspondence. Alternatively, Panther Curtis Powell later reflected on this period: "Around October I started working with SNCC; but they weren't going far: there was something missing. At about this time, the pigs attacked the Panthers in a courthouse. I started checking the

Panthers out, and they looked pretty cool" (Curtis Powell, in *Whirlwind*, 450); Noel Ignatiev, personal correspondence.

27 David Burnham, "New York's 'Finest' Want Pay to Be Finest, Too," *New York Times*, October 22, 1968; Peter Millones, "Police 'Sick' Calls Are Put at 2,000," *New York Times*, October 22, 1968.

10. A City in Itself

1 DOC, *Annual Report for 1967* (New York: DOC, 1968), 10, 12, 15.
2 DOC, *Annual Report for 1966* (New York: DOC, 1967), 10, 17–19.
3 DOC, *1966*, 20–21, DOC, *1967*, 27.
4 DOC, *1966*, 32; George McGrath, "Building a Sound Correctional Environment," in *Annual Report for 1968* (New York: DOC, 1969), 7–8.
5 DOC, *1968*, 15.
6 Barry Gottehrer, *The Mayor's Man* (New York: Doubleday, 1975), 212–13. *Mayor's Man* depicts the Lindsay administration as hopping from one crisis to the next. Later, the administration even kept regular "crisis calendars" chronicling the areas of the city likeliest to witness turmoil in the streets. See also Lindsay Papers, Boxes 53–8, Yale University.
7 Gottehrer's *The Mayor's Man* is a comprehensive account of this project, first called Summer Task Force, then Urban Action Task Force, meant to defuse riots before they occurred, by building relationships with the local players in the city's most fraught areas. See also Nicholas Pileggi, "Barry Gottehrer's Job Is to 'Cool It,'" *New York Times Magazine*, September 22, 1968; Ira Katznelson, *City Trenches: Urban Politics and the Patterning of Class in the United States* (Chicago: University of Chicago Press, 1981), 136–44; Jarrod Shanahan and Zhandarka Kurti, "Managing Urban Disorder in the 1960s: The New York City Model," *Gotham Center for New York City History* (blog), January 7, 2020, gothamcenter.org.
8 Karen Ferguson, *Top Down: The Ford Foundation and the Reinvention of Racial Liberalism* (Philadelphia: University of Pennsylvania Press, 2013), 24–5, 59, 63; Robert Allen, *Black Awakening in Capitalist America* (Trenton: Africa World Press, 1992), 70–9.
9 Malcolm M. Feeley, "How to Think about Criminal Court Reform," *Boston University Law Review* 98 (2018), 673–730;

"Our History," Vera Institute of Justice official website, vera.org.

10 Mayor's Committee on the Administration of Justice Under Emergency Conditions, *Report* (New York: City Hall, 1968), 18–19; David Bird, "City Ready for Mass Arrest in Civil Disorders," *New York Times*, August 5, 1968. Vera followed the 1968 report with a far more detailed plan for a militarized-police crackdown on social unrest, written in conjunction with Lindsay's Criminal Justice Coordinating Council: CJCC, *The Administration of Justice under Emergency Conditions* (New York: City Hall, 1969); Sylvan Fox, "Pickets Circle Columbia; Class Reopening Delayed; 720 Protesters Arraigned," *New York Times*, May 1, 1968; Shanahan and Kurti, "Managing Urban Disorder."

11 Robert Allen, *Black Awakening in Capitalist America*, 70. Richard Reeves, "Marchi Defeats Lindsay in G.O.P. Primary," *New York Times*, June 18, 1969; Vincent Cannato, *The Ungovernable City: John Lindsay and His Struggle to Save New York* (New York: Basic Books, 2001), 414; Richard Reeves, "Lindsay, Garelik and Beame Victors," *New York Times*, November 5, 1969.

12 DOC, *1969 Annual Report* (New York: DOC, 1970), 13; Chick, in *To My Brother Who Did a Crime*, ed. Barbara Habenstreit (New York: Doubleday & Co., 1973), 22.

13 DOC, *1968*, 16; David Burnham, "23 on Rikers Island Indicted for Beating Negroes," *New York Times*, August 13 1968.

14 John R. Dunne, *Report of the Senate Committee on Penal Institutions on the Problems of Correction in Local Jails and Penitentiaries* (Albany: State Senate, 1969), 2–7; Andrew Schaffer, *The Problem of Overcrowding in the Detention Institutions of New York City: An Analysis of the Causes and Recommendations for Alleviation* (New York: Vera Institute of Justice, 1969), v; Harvey Swados, "The City's Island of the Damned," *New York Times Magazine*, April 26, 1970; "Reformatory Guard Is Accused of Assault on Young Prisoners," *New York Times*, August 8, 1969; Lawrence Van Gelder, "Guard Is Arrested in Rikers I. Abuse," *New York Times*, December 23, 1969.

15 DOC, *1968*, 14, 16–17; Lawrence Van Gelder, "Crowding Turns Rikers into an Island of Idleness," *New York Times*, December 24, 1969.

16 Swados, "Island of the Damned," 25, 112; DOC, *1966*, 15; DOC, *1969*, 20; "City Is Chided for Letting Rikers Island Program Die," *New York Times*, November 3, 1969.

17 "Four at N.Y.U. Spurn Awards as Protest," *New York Times*, March 1, 1970; Schaffer, *The Problem of Overcrowding*, esp. 59–61.

18   Nancy Hicks, "Director of Psychiatry Leaves Correction Agency in Protest," *New York Times*, August 27, 1970.

19   Schaffer, *The Problem of Overcrowding*, iv–v; DOC, *1969*, 11–13, 17; Richard Severo, "City's Jail Population Rated 183% above Capacity," *New York Times*, October 4, 1970; "Nassau Jailers Picket Board in a Demand for More Guards," *New York Times*, September 15, 1970.

20   DOC, *1969*, 16; Swados, "Island of the Damned," 111; Martin Arnold, "Rockefeller Refers Jails Crisis to City," *New York Times*, August 13, 1970.

21   Richard Reeves, "Lindsay Is Adding Up to $5-Million for Summer Jobs," *New York Times*, July 12, 1968; Charles G. Bennett, "O'Connor Aides Ask City to Pay for Damage to Cars at Protest," *New York Times*, July 23, 1968; Martin Tolchin, "P.B.A. Head Tells Police to Enforce the Laws 100%," *New York Times*, August 13, 1968.

22   Schaffer, *Problem of Overcrowding*, 21–3.

23   Toussaint Losier, "Against 'Law and Order' Lockup: The 1970 NYC Jail Rebellions," *Race and Class* 59: 1 (2017); Joshua Bloom and Waldo E. Martin Jr., *Black against Empire: The History and Politics of the Black Panther Party* (Berkeley: University of California Press, 2013), 213–14; Safiya Bukhari, *The War Before* (New York: Feminist Press, 2010), 24–5; Orisanmi Burton, "Revolution Is Illegal," *Spectre Journal*, April 21, 2021, spectrejournal.com.

24   Michael T. Kaufman, "Ex-Prisoner at Tombs Feels Close to Cellmates," *New York Times*, August 19, 1970; "The Lincoln Hospital Offensive," *Palante*, July 17, 1970; Alfonso A. Narvaez, "Young Lords Seize Lincoln Hospital Building," *New York Times*, July 15, 1970; Losier, "Against 'Law and Order' Lockup," 12; Orisanmi Burton, "Organized Disorder: The New York City Jail Rebellion of 1970," *Black Scholar* 48: 4 (2018), 29.

11. Power to the People

1   C.L.R. James, *The Black Jacobins* (New York: Vintage, 1989), 138.

2   "Rikers Prisoners on Hunger Strike," *New York Times*, March 14, 1970; Rudy Johnson, "Protest Is Ended on Rikers Island," *New York Times*, March 17, 1970.

3   "City Prison Guards Conduct Slowdown," *New York Times*, February 6, 1970; Damon Stetson, "Police 'Sickness' Offset by Shifts," *New York Times*, October 23, 1968; Harvey Swados,

"The City's Island of the Damned," *New York Times Magazine*, April 26, 1970, 111; Johnson, "Protest Is Ended."

4 BOC, *A Report on the Investigation into the Death of Julio Roldan, an Inmate of the Manhattan House of Detention for Men* (New York: BOC, 1970), 1–2; BOC, *Crisis in the Prisons: A Commitment to Change* (New York: BOC, 1971), 14; David Burnham, "The Tombs Called 'Dungeon of Fear,'" *New York Times*, April 8, 1970.

5 Jamal Joseph, *Panther Baby* (New York: Algonquin Books, 2002), 81, 93–4, 100–1, 112–13.

6 BOC, *A Day in Court Means a Day in the Pens* (New York: BOC, 1972), 6–13, 17–26. In addition to the Manhattan pens, where Tombs prisoners spent their time, this report also visited facilities in Brooklyn and the Bronx, where the same conditions prevailed. The study animating this report was conducted after the dramatic events which follow, but was in large part aimed at capturing the conditions which provided the opportunity for militants to take action.

7 BOC, *A Day in the Pens*, 8–9. Broken ceramic toilets during this period exacerbated crowding, as court pens were put out of order, and others crowded well beyond capacity. So too with cells at facilities like the Tombs, where upward of fifty toilets could be broken at one time, thus rendering those cells inoperable and forcing doubling and tripling of prisoners in a single tiny cell. The following exchange from a BOC meeting demonstrates further bureaucratic obstacles to this most basic of jail provisions: "Mr. Schulte then reported that the problem with the delivery of toilets to the City institutions has been a shipping problem. The manufacturer has advised that it is more expensive to ship 99 bowls than to ship 100, so that it waits for an order of at least 100 bowls before it ships them. Mr. Schulte stated that the manufacturer will advise within a week whether it can adapt the bowls to the existing molds in the institutions. The Chairman asked Mr. Schulte to prepare a written memorandum outlining all information pertaining to the delivery and installation of the bowls. Mr. Schulte added that he has been advised that it would be well worth the $350 expenditure per bowl to purchase steel bowls. Mr. D'Elia stated that steel bowls are almost as easy to break as are the china ones. Commissioner Malcolm expressed his appreciation for any assistance which the Board could give in this area" (BOC Meeting Minutes 3/6/72, 1, 3).

8 Toussaint Losier, "Against 'Law and Order' Lockup: The 1970 NYC Jail Rebellions," *Race and Class* 59: 1 (2017), 8; New York State Committee on Crime and Correction, *The Hidden Society*

(Albany: NYSCCC, 1971), 11; Richie, in *To My Brother Who Did a Crime*, ed. Barbara Habenstreit (New York: Doubleday & Co., 1973), 34; "Two Whites Are Seized by Black Prisoners in Tombs Incident," *New York Times*, August 9, 1970; Francis X. Clines, "Inmate's Beating Called Riot Spark," *New York Times*, August 19, 1970; Alfonso A. Narvaez, "Tombs Prisoners Seize 5 Hostages in 8-Hour Protest," *New York Times*, August 11, 1970; Barry Gottehrer, *The Mayor's Man* (New York: Doubleday, 1975), 262; "Text of Tombs' Inmates' Grievances," *New York Times*, August 11, 1970.

9   This last statement would appear in almost identical language the following year, in Manifesto and Demands of the Attica rebellion – a four-day prison takeover at which twenty-eight prisoners and nine staff were killed by New York State Police and other law enforcement officers. See "Text of Tombs Grievances"; Attica Liberation Faction, "Manifesto of Demands and Anti-Oppression Platform," *Race and Class* 53: 2 (2011), 28–35; Barbara Campbell, "Herbert X. Blyden," *New York Times*, September 15, 1971; Herbert X, Blyden, "Interview with Herbert X. Blyden," *Blackside, Inc.*, December 22, 1988, Washington University Digital Gateway Texts.

10   Gottehrer, *Mayor's Man*, 263; Michael T. Kaufman, "Ex-Prisoner at Tombs Feels Close to Cellmates," *New York Times*, August 19, 1970; Clines, "Beating Called Riot Spark;" Orisanmi Burton, "Organized Disorder: The New York City Jail Rebellion of 1970," *Black Scholar* 48: 4 (2018), 31.

11   Joseph, *Panther Baby*, 111, 114–70.

12   Losier, "Against 'Law and Order,'" 5; Narvaez, "Tombs Prisoners Seize 5 Hostages."

13   Martin Arnold, "Prisoners in Tombs Riot for Second Day," *New York Times*, August 12, 1970; NYSCCC, *Hidden Society*, 11; Burton, "Organized Disorder," 30.

14   NYSCCC, *Hidden Society*, 11; Losier, "Law and Order," 14; Francis X. Clines, "Tombs Prisoners Boycott Hearings," *New York Times*, August 18, 1970; Herman Badillo and Milton Haynes, *A Bill of No Rights: Attica and the American Prison System* (New York: Outerbridge & Lazard, 1972). 15; C. Gerald Fraser, "Dispute Arises between Correction Commissioner and Senator Dunne on Inquiry into Tombs Conditions," *New York Times*, August 17, 1970.

15   "Jail Guards Push Plan on Security," *New York Times*, August 19, 1970; Lesley Oelsner, "Guards at Tombs Regain Control of Seized 4th Floor," *New York Times*, August 21, 1970; Badillo and Haynes, *No Rights*, 15; Burton, "Organized Disorder," 33.

16 Fraser, "Dispute Arises"; Clines, "Beating Called Riot Spark"; Badillo and Haynes, *No Rights*, 16; BOC Meeting Minutes 11/5/70, 2, not a direct quote in cited text.

17 Francis X. Clines, "Tombs Study Said to Mislead Inmates," *New York Times*, August 25, 1970; Oelsner, "Guards at Tombs Regain Control"; NYSCCC, *The Tombs Disturbance: A Report* (Albany: NYSCCC, 1970), 1.

18 NYSCCC, *Tombs Disturbance*, 9–25, 55.

19 Michael T. Kaufman, "Sick-Out at Rikers; City Prisons to Get 300 More Officers," *New York Times*, September 3, 1970; Michael T. Kaufman, "Jail Guards' Sick-Out Spreads; City Orders Paychecks Held Up," *New York Times*, September 4, 1970; "Guards Back on Job at Two City Prisons," *New York Times*, September 5, 1970; Martin Gansberg, "McGrath Blames 'Our Times' for Recent Riots at the Tombs," *New York Times*, August 31, 1970; Craig R. Whitney, "Suit Seeks to Shut and Improve Tombs," *New York Times*, September 11, 1970.

12. Shaping Destiny

1 Stanley Eldridge, "The Black Man Is Unique," in *Return Me to My Mind* (New York: Fortune Society, 1970).

2 Jamal Joseph, *Panther Baby* (New York: Algonquin Books, 2002), 120; Toussaint Losier, "Against 'Law and Order' Lockup: The 1970 NYC Jail Rebellions," *Race and Class* 59: 1 (2017), 16.

3 Barry Gottehrer, *The Mayor's Man* (New York: Doubleday, 1975), 264–6; John Sibley, "Prisoners Seize Hostages, Take Over Jail in Queens," *New York Times*, October 2, 1970; Kuwasi Balagoon, in *Look for Me in the Whirlwind: From the Panther 21 to 21st Century Revolutions* (Los Angeles: PM Press, 2017), 497–8.

4 Balagoon, *Whirlwind*, 371–2, 498; Burton, "Organized Disorder," 34; Emmanuel Perlmutter, "Assault on 5 Guards at Rikers Brings Union Warning That Jail Is a 'Bombshell,'" *New York Times*, October 8, 1970; Losier, "Against 'Law and Order,'" 17.

5 *Mayor's Man*, 267; Orisanmi Burton, "Organized Disorder: The New York City Jail Rebellion of 1970," *Black Scholar* 48: 4 ([2018]), 24–5.

6 Ricardo de Leon, "Rebellion in the Tombs: An Inmate's Chronicle," *Village Voice*, November 5, 1970, 9, 12; New York State Committee on Crime and Correction, *The Hidden Society* (Albany: NYSCCC, 1971), 11; Robert D. McFadden, "All Hostages Out: Holdout Inmates in Queens Yield," *New York Times*, October 6, 1970.

7   McFadden, "Rebellion in the Tombs;" Alfred E. Clark, "Prison-
    ers Citing Old Grievances," *New York Times*, October 3, 1970;
    Losier, "Law and Order," 19; NYSCCC, *Hidden Society*, 13.

8   Herman Badillo and Milton Haynes, *A Bill of No Rights: Attica
    and the American Prison System* (New York: Outerbridge &
    Lazard, 1972), 21.

9   Robert D. Mcfadden, "Rioting Spreads to a Fourth Jail; 5 Hos-
    tages Freed," *New York Times*, October 4, 1970; Gottehrer,
    Mayor's Man, 269–270; Badillo and Haynes, *No Rights*, 21;
    Balagoon, *Whirlwind*, 502.

10 McFadden, "Rioting Spreads"; Balagoon, *Whirlwind*, 501;
    NYSCCC, *Hidden Society*, 11; "Sieze the Jails," *Palante*, August
    1970.

11 McFadden, "Rioting Spreads;" Robert D. McFadden, "Tombs
    Prisoners Free 17 as Mayor Warns of Force; Two Other Jails
    Retaken," *New York Times*, October 5, 1970.

12 McFadden, "Tombs Prisoners Free"; Gottehrer, *Mayor's Man*,
    237–73.

13 Badillo and Haynes, *No Rights*, 22; "Days Development in
    the City Jail Crisis," *New York Times*, October 5, 1970; Bala-
    goon, *Whirlwind*, 499–502; de Leon, "Rebellion in the Tombs";
    Balagoon, *Whirlwind*, 501.

14 Balagoon, *Whirlwind*, 503–4, 508.

15 Gottehrer, *Mayor's Man*, 275–6; de Leon, "Rebellion in the
    Tombs."

16 Corporation Counsel of the City of New York, *The Evacua-
    tion of Inmates from the Branch Queens House of Detention
    for Men on October 5, 1970* (New York: City Hall, 1971), 3;
    Joseph, *Panther Baby*, 170–1; Balagoon, *Whirlwind*, 508, 506–8.
    As Losier notes (34 n129), there is disagreement on the timetable,
    and the existence of two separate votes. Balagoon recalls one
    vote. I have followed Gottehrer, Badillo, McFadden, NYSCC, and
    the Corporation Counsel, all of whom describe two votes, erring
    on the side of the likelihood that separate events were conflated
    in Balagoon's account, rather than nonexistent events imagined
    in the others. Badillo provides additional details, including first-
    hand accounts of multiple city officials (23–4).

17 Balagoon, *Whirlwind*, 510–11; McFadden, "All Hostages Out."
    Corporation Counsel, *The Evacuation of Inmates*, 3–8; Burton,
    "Organized Disorder," 38–9.

18 Gottehrer, *Mayor's Man*, 279–81; Corporation Counsel, *The
    Evacuation of Inmates*, 11, 20–2.

19 Corporation Counsel, *The Evacuation of Inmates*, 15–19;
    McFadden, "All Hostages Out."

20 Balagoon, *Whirlwind*, 513; Gottehrer, *Mayor's Man*, 282–3; Joseph, *Panther Baby*, 171; Burton, "Organized Disorder," 39.

13. Free Angela Davis!

1 Stephan Cohen, *The Gay Liberation Youth Movement in New York: 'An Army of Lovers Cannot Fail'* (New York: Routledge, 2007), 107–8.
2 Cohan, The Gay Liberation Movement, 98, 137, 146.
3 Linda Charlton, "F.B.I. Seizes Angela Davis in Motel Here," *New York Times*, October 14, 1970; Davis, *Autobiography*, 18, 22–3, 50.
4 Angela Davis, *An Autobiography* (New York: International Publishers, 1988), 33–7, 41–2, 44; 48–9, 58.
5 Craig R. Whitney, "City Aides Oppose Solitary Confining of Angela Davis," *New York Times*, November 3, 1970; BOC Meeting Minutes 10/30/70, 3; BOC Meeting Minutes 11/3/70, 3; "Angela Davis Is Transferred to a Regular Cell," *New York Times*, November 7, 1970; Davis, *Autobiography*, 47. In his 1991 memoir *Exposing Myself*, Rivera scrupulously recalls himself as the "ringmaster" of a raucous courtroom scene culminating in Davis's release from jail—thereby exposing himself to serious questions of narrative credibility. Geraldo Rivera, *Exposing Myself* (New York: Bantam, 1991), 100–1.
6 Davis, *Autobiography*, 47, 51–2, 56, 62
7 Davis, *Autobiography*, 20, 43–4, 49–61.
8 Davis, *Autobiography*, 22, 44–6, 60, 64; Barbara Campbell, "Mrs. Davis Loses Extradition Plea," *New York Times*, December 22, 1970.
9 Davis, *Autobiography*, 66, 68–70; Linda Charlton, "Removed in Secret," *New York Times*, December 23, 1970.
10 Joan Bird, in *Look for Me in the Whirlwind: From the Panther 21 to 21st Century Revolutions* (Los Angeles: PM Press, 2017), 485–94; Assata Shakur, *Assata: An Autobiography* (New York: Lawrence Hill, 1988), 83.

14. Aftermath

1 Ricardo de Leon, "Rebellion in the Tombs: An Inmate's Chronicle," *Village Voice*, November 5, 1970; Homer Bigart, "Visitors Say Conditions in the City Prisons Are Worse Than Before Inmate Riots," *New York Times*, October 19, 1970.

2   Toussaint Losier, "Against 'Law and Order' Lockup: The 1970 NYC Jail Rebellions," *Race and* Class 59: 1 (2017), 26; Denise Oliver, "¡murder!," *Palante*, October 30, 1970; "Pig of the Week," *Palante*, October 30, 1970.

3   BOC Meeting Minutes 10/30/70, 2; Losier, "Law and Order," 26.

4   Barry Gottehrer, *The Mayor's Man* (New York: Doubleday, 1975), 271–4, 286; Maurice Carroll, "McGrath Quits Jail Post, Says He Was Not Ousted," *New York Times*, November 20, 1971.

5   Criminal Justice Coordinating Council, "Criminal Justice Plan for 1971" (New York: CJCC, 1971), 46; BOC, *Reforming the Reformatory* (New York: BOC, 1971), 8; BOC Meeting Minutes 4/2/73, 2–3.

6   Roy Caldwood, *Making the Right Moves: Rikers Island and NYC Corrections: Being Calm in the Storm* (New York: Creative Space, 2015), 117.

7   Curiously, Claire Feinman attributes these changes to the rebellion at Attica, making scant reference to the rebellions in DOC custody. While Attica certainly provided additional impetus for reform in the city jails, as I demonstrate, these reforms were already underway and made with explicit reference to the New York City jail rebellions. See Claire Feinman, *Imprisoned Women: A History of the Treatment of Women Incarcerated in New York City (NY), 1932–1975*, PhD Diss., New York University, 1976, 257.

8   BOC, *Crisis in the Prisons: A Commitment to Change* (New York: BOC, 1971), 3; Edward C. Burks, "Mayor Fills Six Vacancies on Board of Correction," *New York Times*, October 28, 1970; New York State Committee on Crime and Correction, *The Tombs Disturbance: A Report* (Albany: NYSCCC, 1970), 16–25; Robert D. McFadden, "Mayor Reactivating Jail Watchdog Unit," *New York Times*, October 19, 1970; Burks, "Mayor Fills Six Vacancies."

9   New York State Committee on Crime and Correction, *The Hidden Society* (Albany: NYSCCC, 1971), 35; BOC, *Crisis in the Prisons*, 3"; "Pig of the Week"; BOC, *A Report on the Investigation into the Death of Julio Roldan, an Inmate of the Manhattan House of Detention for Men* (New York: BOC, 1970), 1–4.

10 BOC Meeting Minutes 11/5/70, 1; BOC, *A Shuttle to Oblivion: A Report on the Life and Death of a Citizen, Raymond Lavon, in the Manhattan House of Detention for Men, also Known as "The Tombs"* (New York: BOC, 1970); "Young Lords Decry Lavon-Death Study," *New York Times*, December 5, 1970.

11 William vanden Heuvel, "Agenda for 100 Days," *Village Voice*, February 18, 1971, 1, 60–2.

12 BOC, *Crisis in the Prisons,* 14; BOC, *A Year of Hope* (New York: BOC, 1973), 1–7; BOC, *1973 Annual Report* (New York: BOC, 1974), 1–17.

13 Juan M. Vasquez, "Correction Aides at Work in Tombs," *New York Times,* September 21, 1971; "Guard-Union Head Assails 'Aide' Plan," *New York Times,* October 11, 1971; BOC Meeting Minutes 10/18/71, 2; 12/9/74, 5.

14 BOC Meeting Minutes, 4/19/71, 4–5, quoted text is a paraphrase in the meeting minutes; 2/5/73, 1–2; 4/2/73, 2; 4/23/73, 2; 10/2/73, 5–6; 10/12/73, 3; 1/25/74, 9; 5/13/74, 2; 7/23/74, 2; 11/18/74, 2.

15 BOC Meeting Minutes 2/3/71, 1–3; 3/4/74, 2; 1/25/74, 3.

16 BOC, *1973,* I-5; These reports include: BOC, *The Death of John Wayne Wilson* (New York: BOC, 1973); BOC, *Report on the Death of Juanita Robinson* (New York: BOC, 1975); BOC, *The Death of John Wesley Thompson* (New York: BOC, 1976); BOC, *Report on Prison Suicides and Urgent Recommendations for Action* (New York: BOC, 1972); BOC, *The Cases of William L. and Larry T.: The Problems of the Mentally Disturbed Defendant* (New York: BOC, 1972); BOC, *The Case of Ralph G.: Legal Representation of Indigent Criminal Defendants* (New York: BOC, 1972); BOC, *Through The Veil of Partial Comprehension: New York City's Hispanic Defendant and the Criminal Justice System* (New York: BOC, 1973); BOC, *Reforming the Reformatory.*

17 BOC, "Report on the Prisons 1970–1973," BOC Archives (BOCA); BOC, *1973,* 1–36; BOC, *1974 Annual Report* (New York: BOC, 1975), 11.

18 Lesley Oelsner, "Jail to Expand Methadone Use," *New York Times,* March 29, 1970; Maurice Carroll, "City Council Overrides Lindsay, Orders Jail Methadone Program," *New York Times,* September 10, 1969; Maurice Carroll, "Councilmen Push for Methadone Plan," *New York Times,* February 15, 1970; Edward Ranzal, "City Plans to Double Methadone Project," *New York Times,* September 30, 1970; BOC, *Crisis in the Prisons,* 9.

19 Noga Shalev, "From Public to Private Care: The Historical Trajectory of Medical Services in a New York City Jail," *American Journal of Public Health* 99: 6 (June 2009), 990–1; Clifton Ping Lee, *An Analysis of the New York City Prison Health Services: A Comparison of Contractor and Direct Services,* MA thesis, Yale University, 1989, 15–16; Lloyd F. Novick, "The Contractual Model for Prison Health Care," *Medical Care* 14:8, (1976), 695–6; Lee, "Analysis," 16; Novick, "Contractual Model" is an early favorable assessment.

20 Geraldo Rivera, "Conditions in New York City Prisons," *New York Times*, January 12, 1971.

21 "Up from the Ranks: Benjamin Joseph Malcolm," *New York Times*, January 20, 1972; Tom Goldstein, "New U.S. Parole Board Member: Benjamin Joseph Malcolm," *New York Times*, November 12, 1977. While McGrath failed to formally abolish the board, it is hardly coincidental that it found no support with Lindsay, who refused not only to appoint new members, but even meet with the members hanging on from the days of rebellion. In 1967, board member David Schulte speculated that the mayor, who showed little interest before, hadn't read a single BOC report. See Ronald Maiorana, "Correction Chief Scores Lay Board," *New York Times*, December 14, 1967.

22 Martin Tolchin, "Malcolm, a Black, Named Correction Chief by Mayor," *New York Times*, January 20, 1972; John Corry, "Spokesman for the City of Unwanted," *New York Times*, May 15, 1974; David Garland, *The Culture of Control: Crime and Social Order in Contemporary Society* (Chicago: University of Chicago Press, 2001), 142.

23 BOC Meeting Minutes 5/12/72, 1; 6/12/72, 2; Alfred E. Clark, "14 Are Suspended over a Jail Riot," *New York Times*, June 3, 1972; BOC Meeting Minutes 8/7/72, 2; 9/11/72, 2.

24 BOC Meeting Minutes 1/8/73, 3; 2/5/73, 4.

25 Sylvia Kronstadt, "The Prison Guards: An Unhappy Lot," *New York Affairs* (Fall 1974), 62–63.

26 Michele Hermann, "*Rhem v. Malcolm:* A Case Study of Public Interest Litigation: Pretrial Detention," MA thesis, Harvard University, 1977, 1–8. This deft study of *Rhem* benefits not only from the author's access to extensive unpublished documents, but also from interviews with several principal participants.

27 Hermann, "*Rhem v. Malcolm*," 9–10; Whitney, "Suit Seeks to Shut and Improve Tombs"; *Rhem v. McGrath*, 70 Civ. 3962 (S.D.N.Y. 1970); *Rhem v. McGrath*, 326 F. Supp. 681 (S.D.N.Y. 1971); Hermann, "*Rhem v. Malcolm*," 15; *Rhem v. Malcolm*, 371 F.Supp (S.D.N.Y. 1974) 594.

28 Quoted in Hermann, "*Rhem v. McGrath*," 16; Hermann, "*Rhem v. Malcolm*," 16–17.

29 *Rhem v. Malcolm*, 371 F.Supp (S.D.N.Y. 1974) 594, 636; Hon. Harold Baer, Jr. and Arminda Bepko, "A Necessary and Proper Role for Federal Courts in Prison Reform: The Benjamin v. Malcolm Consent Decrees," *New York Law School Law Review* 52 (2007/08), 3–64; *Rhem v. Malcolm*, 371 F.Supp (S.D.N.Y. 1974) at 604, 615; BOC Meeting Minutes 1/14/74, 4.

30 Herman, *Rhem v. Malcolm*, 21; *Rhem v. Malcolm*, 377 F.Supp. (S.D.N.Y. 1974) at 995–6.

31 *Rhem v. Malcolm*, 507 V.2d (U.S.D.C.S.D 1974) at 333; Max H. Siegel, "Tombs Closing, Inmates to Go to Rikers," *New York Times*, November 16, 1974; Baer and Bepko, "A Necessary and Proper Role for Federal Courts," 21–2; Tom Goldstein, "Rikers Island Problems Now Resemble Tombs's," *New York Times*, February 23, 1975; Nathaniel Sheppard Jr., "Tombs Closes as the Last of Its Inmates Depart," *New York Times*, December 21, 1974. In the following chapter I will examine this subsequent litigation.

15. Out of Control

1 BOC Meeting Minutes 5/1/72, 3, quoted text is a paraphrase in the meeting minutes. It is unclear whether DOC chose May Day to discuss this issue out of respect for the international workers' revolution, or if it was simply a coincidence.

2 BOC Meeting Minutes 5/1/72, 3, quoted text is a paraphrase in the meeting minutes.

3 "16 Hurt on Rikers in Inmate Brawl," *New York Times*, February 2, 1972; Roy Caldwood, *Making the Right Moves: Rikers Island and NYC Corrections: Being Calm in the Storm* (New York: Creative Space, 2015), 66; BOC Meeting Minutes, October 30, 1970, 2; Robert D. McFadden, "100 Hurt as Rikers Attack Frees 5 Hostage Guards," *New York Times*, February 28, 1972; Caldwood, *Right Moves*, 48–52; Caldwood, *Right Moves*, 10. Curiously, DOC evaded adopting a coherent and documented plan for managing uprisings. Appearing before BOC in early 1974, Director of Operations Joseph D'Elia "stated that each institution has its own contingency plan. However, the tour commander must be allowed the flexibility of determining what action should be taken in each specific case. Therefore, plans must be general in nature." Barry Gottehrer, now a BOC member, reminded D'Elia of his own experience at the Tombs in 1970, when there was no plan at all. In response, "Mr. D'Elia stated that good leadership was more important than good plans. It was crucial that the commanding officer be in control of any situation" (BOC Meeting Minutes 4/4/74, 6). Effectively: riots would be repressed by brute force, diplomacy, or whatever else moved whoever happened to be in charge at the time.

4 Michael T. Kaufman, "A Militant Handful Blamed for Rikers

Island Prison Revolt," New York Times, February 29, 1972; BOC Meeting Minutes 3/6/72, 2; Caldwood, *Right Moves*, 3–6; McFadden, "100 Hurt." See Caldwood, *Right Moves*, 6.

5 Caldwood, *Right Moves*, 58; McFadden, "100 Hurt"; Kaufman, "Militant Handful"; *New York Times*, "Four Rikers Inmates Get 5-Year Terms for Actions in Riot," June 30, 1972.

6 Akinyele Omowale Umoja, "Repression Breeds Resistance: The Black Liberation Army and the Radical Legacy of the Black Panther Party," in *Setting Sights: Histories and Reflections on Community Armed Self-Defense*, ed. scot crow (Oakland: PM Press, 2018), 154–60; Bryan Burrough, *Days of Rage: America's Radical Underground, the FBI, and the Forgotten Age of Revolutionary Violence* (New York: Penguin, 2015), 173–6, 183–9, 193–8; Edward Jay Epstein, "The Black Panthers and Police: A Pattern of Genocide?," *New Yorker*, February 13, 1971. I share Jeremy Varon's critique that *Days of Rage* narrates events, however factually, in a way devoid of political context, and does not take seriously the central question of why its subjects did what they did (Jeremy Varon, "Dumbing Down the Underground," *Los Angeles Review of Books*, April 19, 2015). For the time being, however, it remains the most detailed history of the long arc from the Black Panther Party to the BLA's final days. By contrast, Safiya Bukhari, *The War Before* (New York: Feminist Press, 2010) offers a firsthand account of the BLA's formation amid state repression of the Panthers, intra-party conflict induced in part by COINTELPRO, and persistent poverty, degradation, and police murder of black people in the United States (see especially 119–23). For profiles of thirty-two black liberation fighters slain between 1968 and 1981, see Bukhari's "Lest We Forget," reprinted in *The War Before*, 135–55.

7 Boroughs, *Days of Rage*, 192; Lacy Fosburg, "7 Saw Their Way Out of the Tombs," *New York Times*, October 24, 1972; Glenn Fowler, "Two Accused of Smuggling Saws to Tombs Escapers," *New York Times*, February 7, 1973.

8 Boroughs, *Days of Rage*, 210–17, 237–42; Judith Cummings, "2 of 3 Black 'Army' Suspects Are Held without Bail," *New York Times*, September 19, 1973; Michael T. Kaufman, "Woman Captured in Shoot-Out Called 'Soul' of Black Militants," *New York Times*, May 3, 1973; Michael T. Kaufman, "Slaying of One of the Last Black Liberation Army Leaders Still at Large Ended a 7-Month Manhunt," *New York Times*, November 16, 1973; Bukhari, "Lest We Forget," 150–1; Kaufman, "Slaying."

9 Glenn Fowler, "Brown Is Recaptured with Four in Raid on a Brooklyn Tenement," *New York Times*, October 4, 1973; Alfred

E. Clark, "Jail Escape Is Foiled, Officials Report," *New York Times*, July 28, 1973.

10 BOA Meeting Minutes 10/2/73, 7–9; Fowler, "Brown Is Recaptured."

11 BOA Meeting Minutes 10/2/73, 3, 7–9, quoted text is a paraphrase in the meeting minutes.

12 BOA Meeting Minutes 10/2/73, 9, quoted text is a paraphrase in the meeting minutes; Fred Feretti, "Beame Orders an Investigation of Jails, Covering Escape and Bribe Charges," *New York Times*, March 7, 1974.

13 Pranay Gupte, "Suspect in Slaying of 2 Officers Flees," *New York Times*, September 28, 1973; Paul L. Montgomery, "4 Seized Near Manhole in Alleged Plot to Free Black Army Friends in Tombs," *New York Times*, December 28, 1973; Feretti, "Beame Orders an Investigation"; Dan Berger, *Captive Nation* (Chapel Hill: University of North Carolina Press, 2014) 249n77; "3 in an Alleged Plot to Free 6 at Tombs Released by Judge," *New York Times*, January 24, 1974.

14 "Times Receives Key Set Stolen in Tombs Break In," *New York Times*, May 7, 1974; Max H. Seigel, "4 Others Linked to Prison Escape," *New York Times*, May 28, 1975.

15 "New X-ray Machine Foils Blade-Smuggling at Jail," *New York Times*, August 7, 1974; Alfred E. Clark, "Brooklyn Escape by 3 Is Thwarted," *New York Times*, August 16, 1974; Robert McG. Thomas, Jr., "Fleeing Prisoner Falls to Death, 2d Inmate Captured in Brooklyn," *New York Times*, May 26, 1975; Seigel, "4 Others Linked to Prison Escape."

16 BOC Meeting Minutes 3/3/75, 7; Robert D. McFadden, "Rikers Escape Attempt Reassessed as Stronger," *New York Times*, February 22, 1975; David Bird, "Police Investigate Apparent Escape Attempt by Black Liberationists," *New York Times*, February 18, 1975; BOC Meeting Minutes 3/3/75, 7.

17 Alfonso A. Narvaez, "Prisoner Shoots 2 Guards and Patient and Flees from Kings County Hospital," *New York Times*, September 10, 1975; BOC Meeting Minutes 3/3/75, 6.

18 Robert D. McFadden, "15-State Alarm Issued for 2 Fugitives from Brooklyn's House of Detention," *New York Times*, May 5, 1974; Robert Hanley, "Injured Fugitive Held in Brooklyn," *New York Times*, May 6, 1974; Robert Hanley, "Rikers I. Fugitives Commandeered a Tug," *New York Times*, May 7, 1974; Nathaniel Sheppard Jr., "Captured Inmates Report Paying Officer for Saw," *New York Times*, May 8, 1974; Wolfgang Saxon, "Prisoner Escapes from Queens Jail," *New York Times*, May 26, 1974.

16. Farewell, Anna Kross

1 Ted K. Raderman, "Rikers Island Past Present Future," *Municipal Engineers Journal* 58 (1972), 132–53.

2 BOC Meeting Minutes 10/18/71, 1; Paul L. Montgomery, "Jail for Women Dedicated Here," *New York Times*, June 19, 1971; Raderman, "Past Present Future," 145, 151.

3 BOC, *Crisis in the Prisons: A Commitment to Change* (New York: BOC, 1971), 28.

4 BOC, *Year of Hope*, 1–18; Raderman, "Past Present Future," 147; DOC, *Jails for the 80s* (New York: DOC, 1980), III–37; BOC Meeting Minutes 7/9/73, 2; Raderman, "Past Present Future," 147. Today this facility bears the name Robert N. Davoren Center.

5 Lesley Oelsner, "Voicing Regrets on Need, City Opens a Youth Prison," *New York Times*, June 30, 1972.

6 Raderman, "Past Present Future," 147.

7 Montgomery, "Jail for Women"; "Prison Architects Break Tradition's Bars," *New York Times*, August 11, 1971; Murray Schumach, "City Begins Demolishing Women's Jail," *New York Times*, October 10, 1973.

8 BOC, *Crisis in the Prisons*, 29; Chris, in *To My Brother Who Did a Crime*, ed. Barbara Habenstreit (New York: Doubleday & Co., 1973), 154; BOC Meeting Minutes 7/19/71, 3.

9 Raderman, "Past Present Future," 145; BOC Meeting Minutes 10/18/71, 3; 6/18/73, 4–5.

10 BOC, *Report on the Death of Juanita Robinson* (New York: BOC, 1975), 1.

11 Denise Oliver, "Women in Prison: A Special Report," *Rest of the News*, September 3, 1973, my transcription, Accessed from Indiana University via Inter-Library Loan.

12 Assata Shakur, *Assata: An Autobiography* (New York: Lawrence Hill, 1988), 81–2, 84.

13 Assata Shakur / Joanne Chesimard, "Women in Prison: How We Are," *Black Scholar* 9:7 (April 1978), 10; Shakur, *Assata*, 84. Contemporaneously, Roy Caldwood describes a Rikers doctor who was legally blind. "It was hard to imagine he could do a thorough exam," he recounts (*Making the Right Moves: Rikers Island and NYC Corrections: Being Calm in the Storm* [New York: Creative Space, 2015], 67).

14 Shakur / Chesimard, "Women in Prison," 9–10.

15 Shakur / Chesimard, "Women in Prison," 9–13.

16 Shakur / Chesimard, "Women in Prison," 10–11; Shakur, *Assata*, 83.

17. Burn, City, Burn

1 William K. Tabb, *The Long Default: New York City and the Urban Fiscal Crisis* (New York: Monthly Review, 1982), 19, 23–4; Kim Phillips-Fein, *Fear City: New York's Fiscal Crisis and the Rise of Austerity Politics* (New York: Metropolitan Books, 2017), 21, 44.

2 Vincent Cannato, *The Ungovernable City: John Lindsay and His Struggle to Save New York* (New York: Basic Books, 2001), 548–9; Phillips-Fein, *Fear City*, 21; Joshua Freeman, *Working-Class New York: Life and Labor Since World War II* (New York: The New Press, 2001), 257–8.

3 Robert D. McFadden, "Abraham Beame Is Dead at 94; Mayor during 70's Fiscal Crisis," *New York Times*, February 11, 2001.

4 Tabb, *Long Default*, 12, 20, 30.

5 BOC, *1975–1976 Annual Report* (New York: BOC, 1977), 1; BOC Meeting Minutes 5/21/74, 1–2; 10/7/74, 6; 11/18/74, 3; 12/9/74.

6 BOC Meeting Minutes 12/9/74, 2–4; Tabb, *Long Default*, 30–1.

7 BOC Meeting Minutes,12/9/74, 2–4; 11/18/74, 6, quoted text is a paraphrase in the meeting minutes.

8 Phillips-Fein, *Fear City*, 118–19; BOC Meeting Minutes 12/9/74, 5; 1/16/75, 1; Malcolm W. Gordon, "Report on the New York City House of Detention for Men," February 28, 1975, BOC.

9 BOC Meeting Minutes 3/3/75, 3, quoted text is a paraphrase in the meeting minutes.

10 BOC Meeting Minutes 12/17/74, 1, 3; 12/20/74, 1, quoted text is a paraphrase in the meeting minutes.

11 Phillips-Fein, *Fear City*, 35; Gordon, "Report on the New York City House of Detention for Men," 1.

12 BOC Meeting Minutes 3/3/75, 5, 6, 8; 11/3/75, 6; BOC, *1974*, 2.

13 BOC Meeting Minutes 6/2/75, 4; 9/23/75, 2. Peter Kihss, "Rikers Island Revolt Leads City to Add 69 Correction Officers," *New York Times*, November 26, 1975; BOC, *1975–1976*, 10–11; John M. Wynne Jr., *Prison Employee Unionism: The Impact on Correctional Administration and Programs* (Washington, DC: National Institute of Law Enforcement and Criminal Justice, 1978), 28.

14 BOC Meeting Minutes 11/3/75, 4; 6/2/75, 4; 7/8/75, 1–2; 11/3/75, 2–3, quoted text is a paraphrase in the meeting minutes; Rebecca Hill, "'The Common Enemy Is the Boss and the Inmate': Police and Prison Guard Unions in New York in the 1970s–1980s," *Labor: Studies in Working Class History of the Americas* 8: 3 (2011), 86.

15 Leslie Maitland, "Guards at Prison Protest Layoffs," *New York Times*, July 8, 1975; Hill, "Common Enemy" deftly chronicles the statewide and national context of this movement; Selwyn Raab, "Laid-off Policemen Block Brooklyn Bridge Traffic," *New York Times*, July 2, 1975; Phillips-Fein, *Fear City*, 133.

16 "Inmates Take Over Queens Jail Floor; Three Guards Hurt," *New York Times*, July 15, 1974.

17 Selwyn Raab, "Policemen Block Brooklyn Bridge"; Council for Public Safety, "Welcome to Fear City" (New York: Council for Public Safety, 1975); Glenn Fowler, "Union 'Guide' to 'Fear City' Is Banned by a Court Order," *New York Times*, June 13, 1975; Eric Lichten, *Class, Power and Austerity: The New York City Fiscal Crisis* (Hadley, MA: Bergin & Garvey, 1986), 12.

18 Lichten, *Class, Power and Austerity*, 2.

19 Ruth Wilson Gilmore, *Golden Gulag: Prisons, Surplus, Crisis, and Opposition in Globalizing California* (Berkeley: University of California Press, 2007), 83–4.

20 Samuel Stein, *Capital City: Gentrification and the Real Estate State* (London and New York: Verso, 2019), 48.

21 Hill, "Common Enemy," 85–7; Phillips-Fein, *Fear City*, 182; Gilmore, "In the Shadow of the Shadow State"; Stein, *Capital City*, 52–6.

22 David Burnham, "Arrests Fall Off," *New York Times*, January 16, 1971; Hill, "Common Enemy," 80.

23 Robert F. Wagner, Oral History Archive at Columbia University, 465; Hill, "Common Enemy," 85; Tabb, *Long Default*, 30; Phillips-Fein, *Fear City*, 217.

24 Wynne, *Prison Employee Unionism*, 164–5; Edward B. Fiske, "City Is Rated High in Teacher Pay," *New York Times*, September 8, 1986.

25 "This Former CO Aimed High," *On the Gate*, Spring 1996, reproduced on correctionhistory.org; Hill, "Common Enemy," 87; Freeman, *Working-Class*, 287.

26 Tabb, *Long Default*, 43.

27 BOC, *1975–1976*, 9; Benjamin J. Malcolm, *A Report to the Mayor of the City of New York on the Riot in the New York City House of Detention for Men on Rikers Island on November 23 to November 24, 1975*, 2–3, BOCA; Caldwood, *Right Moves*, 144–5.

28 Malcolm, *Riot on November 23*, 6–8; John T. McQuiston, "Rikers Rioters Seize Five and Hold Two Cell Blocks," *New York Times*, November 24, 1975; Malcolm, *Riot on November 23*, 6–9.

29 Peter Kihss, "Rikers Island Revolt Ends with Release of

Hostages," *New York Times*, November 25, 1975; Malcolm, *Riot on November 23*, C-1; also reproduced in Caldwood, *Right Moves*, 151.

30 Malcolm, *Riot on November 23*, 11–12; Joseph B. Treaster, "Mayor Tours the Scene of Rikers Revolt," *New York Times*, November 27, 1975.

31 Baer and Bepko, "A Necessary and Proper Role for Federal Courts," 22; Peter Kihss, "Rikers Island Revolt Leads City to Add 69 Correction Officers," *New York Times*, November 26, 1975.

32 Wynne, *Prison Employee Unionism*, 64; BOC, *1975–1976*, 9.

33 Caldwood, *Right Moves*, 125–6, 153–61. Caldwood anonymizes Greco's name to "Graziano."

18. Law and Order

1 Ralph Blumenthal, "Koch Eats Christmas Dinner with Rikers Island Inmates," *New York Times*, December 26, 1977; Kim Phillips-Fein, *Fear City: New York's Fiscal Crisis and the Rise of Austerity Politics* (New York: Metropolitan Books, 2017), 284–6; Jack Newfield and Wayne Barrett, *City for Sale: Ed Koch and the Betrayal of New York* (New York: Harper & Row, 1988), 105–16; Benjamin Ward, Oral History Archive at Columbia University, 84.

2 Newfield and Barrett, *City for Sale*, 116–22, 126–8; John Hull Mollenkopf, *A Phoenix in the Ashes: The Rise and Fall of the Koch Coalition in New York City Politics* (Princeton: Princeton University Press, 1992), 100–1; Andy Battle and Jarrod Shanahan, "The Second Time as Farce," *Jacobin*, April 13, 2018, jacobinmag.com.

3 Mollenkopf, *A Phoenix in the Ashes*, 109–10; Phillips-Fein, *Fear City*, 193–4. Zuccotti, the law partner of Peter Tufo, went on to become a successful developer in his own right, and helped launch the career of Donald J. Trump. His name adorns the park that served as ground zero for the 2011 Occupy Wall Street movement. See Sam Roberts, "John E. Zuccotti, Urbanist, Financier and Would-Be Mayor, Dies at 78," *New York Times*, November 20, 2015.

4 Blumenthal, "Christmas Dinner."

5 BOC, Meeting Minutes 5/31/77, 2, not a direct quote in cited text.

6 Mollenkopf, *Phoenix in the Ashes*, 130–1; Ronald Smothers, "Koch Calls Lower Goals 'Common Sense Approach,'" *New York Times*, January 27, 1980.

7   BOC, *1978–1979*, 1; Hermann, *"Rhem v. Malcolm,"* 27–32; BOC, *1977*, 14.

8   New York City Charter, Chapter 25, Section 626, excerpted in BOC, *1977 Annual Report* (New York: BOC, 1978), 43–4; BOC, *1977 Annual Report* (New York: BOC, 1978), 4.

9   New York State Commission of Correction, *Inquiry into the Disturbances on Rikers Island, October 1986* (Albany: NYSCOC, 1987), 1–3; BOC, *1977*, 5–6, 14, 42; BOC, *Report to the Mayor 1978–1979* (New York: BOC, 1979), 15; Todd Matthews, "A Long Road toward Reform: An Interview with John Boston, Director of the Prisoners' Rights Project of the New York City Legal Aid Society," *Prison Legal News* (July 2008), 20.

10 Selwyn Raab, "Inmates' 'Bill of Rights' Is Proposed to Upgrade City Prison Conditions," *New York Times*, May 5, 1977; BOC, Draft Meeting Minutes 5/5/77, 3; Carey Winfrey, "Guard's Union Head Urges Ouster of Tufo as Correction Panel Chief," *New York Times*, November 12, 1977.

11 BOC, *1977*, 16; BOC, *1978–1979*, 3; BOC, *Minimum Standards for New York City Correctional Facilities* (New York: BOC, 1978); Hon. Harold Baer Jr. and Arminda Bepko, "A Necessary and Proper Role for Federal Courts in Prison Reform: The Benjamin v. Malcolm Consent Decrees," *New York Law School Law Review* 52 (2007/08), 23.

12 BOC, *1978–1979*, 1; Charles Kaiser, "Koch to Name Sturz Deputy Mayor and Lupkin to Investigations Post," *New York Times*, January 4; 1978; Robert Fitch, *The Assassination of New York* (London and New York: Verso, 1993), 49, 222.

13 BOC, *1978–1979*, 18; DOC, *Jails for the 80s* (New York: DOC, 1980), III, 19–44.

14 Mollenkopf, *Phoenix in the Ashes*, 110, 113; Phillips-Fein, *Fear City*, 290; BOC, *1977*, 33; CUNY Struggle, CUNY at the Crossroads (New York: CUNY Struggle, 2016), 4–10.

15 Goldstein, "New U.S. Parole Board Member: Benjamin Joseph Malcolm"; Maurice Carroll, "4 Men Are under Consideration by Koch for Top Correction Post," *New York Times*, December 21, 1977; "Debate Rages over Policies of City Correction Chief," *New York Times*, March 5, 1979.

16 Selwyn Raab, "City's Corrections Chief Realigns Jobs of 65 Top Prison Officials: 'Monday Morning Massacre,'" *New York Times*, November 7, 1978; "Debate Rages."

17 Edward I. Koch, Memorandum to Agency Heads, March 15, 1979, Edward I. Koch Papers, Box 112, Folder 6, LWA; William Ciuros Jr., "Declaration of Emergency," August 11, 1978, Koch Papers, Box 112, Folder, LWA; William Ciuros Jr., "Management

Development Program," March 13, 1979, Koch Papers, Box 112 Folder 2, LWA.

18 William Ciuros Jr., "Management Responsibility and Accountability (Managers Dialogue #1)," February 21, 1979, Koch Papers, Box 112, Folder 5, LWA; William Ciuros Jr. to Hon. Edward I. Koch, December 7, 1978, Koch Papers, Box 112, Folder 2, LWA; William J. Ciuros, "Review of Planned Actions," October 5, 1978, Koch Papers, Box 112, Folder 2, LWA; John Alexander Associates, "Development System for Planning and Performance Appraisal, For: The New York City Department of Correction," February 22, 1979, Koch Papers, Box 112, Folder 6, LWA.

19 William Serrin, "A Lasting Uniformed Coalition Planned," *New York Times*, July 3, 1980; Mark Maier, *City Unions: Managing Discontent in New York City* (New Brunswick: Rutgers University Press, 1987), 172.

20 William Serrin, "How Union 'Amateurs' Won High City Pact," *New York Times*, July 14, 1980, quoted text is a paraphrase in the story; Phil Caruso, Phil Seelig, Nicholas Mancuso, Jack Jordan, and Vincent Bollon, "What Is Justly Due New York's Uniformed Workers: An Open Letter to the Mayor of New York about Why We're Marching on City Hall Tomorrow, July 7th," *New York Times*, July 6, 1982; United Press International, "14 New York City Unions Plan to Endorse Reagan," *New York Times*, July 21, 1984.

21 William Ciuros Jr. to Hon. Edward I. Koch, February 2, 1979, Koch Papers, Box 112, Folder 4, LWA; Edward I. Koch to William Ciuros Jr., February 5, 1979, Koch Papers, Box 112, Folder 4, LWA.

22 Edward I. Koch to Bill Ciuros, November 20, 1978, Koch Papers, Box 112, Folder 2, LWA; William Ciuros Jr. to Hon. Edward Koch, December 12, 1978, Koch Papers, Box 112, Folder 2, LWA.

23 William Ciuros Jr., "Anonymous Letter from 'The Coalition of Concerned Correction Personnel," February 22, 1979, 1–6, Koch Papers, Box 112 Folder 4, LWA.

24 William Ciuros Jr., "Bi-Weekly Report," September 29, 1978, Koch Papers, Box 112, Folder 2, LWA; Edward I. Koch to Bill Ciuros, October 3, 1978, Koch Papers, Box 112, Folder 2, LWA; BOC Meeting Minutes 2/19/80, 5; Tony Schwartz, "Guards at Rikers Stage a Walkout over Conditions," *New York Times*, July 12, 1979; Peter Kihss, "Commissioner Agrees on Hardship at Rikers but Disagrees on Strike," *New York Times*, July 13, 1979; Josh Barbanel, "Correction Officers in 2 Boroughs Stage Brief Unauthorized Protests," *New York Times*, August 14, 1980.

25 William Ciuros Jr. to Hon. Edward Koch, February 1, 1979, Koch Papers, Box 112, Folder 4, LWA.

26 Edward I. Koch to Herb Sturz, September 14, 1978, Koch Papers, Box 112, Folder 4, LWA.

27 Herb Sturz, Oral History Archive at Columbia University, 65, 68.

28 A *Times* report corroborates Sturz's assessment that despite Ciuros's unpopularity among guards and negative press surrounding high-profile suicides and escapes, opposition to the Rikers deal ultimately did him in. See Anna Quindlen, "Correction Chief Quitting; Ward Named to Fill Post," August 10, 1979; William Ciuros Jr. to Diane M. Coffey, August 10, 1979, Koch Papers, Box 112, Folder 8, LWA.

29 Benjamin Ward, Oral History Archive at Columbia University, 1, 11–12, 29–32, 50; Quindlen, "Correction Chief Quitting."

30 Tom Goldstein, "Prison Chief, From Frying Pan into Fire," *New York Times*, September 23, 1979; Ward, Oral History Archive, 71.

31 Frank Bruni to Hon. Edward I. Koch, September 30, 1981, Koch Papers, Box 69, Folder 22, LWA. On the KKK, see Goldstein, "From Frying Pan into Fire"; Frank Bruni to Hon. Benjamin Ward, September 30, 1981, Koch Papers, Box 69, Folder 22, LWA.

32 Benjamin Ward, "Monthly Management Report," July 12, 1982, 4–5, Koch Papers, Box 112, Folder 12, LWA; William Serrin, "Matching Wits on Rikers: Correction Officers' Exacting Craft," *New York Times*, March 26, 1982; Koch Papers, Box 112, Folder 2, LWA.

33 DOC, *Jails for the 80s*, III, 29–31, 42; BOC Meeting Minutes 11/7/77, 2.

34 DOC, *Jails for the 80s*, III, 31–2.

35 BOC, Draft Meeting Minutes 12/5/77, 1; William J. Ciuros, "Review of Planned Actions," October 5, 1978, Koch Papers, Box 112, Folder 2, LWA; BOC, *1978–1979*, 1; BOC Meeting Minutes 2/27/79; 9/18/79, 5–6; 5/31/77, 1; 6/28/79, 7; 4/19/77, 2; 6/28/79, 7–8.

36 Ward, Oral History Archive, 82–3, 91.

37 BOC Meeting Minutes 6/28/79, 1; 7/23/79, 2, 4; 2/19/80, 3; 3/26/79, 4.

38 BOC Meeting Minutes 3/26/79, 3–4; BOC *1978–1979*, 9.

19. Lines of Flight

1 *Benjamin v. Malcolm* 495 F.Supp (S.D.N.Y. 1980) 1357; BOC, *Report on the Board of Correction of the City of New York on*

the *Proposed Rikers Island Transfer,* 1980; NYSCOC, *Rikers Island as a Permanent Site for City Corrections, Long-Term Problems* (Albany: NYSCOC, 1980); William Ciuros Jr., "Chronology of Events—Phasing of Rikers Island Transfer," 1979, 1, Koch Papers, Box 112, Folder 6, LWA; BOC Meeting Minutes 4/24/79, 3.

2 BOC Meeting Minutes 6/28/79, 1–3; Phil Seelig, "Rikers Island Is Cheap and Safe," *New York Times,* November 17, 1979; *New York Times,* "Queens Residents and Corrections Officers Oppose State Takeover of Rikers Island," March 17, 1980.

3 Joyce Purnick, "Dispute Threatens Rikers Takeover," *New York Times,* April 24, 1980; BOC Meeting Minutes 5/21/80; Joyce Purnick, "Takeover of Rikers by State Canceled by City, Koch Says," *New York Times,* May 22, 1980; Lee A. Daniels, "City to Offer Plan to Renew Deteriorating Jail System," *New York Times,* August 17, 1980.

4 *Benjamin v. Malcolm* 495 F.Supp (S.D.N.Y. 1980) 1357; DOC, Jails for the 80s, III, 11, 39.

5 DOC, *Jails for the 80s,* ii–iii, 4–11.

6 DOC, *Jails for the 80s,* 2.

7 BOC, *1979–1980,* 19; Ward, Oral History Archive, 84.

8 BOC, *1977,* 25; BOC, *Annual Report 1980* (New York: BOC, 1980), 11–12; Joseph L. Jacobson, "Escape of Eight Inmates from Maximum Security Section, Block 1B of the N.Y.C. House of Detention for Men—September 24, 1979," Koch Papers, Box 112, Folder 8, LWA.

9 BOC, *1977,* 25–6; BOC Meeting Minutes 3/5/80, 1–2; BOC, *Report to the Mayor and the City Council on Safety and Security in New York City's Jails* (New York: BOC, 1982), 8.

10 Benjamin Ward, "Escape of Howard 'Buddy' Jacobson," June 17, 1980, Koch Papers, Box 112, Folder 9, LWA; BOC, *Safety and Security in New York City's Jails,* 3–4.

11 BOC, *Safety and Security in New York City's Jails,* iv–v, 2; Benjamin Ward, "Rikers Island's Future," *New York Times,* April 19, 1980; BOC, Draft Meeting Minutes 2/22/77, 2, quoted text is a paraphrase in the meeting minutes.

12 Bryan Burrough, *Days of Rage: America's Radical Underground, the FBI, and the Forgotten Age of Revolutionary Violence* (New York: Penguin, 2015), 461–4.

13 "Morales Is Sentenced to 29-Year Minimum on Weapons Charges," *New York Times,* April 21, 1979; Boroughs, *Days of Rage,* 471–4, 544–5; Robert McG. Thomas Jr., "16 in Correction Post Accused of Negligence in Escape by Morales," *New York Times,* December 17, 1979.

14 BOC Meeting Minutes 4/19/77, 1; Hermann, "*Rhem v. Malcolm*," 34–7; *Benjamin v. Malcolm*, 564 F. Supp. 668 (S.D.N.Y. 1983); BOC Meeting Minutes 1/13/81, 1; 2/25/81, 1; 6/30/81, 2.

15 Benjamin Ward, "March 1981 Monthly Activity Report," 1, Koch Papers, Box 112, Folder 10, LWA; Benjamin Ward to Hon. Edward I. Koch, August 11, 1981, Koch Papers, Box 112, Folder 11, LWA; BOC Meeting Minutes 4/8/81, 2; 10/7/81, 1; 5/19/82, 2; 12/16/82, 3; 12/2/81, 1.

16 BOC Meeting Minutes 10/14/81, 3–4; 10/7/81, 2, quoted text is a paraphrase in the meeting minutes; Jack Norton, *Little Siberia, Star of the North: Prisons, Crisis, and Development in Rural New York, 1968–1994*, PhD diss., CUNY Graduate Center, 2018.

17 Kim Phillips-Fein, *Fear City: New York's Fiscal Crisis and the Rise of Austerity Politics* (New York: Metropolitan Books, 2017), 273; BOC, *1977*, 22; BOC, Draft Meeting Minutes 7/18/77, 2; 10/4/83, 3, quoted text is a paraphrase in the meeting minutes; Richard E. Wener, *The Environmental Psychology of Prisons and Jails* (Cambridge, MA: Cambridge University Press, 2012) 56–7.

18 Philip Shenon, "Tombs to Reopen with a New Look," *New York Times*, October 17, 1983; David C. Anderson, "New York's 'New Generation' Jail," *New York Times*, October 25, 1983; Philip Shenon, "Koch Says He May Have to Free Some Inmates in City's Overcrowded Jails," *New York Times*, October 28, 1983.

19 Sam Roberts, "Koch vs. the Courts: New York City's Crowded Jails and the Inmate Release," *New York Times*, November 9, 1983.

20 Philip Shenon, "Jail Release: Why?" *New York Times*, November 5, 1983; Benjamin Ward, "Monthly Management Report," July 12, 1982, Koch Papers, Box 112, Folder 12, LWA; Peter Tufo to Hon. Edward Koch, October 22, 1982, 1, Koch Papers, Box 112, Folder 2, LWA; Benjamin Ward to Hon. Edward I. Koch, November 5, 1982, Koch Papers, Box 112, Folder 12, LWA; DOC, *Jails for the 80s*, III, 32. These conditions catalyzed the 1983 filing of *Fisher v. Koehler*, the first lawsuit against DOC that unified sentenced prisoners and detention prisoners as plaintiffs, to which I will turn in the next chapter.

21 BOC Meeting Minutes 6/16/83, 3–6; 3/3/82, 2; 2/14/83, 3; quoted text is a paraphrase in the meeting minutes; E.R. Shipp, "Bid to Raise Rikers Jail Limits Denied," *New York Times*, May 20, 1983.

22 BOC Meeting Minutes 3/9/83, 1–2; *Benjamin v. Malcolm*, 564 F. Supp. 668 (S.D.N.Y. 1983).

23 Sharon Churcher and Mary Murphy, "Benjamin Ward Involved in Night-Court Fracas," *New York*, May 7, 1984, 13; BOC

Meeting Minutes 3/9/83, 2, quoted text is a paraphrase in the meeting minutes. Confronted with a DOI report detailing these events, and reports of his drunken antics at a police convention in 1984—by which time he had become commissioner of NYPD— Ward vowed to stop drinking, so long as he remained a public servant (Michael Goodwin, "Ward Is Under Fire over Conduct," *New York Times*, October 19, 1984).

24 Michael Goodwin, "Correction Chief Warns of Effects of Inmate Limit," *New York Times*, March 16, 1983; Philip Shenon, "Koch Says He May Have to Free Some Inmates in City's Overcrowded Jails," *New York Times*, October 28, 1983; Philip Shenon, "City Officials Prepare Plan to Set Some Prisoners Free," *New York Times*, November 1, 1983; BOC Meeting Minutes 11/1/83, 2; Philip Shenon, "341 City Detainees Will Be Released to Ease Crowding," *New York Times*, November 2, 1983; Maureen Dowd, "City Meets Court Order in Freeing 423 Inmates," *New York Times*, November 7, 1983; Philip Shenon, "Inmates Are Freed without Any Bail," *New York Times*, November 12, 1983; Ward, Oral History Archive, 89.

25 Ward, Oral History Archive, 89; Philip Shenon, "12% of Those Freed on Low Bail Failed to Appear," *New York Times*, December 2, 1983; Philip Shenon, "Inmate Released on Low Bail Cleared of Later Rape Charge," *New York Times*, May 1, 1984; Shenon, "Jail Release: Why?"

26 Thomas J. Main, *Homelessness in New York City: Policymaking from Koch to de Blasio* (New York: New York University Press, 2016), 31.

27 Philip Shenon, "City Plans to Add Jail Space for 2,200 Inmates," *New York Times*, December 10, 1983; Edward Koch to Benjamin Ward, December 14, 1983, Koch Papers, Box 113, Folder 1, LWA.

20. Show This Motherfucker Who Is Running the Jail

1 Tom Wolfe, *Bonfire of the Vanities* (New York: Picador, 1987), 39–40.

2 John Hull Mollenkopf, *A Phoenix in the Ashes: The Rise and Fall of the Koch Coalition in New York City Politics* (Princeton: Princeton University Press, 1992), 131–9.

3 Edward Koch to Peter Tufo, February 6, 1984, Koch Papers, Box 113, Folder 2, LWA; BOC, *Proposed Jail Construction Plan: Recommendations of the New York City Board of Correction* (New York: BOC, 1983), 10.

4 BOC, *Proposed Jail Construction Plan*, 1–4, 6, 10.
5 Seth Mydans, "New Corrections Chief: Jacqueline Montgomery McMickens," *New York Times*, January 19, 1984.
6 DOC, "Rikers Island Developlment Plan," 1985, Koch Papers, Box 37, Folder 13, LWA; Jacqueline McMickens, "Rikers Island Development Plan Priorities," May 6, 1985, Koch Papers, Box 113, Folder 4, LWA Benjamin Ward to Hon. Edward I. Koch, January 13, 1986, Koch Papers, Box 37, Folder 13. LWA.
7 DOC, "Rikers Island Development Plan," 4.
8 Jacqueline McMickens, "Declaration of Emergency," May 14, 1985, Koch Papers, Box 113, Folder 4, LWA. A number of these emergency orders can be found in Koch's papers at LWA, including Box 113, Folders 6 and 7.
9 Jacqueline McMickens, "July Monthly Report," July 1985, Koch Papers, Box 113, Folder 7, LWA; DOC, *Response to Draft State Commission of Correction Report "Inquiry into Disturbances on Rikers Island, October, 1986,"* 4, appended to DOI, *The Disturbance at Rikers Island*. For a detailed account of the like construction of a subsequent (and more sophisticated) facility, the George R. Vierno Center, see William Gove and Tom Rotundo, "Addition to Rikers Island Correction Facility," *Concrete International* 17: 8 (1995), 24–6; DOI, *The Disturbance at Rikers Island Otis Bantum Correctional Center, August 14, 1990: Its Causes and the Department of Correction Response* (New York: DOI, 1991), 24–7; A-16–A-18; DOC, *Saga*, 24–5.
10 BOC Meeting Minutes 5/16/86, 3, 4/26/84, 4–5; 11/29/84, 1–2, 4; Josh Barbanel, "Sharp Increase in Inmates in City Jails," *New York Times*, July 28, 1986; Peter Tufo to Hon. Edward I. Koch, January 6, 1986, Koch Papers, Box 114, Folder 1, LWA.
11 Jennifer Bleyer, "It's Curtains for the Brig, with Smiles All Around," *New York Times*, April 10, 2005; Shenon, "City Plans to Add New Jail Spaces"; Joseph P. Fried, "Conversion of Brig to Jail Is Opposed in Brooklyn," *New York Times*, April 30, 1984; "Former Navy Brig Gets Its First Inmates," *New York Times*, May 16, 1984.
12 Jacqueline McMickens, "May and June Management Report," 1984, 4, Koch Papers, Box 113, Folder 2, LWA; Jacqueline McMickens, "April Management Report," 1985, 3, Koch Papers, Box 35, Folder 15, LWA; Maurice Carroll, "Action on Chinatown Jail Put Off after Protest," *New York Times*, November 19, 1982; Suzanne Daley, "Chinatown Jail Might Put Space to Private Uses," *New York Times*, September 11, 1982.
13 COBA, "McMickens' Policies Are Oppressive and Inhumane," *Chief-Leader*, Friday, October 19, 1984; Jacqueline McMickens

to Stanley Brezenoff, October 15, 1984, Koch Papers, Box 113, Folder 2, LWA.

14 Jacqueline McMickens, "September Management Report," 1985, 6, Koch Papers, Box 113, Folder 7, LWA; *New York Times*, "Jail Guard Seeks Dismissal of Chief," August 12, 1985; Joyce Purnick, "Correction Chief to Be Replaced Today, Koch Aides Say," *New York Times*, August 6, 1986.

15 Travis Linnemann, *Meth Wars: Police, Media, Power* (New York: New York University Press, 2016).

16 Richard Stetson Curtis, *The War on Drugs in Brooklyn, New York*, PhD diss, Columbia University, 1996, 10–22; *New York Times*, "The Crack Crackdown's Jail Backlash," October 22, 1986.

17 New York State Commission of Correction, *Inquiry into the Disturbances on Rikers Island, October 1986* (Albany: NYSCOC, 1987), 5–7, 58–9; *Lareau v. Manson*, 507 F. Supp. 1177 (D. Conn. 1980); NYSCOC, *Inquiry into the Disturbances at Rikers Island*, 46–7; Richard Koehler to Hon. Edward I. Koch, September 11, 1986, Koch Papers, Box 114, Folder 3, LWA; M.A. Farber, "Rikers Island Violence Was Worse Than Reported, Investigators Say," *New York Times*, October 30, 1986.

18 Alexander Reid, "Yet Another Crisis in the City's Jails," *New York Times*, August 10, 1986; John T. McQuiston, "Prisoners Take Over Dormitory," *New York Times*, August 7, 1986; Joyce Purnick, "City Plans to Add 2,300 Jail Spaces," *New York Times*, October 7, 1986.

19 Alan Finder, "Police Official Named to Head the City's Jails," *New York Times*, September 23, 1986; Crystal Nix, "161 Inmates Block Two Dormitories to Protest Conditions at Rikers I.," *New York Times*, October 14, 1986; NYSCOC, *Inquiry into the Disturbances at Rikers Island*, 63–8.

20 Farber, "Rikers Island Violence Was Worse Than Reported"; NYSCOC, *Inquiry into the Disturbances at Rikers Island*, 63–6.

21 Farber, "Rikers Island Violence Was Worse Than Reported"; Bruce Lambert, "60 Guards Stay off Job in Rikers Island Protest," *New York Times*, October 15, 1986; NYSCOC, *Inquiry into the Disturbances at Rikers Island*, 71–2.

22 New York Times, "4½ Hour Protest Held on Rikers I.," *New York Times*, October 17, 1986; NYSCOC, *Inquiry into the Disturbances at Rikers Island*, 73–4. It's worth noting that NYSCOC was invested in blaming DOC's decision to negotiate with prisoners for much of the prisoner militancy that followed. While they produced several anonymous prisoner sources to this effect, the scope of this explanation is narrow and discounts the general

tendency of prisoner militancy that arises when poor conditions enable effective mass action.

23 NYSCOC, *Inquiry into the Disturbances at Rikers Island*, 75–9; Inspector General Judith A. Schultz, "Rikers Island, October 17, 1986," 1986, 2, David N. Dinkins Papers, Box 21 Folder 167, LWA.

24 Robert D. McFadden, "12 Guards Are Injured in 2 Clashes on Rikers I.," *New York Times*, October 18, 1986; NYSCOC, *Inquiry into the Disturbances at Rikers Island*, 75–9. The former quotation is presented as a paraphrase, the latter a direct quote; Schultz, "Rikers Island, October 17, 1986," 2.

25 Schultz, "Rikers Island, October 17, 1986," 2–3.

26 NYSCOC, *Inquiry into the Disturbances at Rikers Island*, ix, xii, 75–86; Michael Caruso and Richard Pagan, "Investigation into the Incident Involving the Correction Emergency Response Team with State Inmates in the New York City House of Detention Receiving Room Yard Area on October 17, 1986," 1986, Dinkins Papers, Box 21, Folder 167, LWA; 11. The accounts of almost thirty prisoners interviewed immediately after the fact by IG demonstrate a remarkable consistency around basic facts: guards entered the bus unprovoked and began violently ejecting prisoners. In some accounts the guards are beating prisoners with clubs on the bus, in others they roughly eject prisoners to beat them outside. Guards' subsequent accounts, by contrast, contradict one another, appear evasive and at times clearly false—even to the point of this being noted by IG. Most guards report having seen nothing at all, sometimes due to darkness that miraculously lifts and falls throughout their stories, with the added impairment of amnesia that sets in around the recognition of names and faces of their colleagues, including prominent wardens and DOC's uniformed chief. Where the guards' accounts largely agree, they deny forming a gauntlet. Those who admit to using force at all present a uniform line on using sanctioned "barrel-thrusts" or "breast thrusts," a jabbing motion made with club parallel to the ground, in response to being charged by unruly prisoners. One guard claims, quite improbably, that a group of handcuffed prisoners charged the riot squad while shouting, "Fuck you, correction officers!" Civilian observers from multiple agencies contradict the guards' accounts at numerous points, especially on the "barrel-thrusts" and the formation of a gauntlet. In a rare instance of what could only be honesty, one guard, Joe Rodriguez, admits to a post-festum meeting of rank and filers intent on getting their story straight for the filing of incident reports.

27 Schultz, "Rikers Island, October 17, 1986," 3–4; M.A. Farber,

"Rikers Island Violence Was Worse Than Reported, Investigators Say," *New York Times*, October 30, 1986; NYSCOC, *Inquiry into the Disturbances at Rikers Island*, 86–9; Caruso and Pagan, "Investigation into the Incident," 20–1.

28 NYSCOC, *Inquiry into the Disturbances at Rikers Island*, 86–9.

29 NYSCOC, *Inquiry into the Disturbances at Rikers Island*, 86–94.

30 NYSCOC, *Inquiry into the Disturbances at Rikers Island*, 94–7; John Maguire, "October 17, 1986 Anna M. Kross Center Disturbance," October 24, 1986, 5–6, Dinkins Papers, Box 21, Folder 167, LWA; John Maguire and Ralph Mierzejewski, "October 17, 1986 Disturbance at Anna M. Kross Center," November 10, 1986, 4–5, Dinkins Papers, Box 21, Folder 167, LWA.

31 Maguire, "October 17, 1986," 4; NYSCOC, *Inquiry into the Disturbances at Rikers Island*, 94–97; Schultz, "Rikers Island, October 17," 5.

32 The letter was also released to the public, along with a press release emphasizing: "Its basic theme is that the Commissioner reaffirms his support for correction staff, commends their professionalism, and outlines his stance with regard to the issues that have recently become public." (Richard J. Koehler, Letter to DOC Guards, October 22, 1986, Koch Papers, Box 114, Folder 3, LWA); Robert D. McFadden, "72 State Inmates at Rikers I. Sent from City Jails to Upstate Prisons," *New York Times*, October 19, 1986; Jane Perlez, "City Checks of Reports of Beatings at Rikers," *New York Times*, October 20, 1986; Josh Barbanel, "3 Wardens at Rikers Ousted in Response to Brutality Complaints," *New York Times*, October 21, 1986; Todd S. Purdum, "100 Jail Guards Reportedly Quit Emergency Unit," *New York Times*, October 22, 1986.

21. A Bridge to the Twenty-First Century

1 Bruce Lambert, "City's Prison Boat Is Late and Costly," *New York Times*, March 24, 1987; Betsy Shirey, "Rikers Island Expansion: Modular Construction Strategy Works," *Corrections Today* (April 1989), 22; BOC, *Annual Report 1988* (New York: BOC, 1989), 33–5; Selwyn Raab, "2 Jail Barges to Be Closed and Removed," February 15, 1992.

2 "Rose M. Singer Center Opens at Rikers Island," *Correction News*, July 1988, 1–2; M.A. Farber, "Rikers Island Violence Was Worse Than Reported, Investigators Say," *New York Times*, October 30, 1986; "CPSU Opening Reduces HDM Incidents," *New York City Department of Correction Newsline*, March 31,

1988, Koch Papers, Box 87, Folder 1, LWA; Allyn R. Sielaff, "Adoption of a Rule by Emergency Pursuant to section 1043.h.1 of the City Charter," Dinkins Papers, Box 20, Folder 158, LWA.

3 John Grosfield (The Grosfield Partnership/Architects) and E. Eugene Miller (C.M. Security Group, Ltd.), "Alternative Construction Methods for Jails," 1990, 1–4, Dinkins Papers, Box 20, Folder 158, LWA; BOC Meeting Minutes 7/14/87; BOC, *Annual Report 1987* (New York: BOC, 1988), 10–11; 7; BOC, *Annual Report 1988*, 3–4.

4 NYSCOC, *Acquired Immune Deficiency Syndrome: A Demographic Profile of New York State Inmate Moralities, 1981–1985* (New York: NYSCOC, 1986); Jessica Loughery, "Building an Icon Out of Kuwasi Balagoon," *Philadelphia City Paper,* December 13, 2006; Nicholas Freundenberg, Marianne Fahs, Sandro Galea et al., "The Impact of New York City's 1975 Fiscal Crisis on the Tuberculosis, HIV, and Homicide Syndemic," *American Journal of Public Health* 96: 3 (2006), 426–8. In this early period DOC was testing for AIDS. HIV tests appeared slightly later.

5 Jacqueline McMickens, "June Monthly Report," 1985, 4, Edward I. Koch Papers, Box 1113, Folder 5, LWA; Richard J. Koehler, "Post Bid Declaration of Emergency for the Site Utilities for a Medical Dormitory for Housing Inmates with Aides," 1988, Koch Papers, Box 114, Folder 7, LWA; Pierre Raphael, *Inside Rikers Island: A Chaplain's Search for God* (Maryknoll, NY: Orbis Books, 1990), 40.

6 Edward Koch, Remarks to DOC "Medal Day," September 29, 1989, Edward I. Koch Papers at LWA, Box 8,081, Folder 6, LWA.

7 Richard Koehler, "Re: Report of the Commission on Black New Yorkers," 1989, Koch Papers, Box 114, Folder 8, LWA; John Hull Mollenkopf, *A Phoenix in the Ashes: The Rise and Fall of the Koch Coalition in New York City Politics* (Princeton: Princeton University Press, 1992), 154. The figure for Latinos comes from 1987, when black guards accounted for 51 percent of DOC.

8 Mollenkopf, *Phoenix in the Ashes,* 136–9; Douglas Martin, "Violence Grows in Crowded New York Jails," *New York Times,* April 15, 1987; New York State Commission of Correction, *Inquiry into the Disturbances on Rikers Island, October 1986* (Albany: NYSCOC, 1987), 100–2; *Fisher v. Koehler,* 692 F. Supp. 1519 (S.D.N.Y. 1988), 1523.

9 *Fisher v. Koehler,* 692 F. Supp. 1519 (S.D.N.Y. 1988), 23–6.

10 *Fisher v. Koehler,* 692 F. Supp. 1519 (S.D.N.Y. 1988), 1555; Edward I. Koch, "Executive Order No. 105," December 26, 1986; *Fisher v. Koehler,* No. 83 Civ. 2128, (S.D.N.Y. Nov. 8, 1989).

11 Jacqueline McMickens to Hon. Stanley Brezenoff, June 6, 1986, Koch Papers, Box 114, Folder 2, LWA; William G. Blair, "Three Flee from Rikers Island Hospital Ward," *New York Times*, December 6, 1987; BOC, *1987*, 24–5.

12 BOC, *1987*, 26–7; Douglas Martin, "New York City Jails: System in Turmoil," *New York Times*, December 12, 1987.

13 Harold L. Jamison, "Rikers Inmates Strike over 'Bad' Food," *Amsterdam News*, June 18, 1988; Douglas Martin, "Hundreds of Prisoners Take Over 12 Dormitories at Rikers I.," *New York Times*, February 19, 1988; Douglas Martin, "When Rikers I. Erupted," *New York Times*, February 28, 1988.

14 Richard J. Koehler, "September Monthly Report, 1989," 1–2, Koch Papers, Box 114, Folder 10, LWA; Dennis Hevesi, "Guards Quell a Disturbance in Rikers Jail," *New York Times*, September 29, 1989.

15 Mollenkopf, *Phoenix in the Ashes*, 166–185.

16 Sam Roberts, "Giuliani Discounts Color as an Issue," *New York Times*, November 1, 1989; Raoul Lionel Felder, "Against Dinkins and for Giuliani," *New York Times*, November 3, 1989; Sam Roberts, "Crime Is the Crucial Issue for New York's Mayoral Rivals," *New York Times*, August 30, 1989; Martin Gottlieb, "After the Conflict at Rikers, a War of Words," *New York Times*, August 27, 1990.

17 Todd S. Purdum, "Cleveland Expert Hired to Run New York Jails," *New York Times*, March 6, 1990; Leonard Buder, "Jail Chief Receives Volatile Welcome," *New York Times*, March 19, 1990. The use-of-force figure is from 1990 (DOI, *Disturbance at the Rikers Island Otis Bantum Correctional Center*, 30n30).

18 Andrew H. Malcolm, "Explosive Drug Use Creating New Underworld in Prison," *New York Times*, December 30, 1989.

19 DOI, *Disturbance at the Rikers Island Otis Bantum Correctional Center, August 14, 1990: Its Causes and the Department of Correction Response* (New York: DOI, 1991), 29–33, 57n65. The "use of force" directive under Fisher is excerpted in the appendix, A-36.

20 The Friends of Officer Narby to Hon. Allyn R. Sielaff, August 10, 1990, reprinted in *DOI, Disturbance at Rikers Island Otis Bantum Correctional Center*, A-21.

21 DOI, *Disturbance at the Rikers Island Otis Bantum Correctional Center*, 34n36, 38–9. DOI investigators, who faced a stone wall in practically every attempt to speak with guards, never recovered any of this literature; Allyn R. Sielaff, "Events Leading to the Disturbance at the Otis Bantum Correctional Facility on August 14, 1990," 1–2, Dinkins Papers, Box 5, Folder 39, LWA; DOC,

"Time Sequence Narrative," 14; DOI, *Disturbance at the Rikers Island Otis Bantum Correctional Center*, 42–5.

22 DOI, *Disturbance at the Rikers Island Otis Bantum Correctional Center*, 35–7.

23 Sielaff, "Events Leading to the Disturbance at the Otis Bantum Correctional Facility," 4–5; DOC, "Time Sequence Narrative," 4, 8; Katie Lapp, "Rikers Island Incident," November 28, 1990, Dinkins Papers, Box 22 Folder 169, LWA; DOI, *Disturbance at the Rikers Island Otis Bantum Correctional Center*, 51–2.

24 Martin Gottlieb, "Behind Rikers Melee: Tensions Wrought by Strain of Change," *New York Times*, August 20, 1992; DOI, *Disturbance at the Rikers Island Otis Bantum Correctional Center*, 51–52; James Grillo, "Correction Officers Job Action-8/13–14/90," 2–4, Dinkins Papers, Box 5, Folder 39, LWA.

25 DOI, *Disturbance at the Rikers Island Otis Bantum Correctional Center*, 53n60; Dean Baquet, "Mayor Backs His Handling of Jail Melee, *New York Times*, August 18, 1990; Sielaff, "Events Leading to the Disturbance at the Otis Bantum Correctional Facility," 5, 7; James Barron, "After Uprising at Rikers, Guards Are Said to Have Beaten Inmates," *New York Times*, August 16, 1990.

26 Grillo, "Correction Officers Job Action," 4; Lapp, "Rikers Island Incident," 4–10; DOC, "Time Sequence Narrative," 48; George James, "EMS Worker Indicted over Rikers Injury Report," *New York Times*, September 27, 1990. Grillo (4) follows the DOC line that this was unnecessary on the part of the EMT, but Lapp's collection of accounts from NYPD and HHS casts considerable doubt on this contention.

27 DOI, *Disturbance at the Rikers Island Otis Bantum Correctional Center*, 37; DOC, "Time Sequence Narrative," 18, 49; Sielaff, "Events Leading to the Disturbance at the Otis Bantum Correctional Facility," 7; DOC, "Time Sequence Narrative," 9. The list of demands is taken from the final agreement between COBA and the city, reproduced in full in the appendix to DOI, *Disturbance at the Rikers Island Otis Bantum Correctional Center*, A-23–A-29.

28 DOI, *Disturbance at the Rikers Island Otis Bantum Correctional Center*, 3–4, 56–7.

29 Annette Fuentes, "Rumbling in Rikers Ranks," *Village Voice*, October 23, 1990; DOI, *Disturbance at the Rikers Island Otis Bantum Correctional Center*, 56–7; Dean Baquet, "Mayor Backs His Handling of Jail Mischief," *New York Times*, August 18, 1990.

30 DOI, *Disturbance at the Rikers Island Otis Bantum Correctional Center*, 57–69. In what follows I am forced to follow DOI's report

almost entirely, due to the patent falsehood of DOC's accounts of these events—itself a theme running throughout DOI's report.

31 DOI, *Disturbance at the Rikers Island Otis Bantum Correctional Center*, 96–105, 104–7, 122–5.

32 DOI, *Disturbance at the Rikers Island Otis Bantum Correctional Center*, 111–14, 117–20.

33 DOI, *Disturbance at the Rikers Island Otis Bantum Correctional Center*, 127–9; DOC, "Time Sequence Narrative," 16, 43, quoted text is a paraphrase in the report.

34 Sielaff, "Events Leading to the Disturbance at the Otis Bantum Correctional Facility," 11; DOC, "Time Sequence Narrative," 31–2, 44, quoted text is a paraphrase in the report; DOI, *Disturbance at the Rikers Island Otis Bantum Correctional Center*, 128–9, 143.

35 DOI, *Disturbance at the Rikers Island Otis Bantum Correctional Center*, 131–98.

36 DOI, *Disturbance at the Rikers Island Otis Bantum Correctional Center*, 185–6; Martin Gottlieb, "Some Link Rikers Melee to a Dismissal," *New York Times*, August 21, 1990.

37 DOI, *Disturbance at the Rikers Island Otis Bantum Correctional Center*, 136, 266, 295.

38 Felicia R. Lee, "Guards' Chief Says Dinkins Backs Inmates," *New York Times*, August 24, 1990; Jack Curry, "Union Leader Fights to Control Rikers Ranks," *New York Times*, August 28, 1990; Jack Curry, "Guard Leader May Be Asked to Step Down," *New York Times*, August 12, 1990; Jarrod Shanahan, "Solidarity Behind Bars: New York City's Correction Officers' Benevolent Association," *Brooklyn Rail*, September 2017.

39 Curry, "Guard Leader May Be Asked to Step Down," quoted text is a paraphrase in the story.

40 Susan E. Shepard, "Rikers," Letter to Norman Steisel, August 16, Dinkins Papers, Box 21, Folder 168, LWA; Kevin Sack, "Panel Faults Rikers Staff in Riot Study," *New York Times*, April 24, 1991; Gottlieb, "Behind Rikers Melee."

Afterword

1 Naomi Murakawa, *The First Civil Right: How Liberals Built Prison America* (Oxford: Oxford University Press, 2014), 22.

2 Jarrod Shanahan, "Solidarity Behind Bars: New York City's Correction Officers' Benevolent Association," *Brooklyn Rail*, September 2017; J. Zamgba Brown, "Norman Seabrook Threatened by a Multi-million Dollar Lawsuit," *New York Amsterdam*

News, June 18, 1994; Greg Wade, "Corrections Officer Seeks Union Presidency," *Network Journal*, August 1, 1994; Al Guart, "Union Big's Merry Widow Finds Husband's $2m Cache,' *New York Post*, July 2, 2000.

3 Wade, "Corrections Officer Seeks Union Presidency;" Michael Schwirtz and Michael Winerip, "At Rikers Island, Union Chief's Clout Is a Roadblock to Reform," *New York Times*, December 14, 2014; Shanahan, "Solidarity behind Bars"; Wade, "Correction Officer Seeks Union Presidency."

4 Frank Lynn, "Mayor Offers Help," *New York Times*, September 13, 1989; "The Mayoral Candidates' Basic Speeches: Laments Followed by Proposals," *New York Times*, October 31, 1989; Wilbur C. Rich, *David Dinkins and New York City Politics: Race, Images, and the Media* (Albany: SUNY Press, 2007), 145–64; Joe Klein, "Fantasy in Blue," *New York Magazine*, October 15, 1990.

5 Ralph Blumenthal, "Dinkins Proposes Record Expansion of Police Forces," *New York Times*, October 3, 1990; Selwyn Raab, "New York City Prison Chief Quits after Rebuke on Contract Bidding," *New York Times*, December 24, 1991; Sam Roberts, "As Crime Rate Drops, New York's Jail Population Falls to Lowest Level in 24 Years," *New York Times*, June 10, 2010; Selwyn Raab, "Jail Chief Is Selected by Dinkins," *New York Times*, March 24, 1992; Marc Santora, "Catherine M. Abate, 66, Ex-State Senator," May 23, 2014.

6 Betsy Shirey, "Rikers Island Expansion: Modular Construction Strategy Works," *Corrections Today* (April 1989), 22; "Rikers Island," Petracca & Sons official website psina.weebly.com.

7 Tom McCarthy, "Before Buono Bridge Construction, Vehicles Only Accessed Rikers by Boat: True or False?," *Corrections History*, correctionhistory.org; "George R. Vierno, 50, Ex-Correction Official," *New York Times*, January 1, 1991; John Gregerson, "Modular Precast Expedites Prison Addition," *Building Design and Construction*, March 1994, 62; "$100 mil. Rikers Island Addition Completed," *Real Estate Weekly*, December 8, 1993; Gove and Rotundo, "Addition to Rikers Island Correctional Facility."

8 Selwyn Raab, "2 Jail Barges to Be Closed and Removed," *New York Times*, February 15, 1992; Bruce Lambert, "City's Prison Boat Is Late and Costly," *New York Times*, March 24, 1987; Selwyn Raab, "Bronx Jail Barge to Open, Though Cost Is Steep," *New York Times*, January 27, 1992; Matthew Haag, "A Temporary Floating Jail Is Still Open after 27 Years," *New York Times*, October 10, 2019.

9 Selwyn Raab, "Rikers to Bring Judges to Inmates, Instead of Inmates to Judges," *New York Times*, April 8, 1991.

10 Rich, *David Dinkins*, 163–4; James C. McKinley Jr., "Dinkins Names Corruption Panel and Urges Civilian Police Review," *New York Times*, June 26, 1992; John Kifner, "Clashes Persist in Crown Heights for 3d Night in a Row," *New York Times*, August 22, 1992.

11 Dennis Hevesi, "Upper Manhattan Block Erupts after a Man Is Killed in Struggle with a Policeman," *New York Times*, July 5, 1992; James Dao, "Police Report on a Slaying Is Challenged," *New York Times*, July 6, 1992; David Correia and Tyler Wall, *Police: A Field Guide* (London and New York: Verso, 2018), 15–16; James Dao, "Amid Dinkins' Appeal for Calm, Protesters Skirmish with Police," *New York Times*, July 8, 1992; David Gonzales, "Events Don't Surprise Dominican Residents," *New York Times*, July 8, 1992; Alison Mitchell, "Dinkins and Brown Walk to Calm Troubled Streets," *New York Times*, July 9, 1992.

12 James Dao, "Police Union Says Dinkins Fueled Unrest," *New York Times*, July 14, 1992; Alan Finder, "Dinkins, amid Crowd, Nurtures Fragile Peace," *New York Times*, July 9, 1992.

13 James C. McKinley, "Officers Rally and Dinkins Is Their Target," *New York Times*, September 17, 1992; Catherine S. Manegold, "Rally Puts Police under New Scrutiny," *New York Times*, September 27, 1992; "'Dunk the Dink, and Much Worse," *New York Times*, September 27, 1992; "Politics, Racism and Little Control," *New York Times*, September 27, 1992; Catherine S. Manegold, "Commissioner's Report Cites Series of Failures," *New York Times*, September 29, 1992.

14 Todd S. Purdum, "Slurs from Police Are Not New to Dinkins," *New York Times*, September 19, 1992; "Put Out the Police Fire," *New York Times*, September 24, 1992.

15 Phil Caruso, "Righteous Anger Spilled Over at Police Rally," *New York Times*, September 25, 1992; James McKinley Jr., "Dinkins Denounces Police Protest as Furthering an Image of Racism," *New York Times*, September 18, 1992.

16 Neil Smith, "Giuliani Time: The Revanchist 1990s," *Social Text* 57: 16, no. 4 (Winter 1998), 1–20.

17 Smith, "Giuliani Time," 2, 4–8.

18 George L. Kelling and James Q. Wilson, "Broken Windows," *The Atlantic*, March 1982. Correia and Wall's *Police* (195–9) provides a more comprehensive refutation of "Broken Windows"; Correia and Wall, *Police*, 34.

19 Craig Horowitz, "The Dirty Secret of Cellblock 6," *New York Magazine*, October 10, 1994, 35; Bernard Kerik, *The Lost Son:*

A Life in the Pursuit of Justice (New York: Regan Books, 2001) 250–1; Craig Horowitz, "Does Giuliani Actually *Want* Prison Riots?," *New York Magazine*, November 7, 1994, 22.

20 Alison Mitchell, "Prisons Chief Quits, Citing Family Issues," *New York Times*, January 25, 1995.

21 Mireya Navarro, "After Melee, Security Is Tightened at Rikers Island," *New York Times*, April 15, 1994; Matthew Purdy, "Correction Chief Declares Rikers Island under Control," *New York Times*, November 18, 1994; Francis X. Clines, "Rikers Is Tense as Cuts Loom and Official Warns of Crisis," *New York Times*, November 17, 1994.

22 "Seeking Ways to Cut Expenses," *New York Times*, May 15, 1995; Vivian S. Toy, "Giuliani Formally Appoints Correction Chief," *New York Times*, March 31, 1996; Elissa Gootman, "A Street-Savvy Innovator," *New York Times*, August 20, 2000; Sam Dolnick, "Kerik Enters U.S. Prison to Serve 4-Year Term," *New York Times*, May 18, 2010.

23 Joseph B. Treaster, "Many Cities Skeptical of Giuliani's Drug Strategy," *New York Times*, November 15, 1993; David Brotherton and Luis Barrios, *The Almighty Latin King and Queen Nation* (New York: Columbia University Press, 2004), 315–19; "Dinkins Proposes Record Expansion of Police Forces," *New York Times*, October 3, 1990; National Gang Intelligence Center NGIC), National Gang Threat Assessment (Washington, DC: NGIC, 2009), 27.

24 Kerik, *The Lost Son*, 259–60, 262; Christopher Drew, "An Iron Hand at Rikers Island Drastically Reduces Violence," *New York Times*, November 8, 1999; Paul E. O'Connell and Frank Straub, "Why the Jails Didn't Explode," *City Journal* 9: 2 (1999), 28–37; Shelley Feuer Domash, "Model Correction Program Works Successfully with Police to Gang Up on Crime," *Police* 23: 5 (1999); Bert Useem and Jack A. Goldstone, "Forging Social Order and Its Breakdown: Riot and Reform in U.S. Prisons," *American Sociological Review* 67 (August 2002), 499–525; Kerik, *The Lost Son*, 259–60, 262. Bernard Kerik, "Accountability: The Key to Safety," *Corrections Today*, July 2000, 147.

25 Vivian S. Toy, "For Those Who Clean Up the Streets, 2 Blocks of Glory," *New York Times*, June 20, 1996; Paul E. O'Connell and Frank Straub, "Managing with T.E.A.M.S.," *American Jails*, March/April 1999, 51.

26 Martin Horn, "Data-Driven Management Systems Improve Safety and Accountability in New York City Jails," *Corrections Today* 70:5 (October 2008), 40; Trevor Paglen, "Ways of Seeing," *Bookforum* 20:1 (Apr/May 2013); Thomas J. Ward, "Commissioners,

Chiefs, and COMPSTAT," *Law and Order* 48: 7 (July 2000), 133; John A. Eterno and Eli B. Silverman, "The New York City Police Department's CompStat: Dream or Nightmare?," *International Journal of Policing Science and Management* 8:3 (2006), 219, 222.

27 Correia and Wall, *Police*, 33–8, 190; Eterno and Silverman, "Dream or Nightmare?," 222, 225. The theatrics of Compstat meetings are chronicled in Robert D. Behn, *The PerformanceStat Potential: A Leadership Strategy for Producing Results* (Washington, DC: Brookings Institution Press, 2014), 172–92.

28 Robert Zink, "The Trouble with Compstat," *PBA Magazine*, Summer 2004, nycpba.org. For a more scholarly account of the same problem, see John A. Eterno and Eli B. Silverman, "The NYPD's Compstat: Compare Statistics or Compose Statistics?," *International Journal of Police Science and Management* 12: 3 (2010), 426–49.

29 Kerik, *The Lost Son*, 274; Kerik, "Accountability," 126.

30 O'Connell and Straub, "Managing Jails with T.E.A.M.S.," 49–52; Horn, "Data-Driven Management," 41–2; Michael Winerip, Michael Schwirtz, and Benjamin Weiser, "Report Found Distorted Data on Jail Fights at Rikers Island," September 21, 2014; Laura J. Limuli to Roslyn Midgett (City Law Department), July 16, 1991, BOCA; *Fisher v. Koehler*, No. 83 Civ. 2128, (S.D.N.Y. Nov. 8, 1989); DOJ, *CRIPA Investigation of the New York City Department of Correction Jails on Rikers Island* (New York: DOJ, 2014), 8–9, 17–30; Mary Buser, *Lockdown on Rikers Island* (New York: St. Martin's Press, 2015) 247; Kerik, *The Lost Son*, 278.

31 China Mac, "I Started a Riot on 9/11 at Rikers Island," *China Mac TV*, YouTube.

32 Eric Pooley, "Mayor of the World," *Time*, December 31, 2001; Jennifer Steinhauer, "Bloomberg Takes Oath as 108th Mayor of New York," *New York Times*, January 1, 2002; Roberts, "As Crime Rate Drops, New York's Jail Population Falls to Lowest Level in 24 Years"; Avram Bornstein, "Antiterrorist Policing in New York City after 9/11: Comparing Perspectives on a Complex Process," *Human Organization* 64:1 (2005), 52–61.

33 Zhandarka Kurti and Jarrod Shanahan, "Carceral Non-profits and the Limits of Prison Reform," *ACME: A Journal of Critical Georgaphies* 20: 6 (2021), 597–617. "About," Center for Court Innovation official website, courtinnovation.org/about; "Michael Jacobson to Step Down as President of Vera Institute of Justice," Vera Institute of Justice, January 8, 2013, vera.org; "Our Work," CUNY Institute for State and Local Governance,

islg.cuny.edu/sites/our-work; Zhandarka Kurti and Jarrod Shanahan, "Rebranding Mass Incarceration: The Lippman Commission and 'Carceral Devolution' in New York City," *Social Justice* 25:2–3 (2018), 25–50.

34 "Rikers Officer Charged with Raping Inmate," *New York Times*, October 11, 2003; Paul von Zielbauer, "Rikers Suicide Called a Glaring Example of Poor Care," *New York Times*, April 4, 2005; John Sullivan, "10 Rikers Inmates Complain of Beatings," *New York Times*, October 25, 2005; Benjamin Weiser, "City to Pay $5.75 Million over Death of Mentally Ill Inmate at Rikers Island," *New York Times*, September 27, 2017; "Rikers Horror Story," *New York Times*, January 29, 2009.

35 Michael Schwirtz and Michael Winerip, "At Riker's, Union Chief's Clout Is a Roadblock to Reform," *New York Times*, September 14, 2014; Shanahan, "Solidarity behind Bars."

36 Michael Brick, "Union Sues over Move to Discipline Prison Guards," *New York Times*, August 23, 2003; David Rohde, "City Board Members Fault St. Barnabas Hospital over Prison Care," *New York Times*, September 17, 1998; Eric Lipton, "Company Selected for Rikers Health Care," *New York Times*, September 9, 2000; DOI, *Investigation Finds Significant Breakdowns by Corizon Health Inc., the City-Contracted Health Care Provider in the City's Jails, and a Lack of Oversight by the City Correction and Health Departments* (New York: DOI, 2015).

37 Michael Schwirtz and Michael Winerip; "Close Rikers Island? It Will Take Years, Billions and Political Capital," *New York Times*, March 2, 2016; Jarrod Shanahan and Pilar Maschi, "There Are Abolitionists All around Us," *Commune*, Winter 2020; "Ending Police Collaboration with Mass Deportation Programs: PEP, ICE Out of Rikers, and Ending S-Comm," Immigrant Defense Project official website, immigrantdefenseproject.org.

38 Homer Venters, *Life and Death in Rikers Island* (Baltimore: Johns Hopkins Press, 2019), 2.

39 Correia and Wall, *Police*, 234–5. Graham Raymond, "Rikers Fight Club," *Village Voice*, February 4, 2009; Isolde Raferty, "6-Year Sentence for Guard in Rikers Island Beating," *New York Times*, August 7, 2010; Russ Buettner, "Rikers Extortion Noted before Death," *New York Times*, March 16, 2009.

40 Martin Horn, "Practitioner Reflections on the Use of Evidence in Management of Correctional Facilities; or, 'You Can Never Find a Princess When You Need One,'" presented at the Fall Research Conference of the Association for Policy Analysis and Management, Washington, DC, November 6, 2009.

41 Benjamin Weiser, "New York City Settles Suit over Abuses at

Rikers Island," *New York Times*, June 22, 2015; DOJ, *CRIPA Investigation of the New York City Department of Correction Jails on Rikers Island* (New York: DOJ, 2014); Baer and Bepko, "A Necessary and Proper Role for Federal Courts," 33–5. Mandatory monitor reports, a condition of the city's cooperation in *Nunez*, paint a devastating picture of enduring violence on Rikers Island, and the inability of reformers to stop it. See Nunez Monitor Reports, www1.nyc.gov/site/doc/media/nunez-reports .page.

42 Jennifer Gonnerman, "Before the Law," *The New Yorker*, October 6, 2014; Jennifer Gonnerman, "Kalief Browder, 1993–2015," *The New Yorker*, June 7, 2015.

43 Michelle Alexander, *The New Jim Crow: Mass Incarceration in the Age of Colorblindness* (New York: The New Press, 2010).

44 "Rethinking Rikers Island," *Center for Court Innovation* (blog), June 22, 2017, courtinnovation.org; Darren Walker, "In Defense of Nuance," *Ford Foundation* (blog), September 19, 2019, fordfoundation.org; Insha Rahman, "Closing Rikers Island," *Vera Institute of Justice* (blog), October 8, 2019, vera.org. Michael Jacobson and Herb Sturz both served on the Lippman Commission.

Index